CAN FAITH SURVIVE?

CAN
FAITH
SURVIVE?

by Maurice N. Eisendrath

*THE THOUGHTS
AND AFTERTHOUGHTS
OF AN
AMERICAN RABBI*

McGraw-Hill Book Company *New York·Toronto·London*

"TEMPLE ISRAEL"

CAN FAITH SURVIVE?

Library of Congress Catalog Card Number: 64-25170

First Edition

19128

to
Rosa Brown Eisendrath
in never-failing
remembrance

CONTENTS

"Do I contradict myself?
Very well, then, I contradict myself.
I am large, I contain multitudes."

from Walt Whitman's
"Song of Myself"

INTRODUCTION

Many of my friends have suggested that I commit to writing some of my experiences during the more than a third of a century since my ordination as a rabbi. Some have even paid me the compliment of saying that certain of the events of which I have been a part reflect the course of Reform Judaism during a large portion of the first half of this century. It is true that I have found myself at the swirling vortex of some of these episodes. I have been, for the past two decades, in the thick of all that has affected Reform Judaism—for better or worse only the future will determine. Accordingly, this book records my reflections on some of these crucial matters.

It was especially the encouragement of my long-cherished friend and former teacher, Rabbi Solomon B. Freehof, which now prompts me, as I complete my second decade as President of the Union of American Hebrew Congregations (the central body of Reform synagogues in North America), to discuss some of the volcanic eruptions in American, and especially Reform, Jewish history in which I have played a part.

It was Rabbi Freehof who first made me believe that there might be something of an exhilarating adventure in retracing the way I have come, in reexamining some of the ideas to which I have given expression in the past, reviewing the thoughts and feelings that have dictated positions I have taken earlier in my rabbinical career, reviewing some of the views I have previously espoused and actions I have urged. He encouraged me to subject rigorously and objectively some of the thoughts that had been mine at the outset to the afterthoughts of the so radically different present in which I now find myself. It is to Rabbi Freehof, therefore, that I am most indebted for finally pushing me over the brink and for compelling me to confront, with as much candor as I can command, many of the viewpoints of my long years in the rabbinate.

I had not a scintilla of desire to include in this reevaluation any autobiographical data that would thrust me into the dreary procession of unabashed public denudings that have frequently passed for literature in recent years. But, almost imperceptibly, I have slipped into the first-person singular and it became apparent that the obvious and ofttimes wide divergence between what I said some twenty or thirty years ago and my startlingly altered position today could be illuminated only by references to much in my personal background, to experiences as a rabbi during the past three eventful decades, and, more particularly, to the

1

challenges presented by my role as President of the Union of American Hebrew Congregations. So the reader will, I pray, indulge me in some subjective revelations.

The pages that follow, however, are not intended as a definitive history of the Reform movement throughout the past few decades, much less of the American Jewish community.* That would demand a far more disciplined historian of this now more than three-hundred-year-old American Jewry than I could conceivably claim to be. Nor do these chapters comprise a theological treatise on Reform Judaism. I do not presume to be a theologian. Though originally determined to devote my days and years in the rabbinate primarily to scholarship, I was detoured by life into an activist career, especially during the twenty years during which I have had the responsibilities as President of so far-flung an enterprise as the Union of American Hebrew Congregations, responsibilities perhaps unparalleled in the modern rabbinate. Therefore, I beg that these words be accepted for precisely what they are: an account of those ideas and actions within the Reform Jewish movement in Canada, where I ministered for fourteen years, and in the United States, with which I have been identified and in which I have been deeply and vitally involved during the most momentous and memorable generation in the long, long saga of the Jewish people.

In these pages, I shall dwell primarily upon those areas related to my rabbinical labors—to Judaism and Jews and, more particularly, to Reform Judaism in America. Some of my earlier thoughts have been confirmed and strengthened in the glow of these later afterthoughts. With regard to others, I have drastically changed my mind or, as is perhaps the case with so many of our ideas and sentiments, had them changed for me in the blast furnace of the times in which we dwell.

Thus, though there has been much change, not everything, contrary to Heraclitus, has been in flux—at least not in my stream of consciousness. There have been some constants, some luminous stars to steer by. My craving to be a rabbi has never varied though there have been moments of fearsome wrestling. In the *gestalt* in which I was reared, the very notion itself seemed at first absurd. There had never been a rabbi in my family as far back as we can trace its roots and branches. Though my parents were devoted members of the Reform Jewish congregation of Temple Emanu-El in Chicago, though my father was a trustee and my mother one of its most ardent volunteer workers, nevertheless it seemed at first incongruous that a rabbi should spring from this particular congregation—which was then quite definitely in what

* For such an account read James G. Heller's "Isaac M. Wise," UAHC, New York, N.Y., 1964.

is now known as the "classical," or more nontraditional, stream of Reform Judaism. In fact, in those days it was almost unthinkable that any Reform congregation should produce rabbinical students out of its own ranks, although many young men from Orthodox backgrounds were inspired and prepared for admission to our Reform seminary by Reform rabbis. Rabbinical students actually arising out of a Reform environment were rare indeed. This failure contributed to a general defeatism in Reform ranks during the early decades of this century, so certain did it seem that we would not reproduce ourselves and that our ultimate doom was therefore sealed. It is gratifying to note that this Cassandra-like mood and condition no longer exist; large numbers of aspirants for the rabbinate are now recruited from Reform households as a consequence of our revivified youth and camp programs, in particular. More than 60 per cent of recent inductees into the Hebrew Union College–Jewish Institute of Religion (our Reform theological seminary) come from a Reform family background.

My own resolve to become a rabbi, however, announced at the age of approximately six, was quite unusual. It categorized me—in current slang—as a "square." It made me the butt of much ridicule and childhood abuse. I came to be regarded as the "sissy" of the crowd. But my determination to become a rabbi never faltered and my family never wavered in its encouragement.

In addition to these external influences a powerful social idealism had gestated within me. I wanted then most resolutely to be a "do-gooder," to be of some tangible blessing to my fellow men. To be sure, this aspiration might have been satisfied through medicine, or science, or social service, each of which appealed to me for a time, as did boyhood fantasies of becoming a life-saving fireman or burglar-routing policeman. But other influences were dominant, and to the Hebrew Union College in Cincinnati I journeyed, a lad of barely sixteen.

The beginnings were far from propitious and my career almost ended even before its very preparation began. My first ordeal was the entrance examination during which Rabbi Freehof—now the distinguished rabbi of Rodeph Sholom Temple of Pittsburgh and the eminent first American President of the World Union for Progressive Judaism, then a young professor at the College—did his best to emulate Torquemada in putting us neophytes on an intellectual torture rack. My preparation for the College had been almost nil, my knowledge of Hebrew barely discernible. As I have indicated, in those days there were few zealots for Hebrew in Reform Jewry. It would have been quite easy to have flunked me. And for a while, with Rabbi Freehof enjoying his role, it did appear certain that my desire to become a rabbi was doomed from the start. He would have been fully justified in recommending my rejection. But, generous to me then as he has been throughout the years, he assisted me on my stumbling way through the tests which seem so simple in retrospect.

But two more serious obstacles almost barred my way. I had entered the College in September, 1918. In October, classes were dismissed and we were sent home because of the violent outbreak of the influenza epidemic of that year. A day after I arrived, my father caught the devastating disease; a few days later we sadly buried him. Conscience and common sense dictated that I should now enter his business to help support my widowed mother, and my sister and brother. But their own sensitivity to my burning zeal to become a rabbi made it possible for me to return, bereft and saddened, to my studies.

Not much later still another roadblock appeared. The College physician, Dr. J. Victor Greenebaum, found that my eyes were far too weak, in his judgment, to cope with the demands of a student's career, much less a rabbi's. A Cincinnati eye specialist confirmed both his diagnosis and prognosis. I was cast into the depths of despair, ready to pack up and return home, when Dr. Julian Morgenstern, who had been recently appointed Acting President to succeed Kaufman Kohler, suggested that I see a famous specialist in Chicago. He sent me to Dr. Snydacker, who had taken excellent care of that virtually blind, but spiritually illumined and illuminating, stalwart of Reform Judaism, Emil G. Hirsch.

Snydacker confirmed the Cincinnati diagnosis that I had a most severe case of congenital astigmatism. But he believed that, if I could improve my general health (I was then a five-foot, eleven-inch gangling youngster weighing about 125 pounds), my eyes would follow suit. The College decided that I could remain and Snydacker's optimistic prediction has been happily verified through the years.

The efficacy of my own efforts, however, to improve my physique can best be illustrated by the fact that I almost failed to graduate from the University of Cincinnati because I had deliberately skipped all my classes in gymnasium. This A.B. degree was a *sine qua non* for ordination at the Hebrew Union College a year later and, for some then altogether incomprehensible reason, gymnasium credits were indispensable. I have since learned—at least theoretically, if not by experience or personal exertion—the truth of the adage *mens sana in corpore sano*. But in that spring of 1925, life could never have seemed more absurd than when the University Dean informed me that I could not matriculate because I had consistently played hooky from gym.

Again, Dr. Morgenstern came to my rescue, despite the trouble I had caused him during the early years of his administration as a most restive and rebellious student who had actually led a revolt to have him ousted from his post because of his imposition of even the slightest discipline. He marched forthwith to the University campus and guaranteed that, in the two weeks until graduation, he would personally see to it that I would fulfill the entire four years of my requirement in physical education. The University faculty held a special meeting and accepted Dr. Morgenstern's sporting proposition. I did, too, believing it to be just that: a sporting proposition and not by any manner of means to be seriously carried out. No delusion, past or present, has ever been more rudely shattered. My college mates of that day may still recall the side-splitting spectacle of my ceaseless running, huffing, and puffing around the campus driveway or shakily raising dumbbells in the gym until I was blue in the face, as I so belatedly discharged my athletic requirements under the tireless coaching of Dr. Morgenstern.

Thus, family and physical obstacles did not, in the end, deter me. Spiritual ones, however, almost did. I had to overcome the naive theology of my Sunday school days. I had to surrender my concept of a bearded God atop a cloud and to struggle painfully to a mature concept of divinity. I entered the storm of adolescence from which theological students are far from immune. In many ways they suffer more than others. They are not only seized by the doubts which overtake the unsophisticated faith of others in their first encounter with science, but they are also consumed by guilt that, as theological students, they have no right to harbor such doubts. This was my darkest hour. More study would ultimately have gained me admission to the College even if I had failed the first test. More effective glasses aided my eyesight. But where were the healing for my disillusioned mind, the fit lenses for my distraught spirit? Like those glowering thunderheads which gather so suddenly and so menacingly to eclipse the sun even as its rays glisten on the waters, so were my skies all too swiftly blackened. It was "a day of darkness, of deep, seemingly impenetrable darkness without a ray of light."

Or so, at least, it appeared until two rare spirits drew me out of the morass of my youthful doubting and despair. The first was Moses Buttenwieser, professor of Bible at the College, who restored my faith in "that Power not ourselves which makes for righteousness," who, through his unparalleled presentation of the moral passion of the Hebrew prophets, awakened in me a new appreciation of Judaism as being far from identical with the "Christianized" version of it with which I had grown up. I learned that "In Judaism," as Rabbi Freehof has phrased it, "we do not begin with theology, we only arrive at it. We go from deed to creed, from doing to believing. Not wrong belief, but wrong conduct evokes God's disfavor. That is the Jewish way." Now I had unveiled before my eyes the whole stirring parade of those who asked, "What does the Lord require of thee?" and who answered, first and foremost, "To do justly and to love mercy" and only then added, "To walk humbly before God"—that humility including, I then came to understand, the inability on the part of our finite minds to probe His infinite nature, the capacity to know Him only, as Maimonides taught, by suggesting what He is *not;* never by what He is. Also from Buttenweiser, through his incomparably exalting exposition of the Book of Job, my own questionings appeared trivial in contrast to his travail, spiritual as well as physical. Surely, then, I could affirm with Job: "Though He slay me yet will I believe in Him"—in a "Him," however, that could in no wise be identified with the heavenly grandfather of my misguided childhood days. The transmutation of God from person to spirit was the fruitage of my exposure to that second masterful teacher of my student days.

Eustace Haydon, professor of Comparative Religion at the Divinity School of the University of Chicago, likewise played a by no means insignificant role in rescuing me from the fog of disbelief. Christian though he was, he was steeped in the mysteries of the East, aware of all the disturbing, revolutionary findings of contemporary science, and especially appreciative of the nondogmatic teachings of Judaism. It was from him, more than four decades ago, during the summers that I spent on the Chicago University campus, that I came to feel within my own being that spirit which suffuses the entire universe—which *is,* in the literal meaning of that term, veritably a universe and not a chaos—linking the soaring satellites and flaming suns with an Amos, a Beethoven, an Abraham Lincoln, an Albert Einstein.

To me it is striking indeed that my faith, forged in the fires of ravaging doubt, has been able to withstand all the furies of these latter days which have witnessed the paradox of both man's depravity and man's ever-expanding knowledge.

It is my profound hope and prayer that something of this redeeming faith and prophetic passion, derived from masterful teachers and towering spirits, may find in me a channel to those who will read these pages and thus speed the day when the ideals we profess may be translated into life, so that God's Kingdom may be more swiftly established on earth. If this be so, it will be because many generous-spirited friends and coworkers have assisted me in this work. To them I must record my most heartfelt and genuine gratitude.

The first draft of this book, including this Introduction, was completed during the summer of 1962. My beloved recently departed wife and I were at our island retreat in Canada where we had spent every summer for twenty years. As soon as I finished a chapter she read it she read it with her usual sensitive critical faculty, made notes on it, discussed it with me, and gave her unfailing encouragement to my efforts.

As with this book, so with my life. She shared with me every facet of my thoughts, my activities, my problems, my victories, my failures. There was no halfway with her; she always went all the way.

In July, 1963, she was prematurely and poignantly taken from our midst even as these pages were being revised and prepared for publication. Insofar as they may reflect an abiding commitment to the ideals of Judaism and to our American democratic principles, it is, in a literal sense, her book as much as mine.

I also wish to thank my assistant, Miss Ruth Buchbinder, who by night as well as by day has labored over this manuscript far, far beyond the call of any conceivable duty; to Mrs. Ann Johansen and Miss Ruth Harrison who have valiantly and patiently deciphered my handwritten scrawl and have transcribed my illegible notes into neatly typed pages; to The Macmillan Company of Canada which has permitted me the unrestricted use of some of the brief forethoughts quoted from my book, *Never Failing Stream*.

Most especially do I express my appreciation to Mr. Albert Vorspan, Director of the Commission on Social Action of Reform Judaism, for whom my affection and esteem have deepened through the now eleven years that he has been so devoted and dedicated a member of the staff of the Union of American Hebrew Congregations. His empathy with all that I hold precious and sacred and his courageous comradeship of the spirit and unflagging consecration to so many mutually cherished ideals have been of inestimable assistance to me in the planning and preparation of this volume.

To all these and so many more friends, colleagues, coworkers, lay and rabbinic, professional and volunteer, I voice my deep-felt gratitude.

Needless to say, the thoughts and afterthoughts herein expressed are mine and mine alone. While several of my associates were good enough to offer suggestions and criticisms, the ideas which are here set down in all the vulnerability of print are my responsibility only and do not necessarily reflect positions of the Union of American Hebrew Congregations or any other body.

In the words which I believe undergird the whole of Judaism and especially of Jewish life, words which have enabled the Jew to survive despite all that would have doomed a less confident people to extinction: *Gam zu l'tovah*—May all this be for good.

THE UNVANISHING JEW

FORETHOUGHT

And it came to pass after many millennia that the descendants of Abraham fled from the lash of many nations and came at last to the golden land of a new Jerusalem and it was a place known as America. And America was a country of black soil and much richness and it grew into a mighty nation which was the envy of all the peoples of the earth. And as the nation flourished, so did its Jewish citizens. And the government did not, as other governments had always done, shunt them behind ghetto walls, or put stumbling blocks in their paths, or ridicule them because of their peculiar ways. Thus did the Jews open themselves in gratitude to the new land, like parched soil embracing the gentle rain, and the sons and daughters of the immigrants adopted the tongue of their native soil and they rejoiced and gloried in their freedom and in the blessings of their America.

From time to time, hate-filled men as of yore rose up to malign the Jews, but the law was a shelter and the evil words found no echo in the hearts of the people. And so the Jews waxed successful and their children grew up and they moved from the tenements to fine houses in the country with many rooms and Olympian swimming pools; and many of them had maid servants and man servants, and there was no lack of milk and honey and wine, and sleek speeding vehicles to traverse the ribbons of road to the glittering shops and the magnificent watering-places, to which they repaired as to the temple of old. And some had airplanes that flew through the air with the greatest of ease and with speeds swifter than the wind. And the Jews who were treated without difference were free to raise their own houses of God and to pray or to stay away, with none to make them afraid.

9

And the healthy children, growing tall and straight, went off to vast universities and wore the same fine clothes and imbibed the same filtered teachings as did their fellow Americans. And after a time the ancient memories became dim and the words of the Torah were seldom on their lips, and their heads were full of knowledge of space and science and psychology. Comfort, security, and success, a smug split-level home in suburbia, snobbish schools for their young loomed large in their sight, for America was a place of good living. And, as the rulers did not separate Jew from gentile and all were cherished in the bosom of the law, the young people followed their hearts in love and marriage and many cast off the ancient traditions, beliefs, and distinctive practices. The knowledge of God receded from their minds. And yet synagogues were proliferating as never before. They were large and beautiful and modern and seemed not much different from the church across the street and, indeed, few of those who entered the synagogue or the church allowed the church or synagogue to enter them. And so they flourished in America and—despite a bit of ubiquitous withholding of the government's due, as was the way of the land—they paid large income taxes and loved the theater and the golf course and the television and the permissive way of life and, inasmuch as society did not brand or denigrate them as Jews, they ceased inwardly to identify themselves as such, for why, in a homogeneous society, should they separate themselves from their fellow men? And thus they became fliers of airplanes, and skippers of boats, and hunters for pleasure, and wielders of power, and the taste of good food and good drink was savored by their tongues.

And it came to pass, in the latter part of the twentieth century, that Jews ceased to remember their past and their distinctive ways and they became like everyone else—and often more so—in the blessed land of America. And so it is written that, in the golden land of the new Jerusalem, amidst freedom and plenty and the warm bonds of brotherhood, Judaism died painlessly in its sleep. And there was no rending of garments, nor heaping of ashes, and the voice of the Kaddish was not heard in the land.

Possible Threnody for 1984

AFTERTHOUGHTS

This is a grim picture. Could it happen? I think it could. But I don't think it has to. However there is an increasing band of fear-mongers, in and out of pulpits, who believe that, given current trends, the early demise of American Jewry is inevitable. Rabbi Arthur Hertzberg, projecting the low birth rate and low level of Jewish religious and educational commitment, has predicted that American Jewry will not long survive these disintegrating elements. *Look* magazine has glumly characterized American Jews as a "vanishing" group. And, of course, the immediate past Prime Minister of Israel has also frequently predicted such desuetude of American Jewish life.

There is no lack of surface evidence for the viewers-with-alarm.

In the first place, Jews might well become a vanishing breed. Despite the Biblical admonition to "be fruitful and multiply," the Jewish birthrate in the United States lags behind that of the population as a whole. A social scientist, Dr. Joshua Fishman, has estimated the present Jewish birth rate as only 79 per cent of the national average in the United States. Recent studies suggest that the Jewish fertility pattern in America has actually been falling for at least the past two generations. This low level of procreation seems to be associated with the urban character of American Jewry, its high educational levels (women college graduates in general tend to produce about half as many children as nonuniversity women in America), and its occupational distribution (white-collar workers and businessmen have fewer children than do manual workers, and manual workers are disappearing because of automation).

Thus, while the Protestant and Catholic communities continue to keep pace with the population explosion, at the same time that the Jewish birth rate remains static and low, a projection of current rates indicates that the proportion of Jews in relation to the general population in America will decline from 2.9 per cent in 1964 to 2.1 per cent in 1980 and 1.6 per cent in the year 2000. Such a diminution of relative numbers could very well have adverse effects on Jewish self-identification, morale, and influence in the general community, as well as upon Jewish staying power and collective confidence.

This poses serious, even crucial, and conceivably fatal problems for American Jewry. Past generations of American Jewry looked abroad for the infusion of new blood and numbers which were the indispensable requisite for the growth, the strengthening, the ascendancy of

American Jewry from 1880 to 1920. During those decades, immigration brought some 2 million Jews from Europe to American shores. Since the adoption by the U.S. Congress in 1924 of a restrictive immigration policy, Jewish immigration to the United States has declined sharply, falling during the years between 1924 and 1944 to 10.2 per cent of the total immigration; while between 1944 and 1960, it dipped to 6 per cent. Had it not been for the emergency displaced-persons program of 1948, Jewish immigration to America would have sunk to a mere 4.3 per cent of the total. Moreover, even if American immigration policy were radically liberalized, there no longer remains any large reservoir of potential Jewish immigration to the United States, with the remotely possible exception of the vast silent Jewish community entombed behind the Iron Curtain. American Jewry is now 80 per cent native born and this figure is likely to increase.

In addition to low fertility and low replenishment by immigration, the American Jewish community faces an additional threat now reaching ominous proportions: loss of numbers through intermarriage. While the rate of intermarriage is still smaller among Jews than among Protestants and Catholics, recent evidence demonstrates that Jewish intermarriage is on a rising arc. Moreover, only about 30 per cent of the children born of Jewish intermarriages are reared as Jews or are considered Jews by their parents. The rate of intermarriage apparently increases with each generation. A study in Washington, D. C., recently revealed that the intermarriage rate among third-generation Jews had soared to 17 per cent. A study of Jews in Iowa indicated an intermarriage rate of more than 40 per cent.

I do not minimize the dangers in this growing rate of intermarriage and its potential for weakening and ultimately destroying Judaism in America. But before we beat our breasts in alarm, before we rush into ill-considered "cures," we ought to do some hard thinking as to *why* Jews are intermarrying in such increasing numbers.

It must be emphasized, at the very outset, that intermixture and intermarriage are normal sociological developments when different religious and nationality groups live side by side in freedom for any length of time. America is characterized, as perhaps no nation before it, by mobility, fluidity, and the integration of diverse groups into the mainstream of American life. Ethnic groups tend to dissolve; the individual remains. The rise of an industrial society has speeded the process of individuation. The growth of religious pluralism—the equality of competing religious sects—has exerted a subtle conformity to "belong to a religion in order to be a complete and identifiable American." But the same pluralism has made all faiths equally respectable (and, of course, equally inoffensive) so that the general culture does not stigmatize intermarriage as it did in previous generations. As the Jew, like the Catholic, acculturates to a society in which religious bigotry has declined, incidence of marriage across religious lines is bound to accelerate. The sanctions which the Roman Catholic Church can bring to bear grow weaker in the libertarian climate of America, but the Jewish collectivity can apply only the secular sanction of social disapproval. This is not likely to be persuasive in a culture which exalts romantic love as *the sine qua non* for marriage and in which personal happiness and personal freedom are regarded as supreme values.

Thus, the question of intermarriage haunts Roman Catholic and Protestant religious groups as well, and the proportionate "leakage" from their faiths by intermarriage is still much higher than from Jewry. If there is something about the United States which despises a wall, we may as well recognize that this applies also to the wall which many seek to erect between youngsters of differing faiths. Much as we tend to play down the question of marriage across racial lines—recognizing that this emotional question is used as a bludgeon by racist forces in seeking to defend segregation—the truth is that such marriages too are on the increase and will mount sharply as the Negro is genuinely assimilated into American life. Neither polemics nor hysteria can resist trends which are sociologically inevitable.

Researchers agree that attendance at, and graduation from, college increases the intermarriage rate. This confirms a mass of information and observation which shows Jewish students on campus, despite verbal affirmations about God and Judaism, to be notably defective in Jewish knowledge, weak in real Jewish commitment, nonparticipants in religious services and other expressions of Jewish life on campus. It is quite clear that, while Jewish youngsters on the college campus are quite comfortable with their nominal Jewish identification and have no great compulsion to change their names or to disguise their identity as Jews, the fact of being Jewish is not significant enough for most of them to play a major part in their own lives or to be given special weight in determining the choice of a mate. Judaism is not unpleasant to them, only unimportant.

What should be done to counter the grave threat to Jewish survival, of which intermarriage is the outstanding symptom?

It is not as if Jewish parents were unconcerned about intermarriage. Indeed, the very converse is true. The first and second generation of American Jews were strongly opposed to intermarriage. The bitter experience of anti-Semitism and Christian persecution, plus the sense of historic marginality, created powerful brakes against out-marriage. These brakes are much less effective in the third generation of American Jews. Moreover, the Jewish family itself may be losing its vitality as a bearer of Jewish values. Jewish parents in America do not want their children to intermarry. Every research into attitudes confirms this reality. There is abundant evidence that most Jewish parents seek to discourage social contacts between their children and those outside the faith—and frequently this discouragement exerts itself when the children are as young as ten or eleven. It grows more pronounced as the children grow older. The tendency of Jews to live in strongly Jewish neighborhoods has less to do with religious and Jewish values per se than with a desire for "my children to mix with other Jewish children." Yet, many of these very children, products of voluntary Jewish ghettos and carefully circumscribed social contacts, then go off to college, fall in love, and marry non-Jews. It is quite clear that self-ghettoization by itself is not a prophylactic against interfaith marriage.

The fact that self-ghettoization does not prevent intermarriage does not deter some of my fellow Jews from nonetheless prescribing more and more Jewish separatism as the key to Jewish survival. The pressure for more and more Jewish day schools, Jewish country clubs, Jewish universities, and Jewish recreational centers strikes me as a misguided response to a very real problem. The effort to build higher institutional walls behind which to seal ourselves in voluntary isolation represents, in my judgment, an atavistic throwback to the Jewish life of the *shtetl* (the East European village), a period which can never be resurrected and certainly not on the soil of a democratic America. Pluralism must not be corrupted into "separate but equal" societies under religious umbrellas, for if that happens pluralism will be a way-station on the road to fragmentation in American life.

Most of my rabbinic colleagues believe that the most important preventative against intermarriage is an unconditional refusal by the rabbinate to conduct a marriage between a Jew and an unconverted non-Jew. The Central Conference of American Rabbis follows a policy which declares: ". . . mixed marriages are contrary to the tradition of the Jewish religion and should, therefore, be discouraged by the American rabbinate." The Conservative and Orthodox rabbinate goes further and flatly prohibits rabbinic participation unless the non-Jewish party undergoes a conversion to Judaism. Within the Reform rabbinate there are conflicting interpretations of the CCAR policy. Some rabbis, having tried unsuccessfully to "discourage" the interreligious marriage, feel free to conduct the ceremony. A large group of Reform rabbis, bitterly opposed to such marriage, wish to strengthen the CCAR policy into an unequivocal and binding prohibition—an odd and paradoxical authoritarian position for an allegedly liberal rabbinate to urge. This view has been expressed by an esteemed colleague, Rabbi Joseph Klein of Worcester, Massachusetts:

One can well understand the pressures to which rabbis, and Reform rabbis especially, are put when some youngster decides to fall in love with a non-Jew. The Jewish parents feel guilty and ashamed. They have lost, or fear they will lose, respectability in the Jewish community. But if the rabbi officiates at the marriage, the onus of guilt will fall on him too and they will feel less guilty. Besides, his participation will put a *kosher* stamp on the union and things will not look as bad as they are to grand-parents and other relatives. The rabbi, in other words, is being "used" to cover up what is a bad bargain to begin with. He is putting his *hechser* (approval) on what everybody knows is *tref* (unclean). But for the sake of saving the dubious self respect of a single family, the rabbi who lends himself to being "used" in this manner is at the same time contributing to the ultimate destruction of Jewish life, for he is participating in the destruction of the Jewish family and the Jewish home. He is unwittingly telling the whole community that such destruction has his sanction and approval.

I have dwelt at length on only one aspect of the problem of intermarriage. I realize, of course, that there are many others—the complete freedom young American Jews have to meet and associate with young non-Jews, the whole process of assimilation that is rampant especially in isolated Jewish communities, the sense of inferiority many young Jews feel because they are Jews, the lack of sufficient religious orientation in the home particularly, the recognition by young Jews that great respectability and prestige and high positions of leadership in the Jewish community are achieved by people who participate in Jewish religious life at the barest possible minimum level, so why should anyone be interested in perpetuating Judaism through marriage? But I am concerned about the role some rabbis are playing, or are being forced to play, in the ever-growing tide of mixed marriage, and in so doing are unwittingly becoming a dangerous element in the struggle for Jewish survival. How ironic if after 4,000 years of survival against the cruelest tyrants in history, from Pharaoh to Hitler, the history books of the future should record that Jewish life in America came to an end aided and abetted by men, sworn to preserve and perpetuate Judaism, who could not refrain from officiating at mixed marriages. What is to be done about it? Personally, I feel that the best thing that could happen would be for laymen to recognize the danger and start raising a howl, in much the same way as a congregation did when the people recognized the peril of a rabbi who allowed himself to perform mixed marriages on a wholesale scale.

The rabbi referred to by Rabbi Klein was dimissed by his congregation.

While I have much admiration for Rabbi Klein and respect him for this view, I do not share it. I believe that it is quixotic to imagine that the problem of intermarriage would vanish if only all rabbis became conscientious objectors to it. We rabbis are not omnipotent. Indeed, the very opposite is the case. One of the problems is that the rabbi receives great respect for his station but precious little for his views. We are more ornamental than influential. Our profound problem is not that some rabbis continue to perform interreligious weddings. Frankly, I have often been troubled by the intolerance implicit in the decree that the rabbi should, under no circumstances, conduct a marriage ceremony, even for a loyal member of the congregation, where a Jewish partner is marrying a non-Jew, especially since this rigidity will not deter those determined to wed.

Despite our awareness of the internal hemorrhaging which intermarriage causes to Jewish life, marriage is a private and profound decision by two individuals, and I cannot see how the illiberal rejection by the rabbi at such a crucial moment can do anything but repel the non-Jew—and the Jew as well—from any potential attraction which Judaism might hold. And, practically, our stern hard-nosed policy does not seem to have dissuaded our youngsters from following their hearts. Is it really conceivable that the lovestruck young couple, confronted with rejection by the rabbi, will tearfully kiss each other goodbye and call the whole thing off?

We may as well resign ourselves to the idea that a certain amount of intermarriage is inevitable in a free society and that the rate will increase. Not only must rabbis accept this painful reality, but I think we should help our congregants and other Jews to do so as well. Why do Jewish parents, at least emotionally if not physically, sit *shiva* (a ceremony for the observance of death) when their child marries a non-Jew? The Slotkin Study of 183 Jewish-gentile intermarriages in 1942 indicated that 20 per cent of the Jews were rejected by their own families; 27 per cent of the gentiles were not accepted by the families of the Jewish spouse. Intolerance is no solution to intermarriage, and hatred and rejection are incompatible with both Judaism and civilized human relations. And what is it that throws Jewish parents into such frenzied emotional states, as if the bottom had fallen out of their world? Is it really a fear that Jewish survival has been impaired, that Judaism has been weakened? Perhaps for some, and perhaps unconsciously for many. But the chief factor seems to be a social stigma. What will people say? What will Grandma say? What will our neighbors think? Isn't this a reflection of *my* failure?

Before the moaning of Jewish Cassandras reaches a crescendo of alarm, it is important to put the problems we face into some perspective. Before we resign ourselves to a vanishing future, let us consider some of the other realities of the present and the past.

1) It is not at all certain that the Washington, D. C., and Iowa studies of intermarriage warrant the facile wholesale generalizations about the "vanishing American Jews" which are being spread by the pundits of doom. Washington is a most atypical community, where Jews, like others, come and go, rootlessly, as part of the government bureaucracy. Iowa is equally atypical—a rapidly shrinking Jewish community in the declining hinterland of America. Who can doubt that intermarriage skyrockets there as it does in the small towns of the South? But does this describe the Jews in Cleveland, Baltimore, Philadelphia, Los Angeles, Detroit, New York City, and the other large metropolitan centers where 90 per cent of American Jews are located? The limited studies thus far completed point up one clear need at least —for more serious and penetrating research on the actual state of intermarriage among Jews throughout the United States. I am not enough of a Pollyanna to suggest that further research will prove that all is well with us. But I do insist that the chorus of wailing and the posting of obituary notices is at least premature and, in my judgment, faithless to the stubborn staying power of the Jew who amazingly, miraculously enough, has stubbornly, persistently outlived many extermination attempts of the past.

2) We are not the first—nor the last—generation of Jews to fret that the golden chain is breaking. Indeed, perhaps no generation in Jewish history failed to produce the same direful predictions of onrushing calamity. Even in the most creative periods of Jewish history there arose a Moses, a Jeremiah, an Ezra, a Maimonides, the rabbis of the Middle Ages, to excoriate the people for falling away from God and from Jewish practice and to predict chaos and ruin. We have always had our full quota of peripheral, even of vanishing, Jews. But Jewry and Judaism have quite definitely not vanished, though all other peoples of antiquity have. We are still here today. And I firmly believe some— even if not all, even if not most of our offspring—will be here tomorrow.

3) Our current fears stem in a measure from our preoccupation with numbers. The questions persist: How many Jews do we lose through intermarriage? How many by a low birth rate? How many Jews will there be in the year 2000? How many Jews belong to synagogues? But aren't we being misled by this numbers game? What counts in

survival is not quantity, but quality—not the counting of noses but the commitment of hearts. What is the magic in toying with or boasting of mere figures or lamenting their decline? There were probably no more than 5,000 persons in the Exodus from Egypt, although the Bible implies incorrectly that there were several hundred thousand. Yet this tiny, beleaguered band gave the world the Ten Commandments and a moral code that persists to this day. The number of Jews in Babylonia probably did not exceed one million—if it even approximated that sum. Yet they created the Talmud, the Jewish code of laws for daily life. The Jewish community in Spain until the expulsion in 1492 probably numbered no more than 400,000. But this small group launched a Golden Age of unprecedented spiritual, cultural, and artistic verve which is still the marvel of historians. Numbers are not decisive. Was it numbers that enabled 655,000 Jews in Palestine in 1948 to withstand the combined aggressions of six Arab nations, comprising 40 million people? In short, how many Jews do we need to survive, to survive even creatively?

The Quakers in America exemplify my point. Few religious groups have had so profound an impact on the conscience of America—and the world as well. Why? Is it their numbers? They claim about 122,000 at most. It is because the Quakers, few though they be, do stand for something—world peace and moral concern. The integrity of their sensitivity and service transcends the paucity of their numbers and, because of what they symbolize, they seem—and indeed are—much more powerful in reality than they are numerically. And until some master of this favorite American game of numbers conclusively proves or dolefully predicts that we Jews shall dwindle to 100,000, or even less, I shall not panic. Abraham was willing to settle for a mere ten righteous men to "save the city" and his descendants—until caught in this quantitative contagion—have never predicated the survival of our people or faith on the rise or fall of the Jewish census.

4) The rate of intermarriage is not by itself the measure of Jewish health or sickness. Jews intermarried throughout history; Moses himself was married to the daughter of a priest of the Midianites, while the Messiah, according to centuries-old tradition, was to be of the "sprout of Jesse," a lineal descendant of Ruth, the Moabitess who spoke those tender words to her mother-in-law, Naomi; words echoed by many similar dutiful and loving converts who have been bound by an everlasting devotion to a son or daughter of Israel: "Entreat me not to leave thee; . . . whither thou goest I will go; where thou lodgest, I will

lodge; thy people shall be my people, and thy God, my God. Where thou diest; I will die, and there shall I be buried."

The rate of Jewish intermarriage in the Jewish Golden Age of Spain was high and in pre-Hitler Germany extremely so. Nonetheless, even in prewar Germany, Jewish scholarship flourished. Judaism had a renaissance and Jewish culture was vibrant. It is wrong to assume that every Jew who marries a person of another faith desires to commit race suicide, or is necessarily making the ultimate rejection of his Jewish identity. What will determine Jewish survival is not the number who leave but the quality of those who stay.

I welcome the debate now seizing the Jewish community as to whether American Jewry will survive, but I think much of it misses the point. One who put his finger on it was my friend, Philip Klutznick, who said: "Subtract religion from Jewish peoplehood and you remove the heartbeat." What has happened is that we Jews have subtracted religion from the real substance of American Jewish life. We have striven to sustain American Jews for years on a heady fare of fighting anti-Semitism, building a Jewish state in Israel, giving to philanthropy, and making God Himself a kind of honorary chairman of our never-ceasing charity campaigns. But these foods have become too bland to nourish us any longer since Israel is a fact, anti-Semitism has declined, and Jewish philanthropy has become routine and drab. The causes that once galvanized American Jews have lost their steam, and *this*—not abstract statistics about birth rates and mixed marriages—is the heart of our American Jewish problem. We are the first generation of post-nationalism, post-crisis, and post-philanthropy Jews. We are the warrior, bereft of our battles, who must go home to remember what we really fought for.

Jews will survive in America as essentially a faith—not merely as an ethnic or nationality group. It is for this reason that our obsession with intermarriage may deflect us from our real problems. Judaism spells the difference between life and death for the American Jew. And, since the synagogue is the heart which pumps the life blood of the Jewish faith, the synagogue is the key institution for Jewish survival. This is not to pretend that the synagogue as presently functioning is an ideal vessel for transmitting Jewish values; later chapters make a sharp critique of the contemporary American synagogue with drastic recommendations for change. But I stress that, with all its inadequacies, the synagogue is our only fountain of life-giving water, our only foundation on which to build a meaningful Jewish future in America.

A vibrant, dynamic American Judaism can guarantee Jewish survival. It is interesting to note that even the melancholy studies of Jewish intermarriage indicate that the rate is only half as high among those who have had a religious education. The Jew will not vanish in America— and neither will Jewish values, which is even more important—if we can find the courage to reconstruct the life of the synagogue to make it worthy of the majestic faith which our "unvanishing" forebears bequeathed to us through all the millennia of history. Even then, we will never win all Jews to commitment and deep Jewish consciousness. Our forefathers did not either. But we will strengthen that loyal minority—the "saving remnant" if you will—who are not ciphers, not zeros, not numbers. They are the ones who count. They are the builders of tomorrow.

Those who write off the Jewish community because of our intermarriage rate must do so because they fear the dissolution of Judaism and the Jewish people if our numbers decline. Well and good. Then why do we agree to marry couples who are Jewish by birth only and are negative toward all things Jewish? Why do we tolerate "alimony Jews"?—those willing to pay for it but not willing to live with it. Or "flying buttress" Jews?—those who would support it but only from the outside. Why do we not take the next step and aggressively seek converts to Judaism? Almost all rabbis—and most Jewish laymen —shrink from this proposal. Their response is visceral, but they rationalize it in terms of Jewish tradition and by raising specious doubts about the mental health of would-be converts. Do we really have so low an opinion of our faith that we believe that only the unhinged can be attracted to Judaism? This traditional abhorrence seems to be traceable to the fact that Jews were enjoined on penalty of death by the Roman Empire of Constantine from converting Christians to Judaism. Although there is some evidence that Jews continued to proselytize, even into the Middle Ages, there is an almost universal attitude among contemporary Jewish leaders that conversion is somehow un-Jewish. We do, of course, accept converts when they come knocking at the door, usually on the eve of marriage, and sometimes at the zero hour to avert the tragedy of a "bastard's" birth. And yet, despite the cool indifference of the Jewish community to conversions, not only such luminaries as Sammy Davis, Jr., Elizabeth Taylor, and Marilyn Monroe have joined the Jewish fold, but some 10,000 others have been converted to Judaism during the past decade.

But such paltry numbers comprise a miniscule minority of the millions of those who throughout the world are disillusioned with the orthodoxies of their respective ancestral faiths and have naught but contempt for their rigid and outmoded creeds and cults, dogmas and rites. In Japan, in India, in Thailand, and Burma, I was told by monks and priests and swamis of the flood of renegades from their shrines and temples. Christian missionaries—usually benighted though compassionate—capture a bare handful. I was told that there were more prostitutes in Tokyo than converts to Christianity. The Moslems, with a revitalized crusade for the crescent—so far at least minus the sword— are wooing and winning far more. But the Communists everywhere are persuading more than all the others combined with their Pied Piper promises not of harems of seductive sirens or pie in the sky by and by, but by their tempting offer of bread and shelter in the here and now.

Have we nothing more to offer? Have we not even as much to proffer these religiously anchorless, faithless, frustrated, hopeless, spiritually starving multitudes of the earth than the cold, unpalatable stone of Marxism, than the fantasies of an outmoded orthodoxy: Hindu, Buddhist, Moslem, Christian, Jewish? Surely, we have a far richer, fulfilling faith and program of action than such stultified, frozen, ancient, and obsolete presentments which are driving myriads from the temples, mosques, churches, and synagogues. It is for this reason that I think that our failure to launch an aggressive program of conversion is a serious mistake. It reflects, I am afraid, an unbecoming distrust of the gentile—an unpleasant heritage of our tortured history and of Christian efforts to save *our* souls by fair means and foul. It reflects, in addition, a provincial attitude toward our faith as if it were an exclusive, aristocratic club into which one has to be born. It reflects, also, a flaccidity of spirit in which we do not fully accept what we ourselves say about the glories of Judaism. If Judaism is the proprietary faith of Jews alone, it is nothing more than an ethnic or tribal cult. But Judaism is more than that. It is a universal faith which speaks to all men and whose values are acutely consonant with, and relevant to, the times in which we live.

I believe that hundreds of thousands of people could be won for Judaism if we cast off our timidity and sought them out. We may be living in the post-Christian era, and it is obvious that millions of Americans, not to mention the peoples of other lands, have become disillusioned with their own traditional creeds. In an age of science, men seek a rational faith and ask hard questions about religions built upon miracles, angels, saints, physical resurrections, transmigrations of souls, and virgin births. In an age of racial revolution, men are sickened by churches which have sold out their basic teachings by segregating themselves. In an age of moral challenge, men are impatient with quiescent religions which turn their backs on this world and invoke the nothingness of nirvana. In an age of sexual revolution, men and women are casting off the shackles of religions which equate sexuality with sin. In an anti-ideological age, men seek a religion of passion and action rather than one preoccupied with passive other-worldly creeds. In an age of despair, men seek a faith which, far from besmirching man with innate original sin, affirms instead his capacity, as copartner with God, to shape a world of peace and justice. In an era of population explosions in which mothers prematurely die of breeding too profusely and children perish of starvation, wives and mothers, and husbands and fathers, too, will revolt against and be revolted by faiths that spurn the scientific and hygienic spacing of childbirths. In an age when the church preaches a sterile and abstract love which has little impact upon the ambivalence of its own members, men seek a faith which affirms a compassionate justice. All this Judaism can bring to searching, hungry, thirsting souls; souls thirsting and hungry not for water or bread alone, but for "hearing the word of God," a living God, a God not only of our fathers but of our children also, if we have the courge to remove Judaism's light from the bushelbaskets of our temples and carry it into the dark corners of an aching and weary world. We can replenish far more than are forsaking our ranks—replenish not with numbers only, but with converts far more committed than those peripheral malcontents who so eagerly "loose the band of the yoke," which, I am confident, myriads are ready, willingly and joyously, to assume. Jews have always claimed to be a "light unto the nations." Through the power of mass communications we can now spread that light throughout the world. Either Judaism has something to say to modern man or it hasn't. If it has, we have a duty to share it. If it has not, then perhaps it has outlived its purpose for Jews as well.

No, Jews will not vanish. For even if we do not choose to be Jews, the world needs Jews—and Jewish values. If there were no Jews, the world would have to create us. Jacques Maritain, distinguished Roman Catholic philosopher, described Judaism as " . . . like an activating leaven injected into the mass, it gives the world no peace, it bars slumber, it teaches the world to be discontented and restless as long as the world has not God; it stimulates the movement of history." Jews without Judaism are nothing; Jews, living out their Judaism, are a leaven of civilization, and must survive for the sake of the world.

Though individual Jews will admittedly continue to "vanish," there will ever remain a sufficient number who will emulate that heroic figure of whom Solomon Ibn Verga writes in his *Shevet Yehuda* (*Rod of*

Judah) and who, despite all temptation whether deriving from persecution or the siren-like blandishments of freedom, will vouchsafe our survival. Ibn Verga recounts how at the time of the expulsion of the Jews from Spain, a ship carrying exiles from that land was stricken by pestilence. Its captain set all of them ashore on a desolate place where most of them died of famine. But a few gathered their forces and continued to wander until they reached a populated place. Among them was a Jew, his wife, and their two small sons. The woman, since she was not used to such an effort, grew faint and died. The husband then carried his two sons until they too grew weak from hunger. Then he, too fainted from his exhaustion. When he recovered, he found that his sons had died of starvation. Despite his deep grief he stood erect and declared: "Lord of the Universe, Thou hast done many things to tempt me to abandon my faith. Know Thou that it is my firm conviction, despite the efforts of the heavenly Powers, to be a Jew and to remain a Jew, and that what Thou hast inflicted upon me in the past or will inflict upon me in the future is of no avail. It is a Jew I am and shall ever so remain." And he gathered some earth and green leaves and buried the boys and continued to wander until he found a Jewish community.

It is this historic heritage which leads me to affirm the unvanishing Jew and to foresee the day when the vision of the prophet Isaiah will be fulfilled: "In those days ten men from the nations of every tongue shall take hold of the robe of a Jew, saying, 'Let us go with you, for we have heard that God is with you.' "

2

WHAT'S JEWISH
ABOUT JEWISH VALUES?

Are Jewish values still operative among American Jews? Are American Jews distinctive from other Americans in terms of their value stance? Does any Jewish uniqueness enrich American life? What is the source of any such differentiation? What must be done to perpetuate Jewish distinctiveness and the unique values of Judaism? These are the penetrating and perplexing questions which haunt Jewish life in America today.

In my judgment, American Jews do embody a distinctive and significant heritage of values. I believe—without undue chauvinism—that we are justified in claiming for Judaism and the Jew: an historically unparalleled love of learning; an unprecedented reverence for the probings of the mind; an extraordinary impulse toward charity; a rare sensitivity to social evil and an unsurpassed passion for social justice which reflects itself in social and political liberalism together with an indomitable vision of a better tomorrow for all mankind. These values flow from the religion of the Jews, from the concept of the Jew as an *am segulah,* as a chosen people, chosen not for privilege or pride but for sacrifice and service; a "choosing people," as Israel Zangwill translated the Biblical phrase, choosing to be the *avde Adonoy,* "the servants of God," a "kingdom of priests and a holy people." All this had its origin in the creative spiritual genius of the Hebrew prophets and it has been sustained and deepened through the nightmarish centuries of persecution and confinement to squalid ghettos. In America, for the first time in Jewish history, the Jew has been given the opportunity to translate this millennial vision and historic moral mission into life. Jewish experience in America has been described as "history without tears." In the United States, where religious and cultural groups are encouraged to express their re-

24

spective values in the building of a plural society, Jews and Judaism have flourished. In addition to the disproportionate number of individual Jews who have contributed to all walks of American life— labor, education, science, business, entertainment, literature—the Jewish community, as an entity, has made vital contributions to the enrichment of America. The distinctively colored threads of Jewish values have been beautifully and wondrously woven into the general pattern of the American social fabric.

Love of learning is a special aspect of the unique Jewish heritage. Even in the Middle Ages, when the Jews of Eastern Europe were locked behind ghetto walls in poverty and misery, education was universal among Jews, and Jewish literacy contrasted sharply with the widespread illiteracy of the general culture. When the country crossroad tavern or the town pub in England had to display its name in pictures of the cock and the bull, the golden lion, or the black steer because outside of the clergy barely any of the countrymen could read, every Jewish child, by the time he reached thirteen, was literate enough to become a *bar mitzvah,* a son of the commandment. This commitment to education continues to distinguish the Jew in America. What prompts the puzzled non-Jew to characterize the Jew as "smart" is not a superior native endowment; it is an unquenchable craving to learn, spurred by an ineluctable will and inescapable discipline to acquire knowledge in order to survive repeated attempts to liquidate this people and this faith. Jewish parents during the Depression years often were not certain how they could feed their children each evening, but there was not a scintilla of doubt that, if the child had a "good Jewish *kopf*" (head), he was going to go to college and become a doctor or a lawyer or a teacher. Although in America one hears the jibe concerning one's choice of the rabbinate as a career—"Is that a proper job for a nice Jewish boy?"— no goal was greater in the past. And many a Jewish maid's dowry was the education of her mate. A scholar was the prime object of the *schadchan's* (marriage broker's) search for a son-in-law. To be or to make possible such a teacher always stood at the summit of the Jewish value system.

Today, although Jewish literacy has admittedly decreased from so high a level, familiarity with the world of the mind among Jews is still striking. Jews represent some 3 per cent of the population of the U.S.; but Jews provide some 9 per cent of college registrations. A study disclosed that 41 per cent of the Jewish adults in Washington, D.C., have attended college or post-graduate school. While some argue that three out of four Jewish high school students go on to college because Jewish parents are over-motivated in the direction of education and perhaps make status symbols out of their children's IQ and entrance into the "best" college, there is no question that the Jewish commitment to learning is unflagging. Nor can there be any doubt that this Jewish reverence for education has enriched American life. Jews represent a pressure for good public education with rising standards. Public school officials take it as an axiom: where there are many Jewish families in the neighborhood, there will be good public schools, there will be a willingness to expend money for quality instruction and education, and there will be competition for academic achievement.

This reverence for the life of the mind also characterizes Jewish cultural and political behavior. Jews constitute a high proportion of the readers of such thoughtful and sophisticated magazines as *Saturday Review, Harper's, The Reporter, The New Yorker,* and *Atlantic Monthly.* Book publishers are frank to admit their dependence on the Jewish book market; Jewish readers can make or break a book. Similarly, Broadway plays are produced with one eye focused on the Jewish audience which tends to be a major theater-going (and play-producing) segment of the community. A special issue of *Fortune,* devoted to an analysis of New York City, once described New York's Jewish community as the cultural elite which stimulates the creative and intellectual life of the city. Jews represent a quickening element, a yeast, a cultural stimulus in American life.

Group differences express themselves clearly in social and political issues. During the McCarthy madness in American life, public-opinion polls indicated that 85 per cent of American Jews sharply rejected McCarthy at the very time that almost a majority of Christian Americans held a favorable view of the Senator. Similarly, Jews reveal a higher interest in foreign affairs and international issues than do any subgroup in America. Despite their growing middle-class and suburban characteristics, Jews continue to vote "liberal-internationalist." Jews have given 65 to 90 per cent of their votes to the Democratic Party for the past thirty years, confounding all the standard rules of American political behavior by swiftly rising middle-class groups. In fact, I have had friends tell me that they register as Republicans solely for the purpose of attenuating this political monolith.

Jews make up a large number of the members of almost every liberal cause. Jewish leaders, including the late Rabbi Stephen Wise, helped to found the NAACP. Jewish financial and political assistance is still a mainstay of the NAACP, as well as of the Urban League and newer civil rights bodies such as Martin Luther King's Southern Christian

Leadership Conference. Moreover, national Jewish organizations were among the first in America to plunge themselves into the struggle for racial equality in the belief that freedom is indivisible and that Jewish security can be upheld only if all Americans are free to fulfill their human potentiality. Such organizations as the American Civil Liberties Union, the National Sharecroppers Fund, the League to Abolish Capital Punishment, and even the Friends Service Committee would be gravely weakened if Jewish membership and support were expunged. Jews have contributed mightily to the American labor movement. In the American idiom, the Jewish passion for justice expresses itself with continuing vigor.

Much the same can be said for Jewish philanthropy. It is not widely known that the Community Chest and Red Feather approaches to unified fund-raising were emulations of the Jewish federations which began to emerge in American cities in the early nineteenth century. A recent study conducted by Dr. James N. Morgan of the Survey Research Center of the University of Michigan, with the cooperation of the National Bureau of Economic Research, reported that the proportion of Jews contributing $50 or more to charity was considerably higher than that of any other specific segment of the American populace. Since 1946, Jewish federations in the United States have raised over $100 million a year for local and world-wide (mostly Israel) charitable enterprises, reaching a high-water mark of $200 million in 1948. The *mitzvah* (the obligation) of *tsedakah* (charity)—a cardinal obligation in the Jewish tradition—continues to find expression in the life of the American Jew. In addition, Jews give a steadily increasing proportion of their contributions to nonsectarian causes. That Jews have strengthened the forces of and raised the standards of giving to voluntary fund-raising in American life is irrefutable. Indeed, Jews may have been excessively influential as evidenced by the contagion spreading now beyond the ranks of Jewry—the high-pressure blitzkrieg campaign (including card-calling, big givers, man-of-the-year plaques) which were once the special invention—and bane—of Jewish fund-raising in America.

How account for the persistence of this pioneering leadership in so many worthy areas? Certainly there are practical considerations which help to explain the clinging to these values and the performance of these deeds despite the denigration of both in our general contemporary milieu? Jews are obviously safer in a land purged of discrimination. A history of persecution naturally makes for greater social sensitivity. The insatiable quest for education is inevitable as the key to opportunity for any disadvantaged and humiliated group. It is not surprising that many Jews responded to discrimination by seeking a life which would be "separate but better." Jewish proclivities to culture and liberalism may be attributable, in part, to the fact that most Jews are highly educated, urban, and middle class. It must be admitted that a unique history has been one of the primary sculptors of Jewish values.

Yet, I believe it is undeniable that the religion of the Jew has played a major role in making him what he is. Whether God chose Jews or not, it is certain that the Jews chose God and covenanted themselves to be a special, morally responsible people. Judaism bids man, as copartner with God, to take the world in his hand and place it on the anvil of life in order to beat it into a better shape. A dedication to racial justice should not be unexpected in a people who are commanded by their faith to "know the heart of the stranger, for ye were strangers in Egypt." A love of free speech and an abhorrence of any form of censorship are logical concomitants of a people which, traditionally, reverences Amos' refusal to be silenced by kings and priests; a people which treasures the clash of ideas as found in the Talmud, a veritable sea of conflicting opinions; a people of diverse majority and minority viewpoints, of a liberality of mind regarded even as divine, as evidenced by the well-known and oft-quoted rabbinic adage: *"Elu v'elu divre Elohim Chayyim."* "Both these *and these* are the words of the living God."

Hence, Jewish liberalism became virtually indigenous to this people which maintained a deep sense of forensic give and take, which cherished a constant sensitivity to the treatment of the stranger, the widow, the orphan, the sick, and the weak. Generous giving is natural to a people which has been taught to regard charity as man's obligation to God and which has taken seriously Maimonides' Ladder of Charity, depicting, as the highest expression of charity, the equipping of the poor to stand on their own feet in dignity and self-esteem. These values continue to animate American Jews, even those Jews who are indifferent to, and ignorant of, Judaism as a living faith. Even the most secular and acculturated of Jews is the product, I believe, of a unique past and of a remarkable value stance which continue to find expression in daily life. They may not know it—or admit it—but they are, nevertheless, permeated by the *z'chus avos*—the merits of the Fathers—the exalted heritage of their sometimes unconfessed, unwittingly neglected, or consciously repudiated religious and moral inheritance from the past.

But will these values remain viable? Will American Jews continue to manifest this distinctiveness?

Scattered throughout the chapters of this book are ominous storm warnings. We have seen that the Jewish family, once the proudest jewel of Jewish life, is weakening. Acculturation and assimilation are cutting deeply into American Jewry. Jewishness is becoming a substitute for Judaism—and many Jews find their Jewish outlets in such so-called Jewish treasures as bagel and lox, the folksy colloquialisms of nostalgic reminiscences of the good old East Side New York days of Harry Golden, or dancing the Israeli *hora*. Most American Jews are native-born; the prospects for the infusion of new blood and new zest from immigration are dim. Middle-class, par excellence, Jews tend to adopt the conformist, complacent, acquisitive, and egocentric values which are the stigmata of the American middle class. Jews are servilely and sometimes selfishly fleeing to suburbia, where many live in gilded ghettos, quarantining themselves and their children from healthy contact with the thorny problems of slums, poverty, delinquency, crime, and racial segregation which dominate the center cities of the North as well as the South. Many Jews, despite their liberalism at the voting booths, live out their days in a euphoric nirvana of escape and creature comforts. Membership in synagogues exerts a minimal effect on the actual lives of congregants, and most synagogues have not found the courage or energy to challenge their members to practice what their prayer books profess and to summon them to the high ground of moral purpose and genuine Jewish commitment.

The Jewish community no longer makes any exacting demands on American life. In contrast to the Roman Catholic community, which has stringent requirements for acceptance in the fold, and the Negro community, whose urgent desiderata are invincible, the Jewish community seems rather sleek and contented, as if to say: Things should be no worse than they are. Anti-Semitism is at a relatively low ebb in American life and this contributes to Jewish complacency. When Jews were denied equality they fought fiercely to be superior. Now that Jews are regarded as equals, they tend to accept mediocrity posing as normalcy. Jewish fund-raising and organizational life frequently border on vulgarity. While excellence is the theme of many Jewish functions, it is no longer an undeviating guide-line to performance in Jewish education, Jewish culture, synagogue, and community life.

Despite Jewish history, Jews in America rarely feel themselves part of a holy people, a people with a sacred moral mission. While Jews pray for peace and inform God that they are "the messengers of peace unto the peoples of the world," the reality is that a mere one hundred thousand Quakers comprise a more formidable and effective force for peace than do five million American Jews. The Jewish religion teaches strict morality as applied to the daily practice of businessmen; but no one can pretend that Jewish merchants are, by and large, any more scrupulous or ethical than others in a society in which competition is cutthroat and in which "Thou shalt not get caught" has been generally accepted as the Eleventh Commandment. Jewish youngsters continue to go from high school to college in droves, but for the most part, they are not social rebels at college and they hunger for security, status, and popularity in about the same measure as college students generally. They, too, play it cool. If the ethical values which are still discernible among American Jews stem essentially from a religious source, one cannot but ponder the future with troubled heart as one observes the evidence of the thinness of Jewish knowledge and commitment and the decline of religious faith among American Jews.

What will the future bring? Can we recapture the spiritual resources to keep alive the flame of Jewish distinctiveness, or will it be snuffed out by the juggernaut of the general culture—or lack of culture?

The greatest challenge to American Jewry is to keep alive these ethical and spiritual values which are the end products of a civilization which is almost as old as mankind itself. These values, which have marked the Jew as different, have also enriched civilization. I do not agree with those who superficially prate of the identity of Judaism and Americanism and who insist that what is good for America is invariably good for Jews also. That may have been true when the pristine faith of the Puritans was regnant, when America really believed that "by their *Creator*" all men are created equal, and when its citizens acted upon that credo. But what is deeply disturbing to me today is the clear evidence that the values of the Jewish tradition and the values of what is rapidly becoming the generally accepted American culture are, in many respects, conflicting.

Can the rivulet of Jewish distinctiveness maintain itself against the onrushing sea of mass American mores? Can Jewish values enrich the mainstream without being swamped in the churning tides of the general milieu? Can Jewish institutions fortify Jewish uniqueness so that Jews will increasingly build their lives upon the foundation of Jewish teachings, while participating fully and creatively in the larger culture? Or is it vain to imagine that Jews can withstand the leveling and pulverizing effects of the American steamroller? Is it quixotic to hope that Jews, living by Jewish values, can apply the creativity to continue to serve as a leaven in American life, a cultural and spiritual ferment, a goad to moral conscience?

I do not know the answers to these questions. But of one thing I am certain: our age, our nation, desperately needs the humanizing values which have been fired by thirty millennia of Jewish experience and which have enabled this people, alone of all the peoples of antiquity, to survive the holocausts of history. If Jews surrender these values in the false belief that this is the price one must pay to be American, then Jews will be poorer. And so will America—and mankind.

I believe that the deepest task of religion—particularly of Judaism— is to keep man *human* in an age which conspires to deflate the coinage of the individual personality.

America is in the midst of a crisis of values. Everything is topsy-turvy. We are standing our standards on their heads. Symbolic of this is our top-priority project to land a man on the moon. This still seemingly miraculous achievement will cost a minimum of $40 billion. Such a colossal sum of money could wipe out the wretched slums which destroy human beings in every American city and will continue to do so even after civil rights are finally secured. This sum could build public schools and strengthen our educational system, which is an American disgrace. Such programs of national rebuilding would dramatically reduce our unemployment. But, because we have committed these funds to getting us to the moon first, Congress will certainly not for many years authorize the funds to provide decent education and housing for our own citizens, to eliminate poverty, to clear the slums, and to launch the other vital social and economic programs so urgently needed in our land.

And all because an altogether obsolete chauvinism demands that we must get to the moon first. Questions are raised however, in at least some quarters, as to the prohibitive and wasteful costs of such an effort, as to the greater advantages, fiscal and moral, of a joint effort to reach the moon with the Russians, and as to timing. But practically nobody asks the $64-billion—or is it trillion?—question: Why? Why go to the moon? Is it absolutely essential to American military security? Why? Would it not make more sense to work out an agreement with the Russians to leave the moon alone for a while at least? Are we certain that the Russians, obsessed with the craving to "bury us"—economically at least—and bankrupting themselves in the attempt, would not agree with alacrity to such a moratorium? In the final analysis, the judgment of how to expend our national resources is not only a matter of security or of scientific high adventure. It is a moral judgment, a judgment of values, of what we as a nation prize most highly. I am far from convinced that the entire multi-billion-dollar program is anything more than a fantastic diversion fashioned in the heat of an unhealthy form of competition with the Russians. I see it as another dangerous expression of distorted values in our national life.

But the greatest value distortion of our era has to do with the Bomb. It colors our attitudes and actions. We blandly and blindly accept the categories of thought which technology has made possible. Despite our nagging anxiety, we have come to accede to the necessity of super-weapons which have the capacity to destroy the entire population of the earth eleven times over. We pretty the dread weapons in our arsenal by characterizing them as "military hardware." Having become reconciled to the horrors of such weaponry, we accept the logical extension of the arms race into the development of poison gases and germs for chemical warfare. We read, with only the faintest shudder, of how many megapersons would be expended in an atomic war—100 million, 300 million. Living on the edge of horror has coarsened our moral sensitivities and deepened our feelings of futility. Few Americans, indeed, seem to experience any moral revulsion in a nuclear deterrent policy which seeks to preserve the peace of the world by threatening the slaughter of millions of innocents.

We are immersed in moral evil. Contemplation of the ultimate horror dulls our moral response to world hunger, to exploding populations, to the grinding problems of poverty. It creates an internal tension which often seeks relief in the vicarious enjoyment of violence—in boxing and other sports, murder-ridden television, sex-saturated movies, and the theater of the absurd. It impels us to seek the nirvana of our private and personal satisfactions.

Our values are distorted. We seem to be developing more reverence for death than for life. Jessica Mitford's *The American Way of Death* indicates that burial of the dead has become a grisly racket of gigantic proportions, involving the annual expenditure of over $2 billion. Clergymen of all faiths have echoed Miss Mitford's angry protest at the outrageous costs, the bizarre efforts to prettify the corpse, the development of a macabre ritual and an equally weird vocabulary (casket, not coffin; deceased, not dead; service, not funeral) which reflects a fascination with death. But why do the American people submit to these indignities? Is it to do full honor to the deceased or is it to impress one's friends and neighbors and to carry status competition right into the graveyard?

We must face the reality of these grim examples, symbols, and portents, as well as the additional danger of a serious slippage of ethical values in our business and community life. Judaism and Christianity insist that a man's religious obligations include the way he conducts his business, his "weights and measures," his treatment of his workers, and his relations with his competitors. But today we compartmentalize our lives, sealing religion into the church and synagogue and exempting our daily business pursuits from religious and ethical responsibility. Once again, the church and the synagogue have failed to invest our daily lives with values and purpose. Otherwise how explain the fact that the religious revival coexists with an unprecedented breakdown of moral standards?

I am deeply troubled by such evidence of our failure as a nation to maintain the rigorous criteria of personal ethics which are required of us: the consent by silence to accept and seldom condemn the generally amused expectation that everyone will cheat on his income tax, will not flinch from expense-account padding, will not protest the moral failure of television with its mendacious advertising and prevaricating pitchmen; that which countenances the rigged price-fixing of big business concerns, the payola scandals, the widespread cheating on college examinations, featherbedding by labor organizations, the fantastic amount of shoplifting in our stores, and other such indices of decay and moral rot. Unless our religious leaders can help to reverse this alarming drift toward ethical irresponsibility, toward the worship at the altars of money and success, toward a contempt for competitors and customers, it will ill behoove us as a nation to posit our superiority to the Communists on the grounds that they are "materialistic."

This corruption of values is painfully evident, especially, in the unconscionable abuse of that potentially most blessed of all instrumentalities of instruction and moral uplift, the television screen, of which I have made but passing mention above. In Judaism, sin is not found in petty misdemeanors, but in the failure to hit the mark, to rise to one's fullest potential. In this sense, American TV is perpetrating our most cardinal sins. The impact of television on our society is beyond calculation. The average American youngster of high-school age has spent more time watching television than he has spent in the classroom. Bishop Fulton J. Sheen, who was a television star himself with an audience of some 5 million persons, once said: "Television is the newborn babe of the Fourth Dimension of Space-Time. Newton knocked the boundaries out of space; Einstein knocked the boundaries out of time; but television has annihilated both space and time." Indeed, television has become a key influence in our political and cultural life, capable of shaping a host of American institutions—of which religion is certainly one.

In many ways, television erodes the very values upon which religion stands. The entire thrust of advertising, upon which television depends, is toward consumption. To consume as much as possible, as often as possible, is the admonition of all channels, as if consuming were a paramount desideratum of Americanism. In dredging the depths of human motivation, advertising strives constantly to use our susceptibility to sex, greed, lust, and snobbery as bait to lead the unknowing to the proper hook in the proper store. This obsession with acquisition is in the nature of advertising; it enthrones a materialism which is anathema to religion. Television is devoted to the making of money, not the making of character. Similarly, on the entertainment side of television, the prevailing themes generally undercut the values upon which religion stakes its teachings. Television entertainment seems to say, among other things, that violence is a proper resolution to conflict, that might makes right, that love justifies any immorality, and that our side is always right and the other side is always wrong.

Further demonstration of our decline in values is revealed in the cool and callous way we accept the stark hunger of more than half the people of the world. That the Soviets do not really care either should be no comfort to our conscience. They do not pretend to attach sanctity and worth to the individual. They use the world's hungry as a pawn in the cold war. But in truth so do we. Despite our publicized Food for Peace program and our generous support of the UN Freedom from Hunger campaign, the hard fact remains that recent estimates maintained that our thousands of storage bins, filled with mountains of surplus foods, could provide 60 billion loaves of bread to feed half the people of the world who go to sleep hungry every night. I know it is no simple task to get that food from the bins to the stomachs of the starving —the problems of logistics, of jeopardizing world markets, of cold war pressures, are mammoth. But a nation which can build an atom bomb and send men into space could solve this problem, too, if only there were a national determination to do so. But we, too, have submerged the feeding of the hungry to the exigencies of the cold war. If Russia would only join us in disarming, we say, we could release our energies toward the conquest of poverty and starvation. But who is to say the one is of lesser importance? Who is to say that we have a moral right to postpone doing what our wealth, affluence, and our moral destiny oblige us to do?

Yet, we *are* capable, as a nation, of caring very much about a mere individual human being—provided, I must add, his plight is dramatic and stands out from the mass of misery all about us. Thus, when an American astronaut rockets into the heavens, we experience that incredible throat-choking thrill of adventure and empathy coursing through the entire nation. And when one of them was out of radio contact even for a few moments, we waited with prayerful hearts while our Navy scoured the ocean for this single human being. It is good and proper for us to care so much about the fate of such heroes. But must a man be a hero to be worthy of our love? And can we long countenance the "I-didn't-want-to-get-involved" refrain which callously rationalizes hosts of nonintervening onlookers who watch a lad about to jump from a window, see little children stomped on in a school yard, witness a young girl raped before their very eyes? The religious obligation is to be equally solicitous and compassionate about the anonymous human beings at our doorsteps or throughout the world who cry out for our attention. The millions of ordinary individuals who are down need our love as much as the few who go up in clouds of fire.

Even the blessings of Freud, I fear, have corroded our values rather than enhanced them as they potentially might. They have made us smaller, not larger. No doubt many troubled people have been helped by psychotherapy. But, more and more, I find that we behave as a nation of amateur psychologists who go about in glib super-sophistication, sticking labels upon each other, seeking the "real" (meaning the *nasty*) motives of every good action, every dedicated service to an institution, every offering of leadership. "Why does he *need* religion?" the sophisticates ask condescendingly. "What lack is the temple filling in *his* life?" "Why does he *have* to knock himself out for the Community Chest?" "What *drove* him to be a Freedom Rider?" "What's *in it* for him?" "Is he looking for contacts? Bored at home? Eager for publicity? Tired of his wife? Competing with his brother in sibling rivalry? Does he harbor deeply buried guilt feelings? An Oedipus complex?" Carrying a couch on our backs, we thus go about dissecting, probing, castrating, and cutting human beings down in size. It is, of course, not psychology which is to blame; it is the misuse of its jargon and its insights by a segment of the public which serves to lessen the respect we owe each other and ourselves.

Thus it can be seen how many are the dessicating, denigrating forces which stifle the human spirit. How much greater today than ever before is the challenge to church and synagogue to reassert and to reestablish their profound value systems. Religion ought to be—but rarely is—a countervailing force, making for human sympathy, for truer feeling, for greater creativity, for the life-giving qualities. As our leisure time increases, as the number of retired folk constantly swells, the church and the synagogue need to find ways to enhance and expand the inner life of man. What better agencies than the synagogue and church to infuse meaning into the lives of our people, to stimulate respect for decency and the right to recapture a nobler art as that which they once inspired and harbored within their sanctuaries, and to provide opportunity for contemporary Michelangelos in the church and Yehuda Halevis in the synagogue. We ought to commission young artists, composers, and dramatists. Let us pronounce a moratorium on temple theater parties which attend tawdry sex dramas and, instead, lead our people to express themselves and their own finest talents in the synagogue or church itself.

We ought to cease offering lectures and entertainers and, instead, offer study and serious discussion. My dream of a synagogue project is a Sabbath program in which the members would attend services in the morning and, after a light group luncheon, would spend the afternoon studying around a table, reading silently or aloud together, and discussing any literature which quickens and enriches the spirit—not only the Bible, the Talmud, and Jewish literature, but also such great writings as have been produced by Matthew Arnold, Tolstoy, Dostoevski, Whitman, Arthur Miller, Archibald MacLeish. The range is unlimited. It is said that the Jewish people kept the Sabbath, but also that the Sabbath kept the Jewish people. Such a Sabbath would be a refreshment of the starved and jaundiced human spirit.

Each of us must also be concerned with more than merely existing—we must remain truly and vitally *alive*. Though we frantically pursue a multitude of nostrums, no one else can hand us a ready-made philosophy of life. It is for each of us to shape our values for ourselves and to chart our lives by them. Life is not to be merely endured—it is to be *lived* deeply, zestfully, sensitively, and reverently; to be faithful to the divine spark of humanity within us.

What does this mean?

Human communication is the first imperative. In a poignant novel entitled *Quiet Street,* Zelda Popkin voiced this simple, yet profound, truth: "Alone is a terrible word. The worst word I know." There are few experiences in life more terrifying than the prospect of being utterly alone. Certainly this psychological truth was grasped by the sensitive author of the first Book of Genesis: ". . . it is not good for man to dwell alone." And, in the long centuries since, down to Marcel Proust and Jean-Paul Sartre, Thomas Wolfe and Edward Albee, it is this gaunt consciousness and fear of aloneness, of the incapacity of one human being actually to know, to penetrate the inner soul, to belong utterly to another, which is the characteristic feature of our time. Awareness of the inescapable isolation of every mortal spirit is the theme of much of contemporary literature; it is also the profound religious problem of our era.

My late and beloved friend and colleague, Joshua Loth Liebman, in a deeply penetrating essay posthumously published shortly after his untimely death, wrote:

I am alone. I am alone. I felt it first, Mister, when my mother began to love my little sister. I felt alone then. I felt alone also when I was sixteen years old, Mister. My father and mother never understood my language. There were many dialects in my house but there was no communication between any of us. I tell you it is a lie that people can speak to each other and understand one another. We are all alone. I am in my solitary prison and everybody else is in his solitary prison, behind walls and behind bars. I know that people run to all kinds of herd movements—to drink, to promiscuity, to sex, to all sorts of false and deceptive fellowships, the fellowship of the miserable and the unhappy, people who are trying to gain some warmth around the cold hearth of their isolation. Why don't people see the truth? We are, all of us, walking between tall coffins called skyscrapers. They are the coffins in the streets and we are all walking to many rivers of oblivion. I am alone.

A somber picture—and yet, how true! How true of too many lost and lonely human souls wandering aimlessly through the wilderness of time; of *our* time, especially, with its frightful prospect of wholesale atomic destruction, constrained to run like rats, to burrow like moles in our shelters beneath the earth.

Is there no antidote to such gaunt despair? Is there no bridge that can possibly be erected between man and man? Are we everlastingly doomed to solitary confinement in our prison cell of self? Is there no "balm in Gilead"? Is there no exit whatsoever, as Jean-Paul Sartre suggests?

I believe there is. Judaism is acutely sensitive to all the nuances of the human soul—nuances so recently rediscovered by modern poets, authors, and contemporary analysts. Judaism taught the way, perhaps the only way, whereby spirit could touch spirit and soul might commune with soul. Our Hebrew forebears, with rare insight and vision, wrote these words in the sacred scroll of the Law, which Jews throughout the whole far-flung world recite each year at the High Holy Days: "Ye are standing this day, all of you, before the Lord your God; your leaders, your chiefs, your elders, and your officers; your little ones, your wives; and the stranger who is within your midst, from the hewer of wood to the drawer of water; yea, everyone among you."

A majestic spectacle, this panorama of every single Jew and Jewess— including even the generations yet unborn—standing thus *together* before the Lord their God, deriving hope and sustenance through their spiritual kinship with their ancestors and with their fellow Jews!

For, as our rabbis long since pointed out, the only way to achieve salvation, as individuals and as a society, is by thus standing every one of us before the Lord our God, hearkening to His word and heeding His will. These sages tell us that when the children of Israel heard the fearful curses contained in the closing chapter of Deuteronomy, which immediately precedes the above Biblical passage, they were overcome with consternation and cried out: "Who shall be able to endure such punishment?" Whereupon, so our rabbis tell us, Moses quietly reassured the people: "So long as you, all of you, stand *together,* stand by and with and for each other, you will withstand every trial and tribulation that fate may hold in store for you."

Why have we endured two bestial, bloody wars within the lifetime of most of us? Was it not because we refused stubbornly, almost all of us—races, religions, classes, nations, and individuals—to stand together before the Lord our God, listening to His Law, carrying out His will? Like wayward sons and daughters, who have forsaken home and loved ones to pursue their selfish willful ways and who never give a single passing thought to all the treasure they have left behind, until some fateful message is delivered into their hands summoning them to a harrowing deathbed scene and compelling them to move heaven and earth to speed home to their dear ones, so have we gone our callous, competitive ways, pushing, shoving, jostling our way through life, oblivious to the welfare of our fellows and blind to their needs. We have isolated ourselves in our walled-in cells of self, mimicking the growl of Cain: "Am I my brother's keeper?"

The sense of fellowship which has bound Jews together, despite all their differences, must bind together the family of man. We dare not balance the West against the East, the white against the black, the Christian against the Jew. If we really mean to usher in God's kingdom upon this earth, which is the whole gospel of Christendom and Judaism, we must, indeed, stand all of us together before the Lord our God and save the world from skidding dizzily into chaos.

But it must be *before the Lord our God.* This must be no mere mass solidarity, either of the hosts of Israel or of mankind. Even the beasts of the field huddle together before the onrushing storm. But they build no heaven on earth. So, likewise, the mere crowding together, in expediency or dread, on battleground or in air-raid shelter, may stave off or defeat the enemy, but it will not usher in the Messianic dawn. We ought to have learned this truth as the consequence of two world wars which promised "the parliament of man, the federation of the world" and ended in the whole of humanity crouching in terror before the specter of atomic annihilation. As the gifted French author Saint Exupéry phrased it in his penetrating *Flight to Arras:* "One can be a brother only *in* something. Where there is no tie that binds men, men are not united but merely lined up."

One of the primary factors which keeps us from both God and our fellow man is that we merely "line up," we stand in endless queues greedily seeking more and yet more of our creature comforts. I am not making an un-Jewish plea for asceticism. A comfortable shelter over our heads, a reasonable income, a few pictures, good clothes, books— all these are enlargements of our lives. But we must possess our possessions rather than be possessed by them. There are circumstances in which we must be prepared to relinquish them with equanimity—or at least without inner devastation. After all, even in the unascetic Jewish tradition, Jeremiah was prepared to renounce his precious birthright, the last material thing he owned, and to put on the yoke of a slave because only thus did he feel he could awaken his people to the sin of their own gross materialism. Thus, Jochanon ben Zaccai could rejoice because, though reduced to abject poverty, in his mind he carried the riches of the Torah which he knew he would pass on to all posterity. Thus, likewise, did many a more humble Jew in the concentration camps of Europe, deprived of all material possessions, face death itself with faith undimmed. Leo Baeck, the sainted rabbi of the concentration camps, told me that never in his life had he been so proud of his brethren as he was of those who, shorn of every earthly treasure and faced with torture-ridden death, were nonetheless sustained by a profound faith which not even the brutal masters of the gas ovens could obliterate.

I have spoken of the permanent and the passing. It is also important to get this present flashing moment into its proper perspective. We must view it as Spinoza suggested, and as the whole centuries-long saga of the people of Israel suggests, "under the guise of eternity." In poetic imagery, an ancient legend suggests the boundlessness of time both behind and ahead of us:

Far up in the frigid land of Svithjod, there stands a massive rock one-hundred miles long, one-hundred miles wide, one-hundred miles high. Once every thousand years a bird wings its way into this land to sharpen its beak upon that rock. When that rock will have been worn away to nothingness, a single hour of eternity will have passed away.

The late H. G. Wells gave voice to this same idea of perspective when he bade us take the face of a clock as representing the span of man's life upon this planet and indicate thereon the time covered by the period of man's historic existence since his emergence out of the unremembered muck of the past to the present hour. At the very most, some twenty seconds shall have elapsed. For it is only within the past few instants that man has known anything whatsoever about what we speak of as civilization.

Perspective is important not only in time, but in space as well. If we are too near an object its blemishes mar our appreciation of its beauty; its flaws cry out. Especially is this true of the age in which we dwell. No man can measure the significance, for good or ill, of his own generation, much less the ultimate outcome of what each of us is trying to do in his own time. Only the historian of the future, who will look back upon this era through the lenses of perhaps a thousand years, will be able to judge the happenings of our own day. We live too close to the events of the hour. We keep our gaze fixed upon the daily headlines. In facing the onrushing tidal waves of change, we would all be better equipped if we could occasionally slip outside the immediacy of events and read some history—both Jewish and general—so that we would better appreciate that we are not the first generation to live through days such as these, that our forebears were face to face with similarly foreboding tempests, and yet life beat on.

Another source of human communion is the recognition that we are all in the same boat, that our destiny is interwoven with all mankind. In the normal course of events, we are unaware of any real connection with mankind at large—with the pariah of India, the coolie of China, the migrant worker in our own land. Anyone who has suffered some profound personal sorrow knows the feeling of estrangement from others. Perhaps some precious dear one has died. One rises from the stilled and clay-cold body of the beloved and is stunned by the fact that life moves on, seemingly oblivious to the loss that has been so crushingly sustained. When the funeral cortege wends its way to the cemetery, one becomes amazed and shocked to see that the streetcars are still running, children are still playing in the streets, the sun is still shining, the birds still singing. How is it possible? Here the bereaved and bereft spirit sits in his tribulation and the world does not seem to care.

But let an epidemic strike one's city—or an earthquake or a flood. Let a President be assassinated. Suddenly, a fellowship springs forth out of such common suffering as can only be called divine. Then men rise to heights of compassion and self-abnegation of which they would not ordinarily be capable. The American people, moved in part by the incandescent spirit of President Kennedy's widow, were—at least briefly

—softened and ennobled by the great tragedy which befell them on that black Friday, November 22, 1963. Similarly, let the world suddenly shudder to the edge of the apocalypse, as we did over Cuba in 1962. In a moment, men are bound to each other in both fear and hope, transcending all national borders. Despite everything, the deep emotions of people in Moscow were probably indistinguishable from those of the people in New York City and Paris and Tel Aviv and Cairo. The bitter antagonists, Kennedy and Khrushchev, found a strange human understanding of each other. In the common kinship which our shrinking world and our heavy travail demand lies mankind's greatest hope for the future.

The older I become, the more certain I am that suffering is the surest teacher. This is true for nations as it is for individuals. Much of the political adolescence and self-righteousness of the United States stems from the fact that our own land has never been despoiled by war; we have not known at first hand the suffering which the French, the British, the Japanese, the Russians, and other peoples have had to endure. What is true of nations is, I believe, true of individuals. Without the inwardness which suffering compels, we go through our lives taking for granted the very things for which we should be most deeply and prayerfully grateful. Again, I quote my favorite Hebrew expression. It contains, in my opinion, the secret of Jewish survival/: *Gam zu l'tovah*—even this is for the good. Suffering is not only redemptive; in a sense it is humanizing, as all of Jewish history affirms.

I know of no more instructive tutor than pain. Nothing compels stock-taking like suffering. None of us learns anything in life except through actual personal experience. Caught up in the swirling currents of a kaleidoscopic age, dashing too dizzily to pause to measure the reality or the sham of one's own goals, spinning feverishly in the cage of self, we require a mishap, an illness, or a great loss to awaken us to the vanity of much that we pursue. Then—and perhaps only then—do the genuine values of life emerge crystal clear as the choicest of God's abundant blessings.

First of all, just to be alive—how many of us, each morning and evening, praise the Lord for the gift of life itself? No one can spend a long and sleepless night within confining hospital walls, where the angel of death may visit the room next door or across the hall, without being made more acutely aware of the precious boon of life itself. And yet we stupidly take this most treasured gift for granted so that most of us are continuously committing suicide; taking our own lives—if not dramatically in a single act of self-annihilation, then in a multitude of murderous onslaughts upon and abuses of our bodies: relentlessly over-working them, ruthlessly overtaxing their limited reserves, shortening our days for fortune and fame, forgetting how precious and how brief is the span of our years, that we pass this way but once and should safe-guard that which God has so beneficently bestowed upon us, the very gift of our living, breathing, throbbing, pulsating selves, capable of so much of life's goodness and bounty and joy.

Life, then, and health as well. Most of us are endowed with days and years of buoyant, blessed health. And yet we prize it not. Only he who has writhed in agony and suddenly has felt the shafts of piercing pain slowly begin to ebb, until serenity quietly returns to the erstwhile tortured flesh, begins to realize what an exquisite and ordinarily un-appreciated good is the sheer absence of pain. We grouse and growl and grumble when we are afflicted. How rarely do we rejoice in the sheer positive delight of the glow of good health, of rising each morning with body unfevered and flesh unperturbed by wracking torment.

Life and health and love, too. Misguided and far too puritanic were they who interpreted the Song of Songs as a mere allegory of God's love for Israel, instead of hearing the surging chant of the love of man and woman it indubitably is. And its inclusion in our Scripture is patent proof of the role which our distant forebears ascribed to the relationship between lover and loved. *"Ani L'Dodi v'dodi Li"*—"I am my beloved's and my beloved is mine." What more majestic words have ever been written to articulate the devotion, the dedication, the sacrifice and sensitivity which bind us to our beloved and our loved ones to our-selves? Again, tragically enough, this, too, most of us take too carelessly for granted. Precious hours that might be spent in silent yet eloquent communion with one's dear ones, in happy comradeship and deeply and mutually satisfying love, are heedlessly squandered upon a myriad of meaningless pursuits until suddenly, released for the nonce from that incessantly swirling whirlpool of superficial obsessions, we are reminded once again that "as the lily among the thorns, so is my love among the daughters. As the apple tree among the trees of the wood, so is my beloved among the sons."

And friendship, also, that sweet and generous impulse which would cause a man to "lay down even his life for a friend"; which, regardless of cost or effort to one's self, brings courage and confidence and faith and trust once again to hearts sorely tried. But who was it who so correctly said that "to *have* a friend one must *be* a friend"? In taking stock of ourselves we must highly resolve to earn the treasured boon of friendship for ourselves by being friends to the friendless, by "feeding the hungry, clothing the naked, and taking the homeless into our habitation"; yes, even into the presently rigidly bolted gates of this blessed America of ours.

All this—and the heaven of freedom too. Even momentary confinement within four bare walls, even the most temporary deprivation of one's freedom of movement, drives vividly and dramatically home the priceless treasure of liberty which, once again, most of us take all too nonchalantly for granted. The simple daily freedom to move about at will, to labor at the work of our choice, to worship as we choose, to roam the woods, to drink in the beauty of sky and sun and sea and stars; to revel in nature's wondrous pageantry or to be transported to joyous heights by the artist who holds up his mirror to reflect its grandeur— only thus do we really prize adequately all these gifts of the freedom that we are privileged to enjoy.

To be fully human means giving expression to the inner life which is unique to each human being. As copartners with God, we renew His work of Creation through fulfilling and expressing that which is latent within us. In an age of stupefying passivity, it is imperative that each human being seek outlets for self-expression. Art, music, and literature, like religious faith, are no mere cultural ornaments. They are, and ever have been, ineluctable necessities for the expression of that spirit within man which marks him as man and distinguishes him from the beast. Hence the exquisitely fashioned pottery, the magnificently painted murals created by the most primitive of men, the Parthenon, the Cathedrals of Chartres and Cologne, the mosaics of pre-Christian synagogues, the Ninth Symphony of Beethoven, the rhapsodic psalms of the bards of Zion, the stained-glass windows of Chagall—these creations articulate man's deepest aspirations and ideals. They keep a light aglow within us. They ennoble the work of our hands. As we expose ourselves to them, learn to appreciate them as the most sublime achievements of the human spirit, they help to keep us vital, to keep us alive, to keep us human.

To be fully human means to grow all the length of our days. The moment we put learning behind us, the moment we close the circle of our intellectual interests, the moment we slam the doors of the mind and spirit against unexplored experience, we begin the process of premature death. Is there any more tragic spectacle than that of the aging man or woman, retired from work and no longer needed by his grown children, sitting aimlessly, brooding over the tarnished memories of yesterday, empty, uncurious, waiting for the physical death which has already settled on the mind and the heart? On the other hand, is there anything more inspiring and challenging than the late Grandma Moses starting her career as an artist in her seventies; or of some other grandmothers matriculating at colleges, of scientists, statesmen, businessmen, mapping out new ventures and adventures well on into their so-called old age?

But it is not merely to store up resources for old age that I urge the necessity of constant growth. It is to quicken and savor life as we live it, no matter what the number of our years. "Repent one day before your death," our rabbis said—meaning you know not which day that will be. My paraphrase would be, "Enrich your life each day." Nor am I writing exclusively of intellectual growth. I mean also emotional and spiritual development. We are never too old—or too young either—to meet new people, to explore new ideas, to visit new places, to hear new music, to thrill to the beauty of a new sunrise, to allow our prejudices to be challenged by a fresh view, to identify ourselves with an emergent cause, to lift the heart to prayer.

On the island where these words are being written, I have sat near the shore of the lake just as dusk begins to descend or I have been paddling in a canoe as the sun plunges into the blazing waters. During the twenty summers during which I sought rest and refreshment of spirit in this sequestered retreat, I witnessed more than a thousand such sunsets. No one was like the other in the precise admixture of celestial hues. Now there were flaming, flamboyant scarlets and orange; now quiet pastel purples and pinks. Now the afterglow was brief like passion swiftly spent; now it tarried, reluctant to depart, with the woods and the water swathed in a long-lingering lavender haze. I have watched and heard more than a hundred storms gather. Sometimes out of a sunlit sky, a clap of thunder pealed suddenly and deafeningly overhead and the sky darkened instantaneously. Sometimes the faintest rumble was heard dimly in the distance and the clouds gathered slowly, hesitantly, not yet decided whether to drop their stored-up torrents or not. I have seen tiny saplings, which were once lovingly planted and tenderly nurtured, grow into stately pines and sheltering cedar—adult now and no longer dependent upon our care. What beauty! What wonder! What inner richness!

To be human is to be open to such experiences which abound at our doorsteps, to be capable of spontaneous awe and rapturous wonder and worship. To be fully human means to avoid the false comfort of a rutted life, eschewing the safety of the harbor, preferring instead to sail the broad oceans of life, stretching the horizons, risking the storms, and exploring the adventures of being truly, exhilaratingly alive.

To be fully human means to be involved with the human family. I don't mean merely one's immediate family, which is of course the primary source of our contentment, or the tight knot of one's own friends and neighbors. But the family cannot be an island of decency in a disorderly and decadent society. Reisman writes of the "inner migration," the tendency to withdraw from the problems of society into an exclusive preoccupation with one's own family and surroundings. One of the grave tendencies in American life is that of self-segregation by class, race, religion, ethnic group. Our human relations are limited, shrunken. We tend to resign ourselves to the gray monochrome of one-race, one-language, one-religion, one-class neighborhoods where everybody looks alike, talks alike, and thinks alike. When we travel we seek out Americans first, foremost, and often all the time. We chafe when we can't procure a Coke or our favorite cigarettes in a foreign land. I've heard Americans curse some gentle room clerk in the distant Orient because he couldn't understand or speak English. We Americans will often pass up a spectacular sunset at sea or the exciting splash of the Milky Way because we are imprisoned in the cocktail lounge drinking the self-same Manhattan we have at home or riveted to our tables in the salon playing the same game of bridge or rummy available to us 365 nights a year.

But this narrowness diminishes our own humanity. It denies us the richness and color and salt which come from living in a variegated, multicolored, pluralistic world. I am not recommending that we go forth consciously—and oh so *self*-consciously and *self*-righteously—to cultivate the friendship of a Negro, a Japanese, a Roman Catholic, or other similar or dissimilar acquaintances. Such cold-blooded condescension is the acme of snobbishness. But I am saying that to be fully human means to be genuinely engaged with other human beings whose lives are different from our own. It means to vault the artificial barriers which, by locking others out, fence us in. It means to be open to difference—to cherish it.

We can no longer pretend that the thin, bland slice of life which constitutes our particular neighborhood, our temple, our club, is typical of all human experience. There is a wide, pulsating world beyond. What do we know of it? Of its sufferings as well as of its joys; of its triumphs as well as of its travail? But in this age of jet airplanes, and Telstar, and language schools, and exchange students, and books without end, we can—and should—rise above our petty parochialisms of nation and color and faith, constantly to enlarge our loyalties, identifications, and interests.

This is, of course, important for America as a nation. It is important, in my belief, for each of us to cast out the superior, smug, and ignorant temper of neocolonialism which shuts us off from our fellow men. We cannot achieve wholeness until we are at one with the rest of humanity, until we can feel another man's pain, exult in his freedom, be jealous of his dignity and warm to his needs. I once read somewhere that we will not fulfill our humanity until the pangs of hunger felt by some starving child in distant India causes us to feel actually and physically a similar pain. I believe this to be true, that this is to be wholly human.

To be human means to live a rich emotional life. How starved and sick emotionally is so much of contemporary society. But no long and costly psychoanalysis is required to understand why the entrances to our moving picture houses are festooned with blowups of such sensationally buxom heroines; why advertisements for everything from toothpaste to cigarettes, from motorcars to motorboats, must feature the female bosom; why sex in America has been cheapened and coarsened and debased. It is as a natural reaction to too much emotional starvation and lingering Puritanism that sex runs riot in America today.

Being human means discovering the capacity for tenderness which is regarded as a weak feminine virtue in American culture. We have grown too tough. It is unmasculine for men to weep. We admire the boxer who can pulverize his opponent and we expect the loser, his face smashed into a bloody pulp, to rise again until he is beaten into unconsciousness. We enjoy the high-wire act in the circus so much more if no net is stretched below. We associate tenderness with softness. To quote Ravid Reisman again, we are reminded of his comment that our undeveloped capacity for tenderness is in part a result of the fact that as a nation we have never known the suffering which the war-ravaged nations of Europe have known. This lack of suffering, he writes, ". . . leads to a certain lack of sympathy for the sufferings of others, particularly when this can be rationalized in terms of American ideals and explained as not the result of visible injustice."

And we must be capable of humor—about one's self, one's society, life itself. For humorlessness steals the spice from life. It leads to pomposity, self-righteousness, and fanaticism. Humor has been a redemptive force in Jewish life. It has helped to keep Jews human despite all the inhumanity they have endured through the ages.

To be human is to build one's life on a set of values and to live by these values. To be human is to live a life of purpose. "What does the

Lord require of me?" was the guide which suffused the life of our Jewish forebears with richness. Is this too old-fashioned to withstand the competition of the beatniks of our age, scrambling for kicks and the joyless thrills of empty happiness?

No doubt it is somewhat self-serving to say this, but I cannot help believing that Judaism, more than any other major religion, is ideally equipped to provide these values which truly make us human, which restore our divinity, rekindle the spark God first breathed into us, and by which a modern man can live a purposeful life. Judaism is a life-affirming faith. It has no patience with the asceticism which streaks Christianity and is the basis of Buddhism. Monasteries, celibacy, and retreats from life are not be to found in Judaism. Judaism accepts the needs of the flesh as well as those of the spirit. Where other faiths downgrade this world and this life in favor of some beckoning paradise to come, Judaism is intoxicated with this earth, which God found "good," even "very good." Where other faiths regard man as contaminated by original sin, Judaism exalts man as copartner with God and a little lower than the angels.

Where other faiths view the world through the gloomy prism of theological pessimism, Judaism affirms its optimistic faith in the goodness of life and in man's power to improve society. Where Christianity seeks the salvation of the individual soul, Judaism summons man to save the world. Where Christianity stresses belief, Judaism stresses action. Judaism is, first and foremost, a way of life—a way of sanctifying and ennobling life. *L'chayim* is the toast Jews exchange over wine. *L'chayim*—"to Life"—is the dedication of the Jewish spirit.

To be human means to feel more keenly, to care more deeply, to exult in our involvement with our fellow men. It means to be capable of compassion in the face of another's pain and indignation in the teeth of social wrong. It means to be alive to the needs and aspirations of our fellow human beings everywhere. Is this possible? Isn't it merely pious and unrealistic? If so, then religion is a cruel jest and we should waste no more effort in its behalf. For religion—and especially Judaism—is a blazing affirmation of the value of life and an eternal rebuke to all that seeks to stunt and shrivel the soul of man. The greatest duty we owe to God is to cherish the human spirit He breathed into all His children. The greatest duty we owe to ourselves and to our fellow man is to recapture these redemptive Jewish values and to restore them to a place of primacy in our lives.

3

THE STATE OF ISRAEL—

IS NATIONHOOD ENOUGH?

FORETHOUGHT

Be not deluded! What many of these Jewish nationalists want is a parliament, a law-making and law-enforcing body, an imperium in imperio *which, even if for a time the Jew remains landless, will nonetheless be the focus of Jewish national loyalties.*

A Jewish national state is what these madmen in Israel are seeking, and he who would call a halt to this fulfillment of our enemies' most malicious libel is called a traitor; he who would find any purpose in life other than just to be Jewish in the jingoist connotation of that term, he who would turn to constructive programs of relief or who would devote our splendid Jewish energies to world causes is regarded—almost the very words of the Nazis themselves are sometimes used—as sabotaging Israel's nationalistic dreams, or rather I should say, Israel's fantastic nightmares.

That is the concept against which I so vigorously protest and against which I shall continue to protest, even if I must stand alone contra mundum. *That I am in the minority concerns me not the slightest. That this vision of Jewish national rebirth, whether in Palestine or in the Diaspora, has kindled new enthusiasm in Jewish life, especially among our Jewish youth; that Jewish cultural and spiritual activities are deserted while mass meetings are swarming with youths and maidens, is beside the point.*

Churches are likewise struggling for existence while youthful patriots parade in endless battalions throughout the earth. Fascism appeals to youth, Communism appeals to youth, Hitlerism appeals magnificently to youth, and so does Jewish nationalism—which makes it quite as dangerous to the essential spirit of the Jew as Fascism, Communism, and Hitlerism are to the essence of Christianity.

Toronto, 1934

AFTERTHOUGHTS

Did I say that?!!

Oh, that mine enemy would write a book! In the rash and angry words of the above sermon, I was my own worst enemy. The times have changed radically since I gave vent to that outburst. And so have I.

A famous scientist recently said that mankind has learned more in the past ten years than it learned in all the millennia preceding. I think I can say that, in the brief span of a generation, more Jewish history has been written or rewritten (in both blood and grandeur) than in many centuries preceding. We have known Hitler. And, while Hitler was defeated in battle, he was more successful in his war against Jewry. He destroyed nearly half our numbers. He wiped out, forever, some of the most renowned centers of Jewish life. He made the old country a Jewish wasteland, a cemetery for millions of our people. The center of gravity of world Jewry moved suddenly to the United States. And, in 1948, also to Israel.

The voice of history has answered my youthful arrogance and dogmatism—harshly, peremptorily, and with finality. Life has reduced many of my callow and presumptuous words to hollow rhetoric. It has mocked my false and shallow antitheses. Are we a race, nation, or religion? Let college students debate this proposition, if they will. Life has given its own answers. Hitler did not trouble himself with the niceties of these distinctions. All who were Jews—the assimilated, the Zionists, the Orthodox, the self-deniers, the Yiddishists, the German syncophants, the knowing and the unknowing—all were eligible for the Nazi crematoria. It was a peoplehood of suffering, a brotherhood of agony.

What are we, then, we Jews? We are not a race, it is true. But we are more than a religion only. The truth is that we Jews do not quite fit into any of the pigeonholes of definition. We are, in the end, an *am segulah,* a peculiar people, molded by a sublime and tragic history into something unique under the sun. In my roseate universalism of 1934 I nurtured a dream which was shortlived.

I was as close to being an anti-Zionist in 1934 as my generally fancied liberal antidogmatic bias would permit. My exposure to Reform Judaism derived from my home and temple—both at that time strongly anti-Zionist. My reading of the pioneers of Reform Judaism both abroad and at home reinforced my attitude. My background and training were, in retrospect, grossly parochial, untouched by the warm emotion of much of my people's poignant saga. Surely it must be conceded that anti-Zionism *was* characteristic of "classical" Reform Judaism. The founders of Reform Judaism in both Europe and America were opposed to Jewish nationalism as they were opposed to much, if not most, ritual and ceremony. This was not meanly motivated, as the defamers of Reform, within as well as without Reform Jewish ranks, mistakenly and sometimes maliciously aver. Many among the rank and file may have been prompted by a "what-will-the-gentiles-say" fear that if, in this new world of cosmopolitan enlightenment, we Jews would retain our peculiar ways and seek the restoration of our particular land, we would remain incarcerated, if not physically, then at least culturally, spiritually, and socially, behind ghetto walls of our own creation.

But this was not true of the spiritual and intellectual founders of the Reform movement. They sought no escape from Judaism either for themselves or for their fellow Jews. They strove instead to save myriads of their coreligionists, who were escaping from Judaism long before Reform emerged—escaping from an outmoded and rigid Orthodoxy. However naively and prematurely, the Reformers genuinely believed that the Messianic Era was around the corner and that the time had come to cast aside all nationalistic and particularistic trappings. To them the genius of Judaism was the universalist message of the prophets, a message which had long been buried under the weedy growth of Orthodox ritualism. This optimistic and anti-nationalist view was set forth clearly in the Pittsburgh Platform of the Central Conference of American Rabbis, the Reform rabbinate, in 1885:

> We recognize in the modern era of universal culture of heart and intellect the approach of the realization of Israel's great Messianic hope for the establishment of the kingdom of truth, justice, and peace among all men. We consider ourselves no longer a nation but a religious community, and therefore expect neither a return to Palestine, nor a sacrificial worship under the administration of the sons of Aaron, nor the restoration of any of the laws concerning the Jewish state.

The truth is that even while I was preaching that bitter 1934 sermon on the evils of nationalism, it was Zionism—and not the synagogue—which was keeping Jewish life alive in many parts of the world. The movement started by Theodor Herzl stirred Jewish hearts in great metropolitan centers such as Moscow and Petrograd as well as in the tiny *shtetls* of Galicia and the Ukraine. It revived Jewish morale and quickened Jewish idealism. Herzl affirmed bravely in the face of a dubious world: "If we will it, it is no dream." He also declared that Jews would never be secure in lands long plagued by virulent anti-Semitism until a Jewish homeland was rebuilt. Such teachings irritated the liberal and sentimental clichés of the era. But history vindicated their essential truth. How many more Jews could have been rescued from Hitlerism if a Jewish homeland had existed in the 1930s —the one place where no questions would ever have been asked before extending the hand and heart of welcome, the very definition of home. And how different the post-war world would have been if there were not a State of Israel to reclaim the survivors, the refugees from anti-Jewish persecution in Arab and Communist lands, and to redeem the broken of spirit! Indeed, the Zionist endeavor in the years preceding the birth of Israel was anticipated in the homily by the rabbis of old: "The Holy One, blessed be He, creates the healing before the disease."

Just as my own position on Zionism has changed through the years, so has the official posture of Reform Judaism. In 1935, the convention of the Central Conference of American Rabbis was the scene of a stormy reappraisal of the traditional Reform attitude toward Zionism. By that time, many Reform rabbis had rejected the dogma of anti-Zionism which, they felt, was tearing Reform Judaism from the deepest traditions of the Jewish heritage and forcing it out of the mainstream of Jewish life. Hitlerism cast its long shadow over these deliberations, and against that grim backdrop the optimistic faith in the inevitable progress of mankind toward internationalism and peace seemed cruelly illusory. In 1937, in Columbus, Ohio, the Conference adopted a new statement of principles which jettisoned the historic anti-Zionism of Reform Judaism.

It is ironic that out of this historic change within Reform Judaism grew the American Council for Judaism which, since its inception in 1942, has been a divisive and rancorous influence on American Jewish life. The first steps toward the formation of this dissident group were taken in 1941, when the Central Conference passed a resolution favoring the creation of a Jewish fighting force to serve with the British military to protect the Jews in Palestine against the marauding Arabs.

Today the American Council for Judaism is still an infinitesimally small organization of some 20,000 members at most. But in spite of its numerical insignificance, it has the deleterious nuisance value of a kind of a Jewish-type McCarthyism which impugns the patriotism of American Jews who express their sympathy and support for the State of Israel. By fulminating in the press over alleged "dual loyalties" of Zionists, the American Council for Judaism has worked mischief far beyond its numbers. It has richly earned the unambiguous condemnation of virtually every other Jewish body in America, as well as the contempt of the overwhelming majority of individual American Jews.

My metamorphosis from one who might very easily have become an American Councilite, had it been in existence during my student days, to one who became a committed friend of Israel reborn, began in Toronto. My arrival there was accompanied by a parade—not, however, for my special benefit. Nor was it the usual kind of parade with uniformed men and brass bands. This was a silent parade, a solemn and somber one; it was a rare Jewish parade.

My labors in Toronto began on September 1, 1929. During the closing days of August, the Arabs of Palestine had committed one of their murderous acts of violence upon the virtually defenseless Jewish settlement there. The purpose of the parade was not merely to protest the brutal assault upon our brethren in the Holy Land but, in addition, to press the British into accepting a brigade of young Canadian Jews as part of a proposed Jewish Legion to safeguard the Jews in Zion. I was not so callous in my attitude to the resettlement of Jews in Palestine as to be out of sympathy with the first of these objectives. But those were still my pacifist days—pre-Hitler—and I strenuously disagreed with the second goal which that parade sought to achieve. I did not believe that Israel's mission of peace could be carried out by recruiting a Jewish Legion to fight the Arabs.

At that time I was reading a book by Maurice Samuels, entitled *You Gentiles,* the thesis of which is that we Jews are incurably "pacific," that hunting, fishing, war, and all such sadistic practices are "for gentiles only." These pages smacked to me of unwarranted Jewish chauvinism and were still vivid in my mind when I heard of the parade. It struck me as incongruous to relate Samuel's thesis of the gentle, non-militaristic Jews to this band of would-be warriors, itching to kill Arabs.

Prior to my arrival in Canada, I had been invited to become a contributing editor of the *Canadian Jewish Review.* My first editorial was to be synchronized with my arrival in Toronto. What could be more timely than to write of Maurice Samuel's *You Gentiles* in the light of the seeming paradox of those parading Jews? My first literary expression in Canada was sardonically entitled "We Pacifists."

After developing the contradictory contrast between theory and practice, I offered a suggestion as to what should be done about the tragic events in Palestine that had provoked the parade. By so doing, I committed what I soon learned was the unpardonable sin in Toronto. I supported the so-called "Magnes line," the course urged by Judah Leon Magnes, renowned American Reform rabbi who was then President of the Hebrew University in Jerusalem. He and his group, known as the Ichud, advocated reconciliation with the Arabs and a binational (Jewish-Arab) state in Palestine.

I was immediately subjected to the same stream of vituperation that Magnes was enduring. Just as he was so frequently threatened with dismissal from his post which only his well-earned distinction was able invariably to avert, so too, my first public expression brought demands for my immediate dismissal from the pulpit from which I had yet to preach my first sermon. But I had no distinguished career behind me, nor any well-earned and well-placed friends to buttress me in my now exceedingly precarious position.

The day after the publication of my editorial, the *Yiddische Journal* of Toronto carried a bold headline across its entire front page: *"Verdammte Narishkait und Chutzpah"* which might be translated as "Damned Foolishness and Effrontery." The Yiddish press in Canada then had a fairly large reading public. The great majority of Canadian Jewry were first-generation immigrants from almost exclusively Yiddish-speaking Eastern Europe. Thus, few Jews in Toronto could have failed to know that I had been scathingly indicted as a *mamzer* and a *meshummed,* which mean "bastard" and "convert" or, less politely, "traitor." The press called upon my congregation's leaders to dismiss me peremptorily.

The leaders of the Canadian Zionist movement, some of them members of my congregation (*my* congregation *for a week*), asked for a meeting with my officers. The conference was held and the specific request for my prompt dismissal was officially placed before them.

The congregational leaders refused to be stampeded, however, and the president, who incidentally boasted that he was an atheist, was as enflamed in his anti-Zionism as those who conferred with him were afire in their enthusiasm for a Jewish state. Thus did my opponents overplay their hand. The august board of Holy Blossom Congregation would not be panicked, nor would its members be so unprincipled as to jeopardize a rabbi's entire career because of a single unpopular statement. That was the first of many evidences that the members of Holy Blossom Congregation would invariably support a "free pulpit." To a man, they rejected the arrogant suggestion to send their young rabbi packing before he had even completed his unpacking.

Those who were repudiated, however, did not take their rejection lightly. The ones among them who were members of Holy Blossom Congregation resigned. They were a bare handful, to be sure, and while they were not counted among the leadership of the temple, they were prominent in Toronto and Canadian Jewry, especially in the ranks of Canadian Zionism.

But even my resignation would not have satisfied them—at least not the fanatical president of the Hadassah of Canada who was the chief of the angry tribe demanding my scalp. It did not take me long to master the truth of the saying "Hell hath no fury like a woman scorned." She would not relent—neither then nor since and, wealthy as she was, she spent a fortune to drive me out of town. Her first move, following the aborted attempt to force my resignation, was to found a rival magazine. It was intended to achieve two fiercely avowed purposes: first, to drive the *Canadian Jewish Review* out of business in reprisal against its refusal, despite threatened withdrawal of advertising, to disassociate itself from the "We Pacifists" editorial; and, second, to deport me back across the frontier. To accomplish these objectives she, together with a few cohorts, imported Mr. Meyer Weigal, world-roving journalist, impresario, and promoter extraordinary, as editor of the newly founded Anglo-Jewish periodical, the *Canadian Jewish Standard*. Weisgal was no inconsequential adversary. He has a keen mind, a quick wit, a scorching irony, a slashing pen. But hundreds of thousands of dollars and oceans of ink later the *Canadian Jewish Review*, as well as the *Canadian Jewish Standard*, was still publishing weekly, and I was still rabbi of Holy Blossom Congregation.

All this, however, did not sweeten my sentiments concerning Zion nor did it generate any great affection for Zionists in general and the Canadian breed in particular.

But the transforming experience was the first pilgrimage to Zion which my late wife and I took in 1935. She was Texas born and was reared in a tiny Oklahoma hamlet to which her grandparents had migrated when it was still Indian territory. That crossroads Oklahoma village was *Judenrein* (clean out of Jews) except for her family, the Browns. Her father had, almost singlehandedly, staved off the threatened advent of the Ku Klux Klan to the new state of Oklahoma. He was also one of the founders of the little Reform congregation at nearby Muskogee, which could afford the services of a rabbinic student only during the Holy Days. Though clinging fast to their identity as Jews, there was little in that congregation's rabbi-less existence and virtually non-Jewish milieu to cause the spell of Zion to captivate them.

Our backgrounds had thus been similarly untouched by the thrust of Zionism. We were eager to see for ourselves all that of which the Psalmists had so rhapsodically sung, though we set out with not altogether unprejudiced eyes or hearts. We returned, aglow from our experience, and with an abiding affection for the land and especially for its people.

But it was not the official Zionists that made this change possible. Indeed, several episodes almost engendered, once again, the opposite effect. Our very first day in Jerusalem was marred by the transference there of the battles I had known at home. Soon after our arrival we attended a reception at the then quite new and attractive building of the Jewish National Fund. At that moment a towering figure was the center of a large group. It was Stephen S. Wise, for whom I had always had the utmost admiration. Notwithstanding what I am about to report, he became, subsequently, one of my cherished friends.

Wise was that Jew of our generation whose name was mentioned everywhere in awe and reverence. The instant I was introduced to him at that reception, Wise, not even deigning to acknowledge the introduction, scanned the fairly sizable audience that surrounded him and satisfied himself that the number sufficed for a typical Carnegie Hall oration. He raised his stentorian voice and berated me in a violent denunciation. So this was "the traitorous Jew who had written that treasonable editorial in the *Canadian Jewish Review*!" Six years had passed, yet Wise remembered not only the name of the magazine, the date the editorial had been written, and the substance of the article, but almost every word in it. He continued, to the obvious delight of the audience now swelling every moment, now all hushed in hypnotic silence before that titanic figure pouring forth his prophetic wrath upon my startled self. I had "no doubt come to Palestine to consort with my friends and allies, the Arabs!" Rabbi Elmer Berger, executive head of the American Council, for all his anti-Zionist tirades and actions, never received a more vehement tongue-lashing than that heaped upon me by Wise that day.

Despite this first unhappy encounter with Wise in the Holy Land,

I did not allow his stinging rebuke to prejudice my impressions of all that was to follow during this first visit to Palestine. Besides, Wise's occasional human frailties were insignificant when weighed against his almost superhuman fortitude, his unfailing fealty to his people, to Israel, and to all mankind. Throughout his noble career, he had an unflinching fidelity to justice and decency and the dignity of every human being.

During the six years since my stormy arrival in Toronto, I had established cordial relationships with the Labor Zionist group there. Its leadership did not share the fanaticism which the officials of the General Zionists had sought to enkindle in Canadian Jewry. These humble toilers contributed toward the rearing of what they conceived to be not another nation like all the rest, but a commonwealth of equity and righteousness. All this appealed to my own interpretation of Judaism and I began to share their dream of the possibility of such a grand experiment of social justice in Zion. Consequently, the response to the letters of introduction I had from my local Poale Zion (Labor Zionist) friends was warm and hearty, and I spent most of my time in the company of those pioneers of the Histadrut (corresponding in general to our labor movements of the West but by no means as limited) who are today the indomitable leaders of the State of Israel. Ben-Gurion, Moshe Sharett, and Shazar were among this group which included most of those who had guided the new-born state through its first decade and a half of existence. But there were two others to whom I was—and am to this day—profoundly indebted for whatever conversion they effected in my attitude toward the rebuilding of Zion. One is Golda Meier, now the wise Foreign Minister of Israel, who generously postponed her many pressing responsibilities to the Party (the Histadrut) to be our personal guide for a full week in our tour of the *kibbutzim* (the labor colonies). The other was the doughty directing head of one of the earliest of these communal settlements, Sireni, who, later as a parachutist, gave up his life rescuing Jews from behind the black curtain of Naziland. It was with him and his fellow *kibbutzniks* that we spent a number of never-to-be forgotten days and nights. Through them we came to know the spirit of the founders of modern Israel.

I learned there was a quite a difference between standing in a pulpit decrying the evils of nationalism and the visceral commitment to one's own land; between writing an abstract editorial, advocating nonretaliatory, peaceful coexistence with the Arabs regardless of provocation, and standing on a hillside overlooking the blood-spattered ruins of what had once been a thriving Jewish settlement. At Beer Tuvia, for example, at the very time I had been writing that editorial, the Arabs had savagely assaulted and destroyed the entire colony. One of the most heartrending sights I have ever seen was the charred remains of Beer Tuvia: the ruined water tower, the crumbling stones of the children's home in which helpless infants were scorched to the crisp.

I realized that one could not dismiss with a pulpit phrase the reality faced by those who had so bravely stood their ground against far superior numbers to defend their homes. The spark of conversion fanned brighter as my eyes passed from the devastation of the ravaged Beer Tuvia to what these same *Chalutzim* (pioneers) had wrought in the few years since the bloody massacres of 1929. With the characteristic valor which enabled the Jew to survive similar depredations all through the centuries, the surviving colonists of Beer Tuvia had returned to the scene of the destruction, buried their fallen comrades, and rebuilt their homes only a stone's throw away from the martyred graves.

It was at another *kibbutz,* Givat Brenner, that the spark burst into consuming flame. For it was one thing to preach generalities about God's kingdom, but it was quite another to behold youthful Jews and Jewesses, with hope in their hearts and spades in their hands, building in the here and now just such a cooperative society as was envisaged by the Hebrew prophets. These youngsters were concretizing the laws and *mitzvot* (commandments) of our Torah and Talmud.

Despite their obvious lack of formal religious worship and the absence of synagogues from their colonies (except an occasional tiny shack as a so-called synagogue, built for their parents), these Labor Zionists were translating into life the two-fold meaning of the Hebrew word *avodah* which connotes work as well as worship. In my eyes, they seemed to fulfill the ancient dictum: "Everyone who dwells in *Eretz Yisroel* (the land of Israel) is recorded as if he is without sins." They were transmitting into reality the traditional Jewish concept of *Kibbush ha Avodah,* the conquest of labor, a veritable religious ritual of their own. They were actually practicing our much-vaunted preachment of social righteousness, so often kept in the deep-freeze of the synagogue, unctuously intoned in hymns and mechanically read in rituals, only to be speedily forgotten and blasphemously betrayed in life.

Many of the ideals that I cherished and which were frequently scorned throughout the "real" world seemed to materialize at Givat Brenner, which resembled the social and economic society of the ancient Rechabites from which Jeremiah is said to have sprung, or the Essenes, described in the Dead Sea Scrolls. Here everything was owned in common. No man possessed anything of his own—not even the clothes on his back. When an individual joined the group he relinquished all his possessions—his jewelry, his furniture, his savings, even his legacies, if he had any.

One of the girls at Givat Brenner had received money from a cousin in America. She wanted desperately to go to Tel Aviv to see the Habimah players, the most famous drama group in the Middle East. Now she would be able to see them without asking the secretary of the commune for the money. Yet she did not go. "It would not be comradely to do so when the others are deprived of such a treat," she explained to me. "I decided instead to give the money to the general entertainment fund. Before long there will be enough for all of us to go together."

I found there, likewise, the refutation of so many of the shibboleths of our rugged individualism, such as: "Human nature being what it is, it can't possibly be otherwise." "No incentive without private profit," the scriptures of capitalism insist. But as I strolled among the primitive tents and huts of Givat Brenner, especially when tasks were being assigned, I saw a different facet of human nature. I listened to the grumblings and griping when the women and the girls were denied the right to undertake the same onerous assignments as the men, or when some youth protested he was being dispatched to some easy job.

A young and attractive *Sabra* (native-born Israeli) named Reuben Zaslani Shiloach, who later distinguished himself in the foreign service of Israel, took me to an Arab-Jewish Club where brave, though I fear ill-fated, attempts were being made to fashion an Israeli-Arab liaison, especially among the workers in both groups. I spoke with boys at school whose answer to my query as to what they wanted to be when they grew up was never businessman or banker or broker or lawyer, but rather tillers of the soil like their fathers, workers, engineers, builders of the land. "We want not merely to make a living, but a life and a better world," they said, echoing the prophets of old.

It was on this soil, after all, that this vision had first been captured by these seers of the Hebrew Bible. Here I found men and women toiling far more tediously than any captains of industry I had ever known, but toiling for the joy of labor and the rhapsodic happiness of bestowing rich blessings upon their fellow beings. A promised land, in very truth.

Their very vocabulary was undergoing a radical transformation. The words "I" and "mine," which dominate our own daily speech, were slipping from their vocabularies as they were replaced by "we" and "our."

Never will I forget the quiet joy that radiated from my newly found friend, Sireni, as, one evening toward sundown, we surveyed the lovely orchards and vineyards which he and his comrades had wrested from the stony desert soil. Proudly he pointed to the prize poultry and cattle which these 500 souls had succeeded in breeding in what had so recently been a parched wilderness. We stood upon the crest of a little hill and looked across the fields to the tents and huts of the settlement. The last rays of the sun gleamed on the window panes of the children's quarters. This scion of an aristocratic family of assimilated Italian Jews, whose father had been physician to King Victor Emmanuel, led us across every foot of the *kibbutz*. He had relinquished all opportunities for self-aggrandizement in his native land for the joy of living for nine years in a tent and, now, at long last, tasted the luxury of a single cell-like room in one of the recently constructed barracks.

Pointing toward those rude buildings with rapture throbbing in his voice, he whispered in stumbling English, "I love this place; just look!" As he seized my arm, he cried: *"Our* homes, *our* barns, *our* cattle, *our* vineyards, all *ours* together."

This credo of one for all and all for one extended even to their children. Asked these justice-loving pioneers: "Why should one child be blessed with all the blandishments of life while another, through no fault of its own, be cursed with malnutrition, disease, and pain?" Every child, they believed, was entitled to as much opportunity, care, and love as was one's own. Consequently, they believed in the group-rearing of children and this was their first and paramount concern. Before a single building was constructed, while fathers and mothers dwelt in wind-swept tents, they would pour their every last coin into the children's home, still the most imposing structure in the entire settlement.

To my skeptical inquiry as to how this arrangement affected parental affection and filial love between natural parents and children, the answer came quite swiftly and dramatically. Sireni and I descended from the hilltop where we had conversed long after the sun had set and darkness had descended. The entire colony lay asleep beneath the clear Palestinian sky. Not a sound was to be heard except the occasional barking of a dog. We were passing the children's home, talking in barely audible whispers, as Sireni had placed a finger to his lips to warn me to keep my voice low so as not to disturb the slumbering children. While we were still some distance from the children's house, we suddenly heard a gentle voice inside calling: *"Abba, Abba,"* —"Father, Father." We went to the screened window and looked into the wide glowing eyes of my friend's handsome child. The lad had recognized, even from the distance, his father's softest whisper and had come to the window for another good-night kiss.

It is true that much of what I have related has been seriously altered by an advancing economy, by the exigencies of the state of siege to which Israel has been subjected ever since its inception, by the drift to the cities that is characteristic of our time, and perhaps by the lack of that one indispensable facet of our Jewish heritage that might have given greater staying power to all this exalted idealism—a religious commitment.

Sireni himself once acknowledged this to me. "You know," he said, "we must give our children something more than a state to build, even more than a cooperative society to rear. The Sabbath must become something more to them than merely a day for the cessation of work. The festivals must be transformed into something that transcends the rejoicing over the harvest, however diligently we labored to produce it, and we must relearn the messages of Rosh Ha Shona and Yom Kippur, of the New Year and the Day of Atonement. We must ask questions and seek answers to the ultimates of life—of death, too, and of the universe in which we dwell."

Thus, as early as 1935, one of the early Labor Zionists pronounced the verdict that nationhood is never enough to satisfy the human heart or to slake the spiritual thirst of man's soul. He likewise articulated the need, the growing and increasingly desperate need, for a living Judaism in Israel.

The ideas and emotions growing out of this trip I sought to bring to the Biennial Assembly of the Union in my first comprehensive State of Our Union message in 1946. As I have indicated, the Central Conference of American Rabbis had already abandoned its erstwhile anti-Zionist position at Columbus, Ohio, in 1937, but the body of Reform congregations still retained its generally anti-Zionist disposition and its lay leadership was largely opposed to any official change. In the heat of controversy over continuing our membership in the American Jewish Conference, scorned as pro-Zionist by many of our leaders because of its plea for the creation of a Jewish Commonwealth in Palestine, I strongly urged that the Union Biennial renounce its anti-Zionist policy.

My views represented not only the further ripening of the impressions of my experiences in Palestine, but were inescapably dictated by the holocaust from which a decimated Jewry and a wounded world had just emerged. All that hatred and horror put the finishing touches upon many of my illusions. I urged the Reform leadership not to cling stubbornly to dead clichés in the face of the foul contempt and unconcern of a civilized world. Not only had European Jewry been stamped out in the most efficient massacre of all history, not only was the protest of the civilized community tepid and ineffectual, but the stark truth was there for anyone to see: no country in the world wanted the surviving Jews. Australia, with millions of square miles and a population shortage, seemed to speak for the Christian conscience of the world when it declared that it had "no Jewish problem and did not want to have one." Canada and the United States opened their doors a bare crack. A Jewish Commonwealth in Palestine now passed from the realm of poetic vision to the arena of grim necessity. If only there could be at least one country in a hate-soaked world whose doors would always be open to Jewish survivors of persecution! In this sense, I became a Zionist.

It would be totally wrong to suggest that, under my leadership, the Union of American Hebrew Congregations became a Zionist organization. But the UAHC turned its back—forever I hope—on the nay-saying of anti-Zionism. While the Reform movement was convulsed in a struggle concerning its membership in the American Jewish Conference and the structure of the American Jewish community, everybody knew that the basic underlying issue was Zionism. In deciding by overwhelming vote to sustain UAHC participation in the American Jewish Conference, the delegates wrote finis to the dogmatic hostility to Zion which had long plagued Reform Judaism. The lay leadership of Reform Judaism thus followed its rabbinic leaders in declaring that Reform Judaism is not incompatible with Zionism and that one's attitude toward Zionism is a matter for the individual to decide in his own conscience.

Today the UAHC is a staunch friend of Israel. As a member of the Presidents' Conference of Major Jewish Organizations, the UAHC cooperates with all segments of the American Jewish community to safeguard the security and welfare of the State of Israel. A corner of history has been turned by Reform Judaism and, while there are still voices of displeasure within our movement, they are the echoes of a dead past.

Did all this fervor and enthusiasm, borne of our first visit to Palestine, make me a Zionist? Not if Zionism is equated with the absolute, unqualified centrality of the State of Israel in all Jewish thought and life as some would have it. Mystically and emotionally, I respond to the magnetic pull which that precious land has always exerted upon the minds and hearts of my people. But I cannot be counted among those who insist that a genuine Zionist must be a so-called Negator of the Exile. In the first place, I do not regard myself or my fellow Jews who reside in lands of freedom as being in exile. Though I do not share the naive optimism of the early founders of Reform that the Messianic Age is immediately before us or that America is the Promised Land, our Paradise on earth, nevertheless, deep and inexorable are the roots of many of us in this new world. I still find positive meaning and purpose in our widespread dispersion throughout the earth. As I find inspiration and stimulus in so many other utterances of the Hebrew prophets, so I still cleave to the concept of Israel's mission among the nations. Not the so-called assimilationist Reformers, but an early rabbinic sage, Rabbi Oshia, affirmed: "It was an act of charity and goodness that God did by dispersing Israel among the nations." In many quarters this idea is now considered hopelessly outmoded and as the peculiar latter-day invention of the allegedly Jewishly illiterate, superficial Reformists. But the more profound and learned of the early Zionists did not lightly dismiss this doctrine which permeates the whole of Jewish tradition and teaching.

Strange, that when some of the most passionate of the Jewish nationalists do not quail at the word "mission," some of our Reformers do. "Ours is the mission of translating our religion into terms of a better social order." This quote is not culled from the so-called escapist tenets of Reform Judaism, but rather from one of the foremost of all the pioneers of the rebirth of Zion, Moses Hess. And A. D. Gordon, another trailblazer of the renascent Jewish Commonwealth, was not afraid to write: "We were the first to proclaim that man is created in the image of God. We must now go further and say that the Nation must be created in His image. Not that we are better than others, but because what we have borne and suffered demands this."

I am not a Zionist if to be so categorized is to cling to the notion of the "ingathering of the Exiles," that our Jewish destiny will never be fulfilled until every last Jew on earth migrates to the State of Israel and that there alone a meaningful and creative Jewish life can be fulfilled.

In a magazine article, a German Jew recounted how he had returned to the *Vaterland* after some years of sojourn in *Eretz Yisroel*. He justified his return to that "Chamber of Horrors," the land of Hitler, and his resurrected horde of neo-Nazis, by insisting that "never again would they be able to drive the Jew away because, whereas formerly the Germans thought that it was easy to hound the Jew from their land because they believed that we were yellow, now they know what Israel can teach the Jew."

Israel, to be sure, can teach us much. As the late Rabbi Milton Steinberg wrote, "It teaches us that miracles are possible and that if the Jew could perform such a miracle there is no so-called miracle that cannot likewise come to pass: the emancipation of the downtrodden races of the world, the attainment of equity for all, the dawn of peace itself." But the comment of the German author and so many like him is predicated upon the exclusive power of the land or the state itself to bring inspiration and challenge, spiritual daring, and moral tenacity and purpose to the Jew. This concept denies the whole destiny of the Jew, which affirms that it was his faith in God and his fortitude because of God, faith in his divine mission as coworker with God, which gave him for centuries past spiritual audacity and moral perseverance. It was not mere nationalism which moved a Job to proclaim "though He slay me yet will I trust in Him"; or an Akiba, roasting on the stake, to utter the *Sh'ma*—"Hear, O Israel, the Lord is One."

These great spirits required no specific soil or flag to work that mysterious alchemy which the Jewish faith has continuously distilled in those who have been reared in its teaching, wherever they may have chanced to be. There is much amiss in the life of Jewry in the Diaspora; there is shallowness and dismaying dilution of the wellsprings of Jewish faith and learning amid American Jewry. Nevertheless, there is as great a potential in America for the cultural, moral, and spiritual rebirth of a viable, thriving, living Judaism as there is in Israel. One recalls the rabbinic saying: "Wherever Israel was exiled, the *shechinah* (God's glory) was exiled with them."

Yet as one surveys the lamentable state of religious affairs in Israel, one sees a rigid, petrified Orthodoxy as the only available spiritual alternative presented to its youth reared in the contemporary disciplines of science and technology. It is an Orthodoxy devoid of prophetic dynamism, that passes no moral judgments upon much that is awry not alone in Israel but throughout a morally bankrupt world. Its spokesmen have at least had the honesty to confess that they would rather have the youth of Israel grow up with no religion than be ensnared into the trap of a liberal, non-Orthodox faith.

Contrary to popular misconception, it is not the government of Israel that stands in the way of a spiritual rebirth in Zion. Time and again, Mr. Ben-Gurion has urged me to awaken my fellow Jews to the spiritual as well as the physical needs of Israel, to comprehend that it is not just technical know-how and tractors and factories, but religious ideals and spiritual and moral leadership that Israel requires. In almost every encounter I have had with the former Prime Minister of Israel, he has chided me about our hesitancy in mounting a dynamic attack upon the widespread irreligiosity of the once Holy Land.

No, it is not the government of Israel that impedes the development of liberal Judaism there. It is we liberal Jews who, having poured forth a flood of contributions for the physical advancement and political protection of Israel, have become so hypersensitive to the alleged political influence of the Orthodox in Israel and in America that out of fear of a *Kulturkampf* (a religious war) we have held in the reins of challenge. But this cowardice in the face of entrenched influence is to write off possibly a whole generation of Israeli youth who may discover too late that "statehood is not enough."

Frequently the excuse is given that Israel has troubles enough without risking such internal strife. Surrounded by 40 million hostile Arabs, intent upon their avowed objective to "drive the Israelis into the sea," there is no time for such so-called luxuries as the rearing of synagogues or the cultivation of the religious life. But never in the past have Jews been beguiled by such superficial rationalizations. The American pioneers also, though besieged by Indians, erected churches as well as stockades.

Maurice Samuel has trenchantly expressed the basic need of Israel today in words with which I heartily concur: "The greatest danger to Israel," he wrote in *Level Sunlight*, "lies not in the possibility of Arab invasion or in economic collapse, but in the loss of its character as being Jewish rather than merely Israeli." ". . . Like chemical equations," he suggests that the following statements are reversible: *"Mitzion tetze Torah"*—"For from Zion shall go forth the Law"—may well be transposed to read *"Into* Zion shall go the Law, and the word of God *into* Jerusalem." Into Jerusalem, even from America, he maintains, "for world Jewry has something to teach even to Israel, and American Jewry is world Jewry's continental center. Israel cannot be rebuilt through a repudiation of America. Let world Jewry understand this— in Israel and everywhere else."

Am I, then, a Zionist? If Maurice Samuel is still counted in their number, yes. If Zionism is no longer limited to a Zion-centered interpretation of the whole of Jewish life or faith, yes. If by Zionism is meant fidelity to the dreams and aspirations of our master teachers, the prophets of Israel, yes. They envisaged that "in the end of days, the labor of Egypt and the merchandise of Ethiopia shall come to thee and they shall fall down unto thee"—the "thee" in this case being the children of Israel reconstituted within their own land. All the prophets envisaged such a return for at least a portion of the Jewish people, no matter with what world-redeeming mission they charged the remainder who would be, by God's divine plan and purpose, scattered among the nations.

Yes, if to be a Zionist is to share Leo Baeck's more contemporary version of this ancient prophetic aspiration when he, a non-Zionist, contended:

> It was no patronizing philanthrophy nor plea for asylum which prompted the contemporary rebirth of Zion. Throughout the ages [the Jew] prayed a prayer also for Zion, for Jerusalem's sake. That dream was a permanent one. It grew into an archetype, an element of the collective subconscious traits and trends. The dream thus became a collective one which, therefore, is to be recognized not within a single, but within the common compass of the soul of the Jew. And whenever a Jew, not only unwittingly, but intentionally, for however sincere or significant reason, discontinues dreaming this dream and displaces this vision, he experiences an inward uneasiness.

I was wrong in my early opposition to Zionism, and history has rebutted me. But the Zionists were also wrong in many of their assumptions and dreams. Israel is now a reality, a throbbing reality. No one can doubt that the presence of the vibrant and valorous Jewish state has given heightened pride and dignity to Jews everywhere. American Jews, especially, have thrilled to a sense of participating vicariously in the miracle of the upbuilding and the heroic defense of a Jewish homeland. The fighting Israeli has counterbalanced the image of the tragic, resigned Jew shuffling silently to the Nazi gas chambers. And this is all to the good.

But we now know how quixotic were the notions of the founders of Zionism that a Jewish homeland would "normalize" Jewish life everywhere and would thus bring an end to anti-Semitism which, in Herzl's mind, was the result of Jewish ghostliness—the separation of body and soul. Israel exists and its voice is raised with resonance in the councils of nations against the mistreatment of Jews anywhere. But does this fact of Israel's statehood prevent the dismal plight of almost three million Jews behind the Iron Curtain, whose religious and cultural life is being systematically crushed under the hammer of Soviet tyranny? Does the fact of Israel mitigate Arab anti-Semitism? And, if I may say so, does Israel have any particular relevance to the status of anti-

Semitism in the United States? Anti-Semitism has an irrational pattern of its own. A war, a depression in America, a severe outbreak of neo-McCarthyism—these would have incalculable effects upon the state of anti-Semitism and whether there was or was not an Israel would be of little consequence.

Another assumption is that Zionism would continue to be a positive force in Jewish life even after the Jewish state was created. Ideally, this should have happened. But it didn't. When the heart-pounding drama of Israel's birth was over, the Zionist movement, for all practical purposes, was dead. Its objective had been attained. Membership in all Zionist organizations (except Hadassah) has drained away to a pittance. The Zionist groups have sought desperately to establish themselves as a kind of junior partner in the running of the state, only to be properly slapped down by Ben-Gurion and the other leaders of the independent State of Israel who, of course, will countenance no such meddling by foreign citizens. Thrashing around for new directions, the Zionist movement seized upon the banners of *Chalutziot* (emigration of American Jewish youth to Israel), only to learn that most American Jews have not the remotest intention of moving to Israel. This program proved a spectacular failure, as did Zionist efforts to play an effective educational and cultural role in the life of the Jewish people.

Very bluntly, the Zionist movement is moribund. Its future is hopeless. Although Jewish organizations practically never preside over their own liquidation and rarely concede that their purpose has been served, the fact is that there is no longer any valid difference between the Zionist and the non-Zionist Jew in America. Each is a friend of Israel. Each expresses that friendship largely through his checkbook. Each has a sense of solidarity with Israel and strengthens Israel's defense through political as well as financial support. Each has already visited Israel—or is making plans to do so as soon as possible. And most important, each has every intention of living out the years of his life in America. As New York City is to most Americans, Israel is to American Jewry: "a great place to visit, but . . ."

Another assumption still being articulated in many quarters, and particularly in Israel, is that Israel itself is the primary condition of Jewish survival in the Diaspora. I reject the notion that world Jewry can survive solely by virtue of Israel's existence; that American Jewry lives by proxy only. I think the reverse is true. Despite all the grandiose oratory, Israel has not even begun to enrich the cultural life of the American Jew. Indeed, I believe American Jewry has had more impact on the life of the Israelis than vice versa. To pontificate about the blessings of a two-way bridge between American Jewry and Israel does not mean that such a bridge exists. I do not think it yet does. In fact, I am very much concerned that a large chasm already separates us and that the gap may grow deeper and broader unless real bridges— as opposed to purely oral ones—are built and set down soon.

Contributing to this chasm are the transcontinental ideological missiles which Mr. Ben-Gurion has frequently lobbed into American Jewry. With an insouciance which is exasperating, Ben-Gurion has become a prophet of doom as to the future of American Jewry. He has implied that a positive Jewish life cannot be lived in the Diaspora, that it is the duty of the religious Jew to settle in Israel, and that assimilation is the inevitable fate of American Jewry. These strictures are not calculated to strengthen the bonds of fellowship between American Jewry and Israelis. They stem, in my judgment, from Ben-Gurion's acute and understandable anxiety that the streams of Oriental Jews now flowing into Israel will swamp the Jewish state and convert it into a Levantine nation, unless Western immigration can be greatly accelerated. Ben-Gurion's impolitic darts are not intended to draw blood —only immigrants, preferably the young and the skilled. But his goads may well backfire and create a tragic alienation between our two communities.

Contrary to Ben-Gurion's alarms, American Jewry has never been more vital, visible, and viable. Problems we have aplenty, but on the free soil of America we have the greatest opportunity ever afforded a Jewish community to shape a Jewish life of vigor and vision. I believe this can be achieved, but it will be more difficult if Israel appoints itself a youthful Mother Grundy or a querulous Cassandra to look over our shoulder in order to carp, scold, and scowl; in order to pronounce the eulogy over our demise.

That there is already an incipient alienation was shockingly evident at the so-called dialogue between Israeli and American-Jewish leaders in Jerusalem in 1962 and 1963. The Israelis could not conceal a note of condescension as to the quality of Jewish life outside of Israel. They made it quite clear that the Americans' financial support did not entitle them to any particular deference or special gratitude. The Americans could not conceal an impatience with Israeli dogmatism. If it proved anything, the dialogue confirmed that we have a long way to go to achieve a truly reciprocal and creative relationship between the two great Jewish communities of our time.

Ben-Gurion worries about the future of American Jewry. But I believe, ironically enough, that there are at least equal grounds for concern about the future of Jewish life in Israel itself. For what is emerging in Israel is a people whose religion is the state. The young people reject God and religion as the relics of an earlier age. And why not? The only religious expression of Judaism they see is a stale, irrelevant, and unappealing Orthodoxy that demeans itself by using its political weight in the maintenance of a benighted theocratic spirit. The only meaningful religious option for the Israeli has been Orthodoxy or nothing, because until very recently there was no possibility of a liberal non-Orthodox expression of Judaism. Fortunately, small and highly tender shoots of liberal Judaism are now gaining strength. Their success is crucial if the Israelis are to refine a modern pattern of religious faith which can appeal aesthetically, ethically, and spiritually to a generation of *Sabras*.

The significance of this development can hardly be overstated. If it fails, future generations will regard themselves essentially as Israelis rather than Jews. The historic lines of faith which bind all Jews into peoplehood will be sundered forever. Chauvinistic worship of a state will replace the worship of God. And Israel will become just another nation—more progressive, more energetic, no doubt, but in no fundamental way an exemplar of Jewish values or a fulfillment of the age-old dream of Zion restored. What a monumental travesty it would be if in the decades ahead Jewish leaders must echo the question now perennially asked about Jewish centers, Jewish hospitals, and Jewish social agencies: What is Jewish about the Jewish State?

But it is important to see things in perspective. Israel is a young nation which has survived the implacable hostility of its neighbors, the fantastic test of gathering in hundreds of thousands of refugees, and the ordeal of making the desert wastes bloom like a rose. I have confidence that Israel will evolve new forms which will be based upon freedom of religion and respect for personal conscience. The ferment now evident in Israel will gather force. And some day soon the people will end the imposition of religious laws, bans, and limitations on their personal rights. Moreover, the still inchoate but latent religious yearnings of many Israelis will find fulfillment in a free, flexible, and uniquely Israeli adaptation of an ancient faith to the human values of a modern Jewish state.

Practically all meaning has been rubbed off the word "Zionist" by the torrential oratory which has poured down the mountainside of history. To argue Zionism is an academic exercise. But, as true friends always do, I will be solicitous, sympathetic, and supportive; but I will also be critical when I consider criticism called for. For Israel must be more than a bustling state. It must be the embodiment of those Jewish values and ideals whose source is the Bible and which have sustained the Jewish spirit for two millennia of stirring sacrifice and striving. As the prophet warned, it is "too light a thing to raise up the tribe of Jacob and to restore the remnant of Israel." Rather must that raising up and that restoration be an *os* (a sign) *L'ma'an Sh'mo*—"For the sake of God's name"—"to give thee for a light unto the nations, that My salvation may be *unto the ends of the earth."* (Isaiah 49:6)

4

THE DILEMMA OF A PACIFIST

FORETHOUGHT

Our only hope for mankind rests in those who dare to say, "I am a Jew and therefore I must obey the categoric, unqualified command 'Thou shalt not kill!'" or who affirm "I am a Christian and therefore I cannot without sin take to the sword."

Down from the ancient world with its fortified villages, its walled towns, its bows and arrows, has come the insane idea that armed preparedness is the way to achieve a sense of security. Glance over the entire world, armed as it has never been throughout its entire blood-bespattered history, and then try to tell me that armed preparedness is bringing to anyone a sense of personal or national safety. The very opposite is true. It is our mad and extravagant preparation that is making the clash more imminent with every passing moment. As someone has put it, "You can do almost anything with bayonets, except sit on them." So the more bayonets are fixed, the fewer places are left where anyone can sit down in confidence and trust. Just put this down as the basic axiom of international relationships: armed preparedness is not the cure for international fear. It is rather the major cause of all the frenzy that has seized the nations. The more munitions, the more fear; and out of fear, rather than out of revenge or hate or creed, the spark will soon be set to all this menacing dynamite by some trembling fear-lashed finger, and then the whole world will be set ablaze. . . .

But the Hebrew prophets, Jesus, and the persecuted martyrs of Rome knew long centuries ago that the real enemy of man was not this tribe or clan or nation, but this reliance upon sword and spear and force and fortress; they knew that, while the chariots of Egypt

*and the horsemen of Assyria might triumph for the hour, in the end
all those who placed their trust in military alliances would themselves
be destroyed thereby. They anticipated by many centuries the inescapable truth which only a few are yet beginning to discern, that our true
foe today is not this people or that but the* war system itself *that is our
arch-enemy.*

*Behold this real foe, this traitor within our gates who still endeavors
to misguide our youth and to misdirect the noblest aspiration of man
to march proudly to the strains of martial music and to believe im-
plicitly in his lying slogans. Yes, still through the misled imagination of
the masses march the militarists bearing the mendacious banners, "for
home and fatherland." But those banners lie. The war system has no
right to bear such slogans; the war system is not the defender of any
home or fatherland; the war system is the most flagrant enemy of every
fatherland and every home and some few of us who are not ashamed to
call ourselves pacifists would seek to snatch those banners from the
hands which so long and so undeservedly have carried them and to put
them where they belong—in the hands of the peacemakers whom alone
the prophets and Jesus called "blessed."*

Toronto, 1931

AFTERTHOUGHTS

The above was the credo of an absolute pacifist. It was written in
1931. I was at that time President of the Toronto chapter of the Fellowship of Reconciliation. My wife occupied a position in the Women's
International League for Peace and Freedom. That was the year of our
first trip to Europe. We saw every museum, château, cathedral, synagogue, castle, and tourist-trap available and passionately longed for
our second trip abroad when we wouldn't have to "do" *everything.*
We saw, likewise, the battlefields of World War I. But we were not impressed by their tranquillity, for beneath those peaceful fields and
flowers lay the shattered bodies of once living youth shot down mercilessly at the very dawn of their lives. We visited Flanders Field, "where
poppies grow." But the beauty of those blossoms did not blot out the
desolate parade that we saw everywhere of the bereaved mothers
and premature widows in their black garb of mourning.

It was also the year that I attended my first international conference of any kind: the World Assembly of the Fellowship of Reconciliation at Lunteren, Holland. There may have been other romantics among these delegates from many lands but, in some respects, I was no doubt the most romantic of them all. How moved I was by those candlelight processions through the dark shadowed forest, led by a family of gifted musicians playing their soft-toned woodwinds. My inexorable romanticism may be illustrated by a small incident.

As we were walking along beneath the templed dome of the star-studded night, I would, every once in a while, whisper to my wife my exaltations concerning the incomparably breathtaking fragance of those sharply pine-scented woods. It was not until we returned to camp that I learned why I had had this unique experience. While we had been wandering along, I had stumbled over a root and fallen on my back. Only when I was changing clothes did I discover that in that fall I had smashed a bottle in my pocket—a bottle of pine-fragrant eau de cologne. I have tried to be a little less romantic ever since.

But not all of those attending this world conference were mere romantics. There were many grim realists among them—men and women and youths who had known war in all its horror. Nor were they a gang of revolutionary "Reds," as subsequent witch hunts sought to dub them. There were among them many distinguished community leaders, churchmen, university professors, authors of world-wide repute. All of them had looked into the flaming fires of hell and wanted no more of such suicidal searing.

I was deeply impressed by what I saw and heard and my innate pacifism was confirmed and intensified. I do not know the precise origin of my pacifism. Only the resurrection of long forgotten memories of earliest infancy and a physically frail childhood might shed light on how I came to develop a life-long revulsion against physical violence of any kind. In childhood I flinched from it. Coward? Maybe. But somewhere, somehow, I sensed the truth contained in the ancient Chinese proverb that he who strikes the first blow is in the wrong, loses the argument, surrenders his human distinction from the beast which knows only tooth and fang wherewith to enter combat.

I know I did not derive these feelings—and I underscore the fact that they were *feelings* far more than thoughts—from my Judaism. No, the celebration each year of the Chanukah festival, with its emphasis on the military triumph of the Maccabees, was too vivid in my early religious training to convey any illusions concerning any such absolute pacifism among the early Hebrews. But I never did care for that motif of the Chanukah story. The courage of Mattathias in refusing to capitulate to the tyrannical decree of Antiochus, the rededication of the Temple, the legend of the vial of oil—yes; but the battles that went between had no glamour for me, even in my childhood.

I recognize that I do now enjoy something of a reputation as a fighter—and I must admit that I have been in the thick of many a fray, including no doubt some of my own making. But no public image which depicts me as "spoiling for battle" could be more amiss. This does not mean, I hope, that I shrink from seeking to right wrongs. But I have always been convinced that one can do all this better without physical violence, which inevitably begets still more violence. I have never been impressed with the bromide that one "fights fire with fire." On the contrary, one fights fire with water.

But this conviction was to be rudely jarred, if not altogether shattered, by the years that were immediately to follow. It is not easy to relinquish a long-cherished ideal—especially one that seems to have rootage in one's very blood—particularly an ideal which appears to be the distinctive possession of the human race in contrast to the snarling animalistic past from which we human beings have so painfully, painstakingly, and ploddingly emerged. In the years following the Holland conference, a spiritual turmoil built up within me, almost rendering me impotent to continue to speak from a pulpit from which I had in the past preached the doctrine of undiluted pacifism. I became embroiled in a crisis of conscience which has left some scars, certain as yet unresolved conflicts, and some lingering doubts and reservations to this day.

These thoughts of 1931 had been expressed before Hitler pulled down the columns of liberty; before tens of millions of Jews, Poles, Russians, Frenchmen, Americans, and myriads of innocent but sheeplike Germans as well were consumed in the apocalyptic flames of war; before the State of Israel arose from the ashes of destruction and faced the alternative of fighting for its life or dying still-born; before Korea, before Cuba, before Algeria, before Laos, before Viet-Nam; before the United Nations and before the H-bomb and the test ban. They were spoken in a now seemingly most distant and dead time, as remote as the age of the Caesars. In relation to revolutions wrought, it was many centuries past, though it was incomprehensibly enough only half my lifetime ago. I have no apology for that sermon spoken in so diametrically different a milieu. It reflected, I believe, an idealism both sincere and romantic. Yet, as I re-read it now I must admit that it is subject to strong reservations. It requires grave reappraisal from two important standpoints: (1) its one-sidedness in the light of a larger perspective and a deeper knowledge of the total Jewish tradition, and (2) its too-superficial and wishful evaluation of the complexities and realities of human nature and the dilemma of contemporary man and nations.

Though I have confessed that my innate pacifism did not derive originally from Judaism, there is nonetheless much in Judaism to undergird that viewpoint and feeling with which I was so early imbued. The ideal of universal peace is one of the most sublime contributions which Judiasm has given to the world. Nevertheless, that ideal vision of peace has been rudely shattered by not a few realistic trials by physical force which have pervaded my Hebraic past. I have undoubtedly been too selective and subjective in my quotations from that Hebraic epic. I fear that I must more objectively admit that, despite the exalted prophetic passages on peace, the ancient Hebrews were not unqualified pacifists nor lovers of peace at any price. As with other nations of the time, Israel was rocked by war and strife. The sensitive prophet cried out, "Not by might nor by power, but by My spirit, saith the Lord," but the people of Israel did ofttimes engage in war—not always in self-defense. They even proclaimed that they fought in God's name the *Milchomos Adonoy,* the battles of the *Lord.* It was only after the destruction of Israel's statehood in the year 70 of the Christian Era, that the vision of universal peace was incorporated as the mission of Israel.

As George Holley Gilbert points out, in *The Bible and Universal Peace:*

The ancient Hebrews had a warlike career. They fought the battles of Yahweh from century to century. But when at last their national existence was no more, when they sat and sighed by the ruins of their holy city or far away among the nations, some among them dreamed of a new and wondrous age that was yet to come. They thought of their past, glorified, indeed, in the far retrospect, but they did not long to have those ages returned unchanged. They dreamed of a future that should be far better than the best that their fathers had ever known, and one constant element of that great future—one on which they dwelt with satisfaction—was peace. Out of the soul of centuries of strife and bloodshed blossomed, as a fair lover, the vision of a time when peace should flow as a river. By this vision the Hebrew prophets became leaders of the race toward a future kingdom whose realization is still among the treasures of hope.

The majestic contribution of Israel was not only its proclamation of the ideal of peace at a time when war was the standard state of affairs. It was also the extraordinary dream of a universal peace—for all nations, for all mankind. Uttered at a time when nations were divided by gulfs seldom crossed except by military forces, the prophecies of Amos and Micah sent forth shafts of light which, like the beams of stars that reach the earth only after eons of time, are only now beginning faintly to illumine our world.

Not that I could not find some confirmation of my pacifism in Judaism. I deny the allegation that the all-conquering power of love, the invincible strength of the spirit, is an invention of Christianity (or a unique characteristic of Buddhism) and that one has caught the contagious disease of non-violence—for some strange reason usually condemned as cowardly and contemptuous—from the infectious germs of our surrounding Christian environment. Jews who argue thus play into the hands of those who have for centuries falsely depicted Israel's God as a "Lord of vengeance" and His people as still steeped in a tradition which once spoke of "bashing babes to bits upon the rocks." I refuse to admit that I have become unconsciously assimilated to the Christian gospel if I insist that "turning the other cheek" is not an exclusively Christian notion, that it was not a concept invented or first voiced by Jesus; if I deny that it was utterly alien to the Jewish teaching into which Jesus was born, in which he was taught, by which he lived, and for the espousal of which, I still insist—no matter what epithets will be hurled my way—he died.

How can any Jewish student of the Bible dismiss what was tantamount to turning the other cheek in not only the teaching but in the exemplary life of the compassionate prophet Hosea? Surely he took far more punishment from his wayward, insolently adulterous wife, Gomer, than any mere turning of the other cheek. And yet he anticipated the contemporary dramatist who had one of his characters affirm: "Sometimes one can beat you and beat you and beat you, and you love them still." So did Hosea take back to his heart his faithless wife. Likewise, a Midrashic legend portrays God chastising the angels of heaven who wanted to exalt Him in ecstatic hymns of thanksgiving when the waves of the Red Sea closed over the drowning Egyptians: "My creatures are perishing and you want to sing praises." And what of the far more explicit admonition of the Book of Proverbs which so categorically commands: "If thine enemy be hungry, give him bread to eat, and if he be thirsty, give him water to drink." Similarly: "Rejoice not when thine enemy falleth."

Thus, though Jews did not refrain from battle, much of Jewish lore did avoid glorification of war and military heroics. In Jewish history, the heroes are sages and prophets, not warriors. King David is recalled as the sweet psalmist and great leader, not as a soldier. Indeed, David was not allowed to build the Temple in Jerusalem precisely because his hands had spilled blood in war. Similarly, because Chanukah recalls a military victory, Jewish historians practically ignored it and Jewish source books scantily touched it. Significantly, on the Sabbath preceding Chanukah, Jews recite the passage from the prophet Zechariah: "Not by might, nor by power, but by My spirit, saith the Lord of Hosts."

Yet, granted all this, I must admit that, as one swallow does not make a summer, two or three quotations do not make a philosophy of Judaism. It's the mainstream, not the rivulet, that counts and so I admit that Judaism's broad current has not clung to such absolute pacifism. But, having so conceded, I insist that the rivulet *is there*. It is not utterly alien to Judaism. It is not exclusively Christian. It is not treasonable to aspire still to this as an ideal of Judaism, no matter how otherwise "realistic" history has demanded the Jew to be.

That realism constrained the Jew—while not abjuring altogether the power of love, the might of the spirit—to predicate the pursuit of peace on the prior establishment of "justice within the gates." The "quality of mercy," the attribute to compassion known as *midas Horachamin,* was not lacking in the Jewish concept of God or in His demand upon man; but the *midas Hadin,* "the quality of righteousness," was paramount. "And the effect of righteousness shall be peace."

The pursuit of justice and the pursuit of peace are both moral imperatives in Judaism. But it cannot be denied that in the mainstream of Jewish thought it was possible, as in the Maccabean struggle or in the revolt of Bar Kochba, to countenance war (certainly in self-defense, at the very least), inasmuch as the victory of an evil cause would destroy both the ends of justice and the future goal of peace.

As I projected my own pacifist predilections of 1931 into a perhaps subjective interpretation of Judaism, so did these personal convictions blind me to much of the reality of the world scene of that day. I was so horrified by the wages of the "war system" that I strove to pit theory against fact. And the over-arching fact of that moment was the rising menace of Nazism. Could I have been so altogether naive as to believe that a refusal by the Allies to arm would somehow turn away the wrath of a Hitler or deter him from the unambiguously proclaimed ambitions of *Mein Kampf,* lusting for world conquest and pillage? If so, then my naivete was even more damning because I had no illusions whatsoever about Hitlerism. At some personal peril because of my outspoken condemnation of Nazism, almost a lone voice crying in the Canadian wilderness of complacent isolation, I visited Germany in

1931, 1933, 1935, and again in 1936. Each time I returned, I raised my voice in desperation, hoping to help ignite the conscience of the free world. But that conscience—snugly and smugly nestled in its seemingly secure cocoons separated by three thousand miles of sea—slumbered peacefully on until as in a sudden, terrifying nightmare, the Axis declared war on the Allies, a war they had shouted into our unhearing ears, and blatantly proclaimed in the pages of *Mein Kampf* before our unseeing eyes.

Was I, then, hopelessly unsophisticated and superficial in speaking as I did in 1931? In the light of all that followed, yes. But in the face of so much that went before, I'm still not willing to plead *Chotosi* (I have sinned). Pacifism does not imply passivity, as too many mistakenly contend—abject acceptance of evil, servile nonresistance. It commands courageous, sacrificial resistance long before nonpacifists are usually prepared to stand in the path of evil's early conquests. The difference is that the pacifist insists that the resistance be *nonviolent*. But, in those early thirties when there might still have been time to undermine the as yet tentative thrust of Hitler, who paid heed to the plea of the pacifist? Or even to those nonpacifists who perceived naught but havoc in the path of widespread American apathy and isolationism? Let the Nazis murder a few thousand Jews in faraway Europe—what concern is that of ours—was the implicit even if unspoken response to rising Nazi terror. What does it matter as long as our own national interests are not impaired? Sell oil and arms and scrap metal to the Japanese as long as their piratical plunder is limited to their fellow Orientals. Let's bide our time, grow fat on the profits of our trade with Japan, with the gruesome consequence that when inevitably our own sons were blown to splinters at Pearl Harbor, we then highly resolved to fight like demons and to imprison all those unrealistic pacifists who for years had begged and pleaded that the profiteering in material of war be ended, that the Japanese warlords be boycotted and halted in time from their imperialist design.

And what of those who stood idly by and resisted not as Mussolini sprayed his bombs over defenseless Abyssinia and joined Il Duce's son in this sport, as he termed it, of watching men, women, and children as they coughed out their guts below his death-spitting bombers? Who really cared? They were only black-skinned Ethiopians! And what did it matter that the warmongers of the *Deutsche Reich* were the same Krupps who had brought such havoc upon the world in 1914? Let them stoke their furnaces once more. We'll revel in our prosperity, arm Germany once again—as a bulwark against Bolshevism, to be sure—and silence those who call for a quarantine against our Nordic kinsmen. The way of the pacifist might conceivably have prevailed, short of war, had anyone given heed to his warnings and paid the price which the sacrifice of "business as usual" would have exacted.

But the "might have been" did not occur and *der Führer* did come to power and was prepared to implement every word of his unheeded predictions concerning "tomorrow the world." It was at this juncture that, of course, I had to realize that Hitler might indeed stride triumphantly across the entire earth and snuff out the lamp of human freedom everywhere. We had come to the point of no return and I was forced to compromise with that ideal of nonviolent resistance that I held so dear. In the face of the horrendous consequences that Hitler's conceivable world-wide victory would have brought, and despite my personal anguish of spirit, I made my own choice. I served as an unofficial spokesman of the Canadian government in seeking to awaken the people and leaders of my fellow citizens in my native U.S. to share in the Allies' war effort. And yet, in the blinding flash of today's mushroom cloud, only the future, if there be a future, can render the final verdict as to whether my capitulation, however reluctant, was right or wrong.

At all events, my own exposure during my summer visits of the 1930s to the menacing march of Nazism completed the "agonizing reappraisal" and did result in my hesitant, troubled, guilt-ridden surrender to war. To stand on the periphery of those frenzied Hitler *Jugend* and to hear them shouting their feverish *Sieg Heils* in the vast amphitheaters in Berlin and Nuremberg; to see the ruins of once imposing synagogues; to watch in awe and terror the incessant marching and counter-marching of those brown-shirted minions, their faces contorted with hate and arrogance—all this brought me, however regretfully and poignantly, to the sorrowful conclusion that perhaps some of the doctrines of my company of passionate lovers of peace in the 1930s might, however unwittingly, have been the precursors of Chamberlain's later policy of appeasement.

No, life is not quite so simple as my wishful thinking sought to make it in 1931. Perhaps it never was. My dogmatic pacifism appears to have been pulverized by the events of the last three decades. It is some comfort to realize that I was more or less typical of a generation of high-minded, sensitive idealists whose loathing of war and commitment to pacifism were shattered by the rise of Hitlerism. Albert Einstein was one of them; Stephen S. Wise, Lillian Wald, and many other distinguished pacifists did not surrender their convictions any more lightly than did I. Their pacifism was dashed upon the jagged rocks of reality and, like myself, they laid aside their dreams in heartbreak and writhing of spirit.

And what relevance, we might likewise ask, has this gospel of pacifism to the millions of my fellow Jews slaughtered by the Nazis, whose agonizing days and nights in the concentration camps and whose terrified march into the crematoria put to naught my own private personal anguish over the jettisoning even of a long-cherished and exalted ideal? How did it happen that most of the Jewish victims went so passively—"like sheep to slaughter," as the current cliché of the holocaust literature puts it—to the gas chamber? Why didn't more of the Jews fight, as did the small, gallant forces of the Warsaw Ghetto? Were they immobilized by pacifist attitudes also? *Should* the Jews have fought back? Would it not have been better to make the Nazis pay dearly in blood for the blackest crime of all history? That seems to be the popular theme song of many of my brother, or, to include Hannah Arendt, of my sister Jews today—Jews wholly immersed in and assimilated to the strutting militant mood of the West. I, for one, however, am not persuaded by this current campaign to impugn the courage of those multitudes of Jews who died as martyrs at the hands of the irresistible Nazis. Dr. Bruno Bettelheim has attributed Jewish passivity to an unconscious death wish which destroyed the fiber of resistance. Hannah Arendt has evolved a latter-day "devil" theory in which responsibility for robbing the Jews of their capacity for manly resistance is divided between the Nazis and—fantastically enough—their so-called secret accomplices, the leaders of Jewish communal life in occupied Europe. According to Miss Arendt, Jewish deaths would never have mounted so astronomically high if Jews had not had a fear-ridden, compliant organized community, the leaders of which were made available to the Nazis. I find Miss Arendt's arguments outlandish and repugnant. They have been rebutted by many authorities, including scores of Jewish survivors themselves who did not "separate themselves from the community" or flee from their brethren, who did not, like Miss Arendt, seek a safe haven in Israel, who were eye-witnesses to episodes which she recounts only from hearsay; brave men and women who did witness deeds of noblest heroism such as the now-maligned Leo Baeck's dragging carts of dung by day and surreptitiously—and upon penalty of death—teaching Torah in the darkness and silence of the Theresienstadt nights.

But I am troubled by a deeper question. Why is it that so many Jews, here and in Israel, have come to feel a sense of shame over the conduct of the six million? Why has passionate anguish turned to cool judgment? And, especially, why is it that so many Jewish students of the holocaust now feel constrained to allocate blame, with high impartiality, between the murdered and the murderers? Miss Arendt brushes aside Adolf Eichmann as a mere cog of banality in an evil system, while characterizing the aforementioned and exalted Leo Baeck as a *Führer* who mislead the Jews to their destruction.

Why? Why this morbid recrimination, this almost psychotic self-incrimination, this seeming need to condemn the dead, our own dead? Perhaps it is easier to libel the deceased innocents than to fix responsibility upon the guilty—not only the butchers of Berlin, but Churchill, Roosevelt, the Pope, and virtually all of Christendom and the civilized world which looked on in alleged impotence and seeming helplessness. Many Jews—especially Israelis—appear to have a compulsion to disassociate themselves from the generation of victims. We are not like that, they say. Why didn't they stand up and fight like men? How can we reverence the memory of cowards? Thus, we can, presumably, bury not only our dead but our memories of them also. They were not our flesh and bone. They were the abnormal products of centuries of ghetto life; they were unreal ghosts whom assimilation had drained of blood and muscle, who walked unprotesting to their doom like dumb and bleating cattle in a slaughter house. They were not part of us. They were the final chapter of an obsolete book we can now cast away. They were strange anachronisms, who, of course, could not endure the toughness of the twentieth century. Let the world know we are not only a different generation; we are a different people.

Our six million dead deserve better than such cruel and callous autopsies, such denigrating post-mortems as they are presently receiving at the hands of some of our self-flagellating Jewish "second guessers." Their one crime, their sole sin—if such it be—was to be utterly incredulous that civilized men could be as depraved as to slaughter one another in cold blood, so sadistic as to relish the torturing and murder of millions, to enjoy the sound of babies' bones breaking on pavements, the sight of blood gushing from children's bursting veins, the smell of stinking, burning human flesh. They believed—or chose to believe—that somehow, somewhere, deliverance would come. For most of them had a deeply imbedded Jewish faith such as is contained in the concluding words of the *Diary of Anne Frank,* which bravely affirms, "But I still believe that people are really good at heart." So, too, they cherished a deep and unassailable confidence in man's ultimate decency which persisted to the very end. And so, admittedly, but not with shame or guilt, they died, most of them, without fighting back, without spilling blood. Without proclamations, they perished, as have Jews throughout the long centuries, for what our forbears felt was the glory of God.

Hounded, harassed, and crushed by brutes, they did not become brutish themselves. They became sacrifices, but they did not sacrifice those human qualities of the spirit which bound them to their fathers in an unbroken chain of gentleness through all the trauma of history. They died quietly, but they died civilized. We should bless their memories, not merely because there but for an accident of birth go we, but because they *were* we and in dying they kept alive in us that strain of quixotic tenderness which was described by the Jewish statesman, Agrippa, in the year 70 of the Christian era, when he pleaded with his countrymen for nonresistance to the Romans: "Nothing so much damps the force of strokes as bearing them with patience; and the quietness of those who are injured diverts the injurious person from afflicting." Judaism has always believed that dying is not as abominable— or sinful—as killing.

How ironic that two decades after Hitler the memory of the martyrs has faded in the minds of most non-Jews and has been discolored in the minds of many Jews! And how ironic that Germans and Germany have become the epitome of respectability in the post-war world. Not that the mantle is totally unwarranted. Post-war Germany has made a serious effort to turn its back on totalitarianism. Democratic liberties have been restored. A modicum of de-Nazification has taken place. For the most part, genuine anti-Nazis have assumed political leadership. Some measure of atonement has been effected in legislation against anti-Semitism, reparations are being paid to survivors of Nazism, and substantial indemnities are being made available to the State of Israel. And, irony of ironies, post-war Germany and Israel have established warm trade relationships, exchanging among other things military weapons and armaments!

Germany is no longer regarded as the enemy of America. The Federal Republic of Germany is our proudest ornament in Europe. Under the impetus of large-scale American aid, West Germany has risen from the wreckage in a truly miraculous recovery, outstripping the rest of Europe. See, we say, pointing to the sleek and chic shops of West Berlin under the blaze of neon lights, this is the way of freedom. See, we say, pointing to the gray life beyond the Wall, this is the contrast between freedom and slavery. See, we say, pointing to Germany's participation in NATO and in the burgeoning European Market, the old Germany is dead. The new Germany, made in the image of America, is now an indispensable part of greater Europe and inexorably linked with the Western world. Maybe so. With all my heart I hope so. But I am uneasy. America has too short a memory. We do not bear grudges. We believe what we want to believe. Let bygones be bygones. Whoever is against the Russians is on our side.

Is it only because I am a Jew that I am troubled by our vast reliance upon West Germany? Is it because I am a Jew that I shuddered when the late President Kennedy declared at the Berlin Wall: *"Ich bin ein Berliner"*—"I am a Berliner!"? Perhaps. But I believe that it is also as an American, as a devotee of freedom, that I fear that we may one day rue the day that we are again making Germany the key to our defense of Europe and that we have determined to rearm Germany once more. The Germans have not renounced their claim to the lost Eastern territories. Is it only Russian propaganda which foresees the possibility that a rearmed Germany might one day be ready to fight again, that it may still harbor the illusion of *Gott mit uns* and yet nurture the dream of *Der Tag* and of "tomorrow the world"? It is one thing to seek to integrate a democratic Germany into a unified West Europe. But it is another to bind ourselves hand and foot to a German government and to give it a virtual veto over the possibility of any political settlement in Europe which Germany may disapprove.

I do not believe that a post-war Germany should have been dismembered and permanently quarantined. But I cannot but view with disquiet the growing influence of Germany within the Atlantic Alliance and the fulsome deference accorded Germany by American foreign policy. It troubles me that this development does not even give rise to serious debate or discussion in the United States, although a good deal of soul-searching is taking place in Western Europe. If present trends continue, the time may yet come when West Germany will receive what now is still clearly beyond its grasp: a German nuclear deterrent. In the name of anti-Communism, we may yet complete the circle which will enable a nuclear rearmed Germany to threaten once again the peace of the world.

All this has happened, it seems to me, because of our persistent illusion that Germany alone provides us with a secure buffer against the Soviet Union. Thus, many Americans regard our contest against the Communists as a holy war in which, with God indubitably on our side, we have no recourse but to fight again "the battles of the Lord," to sally forth in behalf of the right. Other Americans have been so sloganized by fifteen years of cold war that they regard the very processes of diplomacy and negotiation as dangerous, if not vaguely subversive.

Still other Americans, unable to bear the tensions of the cold war, are psychologically overwrought to the point that any "hard" action on our part, regardless of the consequences, would offer a relief from intolerable anxiety.

I believe that we Americans must cease the simplistic and stereotyped view of a complicated and ambiguous world. We must stop looking at the world as if it were a television program pitting the good guys against the bad guys, the peace-loving innocents against the satanic aggressors. True enough, in contrast to the Nazis and the murderers of millions of peasants behind the Iron and Bamboo, curtains we are indeed not only the good guys and the peace-loving peoples, but we are veritable angels. But we have not always been good enough by the yardstick of our own ideals, as our domestic racial troubles eloquently testify—and as our use of the atom bomb demonstrated.

Though all of us joined in the war against the Axis powers, I am not sure that we approved of all the tactics employed in its pursuit. That is one of the penalties of compromise with conscience—a consequence of resorting to violence, no matter how warranted it appears. Force begets force and the hatred to sustain it. Then comes inevitably the mimicry of the foe. And while we Americans boiled no bodies into soap nor burned any of our adversaries in gas ovens, we did throw our own Japanese-Americans into concentration camps and we did yield to the mass bombings of noncombatants, and, above all—or is it beneath all?—we dropped the first atomic bomb on hosts of innocent women and children.

I have grave doubt that we were morally justified in loosing those devastating fireballs on the people of Hiroshima and Nagasaki. Surely we could have warned the Japanese with all solemnity before perpetrating such an unprecedented diabolic deed. If they thought we were bluffing and believed we did not have the bomb, we could have dropped it upon some uninhabited island as a somber ultimatum. It is rather pretentious now to protest that we will not drop the first bomb and that only the godless Soviet could commit so colossal a crime. But that first bomb has already been dropped by our God-fearing selves. Nor can I down the nagging question as to whether we would have dropped the atomic bomb on white men under the same circumstances. The Orientals refuse to believe that we would have. Whomever I encountered throughout my travels in the Far East—the coolie in Hong Kong dragging my rickshaw, coughing up his lungs as he ran, the little men and women beneath their broad-brimmed hats paddling through their rice paddies in Viet-Nam, my Japanese guide in Tokyo and Kyoto, students at the University of Bombay—all these genuinely peace-loving common people of this wide, wide world are still all "shook-up" by the shocking remembrance of that most dreadful of all things past: the incredible fact that our so-called Christian West, which has patronizingly dispatched its missionaries of the Prince of Peace to these so-called "heathens beyond the law," was, despite all our pretensions of love and the all-conquering power of the spirit, the first to drop "It" (the bomb). America will bear throughout history the dubious distinction of being the first nation (and, prayerfully, no matter how stinging the exclusiveness, the last) to have dropped an atomic bomb in cold blood upon human beings.

Nor is the habitual American rejoinder to those sullen Orientals to "remember Pearl Harbor" an adequate rationale or alibi. That was a *military* bastion. Hiroshima should have permanently seared our national conscience. But President Truman had no trouble sleeping the night he made the decision and apparently few other Americans have been deeply disturbed by our action. Except for a few over-sensitive souls it has been dismissed here as a so-called "necessary step in shortening the war," although it seems clear now that Japan was already on the verge of surrender. We would perhaps be less righteous if every American could visit Japan and note in every daily paper, as I did, the steady toll of horrible deaths and suicides, of sickened and twisted Japanese who have been dying by inches since that day in 1945. Hiroshima—and the silence of religion in its wake—will live forever as America's moral infamy and continues to render the grim verdict of the depths to which war apparently and inevitably leads.

There is no more salutary check against American self-righteousness than to read the press of other lands—even friendly lands—and to become exposed to something a bit more objective—and truthful—than the self-censored, canned, syndicated, and homogenized news columns and editorials of the vast majority of our American magazines and newspapers. Thus to peruse even the English language publications in Tokyo, Rangoon, or New Delhi—even of our next-door neighbor, Canada—is to be born anew in an altogether strange and different world. It is to realize that, for much of the world, both Washington and Moscow are suspect and that what we do—or fail to do—speaks more loudly than all our self-serving propaganda.

No, the good guys–bad guys syndrome is far too simple—and fallacious—for our complicated time. And how do we rate if we change the verbiage to the haves and the have nots? How will justice

—the effect of which alone, according to our prophetic teaching, can bring peace—ever be achieved if we uphold those who insist that "what we have, we hold"? Are those who have come late to the imperialist banqueting table to be constrained to behave always as paupers on their knees, humbly grateful for the crumbs we let fall from our overladen banqueting tables? And shall we continue to fail to recognize a nation harboring a fourth of the population of the world because, like a famished child, its manners are not of the most genteel as it grabs greedily for some decent share of the abundance which is ours for its babes with bloated bellies? C. P. Snow has pointed out that most of us of the West resemble people sitting in restaurants before huge plate-glass windows guzzling our superfluity of food while most of the peoples of the earth look hungrily in upon us. If half the world is forced to diet in order to avoid obesity, while the other half starves, can the hungry be blamed for the fires of revolution which alone stir their spirits even if they do not sate their stomachs?

There is another misconception inherent in this peace-loving–aggressor dichotomy. The whirling world of our day doesn't stay in one place that long. China may become the most dangerous source of aggression, precisely because China is a have-not nation while the U.S. and U.S.S.R. become equally wedded to the status quo. Supreme Court Justice Douglas has reminded us that when Cornwallis surrendered at Yorktown, the band played "The World Turned Upside Down" and that this is indeed the tune and tone which the submerged multitudes of the earth expect us to pipe for them today. At a time when these have-not nations are "shopping for a revolution," where are yesterday's American revolutionaries today?

The Soviet Union has been in the main an aggressive and imperialistic force. But the Soviet Union is itself undergoing profound and swift transformations. The Russia of Khrushchev is not the Russia of Stalin. The irresistible demands for consumer goods on the part of the masses, the growing insistence on the part of intellectuals and artists for a greater measure of flexibility, the deepening conflict between Russia and China, the aching memory of the tens of millions who died in World War II—all these and other factors have created a ferment within the Soviet Union which cannot be reversed. Russia will change with increasing tempo. The Soviet Union of a decade hence may bear even less resemblance to the present regime than Khrushchev's Russia bears to Stalin's bloody reign of terror. We have other reformed and retired brigands and tired and glutted revolutionaries in our accepted international club. After all, it has not been too many years since the British massacre at Amritsar—at least not so many as to preclude having my memory jogged when I recently visited there.

But the pursuit of peace is not only a governmental obligation. As war is too important to be left to generals, so is peace too vital to be left to bureaucrats. It is also a transcendent obligation of religion. The time has come, I think, for the forces of religion to be heard. There is a moral dimension to this struggle upon which religion has the obligation to speak and act. Too long have religious groups played the ignoble role of invoking God and high-order rationalizations to justify whatever their own nation chooses to do. It is blasphemy for men of faith to demean themselves into amen-sayers for whatever policy their government proclaims. The true role of religion was charted by the late Pope John XXIII in his revolutionary encyclical *Pacem in Terris* which held aloft a vision of how men can live together, despite their deep differences, as children of one God and upon one small planet.

For several years I have urged a Summit Conference of religious leaders of all faiths to seek to apply God's will to the paramount task of our day: assuring the survival in dignity of the human race. What a paradox that competitive business rivals, athletes from countries that snarl in enmity at each other, that even a Chairman Khrushchev and a President Johnson can communicate with one another, but religious leaders, alleged spokesmen of one God and one humanity, have not yet united to seek an end to the blasphemy of war! Instead, religion too often squanders its resources and its influence on parochial and narcissistic self-interest. I have been pleased to see an increasing support for such an interreligious approach on the part of some of the distinguished Protestant, Catholic, and Jewish leaders and I have received encouragement from religious leaders of the Orient and at a recent private audience with Pope Paul.

Increasingly, religious leaders are realizing that it is time to look beyond the walls of our cool and modern sanctuaries to see the fire spreading unchecked into a conflagration which can and will—unless we are roused in time—consume us all. Ecumenical conferences to bind Protestant and Catholic in new solidarity are all to the good. But the Biblical, God-given mandate is even more timely and more urgent:

> And He shall judge between many peoples,
> And shall decide concerning mighty nations afar off;
> And they shall beat their swords into plowshares,
> And their spears into pruning hooks;

Nation shall not lift up sword against nation,
Neither shall they learn war any more.

(Micah 4:3-4)

That vision, I have always believed, laid upon us Jews, the lineal and, I hope, spiritual descendants of that prophet, the special mission of leading the way toward such a warless world. That belief of mine was shared by one of the most fervid Jewish nationalists of the last century. Moses Hess, more than a century ago, wrote a volume entitled *Rome and Jerusalem,* which was the title I appropriated for that sermon of 1931 which triggered these Afterthoughts. In that pioneer treatise on Zionism, Hess used Rome and Jerusalem to symbolize two opposing value stances. Rome symbolized power and military grandeur; Jerusalem represented moral and spiritual strength. Hess envisioned a Jewish homeland which would be the exemplary tangible expression of the values which Jerusalem embodied.

A century has passed since that book was written and the State of Israel does now exist. One wonders what Hess would think if he were alive today. Would he share something of my disappointment over the "failure of a mission"? For, if his distinctions—and my own in 1931— were once valid, they are much less so today. The Rome of ancient splendor and conquering Caesars is, of course, a centuries-old memory. Today Rome is the colorful, self-indulgent capital of a peaceful Italy, a cosmopolitan bridge to a unifying Western Europe. In Rome lies the Vatican, fountainhead of the Roman Catholic Church. And, unlike the distant times of the Holy Roman Empire when a Pope's word sent armies crashing across Europe to shed blood in the name of Christianity, today the Pope is one of the most eloquent and prophetic forces in support of a peaceful world.

Nor is modern Jerusalem any longer the champion of the values which Hess (and I, too) associated with it. The Jewish world has, perhaps unconsciously, rejected the values which Hess idealized. We have apparently wearied of the image of the long-suffering, sensitive, seemingly, spineless, nonviolent Jew. Our current literature reflects the death of this stereotype and the creation of a new breed of Jew as a brave, heroic, virile man of action. This helps us to understand the phenomenal popular success of such shoddy books as *Exodus, Mila 18,* and *Burnt Offering.*

Here we have a new personification of the Jew—as warrior, blunt of speech, morally unsqueamish, and quick on the draw. He is far removed from the spiritual plane on which Jewish thinkers and writers have moved through the centuries. Now for the first time in the history of the Diaspora, Jewish writers are exalting physical courage and violent action at the expense of the humane and compassionate qualities once reverenced by Jewish tradition.

I shall never forget how shocked I was when I first encountered this contemporary image of the new Jew (what makes *him* a Jew?) in that extravaganza written some years ago by the late Ben Hecht and produced as quite a *tour de force* by Meyer Weisgal. Entitled *A Flag Is Born,* the play posed a conflict between faith and works, between piety and revolt. The drama reached its stirring climax when three heavily armed Jewish men in uniform dissuaded a disillusioned youth from the act of suicide he contemplated and persuaded him instead to join the forces of violence which were determined to win the Promised Land, not by spirit but by power and might. Whereupon the youth seized the *talis* (praying shawl) of an aged Jew who had just died, pinned to it a *Mogen David* (Star of David), and, attaching it to a staff, waved it furiously aloft. *A Flag Is Born* indeed, and so was a new philosophy of Judaism—a philosophy which prated: "The new Jewish voice speaks from out these guns." This was indeed, as the late Judah Magnes then indicated in a letter to *The New York Times,* "a new Jewish voice, a voice which is opposed to the whole tradition of the Jewish religion, all our Maccabean heritage notwithstanding."

Akin to the spirit of *A Flag Is Born* was Arthur Koestler's *Thieves in the Night,* whose doctrine was embodied in one of the hero's utterances: "My teacher carried his praying scarf in a velvet bag to the synagogue— Even so carry I my sacred gun to the Temple that its voice may pray for us."

Undoubtedly all this is an understandable reaction to the trauma of Jewish passivity during the Nazi holocaust. But it is a reaction which may lead to the most primitive forms of self-righteousness, to the super-patriotism and chauvinism of "my people right or wrong," to an exaltation of military exploits (note the pride in all the war-like hardware during the parades on the anniversaries of Israel's Day of Independence!), to a sentimentalization of violence, and to a blunting of moral sensitivity.

Today, Jews want to be normal, like everybody else, and physical strength and military power seem to be the key to such normality. This is not only reflected in literature. It is, increasingly, the tenor of Israel itself. In my recent visit to Israel, I found too much mimicry of the materialism and militarism of the West, which the earlier pioneers eschewed. Suffering and self-restraint are no longer respected. They are condemned as the marks of weakness. Ari Ben Canaan, the hero of *Exodus,* like Moses, did lead many of his people to the Promised Land. But he by-passed Sinai. However, this contemporary Redeemer, unlike Moses, who was "very meek," has become the modern symbol of what a Jew should be. On the other hand, the Jew who does not fight back is beneath pity and below contempt.

The Quakers and the followers of Gandhi did not so regard themselves nor are they so regarded by their fellow men. They refused to capitulate to the predominant contemporary credo of power. A new chapter in the potency of the spirit is likewise being heroically written today by the followers of Martin Luther King who suffer humiliations, jailings, and even murder without retaliatory violence. They are far from viewing themselves as poltroons and the fair-minded white man cannot but be stirred by their silent, prayerful, valorous conduct which has given to the contemporary American Negro a new dignity and destiny which somehow do not seem to require military conquest or even militant resistance to command inner self-respect and outward esteem. These Bible-rooted, God-revering, spirit-trusting Negroes have learned a secret known to and practiced by the Jew throughout the centuries: a secret of the power of faith—a power scornfully rejected by too many Jews today in their indiscriminate assimilation to today's faith in power. Such an assimilation is more odious in my sight than actual conversion to other creeds. This new image of the Jew is a transvaluation of the spiritual courage, the moral grandeur, and the hatred of blood-spilling which have characterized all of post-Biblical Jewish history. If Ari Ben Canaan is truly a symbol of Jerusalem, then once Holy Jerusalem has succumbed to pagan Rome and the hero of *Exodus* has indeed failed to "hear and heed" the "Thou Shalt Not Kill!" revealed upon the cloud-covered crest of Sinai.

It would be wrong to leave the impression that all Jews are wedded to this new stereotype. Some sensitive Jewish writers seem to be warning us against it. One of the most haunting of such books is entitled *Dawn,* written by Elie Wiesel. In this book, a young Jew, who survived a Nazi concentration camp and is now a member of the Irgun extremists, has been ordered by his superiors to execute a British officer as a reprisal. The execution is to take place at dawn. Throughout the interminable night the young man's conscience is tormented. Within him rages a war between the traditional Jewish values and the seeming exigencies of a beleaguered nation. The latter presents its argument as follows:

. . . we have no other choice. For generations we have waited to be better, more pure in heart than those who persecuted us. You've all seen the result: Hitler and the extermination camps in Germany. We've had enough of trying to be more just than those who claim to speak in the name of justice . . . if ever it's a question of killing off Jews, everyone is silent; there are twenty centuries of history to prove it. . . . The Commandment, "Thou shalt not kill," was given from the summit of one of the mountains here in Palestine and we were the only ones to obey it. But that's all over. We must be like everyone else.

The rebuttal from traditional Judaism asks: "Where is God to be found? In suffering or in rebellion? When is a man most truly a man? When he submits or when he refuses? Where does suffering lead him? To purification or to bestiality?" The debate lasts through the long night. It is a debate which will persist for decades because it poses a fundamental dilemma of contemporary Jewish life and of modern Israel. The yearning for normalcy is understandable. So is the vicarious gratification which millions of Jews have experienced in the miraculous military prowess of Israel and in the heart-stopping triumphs of the Jewish supermen of contemporary literature. But the question remains: What is the unique contribution which the Jews have given the world and for which we have endured the sufferings of the ages? Was it the Jerusalem which the prophets symbolized and of which Hess spoke? Or is it Jerusalem come to Rome?

My afterthought has come round full circle to where we began and once more I am plunged into the throes of doubt and self-examination. Do the compromises I made in the face of the Nazi threat of "tomorrow the world" still apply in the shadow of nuclear world incineration? Must Rome win in the end or can the Jerusalem of old still point the way, perhaps the only way, to a warless world?

Am I now a pacifist or not? I don't know. Perhaps I am. If the rise of Hitlerism disillusioned my original pacifism, perhaps the fact of nuclear weapons has revived it. In the 1930s, liberals helped push the democracies into war against Hitler. Today it is the right, equating the menace of Communism with the former threat of Nazism, which seeks to heave us to the brink in a vain pursuit of "victory over Communism." Theoretically, even viscerally, pacifism still appeals to me. Practically, I can see the dangers of standing defenseless in the path of mad or predatory men and nations armed with nuclear missiles. I comprehend the danger of being bereft of any even incipient counterforce when we would then be like sitting ducks—fourteen minutes from Moscow by intercontinental unmanned ballistic missile, and a few minutes more, in the not distant future, from Peking. But with all our present possession of such deterrents, of such impregnable underground arsenals of potential overkill that could snuff out the lives of every

Russian or Chinese Red—of every inhabitant of the earth, that could "kill them dead many times over"—do we really feel safe? Are we secure? Whither will all this mad escalation of atomic power and poisonous fallout lead us? How long, O Lord, how long will we endure the tension, this tension of impending world destruction? This strain between the theoretical and the practical (the emotional versus the rational) has been a central dilemma of my life; it is today a central dilemma in a dangerous world which is still afraid to disarm and which is yet increasingly apprehensive over proceeding with this unabated arms race.

I believe that the final resolution of this dilemma is to dare—dangerous though this course admittedly is—once again to hearken unto the voice of Jerusalem and strive, though the price be high and the sacrifice great, to wed words to work and prayer to practice as each Sabbath in our synagogues we entreat the Father of all mankind to: "Grant us peace, Thy most precious gift, O Thou eternal source of peace, and enable Israel to be its messenger unto the peoples of the earth."

5

MUST GOD GO TO SCHOOL?

FORETHOUGHT

There is a red light that I would like to hold up before myself and my fellow Jews in order to stop us from going full speed ahead in opposition to religious practices in the public schools in this province (Ontario, Canada): To remember that there are majority as well as minority rights. Now, I believe that I am as solicitous as anyone about not merely the prerogatives and privileges, but the downright unassailable rights of minorities, of all minorities, be they Jewish, or Mennonite, or Negro, or agnostic.

But the majority has rights likewise. The majority, it seems to me, has rights especially when it becomes apparent that its very survival and the survival of the minority as well become jeopardized by what may sometimes be the stiff-neckedness of the few. Let me illustrate what I have in mind. If the city of Toronto is threatened with an epidemic of smallpox and the danger of plague spreading to myriads of helpless and innocent children is increased by the refusal of a handful of antivaccinationists in its midst, I believe that the majority has rights that should prevail over the minority. Or, if typhoid ravages a certain section of the country and it is found that the stream from which the drinking water is being drawn has become polluted, and one community or another along its banks insists that its drainage continue to pour its poison into that stream because it "doesn't believe in the germ theory of disease anyway," I believe that the majority has every right to impose its will upon the minority. So, too, must it be with regard to the plague of godlessness and irreligion, of materialism and paganism. This spiritual and cultural plague bids well to wipe out all the spiritual values by which men live. I affirm that no minority has the right to

92

stand upon any of its predetermined notions but must, in the spirit of objectivity and solicitude for the rights of all, re-examine its position and seek to effect some compromise which will conspire to the greater welfare of all.

If there must be religion in the schools, then let it be along the line that a group of ministers and myself labored to make possible in the Village of Forest Hill school, stressing instruction and inspiration in regard to God, the Holy Scriptures, immortality, the brotherhood of man, and similar teachings. We were stymied by the insistence that such a curriculum, in the sight of certain churchmen who are seemingly intent upon leaning upon the school as a staff and a stay to support their weakening denominational ties, was not worth carrying through. Against the use of the schools for sectarian *purposes we Jews must steadfastly set our face, conscious, of course, that the majority has its rights and can counter our opposition, but conscious likewise of the truth that in this instance, the minority is not jeopardizing the genuine welfare of the majority, but is seeking, as our prophets of Israel, who were invariably minorities of one in their generation, did before us: to turn men from the externalities, the outward forms of creeds and dogmas, to the inner content and moral commandments which are the essence of all true religion.*

Toronto, 1941

AFTERTHOUGHTS

To be blunt about it, I'm not altogether happy about what I said above. My support for separation of church and state was much too compromising to suit my present philosophy. It smacked too much of expediency. I believe that my attitude in 1941 was colored by the contrasting situations in Canada and the United States regarding church-state relations. The United States has the blessing of a First Amendment to the Constitution; Canada does not separate church and state. And that makes all the difference.

Under strict separation of church and state, both religious liberty and religion itself have flourished in the United States. The history of the United States, which has been spared the religious wars which have marred other nations, has vindicated the judgment of the Founding Fathers that complete separation is best for *both* church and state.

This thought has been expressed most cogently by the United States Supreme Court:

. . . The centuries immediately before and contemporaneous with the colonization of America had been filled with turmoil, civil strife, and persecution, generated in large part by established sects determined to maintain their absolute political and religious supremacy. With the power of government supporting them, at various times and places, Catholics had persecuted Protestants, Protestants had persecuted Catholics, Protestant sects had persecuted Protestant sects . . . and all these had from time to time persecuted Jews. In efforts to force loyalty to whatever religious group happened to be on top and in league with the government of a particular time and place, men and women had been fined, cast in jail, cruelly tortured, and killed. Among the offenses for which these punishments had been inflicted were such things as speaking disrespectfully of the views of ministers of government-established churches, non-attendance at those churches, expressions of non-belief in their doctrines and failure to pay taxes and tithes to support them.

The Founding Fathers—and particularly Madison and Jefferson— were determined that these bloody expressions would not be duplicated on our shores. They were motivated by a love of liberty, a reverence for conscience, and a profound respect for the private and sacred nature of man's relation to his Maker. As Jefferson put it in his famous letter to the Danbury Baptist Association:

Believing with you that religion is a matter which lies solely between man and his God, that he owes account to none other for his faith or his worship, that the legislative powers of government reach actions only, and not opinions, I contemplate with sovereign reverence that act of the whole American people which declared that the legislature should make no law respecting an establishment of religion, or prohibiting the free exercise thereof, thus building a wall of separation between church and state.

To the American Jewish community, as to former Supreme Court Justice Felix Frankfurter, "separation means separation, not something else." The organized Jewish community has made it clear that it wants to see a constitutional wall—not a moat, nor a picket fence—between church and state. Through the Joint Advisory Committee of the National Community Relations Advisory Council and the Synagogue Council of America, the Jewish religious bodies and community relations agencies have developed policy positions on many of the important issues in the church-state controversy.

Why is the American Jewish community so zealous with regard to church-state matters? Why do Jewish groups take such strong positions on these issues that even such a normally responsible Christian pub-

lication as *America* could burst an editorial blood vessel in exaspera-
tion? The answer is to be found in Judaism's noble role in the ancient
struggle for religious liberty. Jews were the first to fight a war for religious freedom. Our holiday of Chanukah is a testimony to man's sacred
right to worship his God in his own way. When the Hasmonean dynasty
violated Jewish doctrine and philosophy by imposing Jewish practices
upon nations conquered in war, the results of this religious coercion
contributed to the ultimate downfall of the state; and, ironically, the
cruel Herod, who ruled so ruthlessly over Judea, was descended from
the people who had been forcibly converted to Judaism.

But, throughout Jewish history, Jews have characteristically been
victims, rather than victimizers, of such tyranny. I do not suggest that
the Jewish Bible or Jewish theology enjoins us to separation of church
and state per se. Rather, I believe that the totality of Jewish history
is a devastatingly powerful argument for church-state separation. No
matter what the land or the era, when any religious group was able to
control the state, Jews were not free.

We have been, throughout the centuries, living—and often dying—
evidence of the two leagued together to extirpate heresy and to compel
orthodoxy of belief. Ostensibly in the name of God, religion, and the
Church, Jewish blood was spilled by the Crusaders, by the Inquisition,
by the Russian mobs incited to pogroms by Czarist priests. Protestants
and Catholics have had—and still have—some congenial experiences
in some lands under established churches. Jews have been invariably
abused and hounded and discriminated against whenever the state
became an engine of religious coercion, no matter which religion commanded. It is no surprise, then, that American Jews are sensitive (sometimes even hypersensitive) to the need of a strict policy of separation
of church and state; for we believe that the freedom and security of
American Jewry—and of all other religious minorities, as well as of
any nonreligious segments of our population—are inextricably rooted
in the blessings of the First Amendment which guarantees religious
liberty to all.

What, then, is my quarrel with my speech of 1941? It is, firstly, with
the concept of majority rights that I then held. Of course majorities have
rights. Our voting must be decided by the right of the majority no matter
how wrong its verdict may sometimes be. Our legislatures must function
by the similar vote of the majority. But man's right to freedom of conscience is not dependent upon the whims or dictates of any majority.
It was precisely to protect such individual freedom from the encroach-
ment of such majorities that the Bill of Rights was framed in the first

place, and the First Amendment was specifically designed to place the citizen's right to religious liberty and free speech beyond the power of any majority—or minority—to demolish or to diminish.

But what of my example of the right on the part of a majority to compel a minority of Christian Scientists to accede to vaccination in the midst of a raging smallpox epidemic? It seems to me, in the after-thought of the years that have intervened, to be a somewhat inexact analogy. Obviously, in an emergency, the power of the state must be exercised to protect the fundamental health and security of the total community. In war, national exigencies have demanded that we con-script citizens, that we establish rigid controls on freedom of movement and occasionally even on free expression. Even then, however, we respect the right of a conscientious objector. Under ordinary circum-stances we respect the dictates of the individual conscience. In the face of an epidemic, of course, the sheer safety of all would require the vaccination even of those whose religious scruples are offended. But there should be no such compulsion where no such dire emergency exists, where the health and very life of the majority are not jeopardized. In the refusal of the Jehovah's Witnesses, for example, to salute the flag in the public school, despite the wishes of the majority, the United States Supreme Court has correctly sustained their right.

I now realize that the concept of majority rule which I espoused in 1941 has had deleterious effects in American life. If the white majority in a Southern community wishes to maintain a decadent sys-tem of white supremacy, are they warranted in denying the rights of the minority? Is the right of a Negro child to attend a public school in Louisiana dependent upon the wishes of a hostile majority? Or, in a predominantly Roman Catholic neighborhood, do the majority have the right to introduce "Hail Mary" into the public schools? If a majority in a neighborhood is Jewish, does it have the hypothetical right to compose a hymn entitled "Jesus Is *Not* the Son of God" and present it at public school assemblies? These examples—real and imaginary— illustrate the naivete of my earlier thinking. Majority rights must never infringe upon the fundamental civil liberties of free men; even of a single solitary soul. That is the genius of democracy. It is the triumph of personal freedom and the right of the individual to fulfill all the potential of his divine image. It was anticipated in the injunction from Exodus: "Do not side with the majority to do wrong."

My analogy limps on another foot. By implication, I was suggesting that the absence of religious instruction, or even of Bible readings and prayers in the public schools, was tantamount to an epidemic of paganism and that, if as the consequence of such a vacuum our public schools became secularized, then, of course, the rights of the majority must prevail over the tender sensibilities of the minority. I must now take serious issue with this view. To be sure, our public education is basically secular—and it ought to be so in a democratic society. Half the problems of public education in Canada stem precisely from this confusion of religious teachings and secular education. But is public education, therefore, "Godless," as so many in America today charge, particularly in the angry backlash of the Supreme Court's decision on prayer?

I do not believe this at all. Our public schools, with all their limitations, are the best instrumentality we have for the inculcation and perpetuation of democratic and moral values, for training our youth for responsibility in democracy. The values of truth, honesty, equality, responsibility, and mercy can be transmitted in the public school through the example of dedicated teachers and are implicit in all that they are called upon to teach. The important role of religion in world history may be objectively transmitted, as it ought to be. That this is not always accomplished may well be due to incompetent teachers and inadequate curricula. But to seek the remedy by proposing, as I did some decades ago, that our public schools should directly teach religious values—or, to use the words I employed in another section of that original address, make "for the seasoning of the entire (educational) repast with a religious flavor"—is improper, undoubtedly unconstitutional (in the U.S., though admittedly not in Canada), and highly unwise.

What I advocated in those days was a "common core" program, which would communicate the common moral and spiritual values of religion. My proposals were rejected by Christian clergymen who wanted, instead, sectarian programs for the teaching of their particular tenets of religious faith to their particular youngsters. And, in retrospect, I believe they were right in their goal, though wrong, according to my present judgment, in the locale in which they clamored to impose their dogmatic and denominational tenets. I am now strongly opposed even to "common core" programs and the teaching in public schools of moral and spiritual values based on religious sanctions.

As to this much touted "common core," my experience over the past two decades has definitely persuaded me that such a program in public education cannot but be watered down to the lowest common denominator, to some insipid, tasteless broth of commonly-held beliefs, thus diluting vital religious teachings and reducing them to pallid platitudes. I intend no injustice to our teachers when I suggest that few of them have the skill of the great rabbi Hillel who was taunted by the scoffing proselyte to teach him the whole of the Jewish Law and Faith whilst he stood on one foot. Even Hillel, however, after admonishing "what is hateful unto thee, do not do unto another," added: "As for the rest, you must go and study."

To be meaningful, religion must be taught in its full integrity, within the emotional and spiritual context of a particular faith, with its own regimen of ceremonies and practice. But this can only be done in the church, the synagogue, and the home. And those are precisely the places where religious teachings belong—not in the public schools. For religion in public education merely divides the children, creates the real danger of a "public school religion" (the ultimate in secularism) which often conflicts with the teachings of the home, all the while degrading religion by reducing it to a routine and vapid (or mechanical) exercise.

In my earlier, youthful, and immature zeal for "majority rights," I ran roughshod over the rights of one large minority which I did not even trouble to mention: the minority of non-believers—agnostics and atheists. What about their rights? If I had been successful in persuading the school board of Forest Hill Village to introduce a common Judeo-Christian curriculum—including "inspiration in regard to God, Holy Scriptures, Divine Revelation, and Immortality"—where would that have left the youngsters who, out of convictions bred in them by their parents, could not in conscience accept even those concepts shared by both Judaism and Christianity? In the United States, to its glory, the parents of such children can go to court in order to invoke their constitutional rights. Those rights would undoubtedly be sustained, as they have been many times in the past. But, constitutional principles apart for a moment, are those children to be second-class citizens in the public school? Do not their parents pay the same taxes? Who gave us the right to single them out for embarrassment and calumny? Who gave us the right to impose our religious beliefs on a captive audience which is compelled by law to attend school? The right *not* to believe is as sacred—and as indispensable—as the right *to* believe. Yet this is a right which today is becoming so imperiled here as well as elsewhere, is becoming so confused with espousing Communism, that few who genuinely believe in such freedom of the mind and conscience dare to lift their voice in defense of such spiritual and moral freedom lest they too be branded with the taint of subversive and Red.

Not that I concur in the opinions of such non-believers, although I must add that my own faith might well be similarly violated if majorities here had the right to enforce their more orthodox views and to suppress my own which are far more heterodox. Paraphrasing Voltaire, I say that though I disagree with their disbelief, I shall fight for their right to maintain even what I regard as their gross error. Nor am I totally lacking in my understanding of the agnostic. He is struggling, searching, and seeking to find his own truth. In humility he admits his doubt and uncertainty. He does not claim to have the answers but neither does he reject the quest. I have no such respect for the atheist. He is the supreme dogmatist—as benighted, bigoted, and blind as the most fundamentalist apostle of orthodoxy. But, of course, this in no wise means that I would not defend his prerogative, if he so chooses, out of conscience rather than mere caprice, to close the windows of his mind. The nonbeliever, too, deserves the full protection of the law. Where would our much vaunted Judeo-Christian concepts be today, the very ones some would now impose upon our children in the public school, if the iconoclasm, even the then seeming atheism of Abraham, had been forever suppressed by his idol-worshipping father, Terah?

And, beyond this, did I really believe, even in those comparatively less complex Toronto days, that Christianity and Judaism could link arms in teaching the shared values of God, Holy Scriptures, immortality? I must have been younger than I realized. Which God? Which Holy Scriptures? The Old? The New? Both? Then what are the differences? Which New Testament? The King James Version of the Protestants? Or the Douay of the Catholics? What Jewish teachings would be advanced? The Orthodox view which accepts the physical resurrection of the dead or the Reform which does not? Are public school teachers qualified to teach these matters objectively? What of the non-believing teacher? Shall we establish a religious test for every public school pedagogue? Perhaps it is just as well that my fellow Torontonians rejected my proposal, for its public schools would soon have been converted into an angry and clamorous cockpit of competing religious sects, maneuvering for position, engendering divisiveness, seeking to indoctrinate callow youths, and causing untold damage to public education and serious harm to religion itself.

Let us be candid about this whole issue. Many a state within our Union has seen religion flourish—and their public schools have not sunk into atheistic paganism—without a scintilla of religious education. Why then all the fuss and fury today? Because of the refusal of the church to recognize its own failures. The real motivation behind the present thrust for religious intrusion into public education in America is the bankruptcy of Christian church education. The Protestants especially have been seeking to reach their children—who are being lost to their totally inadequate, ineffectively and parsimoniously staffed religious schools—through a variety of expedients within the public schools. One of these devices is released time, whereby pupils are dismissed during the school day for their respective sectarian instruction. But whatever the artifice, the public school is being exploited as a desperate last-ditch means to enforce religious instruction by recapturing the children of a religiously indifferent generation—no matter how vapid its monochrome content, or how rebellious its recipients. But such abdication of responsibility on the part of the church further weakens it, while placing intolerable burdens upon the public school. Why place the onus on the public schools which are doing their work manfully under most trying circumstances? Why make the public schools the scapegoat for our failure to shape a moral society? Let us not delude ourselves any longer into thinking that a flavor or patina of religious practice—skimpy, uninterpreted Bible reading, rote prayers, or the superficial observance of unfamiliar festivals and holy days—will affect the moral standards of our youngsters or will immunize them against juvenile delinquency and Communism. It is self-deception to pretend that it will. Extensive research has revealed that juvenile delinquency is at least as high among students of all-day parochial schools as it is among those in public schools, and ethical behavior is not definitely determined one way or the other by the artificial injection of homeopathic doses of religious devotions into public school sessions. Instead, organized religion will be vitiated by yielding its unique function to the state, by dwelling in a fool's paradise of deluded belief that its own responsibilities are now safely in the hands of the public school. A fragile reed for centuries-old religious heritages to lean upon, indeed!

Actually, the increased sophistication of my position on religion in public education has paralleled the emerging attitude of the American Jewish community. Except for the Central Conference of American Rabbis, which spoke out repeatedly for the strict separation of church and state, American Jewry as a whole played virtually no role in this matter until 1946. Prior to that time, most Jews in America were, understandably, preoccupied in large measure with more immediate matters of life and death for the Jewish people throughout the world. But, in post-war America, the Jewish community began to play its proper role in the life of the entire society as it was affected by growing pressures to introduce released time and other religious practices into public education. A Joint Advisory Committee of the National Community Relations Advisory Council and the Synagogue Council of America was organized to provide leadership to the Jewish community in this critical area. Its first major test came in 1946 when the historic McCollom case, testing released time on public school premises in Champaign, Illinois, went up to the U.S. Supreme Court.

It was a painful test for the Jewish community. The McColloms were avowed atheists. Public opinion was decidedly hostile to the legal action which seemed to threaten the religious euphoria which had settled on the land in the post-war period. But the entire Jewish community —Reform, Conservative, Orthodox, plus all the civic defense agencies —joined in a strong *amicus curiae* brief which was submitted to the Supreme Court in support of the McColloms. The brief was hailed by the *St. Louis Post Dispatch* as a major contribution to the American tradition of religious liberty. The Supreme Court ruled the Champaign released-time program unconstitutional. The Court set down the ringing doctrine—"the state may not aid any religion nor aid all religions equally." This has been the basic guide of the Court in all subsequent church-state decisions. It is this doctrine which subsequently evoked an unceasing propaganda onslaught, led by Roman Catholic and some Protestant leaders, and which was rekindled, with vastly increased indignation and wrath, by the Supreme Court decision on prayer in June, 1962.

In 1962-63, prayer became headline news, the subject of an explosive and ugly controversy in our national life. The United States Supreme Court declared that the Regents Prayer recited in the public schools of New York State is unconstitutional in that it represents an "establishment of religion." The almost universal reaction to the Court's 6–1 decision was condemnatory. Cardinal Spellman of New York denounced the decision as one that "strikes at the very heart of the godly tradition in which America's children have for so long been raised." He apparently overlooked the fact that this so-called godly tradition has not been imposed by law in a number of states without producing a generation of little pagans—no distinction being drawn between the prohibition of legally enforced alleged "religious" devotions and official anti-God propaganda. Cardinal McIntyre of Los Angeles declared: "This decision puts shame on our faces, as we are forced to emulate Mr. Khrushchev." Even the liberal Catholic magazine, *America,* poured scorn upon the decision as "a stupid decision" handed down on America's "Black Monday." Bishop James Pike, too, champion of so many unpopular causes and non-conformist extraordinary, lamented that the decision would "deconsecrate" America. A Southern congressman demagogically ranted that "they" (the Court) "put Negroes into the schools and has taken God out of them." Outraged legislators of the North and the South, some sincerely misreading the content and intent of the decision, others blatantly taking God's name in vain, immediately introduced a spate of bills calling for a constitutional amendment to permit prayer in the public schools. Bitter letters cascaded into Washington and into newspapers throughout the country, creating intense and sometimes irresistible heat. Newspapers throughout the nation excoriated the Supreme Court and beat their editorial breasts about the gleeful gain for atheistic Communism and the lamentable loss for "Christian" America stemming from the decision. Many attributed the verdict to the "agitation of a militant and well-organized minority," and the rancid odor of anti-Semitism could be sniffed in many a community which long prided itself on its good community relations and high level of "tolerance."

One of the most disturbing developments in the prayer controversy was the aforementioned most shocking editorial which appeared in the Jesuit weekly, *America,* on August 27, 1962. Entitled "To Our Jewish Friends," it warned the Jewish community that, if it persisted in its support of the Supreme Court's decision on prayer and continued to press its opposition to religion in public education, it would stoke the fires of anti-Semitism and would "paint itself into a corner of cultural and social alienation." The threatening and patronizing manner of the editorial was as disturbing and as alarming as the matter it contained. The response from Jewish as well as from some Protestant, and even from certain more objective, less impassioned Roman Catholic leaders, was immediate and angry.

Had *America* forgotten that it was individual Roman Catholics who, for many decades, had gone to court with great personal courage to challenge religious practices in the public schools, thus contributing to what they now so disparagingly demean as their "secularization"? Of course, those were protests against *Protestant* instruction and ceremonials in communities and in times where the Catholics constituted such decided minorities, which factor today—when it comes to Jews—they disdainfully slough aside. Is the sacrifice of conscientious principle the price to be exacted for a cessation of anti-Semitism? What would the Roman Catholic community have replied if a Jewish publication had warned Catholics to cease their drive for public aid to parochial education, lest anti-Catholicism be increased? One of the few shreds of gratification to be derived from this serious rupture in interreligious understanding was the chagrin expressed by many thoughtful Roman Catholic leaders who felt, as I did, that *America* had done a disservice to religious pluralism, to interfaith amity, and to democracy itself.

Let me say very frankly that I regard the recent Supreme Court decisions on church-state relations as historic milestones in the reinforcement of religious liberty in the United States and as a genuine contribution to religion itself. For religion has flourished in our nation as nowhere else in the world just because, here, religious groups have had to stand on their own feet and not, as in many other lands, lean as dependents and supplicants upon the almighty state. No other nation has built its national life upon the separation of church and state as we have, and I am one of those who regards this as, perhaps, the paramount contribution which the American experiment has made to the evolution of modern civilization. If the church and the synagogue cannot inspire prayer in their people, then the church and the synagogue will fail—and deserve to fail. The entire notion that it is the responsibility of the state to promote religious faith, to sponsor prayer, and to inculcate a belief in God is not only a corruption of *religious* liberty, it is a corruption of *all* liberty, and of religion too. It is a form of idolatry. And to tamper with our precious Bill of Rights, by amending our Constitution's First Amendment, prohibiting any governmental establishment of religion, is reckless and dangerous folly. It would begin an irreversible process of unravelling the treasured fabric of America's unique religious freedom. Some of those most avid thus to emasculate the First Amendment have had the effrontery to contend that the Supreme Court, by "banning God," as they so cavalierly distort and debase the decision, has made it difficult for the public schools to teach moral values. But how can moral values be taught to the impressionable young when the religious and political leaders of the nation demonstrate so irresponsible a contempt for law? Is the fire-eating defiance of clerics railing against the prayer decision any different, morally, from the defiance by Southern racists of the Court's decision on desegregation? Both violate the injunction from Exodus: "Thou shalt not revile a judge nor curse a ruler of the people."

So anxious have some ecclesiastics become to procure even the most measly crumb of that which they accept as *religion* in the schools that one prelate stated that he would be content if the mere words "In God We Trust" were recited in the classroom. He seems to have forgotten that no such third person reference is a substitute for the I-Thou communication of prayer and conveniently overlooks the frequent debasement of our currency despite the engraving of those treasured words on our coins. Plaster signs of "In God We Trust" over all our buildings, mechanically mumble those otherwise hallowed words each day in school, and America will not place one whit more of its trust in the divine nor advance one centimeter farther on the road to His Kingdom.

Do they forget that when Catholic Bishop Hughes in New York City in the 1840s called for the elimination of Bible reading in the public schools (because it was the Protestant Bible), violence sundered the community; that there was rioting in the streets of Philadelphia in 1844 in the wake of Bishop Francis Kenrick's attack on Bible reading and prayer in the schools? And even today, although Roman Catholics generally feel they have the strength to take care of themselves in relation to the kind of religious practices which will be conducted in public schools, there are frequent Catholic objections to such religious practices as baccalaureate services, distribution of the Gideon Bible, and the use of the King James Version of the New Testament (as opposed to the Douay). The Catholics were right then—and they are right now —in these objections.

I was very much impressed and deeply gratified by the contrasting public reactions to the Supreme Court's decision on prayer in June, 1962 and its decision striking down Bible reading and "the Lord's Prayer" in June, 1963. The first, as I have indicated, touched off a wave of hysteria and deeply troubled fear. I believe, however, that the American people had serious second thoughts after the first wave of panic. Much more mature and sober reflections followed the second decision. What caused the difference? It might be interesting to speculate. For one thing, I believe that the Court itself was much more precise on the second occasion as to the implications of its ruling; none but the malicious could possibly regard the ruling as anti-God. Secondly, I believe that the press and the mass media generally, which had displayed a lamentable tendency to shoot from the hip with explosive generalization after the Regents' Prayer case, did its own homework a little better and gave the public a more thoughtful, balanced, and undramatic coverage of the second decision.

Thirdly, of course, the church-state case may have been somewhat blanketed by bigger news, such as the gathering racial revolution. Fourthly, I believe that the religious groups themselves—through interreligious dialogues, through painful reexamination of positions, through painstaking preparation and education of their own people, through study, and through respect for law—helped create a climate in which the new decision was understood and accepted, even by those who might have preferred a different ruling.

In this regard, I believe that the Protestant community went through a kind of internal revolution which had a tremendous impact on American public opinion at large. The clear separationist position of the Presbyterians, the official stand of the National Council of Churches of Christ and of many of its denominations separately in support of the Court's decision—all this helped to frame the issue as an American issue, on which deep and conscientious differences rest, rather than as a Christian-Jewish issue or a God-anti-God or secularist-religionist dichotomy. In my judgment, this was indispensable to a public clarification of the issues. It seems to me that the Supreme Court has stirred us all into an intensive public awareness of the meaning of church-state separation—and our stake in it—and that, too, is a great gain. The Court has both recognized and strengthened the reality of American pluralism.

The problem of religion in public education is not yet fully resolved, however. There remain many gray and shadowy practices on which the Court's decisions shed very little light. In addition, it is already abundantly evident that many school systems—and not all in the South—are going through the same kind of elaborate techniques of evasion and circumvention that we have witnessed in the aftermath of the segregation decisions. If one purpose of religious practices in the public schools is the elevation of moral standards in our youth, it escapes me how this can be achieved by identifying the Bible and religion with contempt for law. Above all, regardless of how we may differ on the wisdom of the Court's decisions, we all share a deep obligation to conduct our conversations in dignity, to agree to disagree agreeably, to preserve the integrity of the courts and the processes of law.

Catholic though he was, our ever-to-be-remembered late President Kennedy withstood the stampede of his fellow churchmen and their Protestant confreres in sounding one of the few notes of sanity voiced by Christians amid all that chorus of vitriol and venom. He calmly called upon the American people to support the law of the land. He reminded us that we are as free to pray and to worship now as we ever were. But he rightly insisted that religious faith cannot be coerced by the state. It cannot be imposed by fiat. It cannot be demanded as the measure of patriotism. It cannot be reduced to a spiritual loyalty oath. Prayer is the communication between God and man, an individual "I-Thou" dialogue, and upon this holy relationship no state may intrude. It must come from the heart and not from the school board. As the rabbis of old taught: "Prayer without the proper intention (*kavannah*) is like a body without soul." Jewish tradition ceaselessly enjoined its adherents not to "make your prayer a fixed routine but one which is an outpouring of the heart." (Sayings of the Fathers 11, 18)

But I fear that the more realistic reason for the intemperate response of some leaders of the Roman Catholic community to the Supreme Court decision is the clear implication that its wide sweep means definitively that federal funds cannot, constitutionally, be made available to parochial schools. That issue runs much deeper and has more practical consequences than the rote recital of a twenty-two-word prayer or Bible reading in the public schools. If the Court's decision means that the door has been closed to the increasing demand for tax support for religious institutions, I rejoice in it. I believe that the public subsidization of parochial education—including Jewish—would destroy public education, would make our public schools the targets of religious bitterness, would violate the entire concept of separation of church and state, and would Balkanize the American people into separate sub-communities with separate school systems in an atmosphere of religious conflict and divisiveness, with each denomination pressuring, lobbying, pressing to get to the public trough first "with the mostest" instead of relying, as they must, as our common Old Testament insists, upon the support of religion out of the free-will offering of the heart.

Most Jews oppose public aid to parochial schools, although the number of dissenters from this position seems to be on the rise within the Orthodox Jewish community particularly. At the same time, the Jewish day school movement is mushrooming within Conservative Judaism as well, due in large measure to dissatisfaction with the religious school and other nonintensive forms of Jewish education. As Jewish day schools increase, and as the staggering burdens of such facilities become even heavier, there is no doubt that commitment to separation of church and state tends to dim in some eyes as the vision of salvation through public largesse looms larger. Indeed, a few Conservative Jewish leaders have already come out for federal aid to parochial schools.

Within our Reform Jewish ranks, we have not as yet been willing to compromise our traditional twin commitments to public education and to church-state separation. We have thus far refrained from favoring the establishment of Reform Jewish day schools. But, I must candidly confess that in our ranks as well there is a small—but vocal—viewpoint that favors experimentation with such Reform day schools, at least for the gifted "elite" youngsters who, so it is maintained, can thus be best trained for Jewish leadership. I for one am still not convinced that parochial schools are the answer to the very real problems of the inadequacy of our religious school system nor of our public schools either. I would not want to break faith with the public school— nor to see its increasing desertion through greater attention and expenditure concentrated elsewhere. But if we should ever decide, as some are presently proposing, to pioneer with Jewish prep or day schools, I would insist that the Jewish community pay for these facilities out of its own resources rather than yield to the tempting aroma of public funds.

When religious groups surrender moral principles to expediency, they risk not only their integrity but their freedom. The late Edmond Cahn was right in my judgment when he wrote that the way to destroy the churches is to give them all they want in the form of tax money because this would make governmental control of these schools inevitable.

The Supreme Court decisions against religious devotions in the public schools will turn out to be empty indeed if the current campaign to use tax-raised funds for parochial schools prevails. And there is increasing reason for concern. There is, of course, little likelihood of across-the-board public aid to private education. But there is already underway a highly complex and successful effort to change both public attitudes and public policies. With regard to public attitudes, the argument runs as follows: In the light of Sputnik and the vast Soviet challenge to our society, we must realize that "private institutions no less than public institutions are dedicated to public service" and the national interest requires that we close ranks behind tax support to improve *all* schools without distinction. Such eminent observers of the American scene as Walter Lippman and Robert H. Hutchins have been persuaded to this position; Hutchins has gone so far as to comment that the separation of church and state has no future in American education. Public opinion polls indicate that a growing percentage of Americans have been impressed by this line of thinking.

Public policies are also beginning to reflect this approach. Passage of the College Facilities Act in 1964 was hailed as a major educational breakthrough—and it was. But it also broke through historic reluctance to utilize tax money to subsidize church-related colleges along with public institutions. It blurred all former distinctions. Its chief supporters fought fiercely—and successfully—to prevent an amendment to the Act which would have permitted judicial review so that the constitutionality of the law could be tested. Similarly, the National Defense Education Act already provides for the financing of classrooms—both private and public—for the teaching of mathematics, science, and foreign languages.

The pressure to expand this assistance will be difficult to resist. These are likely to be supplemented by the extension of federal scholarship aid to individual recipients, rather than to schools, so that the student can pay tuition to the school of his individual choice, including church-related institutions of learning. In addition, there are mounting efforts to grant funds to public school districts to help finance shared-time programs in which parochial school children will utilize the public schools part of the day; and to grant income tax credits or tax deduction to parents for children attending private or parochial schools.

Thus, though there is no present possibility of across-the-board, massive public aid to sectarian schools because the constitutional barrier is too high, the piecemeal programs described above are well on the way to victory. These programs may well create the precedents and climate of acceptance which one day could achieve Dr. Hutchins' prophecy: the end of separation of church and state. Then America may find itself on the road which, for example, the Netherlands has followed, where the constitution was amended to permit government funds for public schools. There, the proportion of children attending public schools prior to the adoption of the constitutional amendment was 80 per cent, whereas today some 25 per cent attend public schools and 75 per cent are enrolled in confessional schools. Such a development would be a tragic denouement to the American school system and to the great American experiment of church-state separation.

I feel constrained to close with a word of solemn warning to those Christian churches and churchmen so fervid to use the state to advance religion. If the church remains content with *this* solution of its own most serious problem of the dearth of religious education, I, for one, have little hope for its persistence as a flourishing institution in the days ahead. Let the church be a parasite upon the state, seeking to hitchhike on its subsidies as its stay and strength, rather than upon God and His righteousness; then the day will come when, as it inevitably did in so many lands across the seas, the state will either bend it to its will or leave it in the lurch. Such has been the history of the church. Whenever it thus leaned on the authority of the state, it became weakest. Whenever, with its back to the wall, it called out the faithful, even though they were few in number, to sustain it, it grew in strength. For the church to renounce its own charter, based on the voluntary offerings of its adherents' hearts and souls and minds and means, is a seeming confession of spiritual bankruptcy which no amount of state support will liquidate.

I pray with all my heart that America's religious groups can rise to the noble challenge which the Supreme Court has unwittingly addressed to the forces of religion: to rely upon our own resources, to carry out our mission, to teach and transmit the spirit and not the slogans of our faiths, and to be worthy of our high calling, as descendants of those who founded our nation as a protest against every form of religious coercion, as a bastion of spiritual freedom.

6

DARE TO BE FREE

Will we never learn? Will we never profit from the sad, yet eloquent, testimony of the past? Each rare spirit whom now we revere and honor was usually a minority of one among his benighted and irate contemporaries. Aside from his unheard of, incomprehensible God, Moses had but Aaron at his side when he sought to realize his mad dream to redeem a race of slaves from their bondage and to lead them to the promised land of "milk and honey". All the prophets were denounced and even oppressed as fools who lacked but cap and bells to amuse—or to anger—the populace; Jesus had twelve disciples, but not even all of these remained loyal to the end; Socrates drank the hemlock with but Crito by his side; Spinoza was driven alone from the synagogue as an alleged blasphemer of his father's faith. In the light of such a sorry saga with its oft repeated and tragic tale, have we the right ever to act as judge of our fellow creature's opinions or to deny him his God-given right to be himself?

"Judge not thy fellow creature," our sages wisely admonished, "until thou hast stood in his place," shared his thoughts, been scorched by his same flame of conscience. No man can be altogether fulfilled who nurses within his heart the conviction that he possesses the truth but dare not utter it; who dreams that if he could but be heard, humanity might be saved from its delusions and its danger, its disintegration and conceivable demise, that if his convictions were only articulated, all mankind might be redeemed. Deny such spirits the right to speak, and their souls wither and become speedily dessicated; spiritual death overtakes them and abject misery dogs them to their unhappy grave.

Such balderdash as has followed in the wake of the present local controversy over freedom of speech would indeed have our splendid Toronto join with Dayton, Tennessee, to become, with it, the laughing stock of the world. [This has reference to the attempt in Toronto in 1931 to suppress the erstwhile free expression of speech in Queens Park where throughout many preceding years the custom of soap-box oratory had been—no matter how heterodox, unpatriotic, or downright treasonable—endured by a whole corps of "bobbies" and public as the salutary and therapeutic "letting off of steam."]

Here stands revealed the cloven hoof of bureaucracy and intolerance in all its naked horror. For censorship of the intellect is not only the worst of all restrictions—it is the only one that is self-perpetuating and self-destructive. All other oppression provokes resistance. Suppression of the mind and the unhampered expression of its opinions by subtle indoctrination converts victims into the staunchest of supporters. It is the most deadly of all restraints. To yield to such tyranny is to spell the ultimate defeat of all our democratic institutions. What respect can youth have for democracy, for which we fought a brutal and bloody war, while even within the walls of the university the funda-mental principle of freedom is betrayed; while those professors who exercise its divine prerogatives are so frequently demoted or expelled, and while the ghastly fear of heresy-hunting and sedition-searching crouches at the gates even of our institutions of higher learning? Better indeed to relinquish the stately structures and costly budgets and to meet as did Socrates and Plato and Aristotle in some outdoor grove of trees than to sell the great birthright of knowledge and truth for so ill-tasting and poisonous a mess of pottage.

If we would rear a generation to tread the path of wickedness which we have trod, to perpetuate the injustices and flagrant inequalities of which we have been guilty, to emerge from colleges and universities with minds warped and spirits stunted, gullible, suggestible, suspicious, prejudiced, and ignorant—the very finest material for the scheming demagogue and incipient "man on horseback"—then let us continue in our blindness to place a ban on truth and permit those who pay the piper to call the tune.

If we would have our young men and women become but indis-tinguishable members of the herd, living their sluggish lives by imitation and conformity, easily stampeded and led whithersoever the hysteria of the moment might direct them, then let us censor their textbooks, gag their professors, and let the taxpayers determine their curricula. If we really want, as the teachers of our youth, the most tightlipped and timorous of creatures—men who have followed the line of least resist-

ance into slavish submissiveness and subservience to their lay masters— to guard well their lips, keep their mouths padlocked, and their minds empty; if we would drive all self-respecting and independent spirits, all men of ability and backbone from our schools and admit only those so weak-kneed and cringing, so devoid of character as to be content to crouch and crawl, to be shackled and suppressed; if we would convert our faculties into spineless petty clerks, kept men, for whose flattery there is silver and for whose silence there is much fine gold; if we would degrade them into some sort of queer sport in the race of men, a third sex, as it were, marching in a perpetual lock-step, then let us turn the control of our educational system over to our professional chauvinists and shouting patrioteers. But on the contrary, if we would restore education to its proud estate as the eternal quest for truth and light, then must the professors and students of our universities no longer be slaves, but free men all; untrammelled, unfettered by any earthly coils; free to mount upon the pinions of thought and to follow whithersoever it leads.

Toronto, 1931

AFTERTHOUGHTS

Such "remembrance of things past," out of which there leaped from my lips and sprang from my heart the preceding comments, is as relevant now as were those heatedly debated words of three decades ago. Those words of 1931 were not spoken in a vacuum, even as these afterthoughts to follow grow out of some of the most tangible problems that confront our free society today.

Canada in the 1930s, like the U. S., was mired in a depression which, more than any other single episode within my lifetime, unmasked the false idols which most of us so obsequiously worshipped. It was during those years that the treasure of a beloved wife and children became more expendable than supposed gilt-edge securities, and many men plunged from the roofs of skyscrapers, abandoning their loved ones and life itself because their material house of cards had collapsed. And there were many who, in terror over the loss of jobs and the shrinking of the general economy, were prepared to jettison the priceless boon of liberty itself. It was this general depressing atmosphere and the consequent breakdown of values which prompted my sermon "In Defense of Freedom."

The particular episode, however, which precipitated that address was the issuance of an order by the Chief of Police in Toronto that no longer would Communists or other "radicals"—whatever that meant—be permitted to gather or speak in Queens Park. Toronto was an exceedingly proud city—proud of many things but proudest of all of its British heritage. And one of the many institutions whereby Torontonians strove to emulate the old country was its own pocket-sized replica of those large and milling circles of listeners crowding around some flamboyant orator in Hyde Park, London. Every Saturday afternoon a small knot of men and women assembled in Queens Park, which surrounds the Ontario Provincial Parliament Buildings, to listen to some speaker expostulating on one issue or another.

It is interesting—and revealing—to note the timing of what follows. For years in Toronto, as in London, such gatherings had been permitted, with the helmeted police in both cities looking on with the precise amount of boredom appropriate to the keepers of the peace. Now suddenly in 1931 came the ukase that all such assemblages and speeches should cease forthwith.

Why? Why *then?* Factories were being closed down. Men were being thrown out of work by the wholesale. The long-recognized European plans of unemployment insurance had not yet reached this so-called new world. The times were indeed out of joint and those who sought to lead the mounting masses of unemployed and who urged prompt and radical revision of antiquated social and economic policies were quickly sullied by the self-righteous custodians of the status quo, with the tar of "socialist" or, still worse, the most execrable curse of all— "Communist."

There were admittedly some Communists in the Dominion at that time and they were largely centered in Toronto. As a matter of fact, I knew their leader. He had been invited by one of my most precious friends, the Reverend Dr. E. Crossley Hunter, a distinguished minister of the United Church of Canada and cofounder with me of the Canadian Conference of Christians and Jews, to his vacation cottage on the Muskoka Lakes. There, with representatives of the Protestant and Catholic Churches, the recognized Canadian labor movement, various political parties, and others, we lived together for several days and discussed the troubled times in which we found ourselves. Contact with a Communist under other circumstances would have been enough to have tabbed me in every black book around as a "Commie" myself and might have resulted in public calumny and exposure long ago.

That leader of the Communist Party in Canada, Tim Buck, was no fire-breathing, bomb-throwing Bolshevik. He was a radical, there can be no doubt of that—but a radical in the literal meaning of that term: one who digs to the root of things. And the root of things at that precise moment was to find the prime causes of the economic collapse in the midst of a nation and a continent unparalleled throughout God's good earth in a superabundance of material blessings. To all of us, in those discussions, democracy meant not only the right to cast one's ballot, to express a choice between what frequently is Tweedledee and Tweedledum, but to move as swiftly as possible toward equality of economic opportunity, to equalize economic suffering—if suffering need be at all in such a divinely dowered commonwealth—rather than to have some living in the lap of luxury while shamefully large numbers of their fellow citizens were queuing up in front of soup kitchens or peddling apples on the streets.

It was to protest against such evils and to propose prompt legislative action that the crowds gathered in Queens Park in somewhat larger numbers than on previous Saturday afternoons. As the speakers became more stridently specific about the economic ills of Canada and more precise in their proposed parliamentary solutions, as their hearers whooped more enthusiastically their "Hear! Hear!", the powers that be, in the banking houses, among the merchants and the industrialists, and in the legislative halls, panicked and forgot all about their pride in being descendants of the authors of the Magna Carta. So the word went out—and Chief of Police Draper issued the edict that there were to be no more speeches in Queens Park.

To be sure, men reared in the tradition of freedom do not take such seemingly arbitrary decrees—even from a Chief of Police—lying down. On the Saturday after the pronouncement, therefore, as might well have been expected, the crowds were larger than ever. (When will men ever learn that suppression doesn't work—except, of course, under a military dictatorship and even then time will tell how long?) But the Chief was not to be caught napping. He ordered out the cavalry. The helmeted mounties bore down upon the men and women and youths and children who had assembled on the green. The crowd was dispersed—but the episode was far from ended.

A hall was then sought by the protesters, but the pressures from the police and the open threats to revoke the license of anyone permitting his hall to be used by these groups virtually gagged all those speakers into silence.

I felt I had to raise my voice amid that stillness. True, I was not a citizen of Canada, and consequently it might well have been deemed brazen nerve on my part to sound a protest. Besides, it was barely over a year since I had come to Canada. As I insist now that one does not have to be a resident of the South in the United States to oppose the suppression of liberty there, so I argued then that citizenship was not a requirement for speaking out against suppression of the human spirit anywhere. Many deemed my action in Toronto the epitome of rash meddling and were outraged that a rank newcomer to the Canadian scene, a Jew at that (Toronto had not yet matured to that stage where recently it elected a Jewish mayor for three successive terms and by the largest pluralities in Toronto history), should inject himself into so feverish a controversy. But I felt that my knowledge of the Anglo-Saxon tradition and of Christian teachings, derived in turn from the Old Testament's passion for freedom, gave me the right, the responsibility, and the inescapable duty to heed the injunction of our own Ethics of the Fathers: "In a place where there are no men, strive thou to be a man."

I challenged the Chief of Police to a debate. I wrote him an official letter, as President of the Fellowship of Reconcilation, asking him to meet me at Queens Park on the following weekend in order to debate the question as to whether "Communists Should Have the Right to Speak." There was no reply—except in the press.

Through the columns and headlines of what was then as yellow a daily as this continent boasted (it has since reformed) came the volley that I expected. It would be gratuitous for me to state that I was not then, am not now, and hope never to become a Communist—nor even one who is remotely sympathetic to their totalitarian, tyrannical ways. As a religious man, I despise the mechanistic determinism and arrogant atheism which are the hallmarks of Communism. As a democrat, I am outraged at Communism's contempt for the free mind and spirit of man. And as a Jew, I cry out against the Soviet's brutal suffocation of the religious and cultural life of a Jewish community of three million souls. But a "Communist" I was most assuredly and vehemently dubbed. When arguments fail, call names. Then came that which I had feared even more and which I knew in advance would cause greater concern to my congregants: an editorial viciously denouncing me as an alien and calling upon my congregation to send me back where I came from.

My prediction that the Communists were but the first to be suppressed was swiftly fulfilled. Soon, precisely as I had prognosticated, the arbitrary Police Chief denied all manner of meeting places to every liberal organization in Canada. But few seemed to care. And because of this, power fed on power.

As for me, I was in deep trouble. For a while, except for my little band of loyal Fellowship associates, I was virtually abandoned and that was not particularly comforting to the leaders of my congregation. Although they were understandably proud of their tradition of a free pulpit, did such freedom extend to challenging the Chief of Police to a debate from a soap box in Queens Park? I often wonder just what might have happened if formidable reinforcements had not rallied to my side. *The Toronto Daily Star* plunged into the fray—on my side. And then, most helpful of all, sixty-eight professors of the University of Toronto issued a ringing manifesto which, predicated both on the Judeo-Christian as well as the Anglo-Saxon tradition, upheld the right of any man to think and speak as his conscience dictates. The manifesto also sounded a solemn warning that the suppression of any liberties sooner or later is contagious and leads eventually to downright tyranny. The professors warned that the muzzling of one group, no matter how unpopular or how dangerous, invariably leads to the muzzling of all except the one in power.

The weight of these eminent professors' moral judgment and social passion tipped the scales. The Chief of Police was compelled to beat a retreat and soon thereafter the crowds gathered again in Queens Park— their numbers diminishing after a few weeks as the need to react to arbitrary tyranny abated—and the speakers held forth once more, often wasting their sonorous oratory on the empty air. But a victory for freedom of speech had been won.

"The price of liberty," as had been so wisely and warningly stated, "is constant vigilance," and that was but one more momentary triumph in an endless struggle. But it is equally true of the present hour in these United States. For individual freedom is still the fountainhead of democracy, the keystone of religious faith in general and of Judaism in particular.

Judaism teaches that the soul is the divine element in man and cannot be violated by other men or governments. "The soul which Thou hast given me came pure from Thee," the Jew declares, and no man has the right to invade that inner and holy sanctum. "By their *Creator*" —and not by any human institution, our Declaration of Independence insists—are men endowed with the inalienable right of liberty—and only God, rather than man-made law, has the right to take it away. The logical sequence of this fundamental article of faith common to both America and Judaism is that only in freedom can man express the full measure of his God-given potentialities. Jewish tradition reveres the right to hold to one's conscientious convictions, to articulate them freely, to debate, to disagree, to challenge.

The Talmud teaches that honest controversies among men of divergent views are conducted to the glory of God. The Bible brims with examples of voicing one's opinions without fear or favor, however unpopular those opinions might be. Man's right to speak his mind extends even to challenging God Himself as did Abraham, Moses, Job, and a host of other defiant heroes of the Bible. Judaism has taught a profound respect for the individual conscience—for that "flaming spirit within" which inspired the prophets and which should move us too to express the convictions of our heart and mind, no matter what the consequence.

There is no hierarchy, no dogma, no catechism in Jewish life to silence dissent. Despite its stubborn insistence on one God and its never ceasing iteration of the *Sh'ma*, "Hear O Israel, the Lord is One," the rabbis of the Talmud dared to represent God as saying "would that Israel had forgotten Me but had kept My commandments." The rabbi himself, in our tradition, is not the expounder of creeds; he is not an intermediary to salvation. He is not a priest but a more Jewishly literate layman; more learned in Jewish lore and law.

Thus healthy argument—sometimes stormy, sometimes foolish, but always free—is the lifeblood of Judaism and of Jewish life. There is a popular bromide, containing more truth than travesty, which asserts that where there are two Jews, there are three opinions, and another which maintains that the only thing two Jews can agree on is what the third should give to charity. In such a scheme of things, suppression and censorship are enemies of that spirit which God breathed into man. Moreover, experience confirmed the conviction which the bitter lessons of Jewish history taught to the effect that the security and well-being of the Jewish people in any land are inseparably linked to the maintenance of freedom for all.

This religious view and historical experience have helped to make contemporary Jewry uniquely sensitive to civil liberties. While it must readily be admitted that we have our reactionaries and bigots, they are the exceptions rather than the rule. On the American scene, I would doubt that any religious group has been as zealous as the Jews in supporting freedom of expression for all people and in opposing censorship, McCarthyism, and such excrescences as the John Birch Society. It is no accident that public-opinion polls during the height of the fever of McCarthyism in America indicated that Jews were overwhelmingly opposed to him at the very time that a majority of non-Jews expressed admiration for the work in which the Senator from Wisconsin was engaged.

I have frequently seen this Jewish commitment to civil liberties at work. In 1953, when McCarthyism was riding high and fear was abroad in the land, I urged the Union of American Hebrew Congregations to enlarge our staff and budget so as to revive our then somewhat desultory social-action program in order to make it an effective force on the American scene. I recall that there were some who, while not disagreeing with the importance of such a step, voiced certain reservations about the timing and were concerned that any strong social-action program launched at that tense moment in American life would get the Union into trouble. My reply was: "What religious institution, what religion, especially what kind of Judaism, can conceivably be worthy of its proud name and heritage if it does not encounter difficulties in a time of moral and spiritual deterioration such as our own? Should religion be anything but difficult, dangerous, and controversial? Was there a prophet of any faith who did not willfully choose a life that would be difficult and dangerous and controversial because of his religious faith?"

I was no doubt right about the prophets, but religious organizations of all faiths have historically been much more cautious. Yet, to their great credit, the officers and leaders of the UAHC supported me to a man. Our Commission on Social Action was reorganized and revitalized, and it has grown through the years into a powerful expression of the conscience and highest idealism of Reform Judaism. Indeed, it was the Commission on Social Action which brought before the Biennial Assembly of 1955 in Los Angeles a bold resolution on civil liberties. The delegates from our synagogues throughout the United States responded to moral leadership by adopting the resolution which reads, in part:

We deny the validity of the proposition that our government can make itself more secure by denying justice to any man. Absolute security for the State is possible of achievement only in a totalitarian regime and is unattainable in a democracy. There can be no freedom without some measure of risk.

We deplore the view that citizens should be encouraged to inform against fellow citizens with respect to their opinons and political associations.

We would defend all constitutional privileges and immunities without regard to the guilt or innocence of those who invoke them. In our view, the preservation of these rights is of greater significance to our way of life than any benefit our law enforcement agencies can derive from curtailment or suspension of these rights.

We abhor the test oath and its loyalty oath derivations. As did our forefathers before us, we reject the notion that the techniques of the Inquisition, the High Commission, and the Star Chamber are to have acceptance by us in any form . . .

Similarly, in 1961, when our Biennial Assembly was held in Washington, D.C., a hard-hitting resolution was introduced which denounced the John Birch Society and the Christian Anti-Communist Crusade as groups which "in the guise of anti-Communism, weaken America by stirring division and hysteria." There were more than 1,000 delegates present. Many were conservative businessmen from geographical areas where right-wing groups were extremely vocal and powerful. Yet the resolution was adopted unanimously.

I do not pretend that Jews are always on the side of the angels when it comes to civil liberties. There are deviations—sometimes flagrant ones. Some Jewish groups, for example, have been panicked into demanding the denial of the pipsqueak George Lincoln Rockwell's right to speak and to demonstrate in behalf of his lunatic-fringe American Nazi Party. A New York rabbinical group stultified itself by protesting against the showing (and subsequent televising) of Shakespeare's *Merchant of Venice* in Central Park. I also heard of a rabbi who actually took the stand as an expert witness to support the censorship of D. H. Lawrence's *Lady Chatterley's Lover.* More recently some Jewish leaders lent themselves to an ill-advised and futile effort to prevent the New York showing of *The Deputy,* by Rolf Hochhuth, the controversial play about Pope Pius XII. But these are aberrations. They are departures from the mainstream of Jewish life in America. In general, American Jewry is cool to censorship campaigns—including even those launched on the ostensible ground of obscenity—and prefers to allow even a Communist, a racist, an atheist, or the advocate of any other unpopular cause to stand up and have his say in accordance with the American tradition. This tradition is viable only if we extend these liberties to those whose views are obnoxious to us. Ends and means must be regarded as indivisible. Noble ends cannot be attained by ignoble means; the means invariably represent the ideal—or the evil —in the making. The means are inevitably the end in process, the latter is preexistent in the former. The end of freedom cannot be vouchsafed by means of its denial.

There are those who say that the reason Jews are opposed to McCarthyism, the John Birch Society, and similar groups is that Jews are "soft" on Communism—the same canard that was hurled at me and my supporters in my Toronto days. Now, as then, I will not deign to answer this libel in that form. The Jewish antenna is sensitive to tyranny, whether of the left or right, and the grim ordeal of Jews in the Soviet Union has certainly reinforced this sensitivity. But to oppose Communism does not require the denial of rights—and of simple humanity—to Americans who are beguiled by its teachings.

Yet having said this, I nonetheless believe that Jews tend to be less hysterical about Communists and more sensitive to civil liberties than do most other Americans. Why? There are historical reasons. In the 1930s, traumatized by economic injustice in the United States and the terrifying rise of Hitlerism abroad, many Jews turned to radical solutions. Jewish membership in the United States Communist Party was high; many Jews fought with the Lincoln Brigade in Spain. Thus, even after disillusionment had devastated Jewish membership and decimated Communist ranks, Jews tended to see a Communist as a human being, however misguided, while most Americans saw Communists through the prism of stereotype as bomb-throwing ogres. How could it be otherwise? Uncle Harry, Cousin Sam, or the young man down the street were or had been Communists, and though they were fanatical, they did not really seem diabolical. Thus, Jews tend to disapprove of the harassment of individual Communists and former Communists, even though Communism has long since lost its attraction even to those American Jews once seduced by it.

Interestingly, in my travels to South America in 1964, I found Jewish youth going through the same radical ferment which seized American Jews a generation ago. And for many of the same reasons. Young Jews in Brazil and Argentina are in revolt against the chronic political corruption and the shameful gap between the economic oligarchy and the hopeless masses of the impoverished. To them, the future requires radical surgery, not the plastic surgery of a U.S. Alliance for Progress. Thus, Castroism evokes an enthusiasm among South American youth—Jewish as well as non-Jewish—which the U.S.S.R. once stirred in the hearts of idealistic young Jews of the United States.

In contrast to such realism and inescapable recognition of the inevitable working of cause and effect, America as a whole has robbed its home-grown Communists of their humanity. We do not regard them as individuals with varying hopes, fears, motives, conflicts, and intelligence. We crush them all equally under the hammer of an undiscriminating proscription: "Are you now or have you ever been a member of the Communist Party?" This is all we care to know. Not "how come?" Why? When? Wherefore? And if the answer is "yes," then he who admits to this most heinous and traitorous crime is by definition an enemy of the American way of life, dedicated to overthrowing the American government by force and violence, part of an international conspiracy, and axiomatically an agent of a foreign power. Illustrating the extreme of this attitude was the indictment by the State of Indiana of three Indiana University students on charges of criminal subversion, under a 1951 state law "to exterminate Communism and Communists and any or all teaching of the same." Not until 1964 was this law declared unconstitutional.

The exploitation of the domestic Communist issue in America is the principal cause of the continuous and alarming erosion of American liberties. I am not talking of the flamboyant rantings and indiscriminate denunciations of the John Birch Society and those who walk on the wild side. I'm talking about the U.S. Government and the vast majority of the people of the United States who believe only what they read in the papers, hear over the radio, or see on the television screen. Indeed, the radical right is merely taking the accepted myth of American life (that our nation is in danger of being overthrown by American Communists) and carrying it to ultimate and bizarre conclusions. But we have all been subtly brainwashed (or have brainwashed ourselves) into a confusion of myth with reality. We have succumbed to a national demagoguery and demonology. We have chipped away treasured liberties because we have accepted a spurious necessity to subordinate individual liberties to the Moloch of "national security." Acceptance of this myth has corrupted American society. It has tended to silence the churches. It has distorted our laws and tainted our courts of justice, sometimes even including the U.S. Supreme Court. How could the United States of America thus outlaw the Communist Party without doing violence to its traditions? And this with only one dissenting vote in the entire U. S. Senate (the late, and fearless and unstamped Senator Kefauver). We are all, psychologically at least, Birchers because we have voluntarily sacrificed some segments of our liberties to feed an alleged over-arching national emergency. This was also the way we sanctioned concentration camps for American Japanese during World War II, even as we have justified subsequent oppression in the name of national security. Some sins can never be erased or reversed.

I am saying precisely what I said in "In Defense of Freedom" thirty years ago because those who shouted the loudest for my scalp and wrote the most venomous editorials calling for my expulsion from the Dominion because of my alleged pro-Communist, pro-Soviet views and words and action, were the first to embrace those very leaders of Communism in the great love affair, the Grand Alliance of World War II. *"Plus ça change, plus c'est la même chose."*

Is our tiny and ineffectual brood of Marxists a greater menace to the stability of this great nation than the large and forceful Communist Parties of Italy, France, or England, none of which is proscribed by law? Is this comparative handful more subversive than the Bull Conners and the Governor Wallaces and Senator Eastlands who so anarchistically deny and defy the spirit and letter of the United States Constitution and Supreme Court? Or are they convenient scapegoats to detour us from the real sources of our problems and to lead us so lazily to remedy them? The question is admittedly rhetorical and the answer is self-evident.

How could a nation with our cherished Bill of Rights enact into law a Smith Act which penalizes *advocacy* to overthrow the government? Not action, but mere *advocacy!* And this measure succeeded (although by a bare 5–4 majority) in winning the endorsement of the august Supreme Court. Each such corruption begets further corruption, until American justice is befouled and traduced. In order to make the Smith Act an effective tool, it becomes necessary to build a vast American secret police and to create a whole road show of traveling ex-Communist informers, a sort of government-approved Murder Incorporated, assassinating characters upon demand. We have demeaned our moral heritage by wrapping the mantle of anti-Communist divinity about the shoulders of embittered and irresponsible fanatics whose claim to authority is that they, too, were once Communists. Some of them have already been exposed as perjurers and pathological liars, and others have now graduated to the faculties of anti-Communist schools of the ultra-right!

In the fight against domestic Communism, the entire nation is handcuffed by a ritualistic dogmatism which treats common sense and human decency as sentimental weakness. It is almost as if we were following the growl of the McCarthy primitive: "You say he's an anti-Communist? Well, we don't care what kind of Communist he is. A Commie is a Commie."

And the litany of our sins in the name of anti-Communism grows longer and longer, leaving a legacy of legislation and precedent which a braver generation of Americans will have to expunge, despite the apparent demise of McCarthyism. We have an Internal Security Act which provides for "detention camps" in America and decrees that any alien who has ever been a member of a "proscribed" organization can be excluded from the United States or can be deported if he is already here. We have already used this formidable weapon to protect our national security from the menace of an immigrant who had joined the Communist Party as a youngster in 1932 and gave 10¢ in dues to the organization which he was informed was set up to oppose unemployment. That was the extent of his violent revolutionary acts. It was enough to deport him. Anyone masochistic enough to follow the benighted work of the House Un-American Activities Committee has seen in its whirlwind trail the wreckage of innocent reputations and has sniffed the acrid smell of the burning stake. In the name of freedom we have allowed a small group of willful and reckless men to impose their own definitions of Americanism upon an entire nation. We have permitted the high investigative powers of the United States Congress to be prostituted into the irresponsible slandering of individuals, the persecution of dissenters, and the destruction of many an honorable American's career.

Our obsession with anti-Communism has opened a Pandora's box of viciousness and cruelty in this land. In seeking to counter the threat of totalitarianism, we have sometimes emulated the very totalitarian tactics we oppose. We subvert the fundamental premise of our Americanism by setting the state above the rights of its citizens "from whom it derives its powers." Ritualistic anti-Communism has entered like poison into the stream of our national life. It has sickened civilized discourse; it has intimidated politicians and infected our political dialogue in the same way that segregation has in the South and Algeria once did in France, and it has frightened many liberals into impotency. As many actual experiments have revealed, most Americans would be afraid to sign a petition which contains word for word the statements that appear in our Bill of Rights and our Constitution. Fear has emasculated the courage that made this nation great—the courage of conviction.

It is not only the fact that we have cut corners on our basic liberties that appalls me. It is that there are so few ready to fight for their reinstatement. What politician will stake his future on such a battle? What religious group, excepting always the Quakers, will risk calumny and abuse to say these things? We are all on the defensive. We are all rationalizing. We all preface our comments with the ritualistic disclaimer: "I'm not a Communist, but . . ." Freedom is not an easy thing with which to live. It is replete with risks, with buzzing confusion, and with manifold dangers. Many Americans are now ready to end the risks and stop the confusion. John Birchers are only the extreme examples of such a point of view. But by fear and apathy we grant them open sesame to spread their gospel of falsely exploited terror. One Congressman recently told me when I testified against altering the First

Amendment of our Constitution that he received more than a thousand letters urging the impeachment of Chief Justice Warren and not one in opposition. Thus do we lethargically and lazily jettison our preciously hard-won liberties! Thus are we all implicated in this flight from freedom which dishonors what America has been and that for which it came into being. And in abdicating the principles—and practices—which have distinguished us from all other nations, we are forfeiting the allegiance of the uncommitted countries we are so eager to win.

We need desperately a bit of sophistication in our political life. The way to fight the real menace of Communism—which is predominantly an external military and political threat—is not through suppression, crying havoc, and scaring ourselves to death. As our Canadian friends have long since learned through their historic experience in Queens Park, a Communist standing on a soapbox is less dangerous to America than denuding ourselves of our impregnable heritage; than ruthlessly—or even subtly—suppressing anyone who, as Thoreau so vividly phrased it, may be "marching to the beat of another drum."

Mulford Q. Sibley, a plucky University of Minnesota professor of political science, recently put tongue in cheek and declared in *The New York Times:*

American culture is far too monolithic for its own good. . . .
Personally, I should like to see on the campus one or two Communist professors, a student Communist club, a chapter of the American Association for the Advancement of Atheism, a society for the promotion of free love, a League for Overthrow of Government by Jeffersonian Violence, an anti-automation league, and perhaps a nudist club.
If we don't sow seeds of doubt and implant subversive thoughts in college, when and where, in Heaven's name (if there be a Heaven) will they be implanted?
And if they are never sown, moral and intellectual progress may be even more doubtful than many of us think.

The professor is perhaps being more colorful than consistent and the full range of ideas should include the far right as well as the far left. But I am with him in his emphasis on genuine freedom of thought.

Studies indicate the abysmal failure of our educational system to provide a genuine understanding of American liberties. Our teen-age youngsters, these studies reveal, show a widespread readiness to approve use of the third degree by police officials, to accept limitations on the rights of Americans "with wild ideas" (including even the deprivation of vote), and to brush aside the rights of atheists and Communists. While some teachers of American problems and social studies do compel their charges to memorize the Bill of Rights, there is disturbing evidence that few of our teachers are qualified—and few even make the attempt—to convey the dimensions of American liberties which underlie that Bill of Rights. Memorization is a substitute for thinking. And it is tragic that the "controversiality" of the material prevents all but a few public schools from teaching the real meaning of the Fifth Amendment. Dr. Louis Pollock of Yale University, an authority on the subject, has said that American high schools devote an average of two to five hours to the meaning of the Bill of Rights. Is it any wonder that, in the stride toward reaction to the racial crisis in America, we see the horrendous situation in which a high proportion of Americans—perhaps even a majority—do not really subscribe to the prohibitions of the Bill of Rights, express mindless impatience with the "technicalities" of the Supreme Court and approve of patently repressive measures to proscribe persons who are not "right-thinking" Americans?

The difference between us and the totalitarians is not economic systems or the race to the moon. It is our conflicting moral and spiritual values. It comes down to how we regard man and his unique personality as the child of God.

Freedom is the very breath of all life and progress. It is the most sacred and treasured gift of God. How truly appropriate are the tender lines of one of America's sweetest poets, Ralph Chaplin, whom that "land of the free and home of the brave" plunged into a dingy prison cell for daring to differ from the herd. How sadly, yet how eloquently, he sings:

> Mourn not the dead that in the cool earth lie
> Dust unto dust—
> The calm, sweet earth that mothers all who die
> As all men must;
>
> Mourn not your captive comrades who must dwell,
> Too strong to strive;
> Within each steel-bound coffin of a cell,
> Buried alive;
>
> But rather mourn the apathetic throng:
> The cowed and the meek,
> Who see the world's great anguish and its wrong
> And dare not speak!

7

THE RACIAL REVOLUTION
FROM LAW TO LOVE

No cause has preoccupied me as long and as passionately as that of racial justice. Since boyhood, I have regarded myself as a supporter of Negro rights. As a rabbi, I have constantly held the issue of racial equality to be a touchstone of my Jewish faith, and I have no doubt belabored many a congregation with my ceaseless exhortations on this theme. Indeed, I have freely staked my own reputation—and that of the organization I head—in the fierce struggle for racial equality. James Baldwin is able to turn my blood to fire, and Martin Luther King can make me weep unashamed.

And yet, as America now sees the clear shaft of light at the end of the tunnel, as the fate of racial segregation is being sealed in our generation, I find myself, for the first time, looking inward at myself instead of outward at the arena where the foreordained struggle plays itself out. For, when segregation goes, the stage will shift from the public dramas of Birmingham and Harlem to the private recesses of my heart—and yours. The Negro will be a free citizen, but whether he will be my neighbor and my brother will depend not on the law of the land but upon the love in my heart and in yours. Thus, painfully, I have tried to burrow through my own incipient self-righteousness to dig down to the core of my being to find the ore of feeling which may be more important in the long run than the brave words on my lips and the liberal convictions of my mind. For what I feel is irrelevant to the securing of the full right of citizenship which is the due of every Negro. But what I feel—and what other Americans feel—will determine whether the legal process of desegregation will be a pyrrhic victory or whether it can be converted into the human and religious goal of genuine brotherhood.

That I believed myself utterly guiltless of the sin of race prejudice can be explained—if not excused—in the light of my childhood and youth. Though the city of my birth and boyhood, Chicago, was already blighted by the blasphemous existence of its black ghetto, I had little early exposure to this area which was largely confined to the South Side. I was brought up in a lily-white neighborhood on the North Side where it would have been unthinkable in those remote days for any Negro to seek to penetrate. In fact, this section of the city is still quite vigilantly guarded against any such invasion. As far as I can remember, there were no Negro children among my playmates and none in the classes of the grammar school which I attended. We didn't even have a colored maid—the vogue, in the North at least, then being to have a German *schwester* as nursemaid or cook. My knowledge of Negroes during those formative years was primarily limited to such stirring accounts as Booker T. Washington's *Up from Slavery,* the loving poetry of Langston Hughes, the magnificent concerts of Roland Hayes, the handclapping, foot-stomping tunes and lyrics of the spirituals which tingle my spine to this day—especially when they find expression in the stirring songs of Mahalia Jackson or in Johnson's "Lift Every Voice and Sing."

What pride I took in my exceptional freedom from this otherwise ubiquitous prejudice. With what obvious overreaction did I go out of my way so swiftly to extend my hand in greeting to the first Negro I encountered in the university classroom. But this very pretentious gesture appears in scrupulously candid retrospect to exemplify my affliction —however mild—with the widespread disease of white supremacy. There was something of a priggish hauteur in this deed, undoubtedly intended, on the conscious level, as an act of solicitude and kindness but in the depths of my subconscious—if I be permitted this analysis without benefit of a couch—a manifestation of instinctive assurance that a superior was indulgently saluting an inferior. That split-second hesitation as to whether to extend the hand or not, that scintilla of added pressure—overtly intended to convey warmth, covertly an overcompensation—were tell-tale evidences of my unacknowledged, supercilious whiteness.

Whence did this derive? My home, my parents, my brother and sister were all happily free of any direct expressions or attitudes of prejudice against the Negro. But the whole ambient of my surroundings most assuredly was not. One does not have to be reared in the South to take on these prejudicial thoughts and feelings, even as one need not be a Southerner to understand the present-day "Negro problem." *Negro* problem, so-called, for surely just as the problem of anti-Semitism is a Christian rather than a Jewish one, so the gravest dilemma which American society presently faces, is most definitely and inescapably a white problem.

How then did I acquire these distorted ideas and emotions? From the insidious newspapers which never failed to use the word Negro in identifying the perpetrator of any crime committed by a colored person. From the neighborhood nickelodeon where the "flickers" invariably assigned to the Negro the role of lackey, porter, menial, obsequious servant, the timid poltroon ready to fall in all directions at once, the criminal, the villain. And from those more subtle nuances: the failure of one's elders to rise when a Negro or even a Negress entered the room, the knowing wink of an eye, the shrug of a shoulder, the smirk of the lip, the lift of an eyebrow, the entire mien and manner whenever some matter pertaining to the Negro was mentioned.

Each of these, no doubt, contributed some share to the make-up of one who so presumptuously prided himself on being altogether free of prejudice. No matter how much my mind revolted throughout those earlier years against the very thought of distinguishing among individuals because of color, no matter how much I accepted intellectually Burns' insistence that "a man's a man for a' that," nevertheless, I cannot obliterate from my memory—much as I would like to—the feeling of resentment I felt the first time a Negro student at the Divinity School of the University of Chicago answered correctly a question that I had muffed. That resentment was not the same as I had felt when a white student had performed similarly. Nor was the reaction different solely in degree. It was different in kind as well. It was without any doubt projected against the fact of his blackness—that a *Negro* dared to be brighter than I!

Though I have striven mightily to become free of all such prejudice, I cannot state categorically that I have fully succeeded. Am I altogether immune from that "nearly inaudible murmur," however unwitting, which shudders within me, too, as I see a Negro youth with a white girl by his side on Broadway or along the Champs Elysees? Does my glance at the latter "flick over her as though she were a whore," as James Baldwin in *Another Country* so bitterly but so intuitively senses the sneer of which we may be totally unaware? Do I not, therefore, become one with the whole so-called superior white race in so denigrating the Negro that my own subconscious would so classify any white woman that consorts with a black partner? I *know* better. But do I always so *feel?* The spirit—the mind, too—is willing. The flesh, the emotions—saturated with too many early false impressions—remain all too weak. I still catch myself every once in a while—to my own amazement, chagrin, and consternation—reacting either with an obvious overdose of warmth and solicitude or with that all too connotative instant of hesitation. How exigent, therefore, that all of us labor prodigiously to transcend those preconceptions to which none of us is immune. For me to overcome this residual prejudice is as important to my humanity as to the Negro's. And it is important—crucial—to me in relation to my faith as a Jew.

For Judaism gave mankind its first civil rights program. It was expressed in the *Sh'ma*, the watchword of the Jewish faith, a prayer as old as Israel itself: "Hear, O Israel, the Lord our God, the Lord is One." As God is one, mankind is one, for every man is created equally in the image of God. It was expressed at Sinai where it was registered in an eternal Covenant, proclaiming liberty and dignity for every child of God made "in His image and likeness." It was voiced by Moses, facing Pharaoh with the demand: "Let my people go!" It was thundered by the Hebrew prophets: "Have we not all one Father? Hath not one God created us? Why do we deal treacherously against our brother?" And: "Are ye not as the Ethiopians unto Me?" It was nourished by the Talmud which asks (in Midrash, Bereshis Rabbah): Why did God create one man, Adam? And answers: Man was created one so that no one in the future can say to his fellow, "My father was greater than your father." It is a concept unqualified, absolute—which sank deep into the Jewish soul and which was tenderly passed down, from generation to generation, as a precious and inviolate heritage.

Christianity, the daughter faith, was built upon these same central truths. The Golden Rule of Jesus and the teachings of Hillel are almost identical in stressing that respect for the humanity of every man is each man's duty to God. This tradition of freedom and equality was the "Hebraic mortar" which the Pilgrims poured into the foundation stones of American democracy. The American experiment was fashioned by such as Jefferson, Madison, and Washington, but its roots are planted deep in the soil of the Hebrew Bible. Judaism and Christianity spread the seeds of revolution in human relationships, and the plants have brought forth fruit—bitter and sweet alike—even unto our own generation.

If Christians had been serious about Christianity, there could have been no problem of race in America. But they weren't. Dr. James Silver pointed out in his book, *Confederate Morale and Church Propaganda,* that there was not one clergyman in the South, of any faith, speaking out against slavery by the time the Civil War began. Indeed, many clergymen in the North, including Rabbi Raphael of New York, preached that slavery was compatible with God's will. According to Silver, slavery would have collapsed for lack of public enthusiasm had it not been for support whipped up by the churches. And, of course, just as in the twentieth century, Hitler lost his war against the world but won his combat against the Jews, so in the Civil War, the South lost the conflict against the Union but won the deeper war against the spirit of abolition. Only a few years after the Civil War, the South was replacing slavery with the rigid patterns of Jim Crow "separate but equal" racism which has persisted to our time—and, of course, almost always, with the acquiescent amen of Protestant, Catholic, and Jewish Houses of God, South and North.

Religion dishonored its teachings and blasphemed its God by adapting itself to the status quo rather than by demanding what ought to be. The Christian churches continued to murmur the pious words of brotherhood but the church itself became a bastion of racial segregation. Even today, 11 A.M. on Sunday morning may still be the most segregated hour in America. With few exceptions, the leaders of religion—Protestant, Catholic, and Jewish—posed no challenge whatever to the moral leprosy of racism which was spreading and being increasingly systematized throughout the land. To the shame of Christianity and Judaism, it was not the trumpet of religion which awakened the conscience of America. It was the Supreme Court in 1954 and today it is the Negro himself.

The school desegregation decision of a decade ago was the first act of what has become the historic American drama of our generation. It set the stage for the revolution which now besets us. The Court's verdict compelled a searching reexamination of American racial mores. The church and the synagogue, which had draped the robes of their respectability over the institutions of racialism, could no longer pretend that race was not a religious problem.

What happened in the months of confusion and turmoil after the 1954 decision? There was a shocked paralysis. In community after community, throughout the South, the "good people"—including religious leaders—reeled from the blow which the Court had dealt their familiar world; and they waited to see what would happen. Into this vacuum of leadership, in state after state, rushed the hate-mongers, the demagogues, the pandering politicians. White Citizens Councils mushroomed.

The few persons of sanity who spoke up in support of the Court were quickly terrorized and silenced. Intimidation, coercion, and fear took over. The Court had pushed open the door of history, waiting for the lovers of decency and freedom to enter. For a moment, the nation trembled on the edge of a new hope. But, alas, the opportunity was lost. The haters were ready to act, and the lovers were not. Churchmen were still gasping, while racists were acting. It was they who rushed in and slammed the door behind them.

But religious groups were still on the spot. They could no longer sweep the racial issue under the rug. Painfully, laboriously, every denomination wrestled with the implications of the Supreme Court decision. Every denomination, including the Southern Baptists, had to come to the same conclusion: that the Supreme Court decision was fully consistent with the teachings of their faith. Stormy controversies marked the deliberations of most denominational gatherings. But what other resolution could an instrumentality of Christianity or Judaism adopt? Could their words be less Christian or Jewish, less humane and God-like than a secular Court's? Indeed, one is compelled still to wonder why religionists had to wait for the Court so sharply to remind them of the basic meaning of their faiths. Now the national church assemblies began at last to speak, to renounce in words the stigma of segregation. These resolutions had certain educational value. They gave some support to the Negro community as well as to the embattled ministers and rabbis in this or that community or to those who had staked their pulpits on an issue of conscience. But, just as the South defied the Supreme Court, so did Christian and Jew often defy their national bodies, thus vitiating their effective implementation. Ministers and rabbis were enjoined by their trustees from engaging in "political controversies." Clergymen who defended the Court's decision were, frequently, dispatched forthwith. Too many "men and ministers of God" bowed to the winds of public opinion, some with broken hearts. Many made silent compromises with conscience.

From 1954 to 1963, religion played a tepid and timid role in the desegregation controversy. It remained for Martin Luther King and other Negro ministers to demonstrate the blazing power which Christianity could bring to bear upon the racial issue when it was seriously applied. White churches, as well as temples, stood by as troubled spectators. The Roman Catholic Church in the South, due in part to its authoritarian structure, was able to move with greater boldness to integrate its own schools and churches, despite the noisy, sometimes violent, protests of Roman Catholic parishioners. But the Church did not play a significant role outside its own institutions. Protestantism was paralyzed by internal hemorrhaging. Far too many Jews, likewise, although sensitive to the injustice of segregation, felt themselves too vulnerable to take a stand; most Jews sought the illusory safety of neutrality and silence.

But in the years following the Decision, some hard truths came into focus. The issue was not only, or even principally, the treatment of the Negro. It was an issue of whether the United States was a nation of laws or of men—of due process or of mob rule. It was an issue of whether or not the South was going to pull down its educational systems in a mindless and futile effort to avoid the edicts of the Court. It was an issue of the moral health of the community—whether or not the dark clouds of race hatred and intellectual vigilantism would permeate the city like a smog. It was an issue of politics—whether or not the political process would be degraded into a foul contest of which candidate could out-demagogue the other. It was a question of civil liberties—whether the right to speak, to associate, to write freely could survive for anybody in a community terrified into a siege mentality. It was a question of the position of the United States in the free world— whether a world, in which whites constitute a small minority, would long tolerate the horrid spectacle of an American *apartheid*. And, above and beyond all else, it was a question of morality, of ethical alternatives, of right and wrong—a religious question.

By the early 1960s, the race problem was clearly moving into a critical stage. Negro sit-ins, Freedom Riders, and other demonstrations indicated a clear and irresistibly rising tide of Negro militancy. Sensitive religious leaders realized that the day of pious platitudes, and even of noble resolutions, was over. There was no longer any place to hide. The forces of religion must either stand up manfully on the paramount moral issue of the land—or confess their bankruptcy.

The year of 1963 was a turning point for American religion. In January of that year there was held in Chicago a National Conference on Religion and Race. It represented the first time in American history that the Protestant, Catholic, and Jewish faiths established a working partnership in the struggle against racial injustice. It was an occasion heavy with the sense of history. Sponsored by the National Council of Churches of Christ, the National Catholic Welfare Conference, and the Synagogue Council of America, that gathering constituted a uniquely religious commemoration of the centennial of the Emancipation Proclamation. It was not merely another gabfest. The delegates, who included the most distinguished leaders of all three faiths, were there in no mood of self-congratulation. The theme of self-searching, of atonement, and of sincere confession was struck at the opening session.

A Protestant layman shocked the delegates with these words: "You are here too little, too late, and too lily-white. What you men of the church and the synagogue can do is to have the decency to weep."

The National Conference on Religion and Race was late, very late. In the war for racial justice, the churches and synagogues had not yet even moved into the battle zone. Religion, far from leading, was bringing up the rear, behind government, behind business, behind the mass media. But hopefully it was not *too* late. For the decisive battles still lay ahead. And if the faith groups could truly unite in a program of action, such spiritual solidarity might stave off impending torrents of bloodshed and truly bring to fruition religion's goal of brotherhood. It would invest the civil rights struggle with a spiritual and moral dimension which it desperately needed. And over and above what the witness of the faiths would do for the Negro is what it would do to save the soul of the church and the synagogue. For, in my judgment, race has become the flame which will test the mettle of religion in this land.

The National Conference on Race and Religion broke the ice floe of religious passivity. The long thaw was over. The Conference was the catalyst. Within weeks, leaders of the three faiths were organizing action programs on race in dozens of American communities. Ten target cities quickly scheduled their own conferences on race and religion. Roman Catholic leaders, inspired and impelled by the urgency of the late Pope John, suddenly became visible and vocal partners on the local scene. The racial revolution, shifting into high gear, had achieved an unexpected result: it had worked a revolution in interfaith relationships. As the racial conflict moved into the streets with mounting intensity, religious leaders of all faiths began to disenthrall themselves. It was late, terribly late, but perhaps not altogether too late.

Protestantism is beginning to march, taking all the risks of an outraged Southern constituency. The National Council of Churches of Christ, representing some thirty major Protestant denominations, has long been criticized as an over-cautious and ponderous structure, incapable of vigorous action on race. Yet at its Triennial Convention in 1963, it set up a powerful crash program of direct action on racial injustice which was hammered out by a group of zealous Negro intellectuals including James Baldwin and Dr. Kenneth Clark. The National Council of Churches joined hands with its Roman Catholic and Jewish partners in presenting unified testimony in behalf of the late President Kennedy's hotly controversial civil rights bill. Similarly, the Council joined enthusiastically in the extraordinary August 28th March on Washington. And to the Interreligious Convocation for Civil Rights in April, 1964, Reverend Eugene Carson Blake solemnly pledged the Protestant churches to a new sense of urgency and commitment to action. Dr. Blake had proved his own bona fides by getting himself arrested, along with a group of rabbis and priests, for defying the racial restrictions at a Baltimore, Maryland, amusement park.

The United Presbyterian Church, also in 1963, voted to devote 500,000 dollars for an action program against segregation in all phases of American life, including segregation in the churches themselves. Other denominations embarked on similar programs. The World Council of Churches of Christ denounced racial segregation as a form of blasphemy. In a small town, Berlin, New Jersey, a young Episcopal priest excommunicated a member of his church because he had protested against attending church alongside Negroes. A new wind had begun to blow in Protestantism. It may well be the spirit of God moving over the void and chaos which had gone before.

But the changes within American Catholicism were even more dramatic. The late Pope John opened the windows to let in the fresh air; Pope Paul has kept them open. Roman Catholic clerics were, until recently, the most inaccessible group in American life. They were seldom seen or heard on general community problems, preoccupying themselves with what many, including some Catholics, criticized as "Catholic ghettos." No more! The aforementioned National Conference on Race and Religion was organized on the initiative of the Roman Catholic community; its sparkplug was the young director of the Chicago Catholic Inter-Racial Council. Attending that extraordinary Conference were two Roman Catholic cardinals, nineteen bishops, and hundreds of other clerics, sisters, and laymen. In Detroit, Michigan, Roman Catholic laymen have organized an Archbishops' Committee to integrate the community by the simple device of putting together Negroes who want to buy and white people who are willing to sell their homes without racial distinctions. Incredibly, in Los Angeles, California, where a conservative Roman Catholic prelate was dragging his heels on the racial front, an aroused group of his own Catholic laymen organized a sit-in demonstration of protest in the Chancery office. A few years ago such a thing would have been impossible. It bespeaks a changing temper of a changing Church.

I do not mean to suggest that the Messiah has come and that all Protestants and Catholics have suddenly become angels of equality. Indeed, I would guess that a disturbingly high proportion of both Roman

Catholics and Protestants are distressed by the emerging boldness of their leaders. The pew lags far behind the pulpit. Too many churches are still segregated. Yet the church leaders are acting, and the ferment is sharp and real. Christian bodies are exposing themselves to the world and pushing off the grip of a dead past. The churches have been seared by the realization that race is not merely a mortal threat to their integrity, but a God-given opportunity for inner renewal. The churches have come late to the battle, but they are now tasting the dust and the smoke of combat and they know they are alive—perhaps for the first time. And there is no turning back.

And what about Jews? I believe that Jews are more liberal, at least in their preachment on the subject of race, than any other segment of the white community. The American Jewish community has been strongly identified with the pursuit of human rights. Indeed, the major goal of synagogue social action and of Jewish community relations has been the protection and enhancement of equal rights and equal opportunities for all persons. It has been said that the security of Jews, as with all other ethnic and religious groups, is dependent upon the fulfillment of democracy for all. Jews can flourish only in an open society.

Given the concepts of Judaism, the unique history which has shaped Jewish consciousness, and the stake of Jews in a free society, it is not surprising that Jewish organizations have been in the vanguard of the struggle for equality of opportunity for all racial and religious groups. Such organizations as the American Jewish Congress, the American Jewish Committee and the Anti-Defamation League have, over the years, championed the fight for fair employment practices and other civil rights laws on the municipal, state, and federal levels.

And yet, as I write these words in the midst of an intensified racial revolution, I am deeply disturbed and anxious of heart. Unlike many of my white friends and colleagues who are worried about the Negro ("He's pushing too hard"), I am worried about my fellow whites and, most especially, my fellow Jews. We would be better off if we had the Christian's problem of desegregating our Houses of God so that our vaunted liberalism could be tested. Then, we could not run away from the hard problem. For many Jews in the North have escaped from the realities of the racial predicament by disappearing into the bland, homogeneous neighborhoods of middle-class suburbia. Jewish liberalism was most impressive when the measure of commitment was verbal. Jewish groups excelled at heroic resolutions and rabbis were eloquent in their sermons. But it is no longer a question of words. Resolutions do not suffice for revolutions; only resolution to act counts now. Civil rights no longer means what goes on in Mississippi; it means what goes on in one's child's school, in one's apartment house, in one's business, and in one's heart. The issue has come home. It is the moment of truth.

I wish I could say that the Jewish community stands as a "light unto the nation" on this central moral issue. It does not. The Jewish community in the South has been torn by the segregation crisis more severely than by any event since the Civil War. Comprising less than half of 1 per cent of the population of the South, made up largely of merchants dependent on the good will of the community, the Jew feels himself the man trapped in the middle. It is my impression that most Southern Jews disapprove of racial segregation and privately support the Supreme Court decisions. But they are afraid to act on this conviction or sense of conscience in the tense atmosphere which clouds the community. They fear, undoubtedly with considerable justification, economic reprisals, social ostracism, and, in some communities, perhaps even the possibility of anti-Semitic violence. Perhaps, even more deeply rooted is the nagging apprehension of upsetting a carefully wrought and still-fragile acceptance by their Christian neighbors.

Divided against themselves, Southern Jews have sought to resolve this dilemma in various ways. A mere handful have joined White Citizens Councils, thus earning the opprobrium of most of their fellow Jews. One such even publicized a vicious prosegregation tract entitled, "A Jewish View of Segregation." One congregation in Mississippi sent me a resolution, adopted *unanimously* at the board meeting of the temple, informing the Union of American Hebrew Congregations that "segregation is neither a moral nor a religious issue and is, therefore, not the business of Judaism." That must mean that neither the spirit of Amos—nor of God Himself—was present at that meeting which adopted so Jewishly and religiously spurious a declaration.

Driven by inner conflict, some Southern Jews have resorted to what has become a popular indoor sport: baiting their rabbis and their national Jewish organizations. Many do not wish to appear to be different from their Southern gentile neighbors and feel threatened by anybody who seeks to identify the Jew with the Negro. Pressures have been exerted by Southern constituents against their national Jewish organizations (all of whom are clearly on record in support of the Supreme Court decisions), including reduced contributions, threats of secession from various organizations, and fiery denunciations on the floor of national conventions. The oft-repeated refrain is: You Northerners don't understand our situation; you act as if we were expendable, and you harm us by statements about segregation in the public press. One Alabama Jewish leader went so far as to say to a representative of a national Jewish agency: "You're like Hitler. You stir up anti-Semitism against us."

Southern rabbis have borne the brunt of this kind of distorted fear. Those who believe that racial segregation is a profanation of Judaism have sought to find a path between the tug of conscience and the real and exaggerated fright of their congregants. In some synagogues, there have been attempts to curb the freedom of the pulpit. As in some Christian churches, a few of these attempts have been successful. One congregation considered a resolution that "no paid employee may speak out on controversial matters without prior approval by the Board of the temple." That means the rabbi.

A president of a congregation said: "I don't know where you get the idea our rabbi doesn't have freedom of the pulpit. We give him freedom of the pulpit—we just don't let him exercise it." Happily, these are as yet exceptions. Most rabbis will not stand for a controlled pulpit. Indeed, some rabbis in the South have courageously espoused the cause of racial justice not only by pulpit preachment but also by public action. Yet, since most Southern rabbis sincerely feel that it is the Christian churches of the South which must lead in this issue, they avoid publicizing their racial views, stay away from the NAACP (which is anathema to most Southerners), and do what they can quietly within Ministerial Associations (in those Southern cities where they are permitted by the Christian clergy to belong).

It is of some pride and comfort to me that the leaders of the Union of American Hebrew Congregations have consistently rejected the counsels of timidity and that we have, as a responsible national organization, continued to speak out and act in accordance with our religious commitment to human equality. Nor do we accept the parochial opinion that one must live in the South to understand this problem. This is tantamount to asserting that one must actually reside in the Soviet Union or in Red China before one has a right to protest against tyranny there, or that only a German citizen could properly have protested against the Nazi pogroms. Brotherhood is indeed indivisible and the right to protest its violation is not contingent upon one's place of residence. So we have not heeded the injunction, "Yankees go home"—or at least be mum.

There is no doubt that our identification with this struggle has cost us much support, financial and otherwise, in many Southern communities where the name of the Union of American Hebrew Congregations frequently engenders the kind of visceral response in the Jewish community that the National Association for the Advancement of Colored People awakens in the white Christian community.

Remiss and laggard as many have been, I do believe that there is a growing awareness, at least among the more sophisticated Jewish leaders of the South, that the destiny of the Jew is joined with the fate of the Negro and all minorities, and that Jews can be secure only where a climate of freedom prevails. Such an awareness is crucial because Southern Jews have been so preoccupied with maintaining what they term "their excellent relations with the white Christian community" (relations that can't be too good, considering the hysterical anxiety of the same Jews to maintain them) that they frequently ignore the question of Negro-Jewish relationships. Reverend Martin Luther King has often commented upon the dearth of Southern Jewish support for Negro rights. Reverend Shuttleworth, Negro minister of Birmingham, Alabama, has accused the Jewish community of turning its back on the Negro: "Why are you silent in our great hour of need, when we stand in a sea of trouble, besieged by hate and terror? It is there we need Jewish support—and it is there the Jews are silent." That there is growing bitterness increasingly touched with anti-Semitism in the Negro communities of the South and North is an important fact of life. For, as more and more Jewish leaders must realize, a new South is being born in pain and travail, and in that new South it is the proud and militant Negro community—not the Neanderthal white politicians who represent the South today—with which the small Jewish community will ultimately have to come to terms.

And what of the North? In Northern communities, Jews have long been identified with civil rights. The Jewish community maintains a substantial network of national and local organizations devoted to this goal. Jewish Community Relations Councils have developed expertise and smooth-working contacts with many groups in the community on equal rights objectives. The new interfaith approach cannot—and will not—displace these existing structures. Complicated adjustments are needed to mesh the Jewish religious forces into an ongoing and intensified program for civil rights. This takes some doing. It requires flexibility on the part of the civic bodies so that they see the growing involvement of rabbis and synagogues as opportunities rather than as threats to the establishment. It requires some humility on the part of the rabbis and synagogues to recognize the long-standing role of civic groups and to avoid arrogating to themselves exclusivity on this issue.

What is called for is a new partnership of the religious and civic forces in Jewish life. It has not yet developed sufficiently to avoid the strains, recriminations, and jurisdictional jostling which have weakened Jewish participation in the civil rights struggle on the national level and in many local communities. No one benefits when veteran leaders of the national Protestant and Catholic communities make wry and knowing comments about the internecine warfare within the American Jewish community in deciding upon representation and spokesmanship.

The emerging three-faith pattern also imposes an obligation upon the synagogues to go beyond preachment to effective practice. If the Jewish religious leadership is to be regarded with respect, it must do its homework—and quickly. Rabbinic and congregational bodies have been on record for many years, some for decades. This is not surprising since Moses was the first to negotiate for "freedom now." There are few rabbis in the entire nation who do not preach on racial equality and many of them have spoken on this subject so often that some of their constituents are persuaded that they are obsessed with it. But the problem for religious leaders is that strong words, strong resolutions, and strong sermons no longer suffice. The measuring rod today is deeds, not words. Words without deeds, in today's atmosphere, smacks of hypocrisy, particularly in Houses of God. Social action once seemed an optional luxury for the synagogue; today it is the necessary price of relevance.

Is the synagogue equipped to carry this increased burden? It will not be easy. Few rabbis have been trained in community relations and social action. Jewish theological seminaries do not even pretend to give student rabbis the practical instruction in social action which Union Theological Seminary and other enlightened Christian institutions offer. Indeed, the paucity of social passion among rabbinical students scandalizes those rabbis who have dedicated their ministries to social service and social justice. Rabbis learn community relations the hard way, if at all, in the school of communal hard knocks and controversy. But the tendency of rabbis, tutored in rabbinics and homiletics, is to exalt the efficacy of words, as if a stirring sermon or a challenging speech to the Kiwanis somehow changes society. The task of implementing words, by involving laymen, is arduous. But it is the only way to translate the sermon into action and to make Judaism pertinent to life.

This brings us to synagogue social action, by which the congregations seek to apply the ethics of Judaism to such issues as world peace, church-state, and race relations. Each of the national synagogue bodies—Orthodox, Conservative, and Reform—now maintains a Social Action Department, seeking to develop social action programs in individual congregations. The Reform Jewish movement has given the highest priority to this program. Of 660 Reform synagogues, some 400 now maintain, at varying levels of effectiveness, Social Action or Community Affairs Committees. In addition to a national Commission on Social Action staffed in New York, the program of Reform Judaism is enhanced by a Religious Action Center in Washington, D. C., to cooperate with other religious faiths on legislative issues of moral significance. Reform, Conservative, and Orthodox Judaism seek to concert their programs through the Synagogue Council of America and the National Community Relations Advisory Council.

But the key is the individual synagogue. Can it really do the job? There are inherent difficulties aplenty. Unlike the civic bodies such as the American Jewish Congress, the members of a synagogue do not subscribe in advance to a credo of social justice positions. Indeed, the motivations that bring people to the synagogue may have nothing whatever to do with social concerns—may, indeed, be coldly antagonistic to such "political controversy." Until recently, social action seemed alien to the synagogue. And many synagogue members still believe that this function lies in the exclusive domain of the civic bodies. The synagogue in America is a middle-class institution and the values which animate it are middle-class values involved in status, prestige, respectability, and success. The overwhelming majority of synagogues are located in the suburban paradises of one-race, one-class neighborhoods where the bland lead the bland. To most, race relations is a sentimental abstraction, not a fact of local community life. The atmosphere is generally one of getting along by going along. Synagogue lay leadership is almost reflexively resistant to the taking of social stands and the carrying out of social action on controversial issues. The American Jewish community is markedly a status quo community.

The surprising thing is not that social action, by its nature, represents an uphill struggle in the contemporary American synagogue. The surprising thing is that, in these circumstances, it has taken hold as much as it has. The deep ambivalences among congregations, and within them, are keenly revealed whenever the national organization takes a forceful action on a controversial issue. The Reform Jewish movement was almost shredded by the three-year controversy which erupted on the question of whether or not to establish a Washington Social Action Center. The social action forces won but it was a bitter, costly struggle with repercussions still to be felt and read about in the press—even in the North. Similarly, when the Commission on Social Action of Reform Judaism issued a model Call to Racial Justice, urging congregations to pledge nondiscrimination in their building programs and in utilizing services in the community, the reaction was sharply polarized. Approximately 150 congregations adopted their own versions of the Call to Racial Justice. One Northern congregation authorized the Call by an extraordinary ballot in the temple during the High Holy Days. None of these actions could be taken without internal strain and controversy. At the same time, many other congregations—and not only South of the Mason-Dixon line—entered bitter objections to the issuance of the Call to Racial Justice by the Union of American Hebrew Congregations—and particularly to its release to the press. Several big contributors canceled their contributions to the national instrumentalities of Reform Judaism. A large Midwestern congregation considered withdrawal from the UAHC. Many Southern congregations demanded the Call be withdrawn lest it further endanger Jewish security in the South. And some rabbis—even in the North—have been jeopardized by their literal application of this manifesto.

The problem faced by the Jewish religious community is that the long-time intoxication with numbers of members conflicts sharply with the achievement of social-action goals.

The coterie of idealistic and social-minded Jews, which exists in every congregation, must maintain a steady cold war against the stubborn forces of apathy, negativism, parochialism, and outright hostility to social action. In some congregations, where this coterie receives the firm leadership of the rabbi, it will prevail and carry the congregation along. In many others, the group will exhaust its energies and patience in a frustrating struggle to persuade the lay leadership. The struggle may itself be healthy for the synagogue by stirring the flaccid waters. But frequently the most sensitive social action devotees, particularly among the youth, will finally despair of finding outlet for their enthusiasm in the synagogue and will flee to the Jewish civic bodies or to the Friends, CORE, or NAACP. This means that the synagogue will have to pay a price—in controversy—for social action; but the synagogue may have to pay a much larger price if it is content with the slow death of status quo affluence. That price will be desertion and ultimate annihilation.

Some congregations have proved that, despite all difficulties, constructive things can be achieved through the synagogue. Several have set up programs to tutor culturally deprived youngsters in the community. Others have arranged parlor meetings with all the members of the congregation to assist individual businessmen— builders, bankers, real estate men—to do more in their business and industry to open doors for Negroes. Several congregations have raised substantial funds for Martin Luther King, the NAACP, and the Conscience Fund to rebuild the bombed-out churches. Many congregations have created good working relationships with the local churches, white and Negro, in joint community concerns. Representatives of many congregations —Reform, Conservative, and Orthodox—participated in the March on Washington as well as in local demonstrations, marching under banners bearing Biblical verses written in Hebrew as well as English. This is not the millennium. But it is an encouraging beginning.

Despite the heroic pledges of the leaders of the three faiths, the harsh reality is that a large percentage of the constituents of these bodies do not honor these promises. The Negro revolution has obviously engendered a present bloody, ugly counter-revolution. Recent public opinion polls indicate that three out of four Americans believe that the "Negro is pushing too fast." (Sic! After a century of denigration, destitution, and delay!). Equally obviously, despite the affirmations of religious leaders, Jews and Christians are deeply implicated in the counter-revolution even while their institutions support the revolution. Negro-white tension is already sharp and it has a particular Negro-Jewish bite, in that Negroes know Jews largely as landlords, pawnbrokers, merchants, employers, sometimes as exploiters, gougers, too—rarely as peers. Tension is now rapidly and bloodily accelerating as Negro demands collide increasingly with white procrastination. Moreover, Negro militancy has frequently led to misguided demonstrations and racist overtones; more mistakes will inevitably occur and timid souls will rationalize their silence and surrender to inaction by forgetting the cause of such errors: the still infinitesimal, total school integration— ten years after the Supreme Court decision—the persisting discrimination in housing and employment. Antagonisms will rise in intensity as the Negro revolution becomes more and more clearly a threat to the middle class. The challenge to racial bars will inevitably move to a cry for deep-seated economic change without which the Negro revolution is foredoomed. Jewish ambivalence and foot-dragging are abundantly evident already in reaction to school bussing and Princeton plans in New York City and racial change in housing there and elsewhere. It will grow.

All this poses vexing problems for the American Jewish community. It confronts the religious community with hard choices. But in the kaleidoscopic social changes of our time, the synagogue has before it an unprecedented opportunity to redeem the historic mission of Judaism to be a "light unto the nations" and to serve as copartners with God in building a better and brighter tomorrow.

To do otherwise is to be false to our entire history and heritage. For in the main, Jews have not throughout their entire past been guilty of the kind of bigoted madness which eventuated in the blood-soaked Crusades, the torture rack, and the incinerating fires of the so-called Holy Inquisition, or the boiling down of human flesh and fat into soap in Nazi abattoirs. This is not because we are made of better stuff than our fellow human beings, nor because of loftier moral teaching. While I deem our teaching among the most exalted revealed by God or distilled by man, human beings learn far more by example and experience than by precept. Rather, it has been the perennial persecution to which we have been subjected throughout the centuries which has made us somewhat less callous, somewhat more empathetic with the sufferings and exclusions of others. Consequently, I do agree, up to a point, with Rabbi Solomon Freehof, when he stated in the course of a searching sermon delivered over the UAHC national radio program, "The Message of Israel":

Having been the prime victims of prejudice in all the world, the Jews are more sensitive to its presence than any other group. Whenever anybody expresses hatred for any other people, the Jew feels pained—whenever some act of generous justice is done, whenever some group hitherto disadvantaged has had the disadvantages lifted from its shoulders, every Jew in America rejoices. He believes in justice and exults in every act of justice for the simple reason that he has sought for justice all through the long unjust centuries.

I agree with these words, I repeat, up to a point. Nevertheless, as we have seen, Jews are not altogether immune from this American idiocy of anti-Negro hatred. I cannot blind my eyes to the Jewish real-estate profiteers who batten on the ignorance and poverty, the gullibility and helplessness of the Negroes of Harlem or of Chicago or of Los Angeles; to the Jewish builders of vast segregated communities; to Jews who delight to refer contemptuously to Negroes as *schwartzes;* to the unseemly flight of Jews—and their synagogues—from neighborhoods experiencing racial change, and to the real reasons which impel many middle-class Jews in all cities to enroll their children in private schools. I cannot deafen my ears to protests from Reform Jews of the North as well as the South against our Union of American Hebrew Congregations' participation in actions for civil rights. We can perhaps ascribe this to acculturation to the most despicable of American mores, to the very real fears of financial loss or social status. Whatever the cause, the reason, the excuse, the alibi, let it be recalled that in Jewish history there have been Jews, individuals and communities, who chose death at the stake rather than to accept the pagan customs and perverted modes of the surrounding society. Mattathias and his sons did not defy Antiochus' decree merely because they might have been forced to eat pork. They defied it because acceptance of his regime and regimen would have entailed the sacrifice of that essential Jewish teaching and principle of faith—the absolute integrity and dignity of every child of God. Rabbi Akiba at the stake did not allow his flesh to be seared by the scorching tongues of flame merely for the right to attend his own service of worship, but because of his insistence upon uttering —even as his body was being consumed—the "Hear, O Israel, the Lord our God, the Lord is One." While there have been courageous individuals, rabbis and laymen, who have refused to become *gleischgeschalted,* adjusted to the bullyings and the brutalities of racist communities, nevertheless, I believe we have a right to expect more of a people whose forebears knew well the tyrannies and exclusions of Egypt and who have been bidden all during their pilgrimage through the years to "remember that ye were slaves in Egypt," to "regard the stranger even as the homeborn."

And even when Jews do not protest or have their congregations pass resolutions or withdraw their cooperation and support in their endeavor to have the Union of American Hebrew Congregations and its President cease and desist from speaking and acting in behalf of the intrinsically Jewish and ineluctably American doctrine of the dignity of all men, even when we, as a Jewish community and as Jewish congregations, cannot be indicted on the grounds of such sins of commission, what of our sins of omission which are ofttimes similarly disastrous in their untoward effects? We who belong in the front lines of the battle for the emancipation of the Negro often permit our silence to be deafening when scores of humble Negro churches are dynamited, when, though lynching may have diminished, civil rights workers mysteriously vanish, when rabbis and ministers are mercilessly beaten up, when many of the noblest Negro preachers and teachers such as Martin Luther King and Reverend Ralph Abernathy spend a good part of their lives in Southern jails.

How truly the arrow shot by the Gandhi of our nation and of our generation, the Reverend King, hits its target in our conscience when he correctly declares:

It may well be that the greatest tragedy of our day is not the glaring noisiness of the so-called bad people, but the appalling silence of the so-called good people. It may well be that our generation may have to repent not only for the vitriolic words and diabolic acts of the children of darkness, but also for the crippling fears and tragic apathy of the children of light. While the good people stood silently and complacently by, the misguided ones acted. If every church and synagogue had added an action program, had worked out plans to implement their righteous resolutions, Federal troops might not have been forced to walk the corridors of Central High School in Little Rock.

Nor, we might add, would the militia have to be called out and curfews instituted in too many Northern hells on earth.

I am worried about Jews, not because I think we will react to the racial crucible differently from other Americans, but precisely because I am afraid we will react like everybody else. Unfortunately, it is not the ethical mandates of the Jewish heritage which now largely shape Jewish attitudes on social issues. It is, in large measure, the middle-class status values which dominate American life: success, money, and comfort. Thus, Jews are increasingly susceptible to the racial ambivalences which afflict American culture. And, in my judgment, as the Negro drive intensifies, the anxieties of the white liberal—Jew and Christian—in America will mount. Indeed, I think the evidence is before us now.

I see a deep and growing breach between the Negro and the white in American society of which the riots in Northern cities and the Alabama and Mississippi bludgeonings are but the faintest beginnings. The white man of good will is quite proud of the Supreme Court decision, of Ralph Bunche and Jackie Robinson, of civil rights legislation and other gains of recent years. With a combination of sentimentality and pride, he feels we are moving steadily in the right direction. Not so most Negroes. The Negro has seen the promise of the Supreme Court decision strangled by Southern intransigence and legal stratagems and this with the virtual acquiescence of the North. He has seen the technique of tokenism approved by the courts and hailed by the liberals of the white community, although it would take until the year 2070 at the present rate of progress to achieve desegregation of all public schools in the South. He has lost his confidence in the sincerity of the white man's belief in equality in the North as well, as overcrowded, stinking, rat-infested slums, educational starvation, and economic strangulation are all either myopically overlooked or smugly countenanced until his inevitable hoodlumism arouses a belated and unjustifiably incensed response. Thus, the Negro has come, more and more, to believe that he can rely only on himself and his fellow colored people to fight for and hold Negro rights. Some Negroes have gone all the way over to the Black Muslim approach to racist separation and frank hatred of the white man. But most Negroes, while rejecting the extremists, have become impatient, angry, bitter and distrustful of the whole of white America. This alienation between the Negro and the mainstream of the American community is the bitter fruit of our failure as a nation to act with dispatch and urgency in fulfilling the American dream. It now walks our streets—North and South—with the terror few perceptive spirits could have failed to predict.

Many white liberals are flinching from the harsh choices now before us. The problem is so omnipresent, it is so difficult of solution, it is so painful to conscience that many people, including Northern liberals, are becoming weary of it. To the white liberal, civil rights is a "good" cause, akin, perhaps, to slum clearance, Medicare, and liberalized immigration. To the Negro, however, it is *the* cause. The white liberal is for civil rights but he thinks of it in the remote terms of Alabama and Mississippi; the Negro thinks of his block, his home, his job. The white liberal is concerned with timing ("You cannot solve this problem overnight"); the Negro is concerned with *now*.

The white liberal would be delighted to see a distinguished Negro leader in a high public position; the Negro wants a Negro Congressman to represent his district, some Negro judges in the courts, Negro storekeepers and salesmen to replace the whites in Negro neighborhoods. The white liberal is concerned about tactics and methods ("I'm all for Negro rights but I don't think demonstrations and boycotts are the right techniques"); the Negro is for results. The white liberal is used to broadly-based educational efforts, drawing on many elements of the community; the Negro is fed up with long-range community education and he's ready to go it alone. (Good-bye, white liberal.) The white liberal proceeds on the silent premise that the Negro must be acclimated to white middle-class values; the Negro has a mounting contempt for the values of white society ("Who wants to be integrated into a burning house?"). The white liberal balances a particular proposal against the value of good community relations; the Negro is ready to pay the price of sharp tension and even conflict to win his rights ("Nobody ever got his rights without fighting for them"). The white liberal is prepared to support "qualified" Negroes for top appointments to public positions; the Negro wants a fair share of Negroes in top office, period. (I didn't say "quota"; I just said "fair share.") All these growing dichotomies are building racial tension and I fear that we face the danger of widespread violence—perhaps more acutely in the North than in the South. I am speaking of what is being called the counter-revolution, the white backlash, and I am praying that we will not be caught in this backlash and in this counter-revolution, and that some of us will not have found at long last the rationale for our noninvolvement because of untoward deeds of which extremists have undoubtedly been guilty.

This would be tantamount to our having withdrawn our entire support of the rebuilding of Zion, of our having asked our government to stand in the way of the creation of the State of Israel, because a few extremists blew up or tried to blow up the King David Hotel and derailed a railroad train in Palestine.

This would have been to have abandoned the century-old dream of the Jew for Zion restored because there were those who committed deeds of which we disapproved.

There will be things of which we disapprove, admittedly, in the days that I see immediately before us, but I beseech those who are committed to the prophetic mission not to use ill-advised deeds as a rationale for noninvolvement.

I must, in conscience, add that I do not feel the Negro community has fully measured up to its own responsibilities. For too long Negro leaders assumed that an end to discrimination will be the panacea for Negro problems. "If the color barrier could be eliminated overnight," Professor Eli Ginzberg of Columbia said in his book, *The Negro Potential,* "that fact alone would not materially improve the position of the Negro." Many Negroes are not yet able to compete in an integrated society. Even where educational and employment opportunities are broadening for the Negro, there is a self-defeating cycle in what the U. S. Civil Rights Commission called the lack of motivation on the part of many Negroes to improve their educational and occupational status. The Negro community has not created the kind of self-help and philanthropic agencies which characterized the growth of the Jewish community in America. Of course, the heritage of slavery and the crippling effects of segregation have left their legacies of social and family disorganization and the high rate of crime, drug addiction, prostitution, and gambling in the Negro sectors. Full equality will not solve these problems; it will accentuate them. Negro leadership must have the courage to follow the admonition of Martin Luther King: "We have become so involved in trying to wipe out the institution of segregation, which certainly is a major cause of social problems among

Negroes, that we have neglected to push programs to raise the moral and cultural climate in our Negro neighborhoods."

But, there is no time to pause while the forces of government exert themselves and the forces of religion disenthrall themselves, and the Negro community achieves the maturity of self-discipline. Events are moving forward with breathtaking intensity. The Negro community is in the midst of a vast migration. Between 1940 and 1960, the Negro population outside the Old Confederacy increased two-and-one-quarter times—from 4 to over 9 million. Twelve large metropolitan areas—New York, Los Angeles, Boston, Philadelphia, Detroit, San Francisco, Oakland, Pittsburgh, St. Louis, Washington, D.C., Cleveland, and Baltimore—now hold 31 per cent of all American Negroes. In addition, Negroes are flocking from the farms to the cities; the percentage of Negroes living in cities leaped from 21 per cent in 1940 to 41 per cent in 1960, and is still rising. Thus, the so-called urban crisis is, in large part, the problem of absorbing and integrating the flood of Negro migrants. Unless we can help the Negro to fulfill his potentialities in middle-class urban America, our cities are doomed. It is no longer a matter of noblesse oblige or altruism. We cannot save our urban centers from blight, delinquency, and chaos unless and until we can help millions of Negroes to help themselves. And we cannot maintain our leadership of the free world until we can realize our principles in our own backyard.

The barriers of discrimination will fall, all right. Many are down already. The rest are doomed and all but the blind know it. But remaining barriers must be leveled swiftly, lest even greater bitterness and more bloody violence consume those now shut behind the walls. The homogeneous, white suburban ghettos of America will not long withstand the pressures of nonwhite "invaders." The winds of change, blowing across Africa and Asia, will gather force in America as well, demolishing all the fences which separate man from man. What is important is not only when, but how, these fences go down. White men of all faiths must not leave it to the anger of the Negro to accomplish this by himself. There must be a meaningful demonstration that to rely on law and the democratic process and the fair play of the American people is not to act the fool.

I am especially concerned at this time with the why and the how. This should have less to do with decisions of a Supreme Court than with the edict of a Supreme Being which enjoined us "to do justly" and to deal equitably with all human beings. This profoundly religious concept, flowing from the deeply-rooted religious faith of the Puritans and the

Founding Fathers, is embodied in our Declaration of Independence, in our Constitution and Bill of Rights. That concept must impel us to lift the struggle from integration to brotherhood, from the legal to the spiritual, from law to love.

I believe that Jews and Christians alike learn something about the application of our faith from the Negro—something of the power of love; yes, and of the power of hate, too—for there is no commandment either in Judaism or Christianity to eschew the hatred of evil. We must learn that we cannot deny the humanity of another, even of a single fellow human being, without diminishing our own. This fundamental truth is suggested in these words of James Baldwin: "This entire issue has something to do with our concept of what God is, for God is, after all, not any particular people's toy."

That's exactly what we've been doing: reducing God to our particular "toy" dipped and dyed to our distinct hue. But to do thus is the very antithesis of the faith we profess. While certain fundamentalist Christian sects may blast the ether waves with their radio gospel concerning their literal interpretation of the opening chapters of Genesis as dictating the eternal separation of the races, liberal Christianity and the whole of Judaism, proclaiming God the Father of all men made in His image and likeness, must cease toying with this God's demand to "love our neighbor as ourselves."

I feel that this summons to consistency between faith and practice applies with special cogency to my fellow Jews. For innumerable centuries—and at no time more poignantly than in our own—we comprised the barometer of civilization; we were the touchstone of man's humanity or bestiality. All too tragically true is the arresting thought by one of the foremost Jewish thinkers of the nineteenth century, Leopold Zunz, who, in his *Poetry of the Synagogue,* wrote:

If there be an ascending scale of suffering, Israel has reached its highest degree. If the duration of afflictions and the patience with which they are borne are ennobling attributes, then the Jew may vie with the aristocrats of any land. If a literature which owns a few classical tragedies is deemed rich, what place would be assigned to a tragedy which extends over fifteen centuries in which the poets and actors have also been the heroes.

Warranted as were these words at the time that Zunz wrote them, this is not the picture of the Jew in America. But it does depict the Negro here and throughout the lands of his oppression. Have we not a right, therefore, to expect that the Jew, sensitized by his own age-old martyrdom, surcharged with his unequivocal teaching of brotherhood, should be in the forefront of the Negroes' present struggle for freedom and fellowship? Have we not a right to expect that we who pray, in our houses of worship on Sabbath and festival and Holy Days, "may the time not be distant when all men shall be united in the bonds of brotherhood" should be more vigorous and vocal in demonstrating the sincerity of those petitions? It is precisely here that God's plumb-line of judgment is being applied and the ancient prophesy from Genesis, once applied to ourselves, seems similarly relevant to the cause of the Negro in twentieth-century America: "Those that bless thee, I will bless; and those that curse thee, I will curse."

Shall America be cursed or blessed in these days that are so decisive for ourselves and for the entire human race? The answer rests with each one among us for, whether in bloody or peaceful revolution, of one thing I am certain: the onward march to freedom, presently begun, cannot be stopped.

But to achieve a true victory we shall need more than the power of law. We shall need the power of the spirit. The courts will not be able to compel good will; they can only punish the physical manifestations of evil. The law cannot banish hatred; it can concern itself only with the hateful act. Court decisions and laws can require desegregation; they cannot, by themselves, achieve integration. In the final analysis, it is not lunch counters that must be integrated; it is the human heart.

And this is the challenge to religion, to every congregation of every faith: that the message of human brotherhood and divine Fatherhood be delivered at long last so that peoples may not only become equal in law, but, paraphrasing Jeremiah, so that they are desegregated in the flesh shall be integrated in the heart.

A prophetic jurist, Judge Learned Hand, once put these ideas into majestic words:

. . . I often wonder whether we do not rest our hopes too much upon constitutions, upon laws and upon courts. These are false hopes; believe me, these are false hopes.

Liberty (and brotherhood) lies in the hearts of men and women; when it dies there, no constitution, no law, no court can save it; no constitution, no law, no court can even do much to help it.

While it lives there it needs no constitution, no law, no court to save it.

What, then, is the spirit of liberty?

I cannot define it; I can only tell you my own faith.

The spirit of liberty (and brotherhood) is the Spirit which is not too sure that it is right; the spirit of liberty is the spirit which seeks to understand the minds of other men and women . . . ; the spirit of liberty is the spirit of Him who, near two thousand years ago, taught mankind that lesson it has never learned, but has never quite forgotten; that there may be a kingdom where the least shall be heard and considered side by side with the greatest.

Breathes there a Jew, breathes there an American of any faith, who does not rejoice that the day of freedom is thus dawning—whatever may be the pain and conflict that accompany its coming? No doubt it is a sentimental conceit, but I covet for religion in general and, even more especially for Judaism and the Jew, a significant role in thus "forcing the end." I pray that we shall not be constrained to confess to our children and our children's children that we heard God's summons to brotherhood sounding more loudly and insistently in our generation than perhaps in any other—and we heeded it not.

An America, an Africa, an Asia, a world destroyed in violence or redeemed by those who proclaim "One God, One Humanity"—which will it be? The answer to this searching dilemma and challenge of our day is suggested in a legend attributed to the foremost Jewish thinker of the Middle Ages, Moses Maimonides. It is told that he was once brought before his ruler under the penalty of death. The sovereign, however, was tempted to toy with him even in his final hours. He offered to spare Maimonides' life if he could give the correct answer to the puzzle he proceeded to place before him. "In my hand I hold a tiny dove," the monarch said. "Tell me, is it alive or dead?" Maimonides sensed the trap. The dove was undoubtedly still alive. And if he answered that it was dead, the ruler could release the living dove and thus would his life be forfeited. If, however, he replied that it was alive, the monarch could instantly and ruthlessly crush it and snuff out its life. After a moment's reflection, Maimonides sagely answered, "The answer, your majesty, is in *your* hand."

The answer to America's racial dilemma and revolution is in our hands and in our hearts.

8

CHILDREN BY CHANCE OR CHOICE

FORETHOUGHT

There are no doubt many timorous souls who take strenuous exception to the discussion of so delicate a problem as birth control from the pulpit. They believe that such subjects should be limited to the cocktail party, the barroom, or the smoking car. Anywhere outside the prurient atmosphere of such spicy haunts especially reserved for smut and sex to them is a decidedly indecent and distasteful subject to be scrupulously avoided in public speech.

But it is this very false and hypocritical "conspiracy of silence" which makes these "good people" really responsible for the fact that our province of Ontario is presenting so ludicrous a spectacle today, a spectacle which may make of our community the foremost rival of Dayton, Tennessee, and its famous—or, rather, its infamous—"Monkey Trial," a spectacle which witnesses a humble and heroic social worker arraigned as a common criminal before the bar. In fact, almost every one of us, by our jaundiced refusal to make legal for all that of which we seem quite willing that the few should make illegal use; yes, all of us, by our flagrant inconsistency between profession and practice, have been responsible for the present trial of Dorothea Palmer, indicted for disseminating information on birth control.

But there is a far deeper sense in which we are responsible for what is taking place in Ottawa at the present hour. Not Miss Palmer, but almost every last one of us should have been charged with the offense of which she is being accused. We should each and all be placed before the bar of judgment. For it is not a question of whether or not this single individual has broken the law by the dissemination of birth control information, but whether it is right or wrong that such

*information be made available for all those who so sorely need it.
If it be right, then Miss Palmer must be acquitted. But what is far
more important, then our laws ought to be immediately and radically
revised. If it be wrong, then not merely Miss Palmer should be punished for her "offense," but every man and woman who feels that it is
the special prerogative of his class to possess information which is
denied by law to the underprivileged and the needy should be similarly
hailed into court and similarly punished—that is, if there would be
jails enough to accommodate them all.*

Toronto, 1936

AFTERTHOUGHTS

When these words were spoken, feelings had reached fever pitch
in Canada and I was vehemently denounced as encouraging immorality,
promoting promiscuity, and destroying the sanctity of holy matrimony
and family life. Of course, nothing could be more absurd then or now.
No one has been more aware or appreciative of the unique contribution
which Judaism and Jewish history have made to the enhancement and
sanctity of marriage and the home. I concur with Mark Twain's conclusion: "That the Jewish home is a home in the truest sense is a fact
which no one will dispute. The family is knit together by the strongest
affections. Its members show each other every due respect; and reverence for elders is an inviolate law of the house."

It may well be that the greatest contribution which Jews have made
to civilization, save only the concept of the unity of God, has been the
creation of an ideal family life. In his book *Hebrew Marriage,* David
R. Mace wrote that "Yet the family unit . . . was preserved. It survived
the upheavals of the monarchy. It survived the disruption of the exile. It
survived the final disintegration of the Jewish race as a national community. And it has made possible that preservation of the separate
unity of the Jew, throughout all the vicissitudes of his tempestuous
experience, which is one of the miracles of history."

Judaism had—and has—a unique attitude toward marriage and the
family. In Judaism, marriage is regarded as an exalted state of profound religious significance. Not merely for biological union or for the
perpetuation of the race, marriage is regarded by Jewish tradition as
a holy communion, a *Kiddushin,* a sanctification, a consecration, a

miraculous metamorphosis of two souls—as well as two bodies—into one. Unlike Christianity, Judaism did not regard marriage as a prurient yielding to the weakness of the flesh. Indeed, Judaism rejected the ascetic attitude toward sex, holding the satisfaction of normal human appetites to be a duty, not a necessary evil. It radically disagreed with Paul's grudging concession that "it is better to marry than to burn."

Celibacy in Judaism was generally looked upon as unnatural, and Jewish law specified that the high priest was not to observe the rites of the Day of Atonement unless he was married. For in Jewish law and lore man achieves wholeness only through marriage. No greater unqualified commentary on the duty as well as the delight of the union of man and woman, of husband and wife, was God's dissatisfaction with his initial creative handiwork and his categoric verdict that "It is not good for man to be alone." Even today, a congregation's discomfort with an unmarried rabbi is almost as great as its anxiety about an unwed mother. Sex is seen by Judaism as a gift from God, which is not only not to be abused but is not to remain unused as well. It is a precious boon to be received with joy and gratitude. Personal fulfillment in the conjugal bed is as legitimate a goal of marriage as is the bearing of children.

Parallel to the Jewish family value of *Taharas ha mishpochoh*—purity of the family—which is based on a wholesome view of sex relationships, is the obligation to obey the command *Peru oov'voo,* to beget offspring and raise them up in the way that they should go. The Jewish attitude toward bearing and rearing of children, however, stood in sharp contrast to that of other nations of antiquity. The Greeks abandoned weak and sickly children on a mountain to die. The Romans permitted a man, with impunity, to rid himself of his own son, even a grown son. Tacitus, the Roman historian, expressed contempt for the people of Judea because "it is a crime among them to kill any child." Jews viewed children as God's highest treasures. They were to be diligently trained in religious and ethical truths, and every facet of the child's education was a parental obligation. The family, not the individual, was the central unit in Jewish society. "Lo," said the psalmist, "children are a heritage of the Lord; the fruit of the womb is a reward. As arrows in the hand of a mighty man, so are the children of one's youth. Happy is the man that hath his quiver full of them."

One of my colleagues, Rabbi Stanley Brav, said at the UAHC Biennial in 1961 that "In Judaism, familyness is not only next to godliness, it is often identical with it."

How are these traditional values being fulfilled in the modern Jewish family? Is the Jewish family in America any longer distinctive? Despite some alarming signs of deplorable acculturation, to the worst rather than to the best in American pseudomorality, I think that generally the answer is yes. At a time when the family in America shows alarming signs of widespread disintegration, Jewish familial ties continue, in large measures, to reflect the qualities of warmth and solidarity. Although divorce, alcoholism, and juvenile delinquency have skyrocketed in American culture, Jews tend to make a disproportionately small (though rising) contribution to these evidences of social pathology. The motivation for education is undimmed, although it has been largely secularized. Despite many stresses, Jewish family cohesion is still evident. A Harvard dean once observed that you do not enroll a Jewish student at a university; you enroll a Jewish family. And the rapid rise of American Jews out of an immigrant, lower-economic environment to the broad reaches of middle-class (usually suburban) comfort affords the American Jewish family unprecedented opportunities.

One of the marked characteristics of the Jewish family in America is its relatively low birth rate. Jews are probably America's most efficient practitioners of birth control. The small family is the norm. Jews tend to limit the number of children, enabling the family to provide the maximum educational and cultural advantages to each child. There are those who, pointing to the relatively low Jewish birth rate, fear that Jews are overdoing their tendency to control family size. Yet, in demonstrating the positive good which stems from children by choice, rather than by chance, Jews stand as living witnesses to the civilized values which derive from planned families as opposed to the spreading chaos with which the population explosion now threatens the world.

Conflicting religious values about family life represent one of the most serious impediments to a solution of the population explosion.

The underlying issue—children by chance or choice—has become a major requisite of human survival, second only to the threat of nuclear war. The menace of the population explosion will hang over man's future on this planet even if the miracle of disarmament were to be achieved.

The United Nations has estimated that the human family is now increasing at the staggering pace of over five hundred million persons in this decade. This astronomical escalation is dramatically depicted at the New York World's Fair where, with a huge flashing electrical display, the Equitable Life Assurance Society's demograph indicates one birth every twelve seconds for the U.S. alone! This skyrocketing growth can best be understood when we realize that it took *thousands of years* for the human race to attain the population of a billion. That milestone was reached in about 1830. It took but one additional century to add the second billion. That occurred about 1930. It is estimated that the third billion will be added before 2000—approximately thirty-five years hence. At this rate, it will require but fifteen years to add the fourth billion. Thus, if the present trends are maintained, some six or seven billion people will be living—or, to be more accurate, will be barely existing—on this earth by the end of the twentieth century when there will be quite literally "standing room only."

It is, of course, not the birth rate alone which has resulted in these swiftly swarming billions. In addition to this largely uncontrolled and wholesale breeding, we have sharply lowered the death rate, thanks to our scientific knowledge, to "the great sanitary awakening" of the last century, the discoveries of the "microbe hunters" who, armed with sulfa and penicillin and a host of other "miracle" drugs, have cured many an erstwhile incurable disease, prolonging life and holding death itself in leash. For example, some two million lives have been saved since 1942 in the United States alone as a result of antibiotics. United States and United Nations technical assistance and foreign aid programs have helped the underdeveloped nations of the world to reduce the ravages and toll of disease. To cite but one of countless examples, the World Health Organization is now embarked on a major campaign to rid the world of malaria, a disease affecting more than 200 million of the world's present population.

In other parts of the world, too, progress has been well-nigh miraculous, surpassing in certain respects the stupendous gains of even our supposedly incomparable scientific West. Sit on an open, unscreened porch, as I have done, in Malaya, in Rangoon, in New Delhi—once scourged by the most deadly of disease-carrying mosquitoes—and enjoy the luxury of an unbitten evening and you will comprehend what public government spraying programs have achieved in so-called backward countries. This is in striking contrast to our own allegedly hygienic —but still annoyingly itchy—land.

But all the blessings of medicine and of our multi-billion-dollar programs of foreign aid will avail mankind nothing if we do not cope with—and soon—the supreme challenge of overpopulation. Before I visited many of the countries of the Far East in 1958, I had, of course, often heard that two out of three people of the world go to bed hungry every night. But hearing about it was no preparation whatsoever for seeing the pinched and hopeless faces of little children, scrounging and scavenging like rats on a garbage dump for a scrap of decaying vegetable, a morsel of rotting meat, a crust of moulding bread; living in their huddled huts slapped together out of petrol tins, Carnation milk cans, and Kotex cartons; sleeping—and dying prematurely—in the slimy and stinking back alleys of Calcutta (which the late Prime Minister Nehru designated as a "horror" when we talked in New Dehli during my visit to India in May of 1958). And still more recently, I encountered well-nigh similar deplorable poverty, disease, and homelessness in not a few South American countries so rich in natural resources but so piratically exploited by their own robber barons as well as ours, where little children with starved, distended bellies and piteous faces bloody with disease bespeak our callousness to want and gaping need at our very doorstep. Is this the destiny for which God created man in His image? And the chilling fact is that, no matter how prodigious the economic plans for the underdeveloped nation, nor how ample the aid from the United States and others, it can never be effective unless and until drastic action is taken to end the degradation of women the world over into mere vessels for the satisfaction of male studs and their conversion into ceaselessly breeding kine.

As Nehru further commented to me, "Our five-year plans have no meaning if the population grows at a rate one can never overtake." Similarly, Ayub Khan, President of Pakistan, has warned: "If our population continues to increase at the present rate, it will ultimately lead to a standard of living which will be little better than that of animals." Eugene Black, then president of the World Bank, minced no words in saying: "Unless population growth can be restrained, we may have to abandon for this generation our hopes of economic progress in the crowded lands of Asia, Africa, and the Middle East." And of South America, too, he should have added. Unless we address ourselves courageously to the population bomb—which, unlike the nuclear bomb, is *already* exploding—we mortgage our future to hunger, political instability, social unrest, human misery, and war.

Need we surrender to this prospect? In decent consistency with all our proud and presumptuous protestations that we Americans are ethically and spiritually superior to our cold-war adversaries, that we believe in the dignity and inviolability of every one of God's children, the United States should stand on this issue, as we do on many others, as the champion of human dignity in the world.

In 1960, a high-level committee of private citizens, headed by William H. Draper, Jr., appointed by then President Eisenhower to assess United States foreign-aid policy, rendered a searching and definitive report. Among other things it recommended that the United States, on request, assist countries in formulating plans designed to deal with the problem of rapid population growth, and support studies and research to meet the serious threat to stability, health, and peace posed by rapidly expanding populations. These conclusions evoked an inflamed controversy which, for a moment, intruded upon the 1960 Presidential campaign. The Roman Catholic bishops of the United States denounced the Draper Committee recommendations as an immoral plan to foist birth control upon the world. In the face of this ecclesiastical onslaught, even Protestant President Eisenhower retreated in a cloud of ambiguous verbiage. On the other hand, some Protestant and Jewish leaders joined with me in protesting the President's swift and timorous capitulation to such clerical pressures. Paradoxical, isn't it, how fainthearted the heroes of the battlefields sometimes become when facing critical barrages on the domestic front? President Eisenhower's bland statement that "that's not our business" struck me as an irresponsible evasion of public responsibility.

But the upshot of it all was that the United States, holding a religious hot potato, had decided, as an article of national policy, to close its eyes to one of the gravest problems of our time.

In June of 1960, Senator J. William Fulbright asked the then Deputy Assistant Secretary of State for Inter-American Affairs what should be done about population growth in Latin America, India, and Pakistan. "I would rather not pronounce on the population problem," Wymberly Coerr replied.

"You talk about health," the Senator persisted. "Why don't you talk about population control? Why is that forbidden to you?"

"I think you are right, sir," Coerr replied. "Probably it should not be forbidden to me. I just recognize it as a political, sensitive subject."

What an ignominious position for a great and proud power. It is one thing—and most proper—for a particular religious group to express its moral judgment on birth control or, for that matter, on any other issue of public policy. But it is quite another for the United States of America, merely to avoid internal controversy, knowingly to sweep under the rug the time bomb which will defeat the very undertakings through which we are trying to bring a higher living standard to all the peoples of the world. This is more than political weakness. It is moral poltroonery bordering upon the schizophrenic.

For the truth is that nobody has proposed that the U.S. *impose* birth control on anyone. The countries of Asia, Africa, and Latin America are desperately aware of the necessities for the proper spacing of childbirths. We cannot continue to export death control without being concerned with birth control. Far from resenting American assistance, most of the nations welcome it. Some have already made distinctive progress by their own efforts to lower the birth rate. Japan is the most striking example. Despite some opposition at home and abroad, she has moved aggressively by encouraging birth control, authorizing legalized abortions and voluntary human sterilization. Since World War II, Japan has cut its birth rate in half. There can be little doubt that Japan's success in population control has contributed significantly to its economic and political stability and vitality in the post-war years.

In recent months, fortunately, the U.S. seems to be inching painfully, guardedly, toward a more relevant approach to the population explosion. Between 1960 and 1963, U.S. governmental leaders began to address themselves to the gravity of the population problem. In December, 1962, the U.N. adopted a resolution on population growth. The U.S. representative outlined what was, practically speaking, a fresh U.S. policy: to "help other countries, upon request, to find potential sources of information and assistance to ways and means of dealing with population problems."

In December, 1962, the National Institute of Health, encouraged by the statements of some Catholic, as well as non-Catholic, spokesmen, augmented its work in the area of human reproduction. But all of this may well be too little and too late as parents with diseased and too numerous offspring listen increasingly to the wily promises of the Communists of more food and shelter while our monolingual plenipotentiaries continue to preach, from behind barbed-wire enclaves, sundered from the purportedly messy masses of "natives," their high-sounding, uncomprehended platitudes of democracy and freedom. The U.S. Government finances only $4 million worth of research projects in this field. The late President Kennedy himself urged more research on the reproduction cycle, and there is growing pressure for the U.S. government to devote more initiative, funds, and priorities to this overarching problem.

Notwithstanding this process and a growing ferment within Catholic thought, such as the recent more sympathetic pronouncements of certain of her prelates regarding the "pill," the church as a whole still holds birth control by most generally accepted contraceptive means to be immoral. Yet the truth is, as Catholic leaders sorrowfully admit, that a substantial segment of Roman Catholics in the United States practice birth control. An intensive study found that more than 70 per cent of Roman Catholic wives in the United States use birth control, more than half of them having used a technique other than the rhythm method. We pretend that public opinion will not permit us to assist foreign countries in regard to birth control. But a recent poll conducted by the *San Francisco Chronicle* found 83 per cent of the people approving such assistance. Birth control is officially discountenanced in two of our states—Connecticut and Massachusetts—but everybody knows that under-the-counter acquisition of contraceptives is as prevalent there as legal sales are in nearby New York State. Again, the hypocrisy and humbug of Prohibition days come to mind. Instead of getting "hooch" with the greatest of ease "for medicinal purposes," of course, every manner of protective device can be procured "for reasons of health," to be sure, provided only that one has the price and some surreptitious source of supply.

As with the Volstead Act, such attempts to suppress and outlaw what comes naturally only breeds contempt for such intolerable and unenforceable laws and gives a clue perhaps to the moral deterioration of our times paralleling, and in some ways even surpassing, the era of Al Capone.

Similarly, throughout the United States, abortions are illegal, except under the most extraordinary circumstances, with the only discernible result that more than one million women each year are driven into a dirty and dangerous traffic flourishing underground where quacks and incompetents, like omnivorous vultures, prey upon their terrified and defenseless victims. We do not know the full extent of untold injury, horror, and even death perpetrated by bootleg abortions.

On the subject of abortion, I believe we sank to new depths of moral degradation in 1962 in the Finkbine case which followed in the wake of the revelation that the use of the drug thalidomide had resulted in thousands of deformed births throughout Europe. Reduced to emotional exhaustion and driven to the depths of desperation, the Finkbines were compelled to fly to Scandinavia in order to do what simple common sense and humanity would seem to have demanded in their own home town where they had established themselves as respectable and respected citizens and decent parents. But no. They had to be dragged by blatant and blazing press headlines through the scum of prurient notoriety and to bear the not negligible expense of a trip abroad to rout the risk of bearing an abnormal child. Nothing could more damningly expose the dogmatic and inhumane character of our indiscriminate, unqualified ban on abortion which, like divorce laws in New York and some other states, is nothing but timorous surrender to the worst of religious primitivism! Most religious spokesmen —Catholic, Protestant, and Jewish, too—solemnly declared in relation to the Finkbine case that abortion was an improper act, unless the mother's physical health was directly jeopardized. The Vatican solemnly announced that the Finkbine's decision and conduct constituted both a sin and a crime. In the name of a pious and inhumane religious atavism, we were quite prepared to doom an entire family to a lifetime of financial distress and emotional anguish, blasting their hopes and dreams—for what? For an obscure dogmatism which debases human dignity and violates every tenet of human compassion.

What I fail to see is how all this inhumanity enhances our moral standards and our profession of reverence for human life. Jewish teaching is not nearly as squeamish as are we who profess to be its teachers today. It is far more realistic and unflinching, even in the face of the presently unmentionable subject of abortion. Shocked as we may be in our abject surrender to the most puritanical of Pauline aversions, Dr. Solomon B. Freehof cites a *Responsum* given by Rabbi Ben Zion Uziel, the late Sephardic Chief Rabbi which, after a general analysis of the subject, concludes that a foetus is not a *nefesh* (soul) at all and, therefore, has no independent life. It is part of its mother and, just as a person may sacrifice a limb to be cured of a worse sickness, so may this foetus be destroyed for the mother's benefit. Of course, he reckons with the statement of the *Tosfos* that a Jew is not permitted to destroy a foetus, although such an act is not to be considered murder. Rabbi Uziel says, of course, one may not destroy it. One may not destroy anything without purpose. But *if there is a worth-while purpose* (italics mine), it may be done. The specific case before Rabbi Uziel concerned a woman who was threatened with permanent deafness if she went through with her pregnancy. Rabbi Uziel decided that, since the foetus is not an independent *nefesh,* but is only part of the mother, there is no sin in destroying it *for her sake.* One has little doubt as to how this humanitarian rabbi, how the whole humane tradition of Judaism, which justified abortion on the grounds of the comparatively minor malady of deafness, would react to the widespread ruination of health, mental and spiritual, which hounds myriads of women— possibly errant but still human—because of our flagrant refusal to face the ubiquitous but subterranean, clandestine fact of abortion squarely.

In recent years, the issue of voluntary sterilization has also become an issue of controversy. In September, 1962, Archbishop Patrick O'Boyle of Washington, D.C., lashed out at the Fauquier clinic in Warrenton, Virginia, charging that the program of sterilization at the clinic, although voluntary, was "immoral" and was designed to reduce the tax burden and the birth rate of indigent Negroes in the county. My reading of the detailed reports persuaded me that the clinic was prompted by no such consideration, but, rather, was pioneering in a most important program for the improved health and welfare of all residents, regardless of race or economic station. Voluntary sterilization was performed under strict medical safeguards, and this procedure was only one aspect of an enlightened total program of prenatal and post-natal care along with modern birth-control guidance.

But the question remains. Is voluntary sterilization moral? I understand and respect the Catholic view that such an operation is, in Catholic doctrine, a violation of natural law. But so, it seems to me, would be any operation which mercifully but artificially removes some lacerating limb or tumor which nature—or God—has brought into being. I must even admit that there is considerable doubt that sterilization is fully compatible with traditional Jewish law, except where there is urgent medical or other extraordinary grounds for such drastic action. Certainly effective birth control is a better solution. Yet, for those couples for whom birth control does not prove to be efficacious for whatever reason, it seems to me that there is no moral impropriety in voluntary sterilization. Basically, I believe the issue is a medical matter, to be considered in the light of competent medical guidance, and to be decided in the sanctity of the individual conscience.

Having thus pleaded for the right—through carefully controlled birth control, abortion, or sterilization—to avert intolerable agony of body and anguish of spirit on the part of both parents and unborn but prenatally doomed children, must I not honestly face a seemingly inevitable query as to whether it is proper and right to abort human life itself? Is euthanasia also legitimate? I have come to believe that there *are* circumstances in which such merciful release should be available to sufferers wracked by ravaging and incurable disease. I have stood helplessly and hopelessly beside those who have endured hideous and horrifying torture. I have seen the tightly drawn lips and clenched fists of indescribable torments, the writhing and twisting of one's pain-haunted body. I know what such suffering does, not only to the person who is afflicted, but also to the loving family whose suffering becomes equally intolerable. And I cannot help but agree with Dr. W. Inge, the former Dean of St. Paul's Cathedral, London, who said, "It seems anomalous that a man may be punished for cruelty if he does *not* put a horse or a dog out of its misery but is liable to be hanged for murder if he helps a cancer patient to an overdose of morphia. I do not think that we can assume that God wills the prolongation of torture for the benefit of the soul of the sufferer."

As one who strongly opposes capital punishment, pleads constantly for man's right to life, and feels deep compassion for those condemned to die, it may seem anomalous for me to support, also, man's right to die. Yet, I cannot but feel the same compassion for human beings condemned to live in futile, frightening, frenzied pain, doomed to a death that creeps with insidious, snail-like, and hopeless agony. Cancer alone has over a half-million known sufferers in the United States today, many of whom are both doomed and degenerative. Many will try, desperately, to take their own lives. Many will beg their relatives and doctors for escape from such torture. But under our present antiquated laws, society turns away coldly, ignoring their poignant, trembling pleas. Is this sensible and humane in an age of science and humanity?

I am aware of the complexities and risks, but the time has certainly come to consider the development of sound legal measures, with stringent safeguards against abuse, that will permit respect for human personality to be expressed, in these tragic cases, through merciful release from hopeless suffering.

The more one examines the various problems related to the family, to life and death, to sex, to birth and death control, the more one's senses are assaulted by the stench of hypocrisy and self-righteousness. Some religious leaders seem to feel that the millennium is reached when a repressive and puritanical law is forced onto the statute books. Is New York State moral because it has a strict and archaic divorce law whose only apparent result is to chase thousands of New Yorkers (including the governor of the state in 1963) to other states or countries, conspiring to establish an ugly pattern of collusion, deceit, and fraud which violates all standards of decency and dignity?

Is the failure of most of our public schools to develop enlightened programs of sex education leading to a strengthening of American life or is it contributing to the lax moral standards which cause consternation among public school educators over an alarming rise in sexual licentiousness among American youngsters, with its concomitant increase in adolescent pregnancies, a startlingly precipitate increase in venereal disease, and a growing mortality from illegal abortions?

A fresh, frank, and enlightened reappraisal of our laws and mores on sex and family relations is long overdue. Many of our present statutes simply do not work. They inspire the utmost contempt for law. They are out of touch with modern knowledge and enlightened concepts of social work and family planning. Religious primitivists have succeeded in converting many such laws and codes into taboos, and politicians who weigh their mail far more diligently than their consciences, know that there are few votes to be gained for courage in reforming such laws and many ballots to be lost by the reprisals of sectarian groups. But the time has come for liberal religious leaders to articulate and fight for the enhancement of human values and human dignity and to war against religious antiquarianism and repression. America desperately needs a twentieth-century reassessment of such issues as abortion, artificial insemination, divorce, sterilization, child adoption, homosexuality, sex, and marriage.

A prime requirement of both religion and democracy is truth. Let us not tarnish it with our self-deceptions and pretensions. "Be fruitful and multiply" is God's commandment and blessing. But if we truly cherish the uniqueness of the human personality, stamped in the image of the Divine, we had better end our conspiracy of silence and surreption in order to make certain that His image of perfection is not blemished. Then let each of His children be conceived in love and delivered—not unwanted—into the arms and hearts of their eager parents. We had better make certain that it is the Kingdom of God and not the bleak vision of Malthus that must become the heritage of the human family.

Make child-bearing the most precious and joyous *choice* of a mother's and father's love, make parenthood voluntary, redeem so holy a responsibility as the creation of a human being, a child of God, from being the accidental by-product of passion or lust, and we will pave the way toward the speedier solution of innumerable of the challenging problems of our time: the greed for colonies for surplus populations; the glutting of the labor market with millions of unemployed; and the fear of early marriage and child-bearing with its inevitable consequences in promiscuity and prostitution.

Not alone will we thus alleviate or overcome these crushing social difficulties of our time, but we will cleanse the whole concept of sex from its scarlet taint of sin and restore it to its place of pristine purity as one of the rarest gifts of God. We will transform the marriage act from an act of shame or sheer utility into a virtual "sacrament," as Olive Schreiner puts it, a sacrament which, as she defines that treasured, meaningful word, is "the outward and visible symbol of an inward and spiritual grace." A spiritual grace wherein, as Havelock Ellis so beautifully describes it—

husband and wife pass to each other the sacramental chalice of that wine which imparts the deepest joy that they can know, which binds them to each other more truly and more firmly than the priest of any church, a spiritual grace in which their lives become as one with that divine act of creative artistry in which old poets fabled that out of the dust of the ground and in his own image some god of chaos once created man.

9

THOU SHALT NOT KILL—PERIOD

FORETHOUGHT

Suppose that I agreed with all the extravagant and lurid language of the tabloid press that the crime of Bruno Hauptmann was the most savage, brutal, and barbaric villainy of our time? Suppose, furthermore, that I were convinced that Bruno Hauptmann had slain the Lindbergh baby; suppose that, beyond a doubt, it were demonstrated that he and he alone had committed this foul deed; suppose even that he confessed and graphically traced every detail of that crime. . . . Should he therefore die? I ask this specific question just because I realize that, for many years to come, this revolting crime will be flung into the faces of those who are opposed to the taking of human life under any circumstances whatsoever. It is because this single case has constrained many an opponent of capital punishment to take cover ignominiously and to capitulate to the vengeful crowd that I have taken this most vehemently castigated atrocity to ascertain whether the execution of its perpetrator is the best, most practical, and truly moral answer which society can give.

But whether practical or not, the belief in redemption rather than retribution is the basic teaching of our respective faiths: Judaism and Christianity. Personally, I believe it is the most practical as well as the only moral way of life (sounded first so many centuries ago by the prophet who said, "I desire not the death of the sinner, but that he should return to me and live"), and reechoed by every prophetic spirit still today, for until not merely the synagogue and the church, but the state as well, has such an unwavering and uncompromising respect for human life will there be hope for our sorely riven contemporary world.

The thunder of war becomes more deafening with every passing day; the monster of revolution crouches at our very doorstep, tense and

166

wrathfully prepared to pounce upon us and to tear us all to shreds; moral degeneration and spiritual decay sap our energies and threaten to drag us swiftly to our doom. And all because we have not mastered this single and simple religious teaching: the sanctity of every child of God; the sanctity of every mortal being whether he be prince or proletarian, whether he abide within or without the borders of our particular land, whether he profess our faith or pay homage to some alien creed. The mastery of this single lesson alone can save us. Only then will civil strife be ended and the rumors of war silenced; only then, when society itself will cease to desecrate a single precious human being, when it will not punish the murderer by stooping to murder. Only then will each and all become secure at last.

Toronto, 1936

AFTERTHOUGHTS

I'm glad I said that. I am still opposed to capital punishment. But if it was almost reckless to declare publicly in 1936 that Bruno Hauptmann should not die at the hand of the state, it is infinitely more difficult to be unqualifiedly opposed to capital punishment today. Certain of my own words above seem to leap from the foregoing pages with startling immediacy. That is why, with Lafayette, I will affirm that "I shall struggle against capital punishment in even the most extreme and dastardly of cases until I have demonstrated to me the infallibility of mortal men." As I write these lines, what weighs upon my heart and conscience is precisely "the most extreme and dastardly of cases."

As I was recently reviewing these words leading to an evaluation of what seemed "the most extreme and dastardly case" of our days—the atrocious unspeakable mass murders of Adolf Eichmann—shots were fired that were indeed "heard around the world." Our renowned and revered President John F. Kennedy, brilliant meteoric mind, liberty-loving and peace-pursuing spirit, was brutally, satanically murdered in Dallas, Texas, in this supposedly civilized U.S.A. In the aftermath of a national disaster and a grief which seemed personal to almost every American, it is hard to force the mind to speculate on what might have been. But it may be important to try, for the moment of horror in Dallas illumined not merely a moment of aberrational madness by a single individual but also a streak of violence in our national character.

Lee Harvey Oswald, the President's apparent assassin, was himself assassinated in a crime hardly less revolting than the shooting of the President. Yet there can be little doubt that millions of Americans were titillated by the drama of the first nationally televised murder. Staged blood-and-thunder shooting TV has provided in abundance, but this was "for real." Millions of Americans, viewing this eye-witnessed deed, cheered Jack Ruby's act; he gratified an almost universal lust for vengeance. Yet, every American who responded thus was trampling on the most basic and fragile values of civilization, was turning law into a plaything of mob emotion, and was driving a nail into that belief in the preciousness of human life which was nourished by our religious traditions and by the wisdom of the ages.

What if Oswald had not been killed in that despicable Dallas spectacle? What would have happened to him? Granted that the evidence against him seems overwhelming, would he have received a fair trial in the face of feverish public passion? There can be little doubt that, in any event, a trial would have found him guilty and the penalty would have been death. Aside from all else, public opinion would have demanded the supreme punishment. And what would have happened then? Would the long-standing opponents of capital punishment—myself included—have had the courage to speak out in behalf of the wretch who snuffed out our generation's brightest candle? If we had summoned such courage, would the public have heard us out, or would we have been shouted down in contempt and anger? And if, as seems certain, Oswald had been put to death, would there be a significant moral distinction between the calculated and cold-blooded murder performed by the state and the blind, frenzied murder by an unhinged citizen? These are unpleasant questions. They are perhaps unanswerable questions. But, I submit, they are questions that cut to the marrow of our national character. They expose our emotional and social health. They raise the supreme question: how do we value the human personality?

As a consequence of the atrocious deed in Dallas, Oswald would have been, for Americans, that "most extreme and dastardly of cases" of which Lafayette wrote. But for Americans of the Jewish faith, and for Jews throughout the world, it was the case of Adolf Eichmann that provided the ultimate test of moral opposition to capital punishment.

Should Eichmann have been executed by the State of Israel? No court has ever convicted a man more satanically stained with the blood of the innocent. If society were ever justified in taking a life, then this exemplar of the "banality of evil," whose office routine was to arrange the daily slaughter of Jews for no reason other than their Jewishness, is the most conspicuous candidate. Some six million of my coreligionists —one-third of the Jewish people of the entire world—were wantonly and wickedly destroyed by the coldly efficient engines of mass slaughter operated by Eichmann and his fellow technicians of wholesale murder. The imagination trembles at the magnitude of so diabolic a deed. The mind questions the credibility of anything so inexcusably grisly and ghoulish. Granted the ease with which a human being erases that which he has not the intestinal fortitude to remember, it seems incomprehensible that, although all this happened only two decades ago, it has already slipped from too many of our minds. Yet, it is all too tragically true. It happened. Santayana is right when he says that what mankind refuses to remember, it is doomed to repeat.

Some maintain that Eichmann's execution was desirable precisely on this score—as an unforgettable message and moral to all mankind. I disagree. On the contrary, I insist that for the abolitionist—and I have been one all my adult years—the Eichmann case was the climax of a series of harsh and spectacular cases, including that of Sacco-Vanzetti, the Rosenbergs, and Caryl Chessman—each of which forced a reluctant public to examine itself as executioner.

Perhaps the most surprising and to me the most penetrating and devastating challenge to the blithe acceptance of capital punishment was penned by Chessman from his death cell just a few hours before the state of California asphyxiated him in its aseptic gas chamber.

In that last night on earth, Caryl Chessman wrote these lines in a letter to Will Stevens of the *San Francisco Examiner*:

Dear Mr. Stevens:

As you know, the California executioner keeps banker's hours. He never kills before 10 o'clock in the morning, never after 4 in the afternoon. When you read this, he will have killed me. I will have exchanged oblivion for an unprecedented 12-year nightmare. And you will have witnessed the final, lethal, ritualistic act. It is my hope and my belief that you will be able to report that I died with dignity, without animal fear and without bravado. I owe that much to myself.

I owe much more to a great many others. These words, accordingly, are addressed to the thousands and thousands of people throughout the world who have taken such a moving, humane interest in my plight. I want first to take this opportunity to say goodbye to them and to express my heartfelt thanks.

The death watch will come for me in a few more minutes. What remains of my life, so far as I know, is less than 18 hours. Those hours will be spent in one of the two cells downstairs just a few short steps from the gas chamber. Morning will mean oblivion. I accept this fact, I do not try to hide from it or delude myself that a miracle will spare me.

And yet, paradoxically, the will to live continues to burn brightly within me. It is that will—that affirmation of life—which makes it possible for me to sit here quietly, reflectively, and write these words. It is what impels me to declare candidly: I did want to live. I believed passionately that I could make a meaningful contribution to both literature and society with my writings. I was determined to repay those people from many nations who spoke out for me, who believed in Caryl Chessman as a human being. It would have given me great satisfaction and a sense of purpose to have survived to vindicate their compassionate judgment. But a harsh fate, wearing judicial robes, has decreed death in a small octagonal room painted green.

How do I feel? Strangely calm. Since this letter will reach you only if the execution is not postponed, it means sometime tomorrow morning I shall have received word of final court rejections. I shall have been told, "It's time"—time to take these few, short steps, time to be strapped down in a straight-backed metal chair, time to be stared at by other men and women come to witness how the sovereign state of California snuffs out human life in the name of justice, time to smell the synthetic odor of peach blossoms, time to inhale and gag and have consciousness recede into an eternal black void. Time, in short, to die. Then, many California officials believe, California will have vindicated itself and its system of retributive justice. It will have claimed revenge. But vengeance against what?

Gas chambers only can kill people, not counterfeit, self-deluding black criminal legends, not "monster" myths. Facing death, I say this again emphatically and without qualification: I was not Southern California's infamous red light bandit. California convicted the wrong man. And it stubbornly refused to admit the possibility of its error, much less correct it. In time the world will have proof of its savage error. It will not be proud then of its deed. But let us put aside here the question of guilt or innocence. What impels me to write this letter is because I earnestly believe more is involved than the death of one man. I am writing it because I have heard humanity's voice raised in my behalf—and because I have seen too much of man-inflicted death. I must believe and I do believe that before too many years have passed we will realize that senseless tragedy and the witless futility of that "relic of human barbarism," capital punishment, and that we will have the courage and the vision to eliminate it.

I must die with the knowledge that I leave behind other men living out their last days on death row. I must say here that I know that the practice of man ritually and premeditatively killing man demeans and blasphemes our civilization while solving nothing. We must learn to forego hatred and vengeance for these breed a milieu that makes a rational or humane approach to the problem of what society can and should do about the man who has turned violently against his fellows—and himself—impossible. That problem cannot be buried with the body of the executed offender and his victims. It will not be buried with me. In my own way, I have done all in my power to focus attention on this problem, to make the world aware of death rows and execution chambers. I regard myself as neither hero nor martyr. On the contrary, I am a confessed fool who is keenly aware of the nature and quality of the folly of his earlier rebellious years. I do not mean to sound grand or didactic. But these are beliefs that burn brighter in me than hope for my own survival. In dying I must affirm them and express the final hope that those who have spoken out for me will continue to speak out against gas chambers and executioners and retributive justice. Surely we are worthy of better. My time has run out. I must close. Sincerely, [signed] Caryl Chessman.

I believe that these words will be heeded by future generations as they were howled down by ours.

It was no more popular to defend Chessman and other persons in the 1950s and '60s against the passion of the blood-thirsty than to oppose the execution of Bruno Hauptmann in 1936.

If such opposition to capital punishment in these cases aroused storms of protest in the community at large, caveats voiced against the death penalty imposed against Eichmann evoked even more violent protests in the Jewish world. What kind of Jew could one conceivably be who had reservations on this score? What manner of sensitivities—or insensitivities—did such a person possess? And yet, Eichmann was the ultimate test. If one opposed capital punishment in principle but felt compelled, because of the enormity of his crime, to except Eichmann, then no principle remained. Either capital punishment is immoral or it is not. We cannot have it both ways. That is why, joining with the miniscule minority of my fellow Jews, including the saintly Martin Buber, who urged that Eichmann's life be spared, I maintained that his death on the scaffold would not summon the six million murdered Jews from their martyred graves.

His death did not end the ache in the hearts of those whose loved ones disappeared into the crematoria. The one thing it might well have ended, however, was a sense of guilt unexpiated. His execution only perpetuated the foul illusion that this one man might somehow be equated with his countless victims and that his annihilation would magically vindicate the dead. How much better it would have been if a Jewish state, above any other, could have achieved the moral grandeur to rise above incalculable sorrow and say: We will not take a life, no matter how wretched. Despite everything, we continue to believe in the sanctity of the human personality.

I do say "a Jewish state *above any other*" despite the protests that rise from those who are content to have the State of Israel be in every respect *Kechol ha-goyim* (like all nations) and who would echo the youthful Israeli zealot who declared that he resented all this appeal for a higher morality on the part of Israel. "Just give us a bit of good old downright normality," he insisted. He protested that Jews have for too long been dubbed subnormal by their enemies and regarded chauvinistically as supranormal by their own "chosen people" theology. He wanted no part of either. Just to be normal. Normal, in the sense, I suppose, of "My country right or wrong." But if we have a right to expect America with its Judeo-Christian rootage to rise to its high-born part—above the sheer level of animal survival—surely we have a similar justification to desire that Israel be unlike any other nation in its fealty to the unique moral teachings of Judaism. The prophets of Israel sought no simple normality either on the part of the individual or the state. They demanded that both be "servants of God," unreservedly obedient to His will.

Max Lerner has written that Adolf Eichmann and the Nazi leaders had placed themselves "above and outside of humanity" and that, therefore, the issue of capital punishment in relation to Eichmann was grotesquely academic. Abba Eban, in an eloquent summation, stated that the theme of the Jerusalem courtroom "was the unending tension between the sublime attributes of man's nature and his unlimited capacity to distort the human image. And, in this conflict our generation has lived the moments of greatest defeat."

Yet, to the contrary, there were those who viewed the execution of Eichmann as a failure of moral courage, as a lost opportunity to say No to the spilling of blood and Yes to the sanctity of the human personality. The Central Conference of American Rabbis, in a dramatic last-minute representation, cabled the President of Israel to exercise clemency. Although, understandably, a few Reform rabbis took sharp exception to this action, the plea was sustained overwhelmingly by hundreds of Reform rabbis at the subsequent national convention of the CCAR. I voted to sustain the action of the officers of the Conference. No one of us had any desire to embarrass the State of Israel or to make a *cause célèbre* out of so ignoble a character as Eichmann. But my conscience was troubled—and still is—by the conviction that Israel must be more than a normal nation "like all the other nations" of the world; and by the profound wish that, however cruel the provocation, Israel could have summoned the strength to rise to the moral heights of mercy, standing tall before the world as a "light unto the nations."

Capital punishment is an affront to the spirit of Judaism. While supporters of capital punishment glibly and piously quote "an eye for an eye, a tooth for a tooth, and a life for a life" from the Old Testament, they neglect to mention the prophet Ezekiel's categoric statement: "Behold I desire not the death of the sinner, but that he should live, saith the Lord." Moreover, the moral genius of Judaism is not confined to the Bible; it was matured and refined in Jewish law as expressed in the rabbinic literature and in the Talmud. Revulsion against capital punishment was clearly evident in the evolution of Jewish ethics. Even the Bible waived capital punishment for the most serious offenses, based on the principle that they cannot be atoned for by execution, and substituted for the death penalty the *Kareth,* i.e., the "cutting off" of the sinner from eternal bliss—but by Providence, not by any human agency.

Of course, in many instances the Bible still prescribes capital punishment, but so numerous were the restrictions as Jewish law evolved (in Mishnah Sanhedrin 8) that it is quite clear that the effect was to nullify the death penalty. The abhorrence of shedding blood is evident in the painstaking procedure the rabbis erected. Only deliberate murder was punishable by death. The murderer had to know and acknowledge the nature of his crime *before* he committed it. At least two eye-witnesses were required. The judges, selected with utmost rigor, were required to examine and cross-examine the witnesses most diligently, and if any one of the witnesses should be incapable of answering one of the inquiries properly, all witnesses were disqualified. The judges had to admonish the witnesses in these words: ". . . the blood (of the accused) and of his descendants clings (to the false witness) to the end of time." The rabbis also taught that "whosoever preserves the life of one person, it is as though he saves a multitude of men. But he who destroys the life of one man, it is as though he destroys the world." We are also told that "the divine presence is sore troubled at the shedding of the blood of the convict."

These—and hundreds of similarly scrupulous regulations—testify to the horror which the rabbis felt at the taking of a life. They had grave doubts about the infallibility of men, including themselves. To them, love and compassion were the foremost duties of man towards their fellow-men.

Rabbi Eliezer ben Azaryah said that, if he were in the Sanhedrin, capital punishment would be applied only once in seventy years. To which Rabbi Tarphon and Rabbi Akiba exclaimed: if we were in the Sanhedrin, nobody would ever be subjected to capital punishment. Thus, while capital punishment was not avowedly abolished in Jewish teachings, the practice of it was so fenced in by virtually insuperable qualifications that, in effect, it was rarely imposed. Today most Jewish organizations, whether liberal or traditional, have condemned capital punishment as antagonistic to the principles and values of Judaism.

And capital punishment is wrong also on practical grounds. The death penalty is an anachronistic relic, out of place in civilized society. Does it deter the murderer? Recently, in Wilmington, Delaware, a city detective got into a heated argument with his minister about this question. The minister insisted that capital punishment does not deter, and he lamented the fact that the state legislature had just restored the practice of capital punishment. The detective mocked his pastor's sentimentality and insisted that the *only* thing which deterred a murderer was the knowledge that his own life would be forfeited if he committed a capital offense. A few weeks later that same detective murdered his wife and became the first person to face the freshly restored death penalty of the state of Delaware.

A growing body of data, including the report of the British Royal Commission, clearly demonstrates the fallacy of capital punishment as a deterrent. Recent evidence also indicates that capital punishment is applied mostly to the poor, the weak, the friendless, and the non-white. A study found that from 1930 to 1952, 1,479 whites and 1,763 Negroes were executed in the U.S. Representing but 10 per cent of the population, Negroes produced over 50 per cent of the victims of capital punishment. Fred Cook concluded: "In seven Southern jurisdictions . . . while seventy-eight Negroes had been given the death penalty for rape during the twenty-four years studied, *not a single white man* had been executed. And this despite the fact that hundreds of whites were convicted in the same period for the same offense."

The late Lewis B. Lawes, long-time warden at Sing Sing, had perhaps as much experience with capital punishment as any other American. He once declared:

> The defendant of wealth and position never goes to the electric chair or to the gallows. Juries do not intentionally favor the rich. The law is theoretically impartial, but the defendant with ample means is able to have his case presented with every favorable aspect, while the defendant who is poor often has a lawyer assigned by the court. . . . Thus it (seldom happens) that a person who is able to have eminent defense attorneys is convicted of murder in the first degree, and very rare indeed that such a person is executed.

Capital punishment is nothing short of ritual murder, no less civilized than the cannibal boiling his brother man in oil. It is an irretrievable judgment perpetrated by fallible man. It brutalizes society. It is not surprising that many sensitive persons refuse, out of conscience, to serve on juries in capital cases. In my opinion, no state can affirm the sanctity of each human being while, at the same time, arrogating to itself the right to snuff out a God-created personality. Benjamin Cardozo, distinguished Justice of the Supreme Court, once wrote: "The next generation may look upon the death penalty as an anachronism too discordant to be suffered, mocking with grim reproach all our clamorous professions of the sanctity of life."

One of the most devastating indictments of capital punishment was contained in Albert Camus' essay entitled "Reflections on the Guillotine." If we really believed that capital punishment is a deterrent, Camus argued, we would not conduct our executions quietly and stealthily but would do so with the utmost of fanfare, preferably on television. Camus cited the innumerable studies which demonstrate no correlation between capital punishment and crime. He recited the many trivial crimes once punishable by death. He recalled some of the most horrendous cases of judicial murder in America and in France. He noted with horror the inhuman suffering inflicted not only upon the condemned but upon his family and loved ones. He showed how capital punishment brutalizes the executioner and the society of which the executioner is surrogate. In agony of spirit and shame of conscience, he cried out for an end to this medieval barbarism:

We scarcely need to point out how inapplicable the law of retaliation has become in our society: it is as excessive to punish the pyromaniac by setting his house on fire as it is insufficient to punish the thief by deducting from his bank account a sum equivalent to the amount he has stolen. Let us admit instead that it is just and even necessary to compensate the murder of the victim by the death of the murderer. But capital punishment is not merely death. It is as different, in its essence, from the suppression of life as a concentration camp from a prison. It is understandably a murder which arithmetically cancels out the murder already committed; but it also adds a regularization of death, a public premeditation of which its future victims are informed, an *organization* which in itself is a source of moral suffering more terrible than death. There is thus no real compensation, no equivalence. Many systems of law regard a premeditated crime as more serious than a crime of pure violence. But what is capital punishment if not the most premeditated of murders, to which no criminal act, no matter how calculated, can be compared? If there were to be a real equivalence, the death penalty would have to be pronounced upon a criminal who had forewarned his victim of the very moment he would put him to a horrible death, and who, from that time on, had kept him confined at his own discretion for a period of months. It is not in private life that one meets such monsters.

It is the value which we place upon the human being—a value derived initially from Judaism and subsequently from Christianity also

—which is the central motif of democracy. It is that—and not our differing economic system—which, at bottom, distinguishes democracy from Soviet Communism. Recently, the Soviet regime has reached a new nadir in degradation by making a variety of economic crimes punishable by death. That the Soviets thus hold human life so cheap is not surprising. But it is no less revolting that we, who cherish the human personality as endowed by God, should fail to sweep away the evil of capital punishment for any and all crimes.

As I indicated in 1936, the belief in redemption rather than retribution is the basic teaching of Judaism and Christianity. But when public passions boil up, it is the primitive roar for retribution—for vengeance —which usually overmasters the religious cry for redemption. If Oswald had not been wiped out, would we have tried to restore him to decency? Would we have called in the psychiatrists—who might have saved him as a youth in New York City—to try to rehabilitate him? To raise such questions is to earn the public opprobrium of "bleeding heart," of being a "softy," a "sentimental slob," an unrealistic "do-gooder." Yet human beings *can* be reclaimed. Human beings seemingly wholly depraved have been rehabilitated and restored to creative roles in society. Such redemptive power has been demonstrated in instances almost as repugnant as the Oswald case. The Leopold-Loeb murder of young Bobby Franks, to take but a single illustration, was dubbed, with excessive melodrama, the "crime of the century." It was a brutal, diabolical, sickening crime. Only the wizardry of Clarence Darrow snatched Nathan Leopold and Richard Loeb from the electric chair which an incensed public demanded. "How can we allow such monsters to live?" their contemporaries, with but few exceptions, challenged. Loeb was murdered in prison by a fellow inmate. Yet, Nathan Leopold, on the other hand, devoted his long years in prison to study, research, and medical service. For him, as for many others, suffering was redemptive. Leopold today is a free man and a useful citizen, dedicating himself to a quiet life of humane service as a medical aide in Puerto Rico. Would mankind be better served if he had been blotted out by capital punishment?

Nothing frightens me quite so much as our stubborn refusal to face such incontrovertible facts of the never-failing flexibility of every human being, of the too frequently overlooked truth that it is the nature of human nature to change, to respond to the redemptive power of care, solicitude, scientific therapy, and all-conquering love. In this nightmarish nuclear era, we bandy about the number of deaths—20 million or 40 million or 60 million—from an atomic attack. Thanks to the cool detachment of the modern breed of nuclear philosopher who does our thinking for us through the good offices of Rand Corporation, we hardly conceive of these possible casualties as human beings. They are megapersons. Automation, mass media, advertising, public relations—all the forces of modern life seem to conspire to rob us of our individuality, of our distinctive personalities. We are in mortal danger of dehumanization. All the more, therefore, does it become the paramount task of religion in our time to proclaim the power and preciousness of each individual child of God, derived from dust, to be sure, but dowered with and destined for divinity, of each human being who bears the stamp, not of a blind technology but of God Himself. Casting off the vestigial barbarism of the death penalty would be a long and heartening step toward a civilization based on humility, compassion, and humanity.

10

JESUS—MAN OF MY PEOPLE

FORETHOUGHT

Jesus was not merely a Jew by heredity. He remained within the Jewish fold until the very hour of his death when in agony of body and anguish of soul, he uttered the plaintive words of the Hebrew psalmist: "My God, my God, why hast Thou forsaken me?" Nor did he, as others maintain, wish it otherwise; he did not strain at the leash and seek to cast aside his Jewish heritage. On the contrary, he was conscious, even proudly conscious, of his Jewish derivation as well as of his debt of gratitude to his Jewish past. His noblest teachings were illustrated by citations from the Jewish scriptures, his most solemn admonitions and his most tender words were directed solely to his Jewish brethren. Jesus would not have been Jesus had he not profoundly loved the people from whose loins he sprang and from whose heart his life blood had been drawn, had he not been fully and gratefully conscious of his Hebraic heritage.

Toronto, 1934

AFTERTHOUGHTS

Those words, spoken in 1934 from my pulpit at Holy Blossom Temple in Toronto, touched off an explosion which, if not precisely as loud or far-reaching as the shots fired at Concord that were heard round the world, nevertheless resulted in a detonation that had its repercussions throughout the whole of Canada. Once again, I was placed on the blacklist by many of my Jewish brethren while, at the same time, I was accorded an unwarranted and embarrassing embrace into the arms of too many churchmen who likewise totally misunderstood and misconstrued my message. I was once more, in the lush and expressive language of the Yiddish press, described as a *mamzer* and *meshummed* and regarded by the Canadian religious press and many ministerial associations as a promising convert to the Christian fold. Both hasty conclusions were totally in error, as I shall attempt to demonstrate in this chapter.

Would those views excite the same violent emotions in today's more liberal climate? After all, as I have indicated elsewhere, the Jewish population of Canada at that time was predominantly foreign born, had emigrated directly to the Dominion from Eastern Europe, had known little, if anything, of the fresh, new currents of thought that were circulating through the academic worlds of the West, and as far as the name Jesus was concerned, still regarded it as anathema. And with good reason insofar as their background and personal experience were concerned. Not only from the blood-bespattered chapters of the early Christian era and the medieval lacerations of Inquisition and Crusades in which tens of thousands of their Jewish forebears had been slaughtered in cold blood; not alone from their scarlet-stained past, but from contemporary massacres and pogroms they knew only too well how frequently the name of Jesus had been taken in vain and his teachings had been blasphemed by the wholesale murder of myriads of Jews—all in the name of a loving so-called Saviour and of an allegedly forgiving, compassionate, redemptive faith. Hence I was neither stunned nor demolished by the explosion of 1934.

But I *was* shocked by a similarly violent reaction which recently attended an even more innocuous statement which I made at the Biennial Assembly of the Union of American Hebrew Congregations on November 17, 1963. Nearly three decades had elapsed since I had first uttered those thoughts. And I was addressing an assembly of delegates who had not just emerged from the incarceration of the ghettos. The great majority there gathered were university graduates, had taken courses in comparative religion, knew something of the forces of liberalism that are coming into the ascendancy in Christendom. I was especially distressed by the reaction of rabbis, reared in our Liberal Jewish tradition, who had supposedly been trained to examine all these facts on the basis of their respective merits. They, at least, it seemed to me, would not be triggered by that primitivism characteristic of the most orthodox of creeds. Most of them knew full well that what I said was not really new. In our own rabbinate, towering titans of the Jewish people such as the late Stephen S. Wise—who could not conceivably be dubbed "renegade" or "apostate"—had given voice to this same point of view. It was as early as December 20, 1925, that Wise uttered similar thoughts from his pulpit then in Carnegie Hall, New York. At that time, reviewing a scholarly book, *Jesus of Nazareth,* written in Hebrew in Palestine by an exceedingly pious and observant Orthodox Jew, Dr. Joseph Klausner, Wise stated:

> It marks the first chapter in a new literature. Such a book could never have been written a few years ago. You all know what would have happened to the Jew who would have dared to express his opinion based on facts—of Jesus a few years ago. Thank God the time has come when men are allowed to be frank, sincere and truthful in their beliefs. This book, overlooked by the press and handled wretchedly by reviewers who have missed the point completely, is the greatest book of its kind ever published.

But the time was not as liberal or as understanding as Wise had anticipated. He, too, was ripped to shreds by the Yiddish press, by the Orthodox rabbinate, while even some of his Reform rabbinic colleagues, such as Rabbi Samuel Schulman, bitterly attacked him from their pulpits. As always, it was not the substance, but the motivation that was subjected to ruthless attack. Said Schulman:

> The sensationalist of the Jewish pulpit seems to be again on the rampage. I have too much respect for the Christian religion to discuss Jesus in any such way. I consider Rabbi Wise's discussion of the whole question most superficial and sensational. . . . Now I have every reverence for the sincere manifestations of any form of the religious sentiment and Jewish teachers have always respected sincere Christian convictions, but as a Jew I differ from these convictions profoundly.

Far more devastating was the onslaught in the Yiddish Press:

> We have no objection when such statements are made by the Christians in Christian churches, but when a Rabbi says such things in a temple before Christians, it must call forth indignation and a feeling of disgust on our part. . . . The only thing this strange Diogenes-Rabbi can be in search of is to curry the favor of the Christian clergy which is extremely undignified for such a dignified Rabbi. . . . Such a Rabbi disgraces every Jewish movement in which he participates because it is not a Rabbi's business to preach Christianity to Jews especially since he is not sincere and merely seeks publicity.

But that was thirty-five years ago. And even then, though Wise had offered to resign from the chairmanship of the United Palestine Fund, his resignation was refused and he remained the titular head and recognized tribune of American and world Jewry despite his further insistence:

> What mournful commentary upon the infinite hurt which the Jew has suffered at the hands of Christendom that a Jewish teacher cannot even at this time speak of Jesus, his completely Jewish background and his ethical contribution to his time and for all time, without being hailed as a convert to Christianity or misunderstood by some of his fellow Jews to whom the centuries have, alas, made the Christian name synonymous with injustice and wrong.

Despite my awareness of this unhappy episode, surely, I thought, by the year 1963 the temper and climate of our time had worked some metamorphosis in the Jewish mind and spirit—the Reform or Liberal spirit and mind especially. It was impossible, I believed, that the mention, the sympathetic approach to the man, the Jew, Jesus, could still be regarded as heretical. I thought that the outreach of the American spirit had permeated the American Reform Jew as it had impelled Dr. Sandmel, the Provost of the Hebrew Union College–Jewish Institute of Religion, to write so vigorous an apologia for similar sentiments voiced still earlier by Isaac Mayer Wise, founder in 1873 of the Union of American Hebrew Congregations.

Thus Dr. Sandmel writes:

> The age-old antipathy, as reflected in the travesties on Jesus as in *Toldot Yeshu,* was inconsistent with an age of enlightenment and broad horizons. Moreover, there was no spiritual or physical ghetto in the United States, and Jews and Christians lived side by side in a relatively high state of harmony and good will. Christianity inevitably intruded into the consciousness of Jews and so did Jesus.
>
> Isaac Wise wrote as he did because he was Wise; he was moved so to write because no Jew breathing the free air of America could refrain from coming to grips in some way with Christianity and with Jesus. Indifference and total lack of contact were possible only in ghettos where medievalism had survived. Wise wrote because he had to write; he could not be the leader of an American Jewish community and not do so.

True, we Jews had known the horror of the Nazi holocaust in the interim—the mass incineration of millions of my brother Jews made possible by the deafening silence, not merely of a single Pope as the German play *The Deputy* rather myopically depicts it, but the roaring silence of virtually all who seemingly lent the consent of a so-called Christian West. As Hitler confessed, he had only to fan the latent sparks of anti-Semitism ever present in the hearts of the European peasant—sparks kindled by the distortions of the life and death of Jesus for which the writers of the Gospels and the early Fathers of the

Church were responsible. Hitler by no means invented the Nuremburg Laws; he merely plagiarized the writings of such early Church Fathers as Cyril of Jerusalem, Ambrose of Milan, and Chrysostom of Antioch whose viper-like reviling of the Jew led to the confiscation of Jewish property and the destruction of Jewish lives. While it must be admitted that there was nothing in those early days to match the ingenuity of Hitler's gas ovens and asphyxiation chambers, nevertheless, his burning of synagogues and his massacre of Jews (whatever the method) were likewise presaged by the similar practice of putting to flames Jewish houses of worship in the early centuries of the Christian Era and by the torture wheels and racks of the Inquisition.

It is this religion *about* Jesus, not the religion *of* Jesus, of which I recently spoke in Chicago, it is this religion about Jesus which I have frequently stressed from the pulpits of synagogues and of a multitude of churches and public platforms that does, with good reason, offend against Jews and truth. It is this religion about Jesus which, beyond any other contributing factor, has indeed whipped flames of anti-Jewish hostility into a centuries-long conflagration that consumed myriads of Jews in medieval autos-da-fé and reached its apogee of ignominy in our present age of Nazi genocide.

His New Testament narrative is so laden with miracle tales, is so psychologically doubtful, and is so self-contradictory that some scholars have even doubted that Jesus ever lived, yet, according to the latest Biblical research, it seems almost certain that Jesus was an historical personality. He was born in Galilee, reared in the tradition of the Pharisees, influenced by John the Baptist, and became a wandering teacher in a feverish time when Palestine knew many such itinerant religious men and alleged miracle workers. Together with his small group of zealous disciples, Jesus came to Jerusalem to observe the Passover Feast. At that festive time, with myriads of pilgrims in the Holy City, Jerusalem was electric with tension, as Jews from all over the nation gathered at the Temple, while the zealots continued to agitate for revolt against the despised Roman rulers. When Jesus was hailed as a Messiah, there was fear of an uprising against Rome. Jesus was seized, arrested, and executed by command of Pontius Pilate, Roman governor.

Jesus' disciples, like Jesus, as I shall seek to demonstrate in this chapter, had no intention of organizing a new religion. Like Jesus, these disciples were devoted Jews. In their visions, the crucified Jesus rose from the dead and promised to return to them. The story of the crucifixion and resurrection was reminiscent of the myth of many pagan cults which glorified great gods who died and were later returned to life.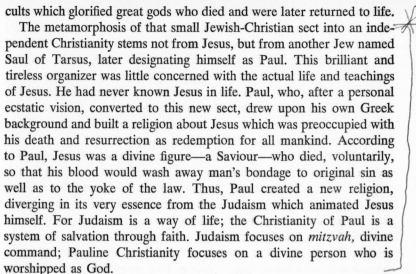

The metamorphosis of that small Jewish-Christian sect into an independent Christianity stems not from Jesus, but from another Jew named Saul of Tarsus, later designating himself as Paul. This brilliant and tireless organizer was little concerned with the actual life and teachings of Jesus. He had never known Jesus in life. Paul, who, after a personal ecstatic vision, converted to this new sect, drew upon his own Greek background and built a religion about Jesus which was preoccupied with his death and resurrection as redemption for all mankind. According to Paul, Jesus was a divine figure—a Saviour—who died, voluntarily, so that his blood would wash away man's bondage to original sin as well as to the yoke of the law. Thus, Paul created a new religion, diverging in its very essence from the Judaism which animated Jesus himself. For Judaism is a way of life; the Christianity of Paul is a system of salvation through faith. Judaism focuses on *mitzvah,* divine command; Pauline Christianity focuses on a divine person who is worshipped as God.

Thus the new faith became not only un-Jewish; it soon became bitterly anti-Jewish. The life of Jesus was reconstructed retroactively by hostile Gospel writers, writing one hundred years or more after the death of Jesus. Thus, Jesus was modified into an enemy of the Pharisees. Jews—some of whom were passionately devoted to Jesus, most of whom had never even heard of him—were portrayed as a howling, blood-thirsty, monolithic mob. The Sanhedrin—which had in reality been banned by the Romans—was portrayed as a foul den of schemers, meeting like a kangaroo court to try and to sentence the heretic in one night—something which was prohibited by Jewish law. A ridiculous custom—of releasing a condemned criminal in observance of the Passover—was manufactured out of whole cloth in order to show the Jews demanding the release of the lecherous, corrupt Barabbas and the crucifixion of the gentle Nazarene. The betrayal of Jesus is symbolized by the loathsome traitor Judas, who has come to symbolize the Jews as a group and has provided the hate-filled denouement of countless passion plays throughout the centuries. The Gospel writers etch the Jews in acid, while they portray Pilate as the epitome of the noble, humane, civilized Anglo-Saxon. Poor Pilate, who has the awesome might of the Roman empire in his person, must bargain with this foul-smelling throng of Jews!

Through the constant reading and rereading of this Gospel account and by witnessing the even more lurid and flesh-tingling Passion Plays enacted and reenacted through the ages—the blood-and-thunder antecedents of today's bang-bang TV fare—the innocence of the Romans, the guilt, the villainy, the venality of the Jews steeped deep into the brain and blood of generations of followers of him who said, "Blessed are the peacemakers." To Pilate comes the infuriated mob. From a soft whisper the oft-repeated refrain, "Crucify him, crucify him," mounts into a mighty, clamorous crescendo as the sky, the earth, the very hills of Jerusalem echo and re-echo and ring with that now deafening wail, "Crucify him, crucify him." But the calm and gentle Pilate remains obdurate and can still see no fault in Jesus.

Of course, neither Passion Play nor the Gospels, nor the ministers and priests who, year in and year out, repeat this tale seem in the slightest degree embarrassed by the inescapable verdict of history upon this same man Pilate. Of all the Roman Procurators whose presence cursed the Jewish nation before, during, and after the time of Jesus, history records the name of none quite so cruel as Pilate. So fiendish was he that even oppressive Rome was obliged to recall him because of his unprecedented tyranny. Even the New Testament recounts how the sword of Pilate mingled the blood of pilgrims with the blood of their sacrifices. The roads of Palestine were literally lined with corpses dangling from crosses which this same Pilate caused to be erected. And, what is far more significant than aught else besides, his own fellow Roman, Tacitus, the great historian, writing but a half-century after the death of Jesus, relates how Jesus had suffered death at the hands of Pontius Pilate and mentions not a single word about the Jews.

All this, however, is ignored in both the Gospels and the Passion Plays they inevitably inspired. Pilate refuses to pass the sentence of death. The Jewish mob, however, is restless and rebellious. So Pilate, although he has all the power of the Roman legions behind him, haggles with these Jews. First he suggests a compromise. Let us scourge the criminal and let him go. "No, no," the mob murmurs; "Crucify him, crucify him." Pilate tries another expedient. At this Passover season, he reminds them, it is the custom to release a condemned prisoner. He will give them the choice between the murderer Barabbas and the preacher Jesus. There they stand: the leering Barabbas; the majestic, silent Jesus. Could there possibly be any mistake as to which of these two men the Jewish masses who had learned so to love the Nazarene would have released? But no; all things satanic are presented as being possible for these Jews. The multitudes demand: "Give us Barabbas!" "Let Barabbas be free; crucify, crucify the Nazarene!" yell the priests and rabbis and people of Judea.

Pilate can no longer deny their ultimatum. Their wish is soon fulfilled. The Nazarene trudges wearily along bearing the heavy cross; he stumbles, he falls; he bids a last tearful farewell to his mother— and not a single Jewish heart relents. Ah no, this is a stubborn and stony-hearted, a "stiff-necked people." At Golgotha he arrives at last; hill of skulls where the common criminals are crucified. The hammers thud against the cross; the nails are driven deep into the tender flesh; the blood streams down over his quivering limbs, and with the whispered words of the Psalmist upon his lips: "My God, my God, why hast Thou forsaken me?" the tortured victim dies. Still no Jew relents; even then their hatred is not appeased as they begrudge him a decent burial place. While, again, it is supposedly through the always kindly intervention of the Roman alone that a suitable sepulcher is secured.

Such is the diabolical and fictitious portrait of the Jew which is burned deeply into the minds of unnumbered multitudes of Christian children the wide world over. Small wonder that often the first taunt a Jewish child hears is the mocking jibe of "Christ killer"; small wonder that, when economic crises come upon us, youthful zealots and fanatical students sally forth in crusades and pogroms of yesterday and in the gas-oven mass asphyxiations of our time to make the earth *Judenrein,* to rid all Christendom of the descendants of those whom early childhood impressions have made into a race of merciless deicides. Childhood suggestion is the most lasting and no amount of later culture and superficial propriety will wipe clean that first unhappy picture of the Jew. In times of emergency and stress, the veneer of civilization is scraped off, and the well-nigh infant memory of the Jew as the bloodthirsty murderer of the Christ plunges to the fore.

In her moving poem, "To a Christian Friend," Marie Syrkin has captured this painful irony of our history:

> There is something between us now:
> The cry you did not raise.
>
> You have washed your hands again.
> Put down the pitcher.
> This water will flow between us.
>
> Give me back Jesus;
> He is my brother.
> He will walk with me
> Behind the gray ghetto wall
> Into the slaughter-house.
> I will lead him into the lethal chamber;

He will lie down upon the poisoned stone;
The little children pricked with the death-bubble
Will come unto him.

Return to him the yellow badge.
Give me back Jesus;
He is not yours.

Now when will Christendom right this wrong? I, for one, welcome every effort, every gesture toward good will. I firmly believe that in every advance we make, Christian toward Jew and Jew toward Christian, we are moving nearer to that more perfect brotherhood to be. But I am realist enough to know that no amount of talking or even of laboring together in those vital causes common to us both will be of true and lasting worth until Christianity itself will have the honesty and courage to rewrite this Gospel tale, to tell to all the world how in those early days an inordinately ambitious church recognized that it could grow to power not through the lowly Jew but through the mighty Roman; how, therefore, in order to achieve this greatest diplomatic feat of all history, it found it necessary to remove from the hand of Rome every vestige of guilt in connection with the crucifixion of the Christ it was asking Rome to worship, and to place the entire stigma upon the Roman-conquered, Roman-persecuted, and now both Roman- and Christian-hated Jew who refused still so obstinately to acknowledge their god as "the Saviour." And may I add that almost every Christian student of the Bible and of early church history worthy of the name admits as much today. Whey then must the church itself, its Popes and archbishops, its cardinals and ministers and priests, once again lag so miserably behind? Why the hesitations, compromises, procrastinations of the Vatican Ecumenical Council to implement the will and testament of Pope John XXIII to right this flagrant historic wrong?

No, it is not the life of Jesus which we must oppose, but the false and murderous anti-Jewish ingredients which were grafted onto the creation of a religion about Jesus. It is no wonder that Jews, hounded and harassed through the centuries in the name of Jesus, should for so long a time have contemplated the very mention of his name with revulsion and fear. Surely, the time has come for Christianity to eliminate its scandalous anti-Jewishness—a Christianity which expects Jews not to blame Christians for the death of six million Jews in this generation, but which still persists in falsely blaming Jews for the death of one man 2,000 years ago.

That is why Jews and even multitudes of Christians, weary of this dreary, demonic record of discrimination and death, look with such eager anticipation to the results of the wrestling of the Catholic Church with this historic libel, with this theological paradox (for if the Passion and Crucifixion and Resurrection of the Christ are prerequisites of salvation, then glory be to whomever may have been God's instrument in effectuating this supposed divine objective and let the Jews be praised "forever and ever, amen," instead of denigrating and massacring them). That is why we are so hopeful that, despite the aforementioned delays, the valiant efforts of the late Jope John and the present Pope Paul, of their more liberal adherents in the far-from-monolithic Church of Rome, will bear rich and far-reaching fruitage; that is why we have been gratified likewise by the rewriting of many a previously prejudice-producing Protestant textbook. That is why, in the light of the new breeze that is blowing throughout Christendom, I was so startled by the adverse reaction of not a few of my Reform Jewish colleagues to my words in 1963.

I firmly believed that the recent ecumenicity of the Catholic Church, under the stimulus and challenge of Pope John XXIII, with his insistence on the deletion of that too-long-repeated reference in Catholic liturgy to the "perifidious Jew" and his determination to cleanse the Church of the charge of deicide against Jews, was a revolutionary event. I felt too that, in the light of the apocalyptic age in which we are living, with unprecedented hatreds and unrestrained violence on the one hand and the thrust for understanding and brotherhood on the other, that the hour had come when the Jew too must manifest his own deeper understanding and more scrupulous reexamination of those aspects of his own teaching—or lack of teaching—that have been predicated not necessarily on historic fact or religious and moral consistency, but upon hitherto understandable existential circumstances. Not as any *quid pro quo* which would be a gratuitous insult to any church that could be so cheaply bribed as well as to any Jew who would so brazenly barter his conviction, but to share in the opening of windows to let in more fresh air, to stretch forth one's own hands to match the outreach of the nobler spirits of our day.

Consequently, quite innocuously, so I thought, I called upon my fellow Reform Jews—not all my brethren—but upon my fellow Reform Jews, who boast of the liberalism of our faith, to reassess our liberal Jewish attitude to Jesus. I sought to suggest, in short, that in the mood and temper of our time, the only counterforce to prejudice, bigotry, and violence must be the stretching of all our minds and spirits beyond the narrow, rigid domain of our own once sacrosanct precepts and precincts. In a day when even such a long-hallowed dogma as the infallibility of the Pope is being subjected by Roman Catholics to reevaluation, when the teaching of the centuries-old doctrine of the "just war" is being reassessed, I inquired as to what conceivable reason there could be for any hesitation on the part of Reform Judaism to reexamine its attitude to Jesus. To Jesus, I repeat, to Jesus, the man, the Jew; to Jesus, the good man and not the sole God-man; not to the Christ, the "only begotten son of God," the so-called Messiah.

I requested a study in order to determine whether our attitude would be precisely the same as it was during the first centuries of the current era when so many thousands of Jews were martyred by Christians in the name of him whom they called "Lord, Lord,"—whether it was identical with the attitude bred of medieval Crusade and Inquisition when once more multitudes of my Jewish forebears were torn limb from limb on wheels of torture or burned to ashes in autos-da-fé in the name of the Prince of Peace. I felt that, despite the barbaric atavism of Nazism and our having more recently jettisoned our erstwhile naivete concerning man's innate humanity to man, we had emerged from the Middle Ages and could look the most heterodox of notions squarely in the face. Hence, in my Presidential Message to the Forty-Seventh General Assembly of the Union of American Hebrew Congregations in 1963, I called for a more rational approach to the name Jesus. I said:

> How long can we persist in ignoring the lofty and yet so simply stated prophetic and rabbinic teachings of Jesus, merely on the grounds that he repeated much that was voiced by his prophetic predecessors and rabbinic contemporaries? Was Micah more spiritually and morally original than Amos and Hosea? Does none of the rabbis we revere and whose utterances we have our children master repeat each other? How long shall we continue to aver that the chief contribution of Jesus was simply a rehash of all that had been said before by his Jewish ancestors? How long before we can admit that his influence was a beneficial one—not only to the pagans but to the Jews of his time as well, and that only those who later took his name in vain profaned his teaching?

I did not predict the outcome of such an exploration. It might conceivably conclude that there has been no change, no fundamental reason for such a transformation of opinion. I would hope and I do believe that such would not be the case. But I made no prognostication. Yet, even this harmless appeal for some objective study of this long controversial subject on the part of liberal Jews was greeted with an almost wholly visceral and vehement rejection—not so much by laymen, but by many rabbis to whom it seems the very mention of the name of Jesus is still forbidden.

I was treated to a vicious attack from one of the leaders of our Reform Jewish movement notwithstanding his own written declaration of respect and esteem for Jesus. *Time* magazine on December 13, 1963 carried a report of the scathing rebuke of my views by Dr. Nelson Glueck, President of the Hebrew Union College–Jewish Institute of Religion. But in his own volume, *The River Jordan,* Dr. Glueck states:

> Jesus was of the spiritual stock of Jeremiah, who spoke in the name of God. Jesus was also of the same prophetic background as Amos, who had said: "The Lord hath spoken. Who can but prophesy?" (Amos 3:8).
> In the same prophetic tradition Jesus continued to teach and interpret the Torah. Few in his generation were more familiar with its basic principles and enduring significance than this young Rabbi.

In his *Rivers in the Desert,* he adds:

> Throughout the entire history of Israel, the physical and spiritual influence of Sinai and the Negev remained paramount. The understanding of God's will achieved there has been transmitted over the centuries through such elect of the Lord as Elijah and Jeremiah and Hillel and Jesus.

Similar sentiments were expressed by the sainted Dr. Leo Baeck, the most distinguished rabbi of Hitlerite Europe. Writing in his *Judaism and Christianity—The Gospel As a Document of History,* he said:

> In the old Gospel which is thus opened up before us, we encounter a man with noble features who lived in the land of the Jews in tense and excited times and helped and labored and suffered and died: a man out of the Jewish people who walked on Jewish paths with Jewish faith and hopes.
> . . . we behold a man who is Jewish in every feature and trait of his character, manifesting in every particular what is pure and good in Judaism. This man could have developed as he came to be only on the soil of Judaism; and only on this soil, too, could he find his disciples and followers as they were. Here alone, in this Jewish sphere, in this Jewish atmosphere of trust and longing, could this man live his life and meet his death—a Jew among Jews; *Jewish history and Jewish reflection may not pass him by nor ignore him. Since he was, no time has been without him; nor has there been a time which was not challenged by the epoch that would consider him its starting point.* [author's italics]
> When this old tradition confronts us in this manner, then the Gospel, which was originally something Jewish, becomes a book—and certainly not a minor work—within Jewish literature. . . . it is a Jewish book because . . . the pure air of which it is full and which it breathes is that of the Holy Scriptures; because a Jewish spirit, and none other, lives in it; because Jewish faith and Jewish hope, Jewish suffering and Jewish distress, Jewish knowledge and Jewish expectations, and these alone, resound through it— a Jewish book in the midst of Jewish books. Judaism may not pass it by, nor mistake it, nor wish to give up all claims here. Here, too, Judaism should comprehend and take note of what is its own.

Much, much earlier one of the greatest Jewish philosophers of all time, Maimonides, writing in the twelfth century, described Jesus as "one who prepared the way for the Messianic King."

And one of the most brilliant leaders of contemporary Conservative Judaism, the late Rabbi Milton Steinberg, affirmed:

> To Jews . . . Jesus appears as an extraordinarily beautiful and noble spirit, aglow with love and pity for men, especially for the unfortunate and lost, deep in piety, of keen insight into human nature, endowed with a brilliant gift of parable and epigram, an ardent Jew moreover, a firm believer in the faith of his people; all in all, a dedicated teacher of the principles, religious and ethical, of Judaism.

Why then in the light of such antecedent statements as these, should there have been an outcry in the United States in 1963 similar to that storm which arose in Canada in 1934?

Primarily because "nobody listens." Nobody actually hears what another has to say in these hectic, hurried, harried days. We talk but we do not communicate. So headline writers splashed across their front pages the altogether inaccurate sensational headlines that "Reform Jewish Leader Urges Jews Accept Jesus" and torrents of letters flooded my desk welcoming me to the fold of Christendom since the word "accept," which I vigilantly desisted from using, has specific implications for the vast majority of Christians. And Jews also reading such misleading headlines acclaimed me anew as a bastard and a renegade.

But, of course, I have never spoken of "accepting" Jesus in the Christian sense of that term. I have called for a reevaluation of his role as a Jewish teacher. And because there is still so much confusion and misunderstanding on this subject it is imperative to repeat some of the reasons for what I regard as a necessary transcendence of past parochial considerations on the part of both Christians and Jews.

Who really was this Jesus? That is indeed the crucial question and upon the answer thereto men have been divided into many hostile camps almost from the very moment of his birth, certainly from the agonizing hour of his death upon the cross of Calvary. Prince of Peace he was called, yet quite literally, in his own words, did he apparently "bring a sword" which has cleft in twain great numbers of his fellow men whom he strove so valiantly, and apparently so vainly, to teach the saving grace of love. Who was this person then who bore the name of Jesus, this name which multitudes repeat in hushed and reverent whispers and others still altogether reject?

"He was the first Christian, the founder of our faith," spontaneously answer the host of followers who call themselves by his name. "He was a renegade Jew, a destroyer of his father's faith, an iconoclastic foe of Israel's sacred Torah," assert great numbers of my Jewish brethren who have often read not a word of the New Testament. "He is a myth," say a few heretical scholars, to which the rabid Communists and the dogmatic atheists shout a unanimous "Amen." "He was a 100 per cent Aryan, nothing less blue than the blood of the Indo-European coursed through his veins," wrote Houston Stewart Chamberlain in his *Foundation of the Nineteenth Century,* while his Nazi compatriots plagiarized these writings and sought to impress the world with their ostensibly original "discovery" that a good and noble Galilean could not possibly have been other than a Nordic.

"Jesus was the first anti-Semite" chimed in *Reichsbishopf* Mueller, swastika-spangled, bemedaled dictator of the official German church as his followers, thus self-righteously assured of the Scriptural validity of their hatreds, proceeded to annihilate the Jew, the people from whom he was descended. The first Christian, a renegade Jew, a myth, an Aryan, the first anti-Semite—such are but a few of the welter of confused and contradictory answers which greet our simple query as to just who was this being to whom Christians pay homage.

And while it would take not merely many chapters but many volumes to present even the briefest summary of all the arguments that have been written to substantiate each one of these divergent claims, I make bold to suggest that Jesus played none of these roles that are more commonly ascribed to him. That he was neither an Aryan nor an anti-Semite we will not even pause to prove since all scholars in this field, as well as all truly pious Christians, recognize that this was but the jaundiced aberration of a megalomaniacal regime which twisted every fact of history to fit its own fantastic theories, which likewise twisted the cross on which a martyred Jew pleaded, "Forgive them, Father, for they know not what they do" into the menacing and murder-mongering swastika.

That Jesus was not a myth, but a living personality, seems to be the accepted conclusion of most authoritative thinkers of our time. There was a period, to be sure, not so very long ago, when the historicity of Jesus was seriously challenged, not merely by Jews, mind you—but by notable non-Jewish scholars. This theory, however, seems to be waning today, and few are the serious students of the past who cling to the notion that the towering figure of Jesus was but the figment of his followers' imaginations. Besides, as the eminent and scholarly Rabbi Solomon Freehof intimates, the image and impact of his personality remain whether he lived or not—precisely as the moral messages of the Hebrew partiarchs are treasured whether they be fact or fiction. Thus, Dr. Freehof writes:

> Jesus was an extraordinary man. It was his version of Jewish ethical idealism which conquered the western world and changed the course of human history. Even granting Paul's exceptional eloquence and the influence and the interplay of historical forces, the power of Jesus' name could only have been so magnetic, if Jesus possessed some particular kinship with the infinite. . . . The genius of Jesus is not one of doctrine nor of organization. These things were added to him. It is distinctly one of direct influence. He brought God near to men, through his presence.

So while I could cover many pages with each one of these suggested answers, suffice it to conclude that the verdict as dictated by an overwhelming number of scholarly evidences categorically denies that Jesus was either an Aryan, or a myth.

But with regard to the other suggestions I cannot be so dogmatic. Hosts of Jews still maintain that he was a renegade Jew while the multitudes in Christendom acclaim him the founder of their church, the first and foremost Christian of them all. To dispute either contention demands much proof and it is to this facet of our theme that I now must turn.

But for what purpose, some inquire? What practical difference does it make? Granted that rabbis and ministers and scholars and teachers may be concerned with such a problem, why consume the average reader's valuable time with such a purely theoretical question? But this is not a *theoretical* proposition at all; it is one of the most practical problems of our day. On it may depend the very survival of Christianity itself. On it hinges the whole future relationship between Christian and Jew even as its former answers dictated the centuries of hatred and persecution that have gone before. On it is contingent our moral justification or our obstinacy in remaining Jews, in resisting still the tendency of all ages, of even our enlightened era as well, the tendency of compelling us to think and act and believe as the Christian. The question as to who actually was this personality whom all Christendom worships is among the most vital and timely and practical problems of our day.

"But surely," the dogmatic Christian and the queasy Jew will challenge, "you will not have the audacity to assert or to try to prove that Jesus was anything but a heretical Jew and a faithful Christian." That he was born a Jew I may well be permitted to maintain, for even the Scriptures written by his most loyal followers specifically assert that "he came unto *his own*" and for 1900 years *his own* have been despised because allegedly they rejected "their flesh and blood." "Granted that

Jesus was by birth a Jew," such will continue, "it cannot be denied in the face of equally antagonistic Jewish and Christian opinion, that he did not depart far from the people from whose midst he sprang to found a new and altogether different dispensation." But that is exactly what I intend to do and I am confident that I shall have little difficulty in doing so except in the sight of those who are too doctrinaire and bigoted to hearken to the argument of history and the irrefutable findings of contemporary Biblical science. For after long and painstaking study of these sources, it is my humble judgment that Jesus was neither an apostate Jew nor an original Christian, but was naught other than a loyal and devoted son of Israel.

Nor need the more pious Christians be angered by this apparent irreverence of a Jew, this seeming—though far from real—desire of a rabbi in Israel to deprecate the teaching of him whom millions call their master. There is no occasion to rise up in protest against what may be designated as this latest example of the "Anti-Christ," for what I have just written is far from new. It is not my original discovery. It is not the satanic affirmation of some "Christ-denying Hebrew." As a matter of fact, it was, ironically enough, Julius Wellhausen, the great German scholar, that renowned Christian student of the Scriptures, who never, by the way, had the reputation of being philo-Semitic, but who, in his *Einleitung in die Drei Ersten Evangelein,* wrote these words: *"Jesus was not a Christian, he was a Jew*. He did not preach a new faith, but taught men to do the will of God, and in his opinion as also in the opinion of the Jews, that will of God was to be found *in the law of Moses and in the other books of Scripture."* It was in 1905 that Wellhausen wrote those words and, while to this day practically every notable Biblical scholar—whether he be a Christian such as Professor Shirley Jackson Case of the University of Chicago, or the Reverend James Parkes, or a Jew such as Dr. Joseph Klausner of the Hebrew University at Jerusalem—both Jewish and Christian thinkers, alike, have added voluminous evidence to prove the conclusion of this German pioneer among the Biblical scientists, still do the masses both in Jewry and in Christendom contend, the former in lamentation and the latter in ecstatic joy, that Jesus was the founder of a new and altogether different faith from that which as a boy he imbibed from his rabbinic teachers.

But, some may aver, even though at first he may have been thus duly appreciative of his native background, at least later he rose far above and beyond it, to proclaim a message that was so radical and revolutionary as to have aroused the frenzied and fanatical opposition of the

Pharisees to such an extent, even though we may be generous enough to grant that they did not themselves put him to death, at least they plotted his downfall and sought to betray him to the political rulers of the day. How else can we explain the vehement denunciations vented against the Scribes and Pharisees whom even the gentle Jesus felt constrained to call "vipers and hypocrites?"

Again the answer to this stock argument is complicated and long and would take us far afield into a historic reconstruction of that entire chaotic period in which Jesus lived. But this much I must ask every interested reader to do. By all means read the great English scholar Trevors Herford's several magnificent volumes on the Pharisees so that it will become crystal clear that, far from the viperous hypocrites which certain passages of the Gospels portray, far from the enemies of Jesus therein depicted, these Pharisees were, in reality, the steadfast guardians of Israel's religious well-being who alone saved its faith and its Scriptures from being polluted and lost amid the threatening paganisms of Jesus' day. As Shirley Jackson Case in his volume *Jesus* puts it: "They were the group who had done most to keep alive the ideal of devotion to the will of God in daily living and—*in his sympathies and aims, Jesus had more in common with them than with any other Jewish party of his day."*

Thus Jesus himself was a Pharisee of the Pharisees. He feasted with them and worshipped at their side. He preached in their synagogues and learned from their law and to these very Pharisees he gave the solemn assurance: *"Until heaven and earth pass away, one jot or tittle shall in no wise pass from the Law. . . . Think not that I have come to destroy the Law or the prophets. I am come not to destroy but to fulfill."* To fulfill, in the sense of amplifying, enlarging, and deepening rather than of abrogating or negating the Torah of the Pharisees and Scribes.

Whence then came such bitter denunciations as we read in the Gospels? Well, do not take my word for it, but read Case and Herford, the late George Foote Moore of Harvard, and James Parkes of England— all eminent Christian scholars—as they unite in telling us that it was only following the death of Jesus that his much too zealous and overly fanatical followers, feeling that the Law was a stumbling block in winning the pagan to their newly founded cult and fearing that the Pharisees were preventing many pious Jews from joining their movement, composed these more venomous passages, and rather dishonestly imputed them to their master, as they interpolated them into the New Testament text.

By this I do not for a moment imply that Jesus had no quarrels with the Pharisees or with the rest of his fellow Jews. Undoubtedly, he had. It was inevitable that he should. So had Amos and Isaiah and Jeremiah battled and challenged their coreligionists. So likewise Hillel differed from many of his contemporaries when he defined the whole substance of Judaism as being but the observance of the Golden Rule. So profound a spiritual being as Jesus, to whom religion was expressed in the intimate relationship of man to God, could not but have grown impatient with much of the minutiae of the Law. But this did not in any wise place him beyond the pale. Even when, in justifying his healing of the sick on the Sabbath, he declared that the "Sabbath was made for man, rather than man for the Sabbath," he was voicing no fundamental heresy. Long before, Rabbi Jonathan ben Joseph had specifically declared: "The Sabbath was given into your hands, ye were not given into its hands." And had not the rabbis asserted that even the most sacred requirements of the Torah, Jews might set aside, even the Day of Atonement fast could be broken, if thereby a human life could be saved. Thus, with regard to this alleged breach with Judaism, Jesus went no further than many of his more liberal rabbinic predecessors and contemporaries.

And surely there was nothing un-Jewish or treasonable in his denunciation of the pompous Temple piety, or in his driving of the money changers from its midst. Long before him, Jeremiah had spoken even more caustically than did he concerning the abuses of its would-be worshippers and priests. Jesus, like his prophetic forebears, bitterly chastised his brethren. But he did not hate them. He was not "the first anti-Semite" merely because he found reason to criticize his compatriots and sought to correct their shortcomings. At no time did he despise them, nor forsake them. He would not have been Jesus, if he had.

Nothing is a grosser distortion of the truth than the long-cherished delusion that Jesus taught a doctrine which alienated him from the main body of his fellow Jews. He may have alarmed a few Sadducean aristocrats, terrorized by his economic radicalism. Even some of the more pietistic Pharisees were probably disturbed by his occasional latitude with regard to rabbinic authority. But this did not lessen the love and pity which he bestowed upon the masses, the *Jewish* masses; nor mitigate the affection wherewith he was cherished by those multitudes of Jews who exultantly welcomed him to Jerusalem and who so solemnly and sadly followed him to the hill of Calvary, those Jews who so bitterly wept for him as the callous Romans cast dice for his garments and taunted him upon the cross.

For there was really no reason for the main body of the Jews to have done otherwise. His entire ministry had been saturated with love for his people and loyalty to it. His kindliness and forbearance, his unbounded humanity, had swiftly won the multitudes to his side and almost inevitably he had become their hope for deliverance from Roman tyranny. Whenever Israel was heavy laden and oppressed, her people longed for "a sprout of Jesse," for a descendant of David who would throw off their yoke and free them from the oppressive foe. Thus under the ruthless rule of Rome never had this hope been so pronounced, so fervent as it was during the lifetime of Jesus.

And, as he gathered the multitudes about him and preached of the imminent coming of God's kingdom, they were indeed tempted to believe him and to proclaim him their long-awaited Messiah who would redeem them—and here I must tread cautiously and make myself clearly understood—redeem them, not vicariously from some metaphysical "original sin" in order to assure them some mystic and magic "salvation," but redeem them quite realistically from the grinding heel of Rome and restore them to their pristine estate as a free and happy commonwealth. And if Jesus allowed his disciples to call him the Christ, or the Messiah, which is the meaning of that word, *that is all that he implied* and that too was in no wise alien to Jewish tradition. It was only later when his disappointed fellow Jews saw that they had been deluded, that none of the promises of the Messianic Age had been fulfilled, that neither peace nor freedom, nor tranquillity nor the reign of righteousness had been established through Jesus' life and death, it was only then that they rejected, *not his character or personality or deed, but merely his alleged Messiahship,* even as Jesus himself would have done had he witnessed the confusion which followed upon his death, had he beheld how far from realization, even to this day, is the kingdom which he had proclaimed.

Surely one cannot challenge so illustrious a Christian theologian as Lyman Abbott, who writes in his *What Christianity Means To Me:*

But when I came to study the teachings of Jesus . . . I found that he never mentioned vicarious atonement nor the Fall of Adam nor the Trinity. . . .

Nor did I find in Christ's teaching any provision of a new theology or a new ecclesiastical system to take the place of the old. . . .

Born a Jew, he remained a Jew to the day of his death. . . .

The notion that Jesus organized a Christian church to take the place of the decaying Jewish church has very little evidence to support it. . . .

The institutions of Christianity, however important they may be, were not framed by Christ and imposed on his followers. They were gradually *developed by his followers after his death.* . . . [author's italics]

Christianity converted paganism, but paganism changed Christianity. . . .

And that paganism, I repeat, which grew up *about* Jesus was far different from the religion *of* Jesus, from the religion which Jesus himself had practiced and preached. The former became Christianity, or the cult which grew out of the concept of Jesus' alleged supernatural Christship, or Messiahship. The latter—the religion of Jesus—was, and is to this very day, *pure and unadulterated Judaism.*

Even those Jews who shout *touché* as they talk of Jesus' celibacy as testimony to his departure from Judaism forget that Jeremiah was a celibate who, according to Professor Max Margolis, in his article in the *Jewish Encyclopedia,* because of his certitude of impending doom, discouraged giving birth to a new generation destined to imminent destruction. To be sure, Judaism as a whole departed far from any such a celibate tradition (and so did Christianity). Judaism has indeed deprecated asceticism because of its emphasis on the blessings of family life and on obedience to the command to "be fruitful and multiply." Yet, as Margolis maintains in this same article, the Essenes too were celibates. According to Josephus, marriage was specifically repudiated by some of the Essenes. Some even went much further and anticipated some of the more extreme statements of Paul, indicating that among the Essenes were those who "regarded intercourse as polluting the aspirations to the highest degree of Levitical purity, and whose passion for sanctity may have led them to the rejection of marriage." So Jesus was not the only Jew to be a bachelor in his early thirties.

And this I say not cheaply to disparage Jesus, which is the rationale of so many of my fellow Jews who disregard him, decline to teach of him in our Jewish schools or quote his writings from their pulpit because of his alleged lack of any originality. For what, after all, is originality?

We could do no better than accept a definition offered by Hazlitt.

Genius or originality is for the most part some strong quality in the mind, answering to and bringing out some new and striking quality in nature. . . . This is the test and triumph of originality, not to show us what has never been, and what we may therefore very easily never have dreamt of, but to point out to us what is before our eyes and under our feet, though we have had no suspicion of its existence, for want of sufficient strength of intuition, of determined grasp of mind, to seize and retain it.

I do so to demonstrate Jesus' genuine fidelity to his Hebrew past and to plead for his retention, or rather his reclamation, as one of Israel's noblest teachers. Granted even that every thought which Jesus uttered had been previously anticipated in Israel, surely this is no valid reason to cast him off or to hold him in disdain, as less truly in the Jewish tradition than Amos or Hosea, or let us say, than Nahum and Nehemiah. And yet, all those are regarded as among our treasured Hebrew masters whose ofttimes repetitive messages are taught to our children, while Jesus' golden words are scrupulously avoided in our Jewish schools.

What was there of originality in Micah? Yet with what rapturous nuances do we repeat his famous definition of religion—"to do justly, to love mercy, to walk humbly with God"—even though this was but a paraphrase, a synthesis of his prophetic predecessors. Granted that from as early as Tertullian, the Sermon on the Mount has been traced back verse by verse to similar sentences spoken by the prophets and rabbis, still that does not in any wise mar the sublime beauty of that sermon as a whole any more than the recurrence of Beethoven's "Ode to Joy" in one of Brahms' symphonies proclaims the latter a thieving plagiarist.

Brahms, like all the other great composers, took a simple tune and through the power of his supreme musical genius converted it into something that was distinctively his own. So did Jesus absorb the ethical ideals and moral values which were an integral part of his Hebraic environment and, through the spiritual genius which was his, gave them a fresh interpretation. In short, *he made them his own.* At no time did he himself profess that he was saying anything that had never been said before. How could he, in view of what he had read in, and what he so frequently quoted from, the Prophets and the Psalms? But he did try, and to a remarkable degree he succeeded, in teaching these essential truths and central principles of the religious life in his own way, through his own experience, and through the power and example of his own personality, a personality which in some respects was more picturesque and magnetic than those of at least some of the prophets who had preceded him, a personality which therefore brought still nearer to the masses the lofty teachings of our Jewish faith.

Would that I could take these teachings one by one in order to demonstrate just how essentially and indubitably Jewish they really are, and how dishonest and benighted are such opinions which often come even from the pens of the scholarly, to the effect that "to the base materialism of the Hebrew, Jesus opposed the loftiest idealism which marked a complete reversal of Jewish ideas." But this too is beyond the scope of such a chapter as this. To the student I might commend the four monumental volumes of Strack and Billerbeck who take each and every phrase of Jesus and trace them back to their Talmudic and Midrashic origins. To the layman, I suggest the more popular digest of these huge tomes in Montefiore's *Rabbinic Literature and Gospel Teachings.* There we find exhaustively presented the substantiation of Wellhausen's contention that "Jesus was not a Christian, but a Jew."

Yes, a Jew even when he proclaimed his fundamental gospel of love which Christians, abysmally ignorant of Jewish teaching, maintain was Jesus' unique contribution to the spiritual evolution of mankind and which even some Jews who, similarly ignorant and for some strange reason eager to find something superior rather than merely diverse in Judaism, insist that Jesus went to an extreme of non-violence which is contrary to the more virile Hebraic teaching. Again both are woefully wrong. How ridiculous for Jews cynically to deprecate Christianity for its alleged softness and impracticality in counseling the "turning of the other cheek" and the "walking of a second mile" when Judaism prescribes that if the possession *even of an enemy* becomes lost, it is incumbent upon the upright Jew not merely to return it if he find it, but actually to set out in search for it.

How unfair on the other hand, for Christians disdainfully to declare that the Jewish law is based on the primitive *lex talionis,* on the crude "eye for an eye and tooth for a tooth" concept of justice. How weary we become of their frequent quotation of the verse, "Ye have heard it said, 'Thou shalt love thy neighbor, but hate thine enemy' "; a verse which merely proves to what lengths the writers of the New Testament went in order to establish the originality of their master and the inferiority of the faith he supposedly supplanted. For while Christians will quote this verse ad infinitum, and self-righteously assert the superior moral caliber of Christianity, I would challenge them to find a single reference in the whole range of Hebrew literature where the Jew is counseled to hate his enemy. On the contrary, long before Jesus, the author of the twenty-fifth chapter of the Book of Proverbs had gone much further than merely a general entreaty to love, by concretely and specifically enjoining: "If *thine enemy* be hungry, give him bread to eat and if he be thirsty, give him water to drink," which injunction, if carried out, would probably be even more useful to the enemy than an abstract principle of love; an injunction which most assuredly belies the so-called primitive and vengeful character of Jewish ethics.

But even further than this did some of the rabbis go, as, for example, when Rabbi Chanina said: "Even though thine enemy has risen up early to kill thee and he comes hungry and thirsty to thy house, give him food and drink." Is then the love of one's enemy exclusively a Christian virtue? Once again, I quote the rabbinic writers as they state that, "although from the commandment 'Thou shalt not hate thy brother in thy heart' we might infer merely that we may not strike him, slap him in the face or curse him, the Scriptures specify 'in thy heart' for the sole purpose that we *'may not hate him even in our own thought.'* " That is Judaism's message to all mankind, a Judaism which as Professor Charles, the editor of the most authentic collection of the Apocryphal writings, is compelled to admit, anticipated Jesus in proclaiming the love of one's fellow creature, friend and foe alike, as the foundation of all faith.

Self-righteously, Christians likewise ask what there can possibly be in Judaism to compare with the cross as a challenge to selfless heroism and as a summons to martyrdom. Aside from the question as to just how much of the present doctrine of the cross was in Jesus' mind, certain it is that his Jewish contemporaries and myriads of his martyred descendants regarded suffering, *al Kiddush Ha Shem,* for the sanctification of God's name, as a prelude to a deeper understanding for the Divine will and as a stimulus to the service of one's fellow men.

Many centuries before Jesus had come into the world, the story of martyrdom had begun in Israel and suffering for convictions' sake had become the badge and business of the Jew. Not only had Deutero-Isaiah drawn his incomparable picture of the "suffering servant," but Jeremiah had tasted of the bitter cup of persecution and exile as well as perhaps murder itself. In the very age that Jesus lived, a Jewish author had written as noble a panegyric of martyrdom as was ever penned: the so-called Fourth Book of Maccabees. In the centuries since, not merely has a single Akiba, in accordance with the rabbinic dictum to "be among the persecuted rather than the persecutors," gone willingly to the fagot with the *Sh'ma Yisroel* upon his lips but, I dare say that if the numbers of martyrs, Christian and Jewish, were placed side by side, proportionately, if not absolutely, the Jews who died for the sake of the Torah would outnumber those who perished for the cross. History refutes the somewhat arrrogant boast that Christianity gave to Judaism something which alone can elicit heroic sacrifice.

From whatever tack we approach this vast and complex subject, the inescapable verdict of Wellhausen stands that Jesus brought nothing radically new or original, that "Jesus was not a Christian, but a Jew"; a Jew who crystallized his entire teaching in those characteristically Jewish words "Hear O Israel, the Lord our God, the Lord is One. And thou shalt love the Lord thy God—and thy neighbor as thyself."

This does not mean that Judaism and Christianity are identical. But it most assuredly does mean that if Christians would recapture the message of *Jesus himself* they will have to cast aside those doctrines

JESUS—MAN OF MY PEOPLE

and dogmas and creeds which have concealed the lowly son of Israel, which not I, but so renowned a Christian leader as Harry Emerson Fosdick maintains: "Jesus never heard of and would have scorned as mint, anise and cummin. The Church," Fosdick continues, "has garbed the simple Jewish teacher beyond all recognition in heavy brocaded garments of sterile theology until the real Jesus has been got rid of altogether."

Pretty stern words those, and yet they were spoken by one of America's outstanding Christian ministers. They are the kind of words which the loyal and steadfast Jews used when they rejected not the real Jesus whom Fosdick is seeking so strenuously to recapture, but the "theological Christ" invented by Paul. That artificially manufactured Jesus alone the Jews refused and will continue to refuse to accept. And because of their refusal to accept these false theological notions they have been erroneously represented as having rejected the gentle teacher himself. For this, they were despised and hated and their children were murdered and turned into a pariah people. And now after 1,900 years, as the liberal Christian frees himself from what Fosdick further designates as the "brocaded velvets and golden crowns of our too conventional and formal adoration" which laid Jesus "in a theological tomb and rolled a great stone at the door"; as the liberal Christian emancipates himself from all this Christology which developed only after Jesus' death, what have they left but another Hebrew teacher who taught and yearned to proclaim Israel's truths to all mankind? And that Jesus, far from desiring a continuation of the breach between Christian and Jew, would indeed praise the Jew for his martyred steadfastness and would plead with the Christian to depart from his always subtle and ofttimes brutal attempt to convert the Jew to a cult of which Jesus had no knowledge, to cease rejecting Jesus by beginning truly to follow in the way of this son of Israel.

And for the Jew, the inescapable verdict of Jesus' Jewishness is likewise fraught with limitless possibilities. While many will minimize this significance upon the basis that nothing new is thus added to our faith, those who are objective and fair will affirm that Jewish life can be richly enhanced by his restoration to a proper place among our Jewish teachers and sages. His life holds a charm, an appeal, and a challenge which only a few great souls among the whole of mankind have possessed. And in a far too pygmied generation, wherein there is so glaring a dearth of spiritual guidance and moral leadership, we can ill afford to relinquish so sublime a character either for ourselves or for the inspiration of our children. Therefore, if it be true that Jesus was a true and loyal Jew, then the time has come for Jews to cease from their fear of being misinterpreted, from their vaunted desire of "saving face," from their vain dread of making what merely appears to be a capitulation, from their supplanting of an erstwhile obsequious inquiry as to "what will the non-Jew say?" to an equally abject "what will the Orthodox prate?" Turning from their immodest boast that "our pantheon of prophets is already filled," they may welcome back into their fold, not this stranger and alien spirit, but this true son of Israel and incorporate this Jewish hero into our never too overcrowded company of saintly spirits.

Nor do I mean a perfunctory gesture of passive recognition, but an active utilization of his outstanding personality as an impetus to a more profound understanding of our Jewish faith. For while, admittedly, there is no lack in Israel of prophets true and brave "who preached righteousness in the congregation," still there are aspects of Jesus' character and career which, in the words of Rabbi Hyman Enelow, were "unequalled in human history." What conceivable objection could there be—other than long-smouldering prejudice, however justified it may have been—to including the majestic sentences of the Sermon on the Mount among the other post-Biblical readings in our synagogues? Are not some of the down-to-earth, homely parables of Jesus of inestimable value as moral instruction for our children and youth? Why—because of all the aforementioned desecration of the life of Jesus by virtue of the libel concerning his death—must we put ethical and spiritual blinkers on our religious-school children by depriving them of the exalted teaching contained in the tale of the Good Samaritan, which we so scrupulously excise from our curriculum and Jewish heritage? I would teach such moving stories and utterances diligently unto our children along with those of Moses and Hillel. I would even dare to show non-Christological pictures of Jesus' life and martyrdom in our religious schools, as we have made exciting filmstrips of other heroic Jewish figures. I would use similar techniques to give our own children dramatic visualization of the true Jesus, both as a positive example of moral rectitude and as an antidote to the fictitious one imbibed with the jibe of "Christ Killer." Thus, I would call a halt to those who shrink in terror or smile superciliously at the mention of his name.

If it be true that Jesus was not a Christian but a Jew, then, although we will never be able to join those who worship him as "the only begotten son of God," as even a Fosdick and the late John Haynes Holmes would not think of doing; then, though we will be unable to accept him as the Messiah, since he himself would have been the first to admit, in disillusionment and despair, that neither his heroic life nor his sacrificial death ushered in the age of righteousness and peace which the Hebrew Redeemer was to bring in his wake; though thus the Christ of Paul we will still reject, perhaps we Jews may be the very instrument whereby the Christian masses might be led to that truth which their own thinkers already categorically proclaim: that here was a Jew, one of the noblest, most loyal, and faithful Jews who ever lived, a Jew who combined in his majestic personality "all that was best and most enchanting in Israel—the eternal people whose child he was."

This Jew, therefore, may yet serve as a bond of union between Christian and Jew, not to merge one into the other, not to submerge one to the other, but to build a bridge across the ancient chasm upon which the still-diverse faiths of Judaism and Christianity might meet in deeper understanding. Through a truer perspective of the man Jesus and his people of the Household of Israel whose Law he came but to fulfill, the age-old enmity between these two honored faiths might be put to flight, the longed-for "peace on earth and good will toward men" might be attained at last. While others may but reluctantly leave their long-cherished illusions and prejudices behind, let us at least be brave and honest enough to say with the poet Florence Kiper Frank:

> O man of my own people, I alone
>   Among these alien ones can know thy face,
> I who have felt the kinship of our race
>   Burn in me as I sit where they intone
> Thy praises—those who, striving to make known
>   A God for sacrifice, have missed the grace
> Of thy sweet human meaning in its place,
>   Thou who art our blood-bond and our own.

11

NEW FRONTIER IN JEWISH-CHRISTIAN

RELATIONS

FORETHOUGHT

*It cannot be gainsaid that the causes of anti-Semitism are many; so
the cure or cures must likewise be found in a pluralistic rather than a
monolithic approach to this age-old, bloody tale. Yet, this admission
having been made, prompted primarily by contemporary conditions,
a wider and deeper grasp of historic perspective lends irrefutable cre-
dence to the unqualified conclusion of Dr. Conrad Moehlman's definitive study of this problem in* The Christian–Jewish Tragedy, *wherein
he states: "The causes for the Christian persecution of the Jew may have
been economic, social, political, and religious. But the* Religious *reasons
always took first honors."*

*There is a plethora of unassailable documentary evidence, painstak-
ingly gathered and candidly presented by such eminent Christian
scholars as James Parkes, Malcolm Hay, Hugo Valentin, George Foot
Moore, Trevors Herford, and others, all of which leads incontrovert-
ibly to the conclusion voiced by the late lamented Catholic author,
Thomas Sugrue, who, in the introduction to his fellow Catholic Malcolm Hay's incomparably challenging volume,* Foot of Pride, *frankly
confesses that:*

*Nothing can be done about anti-Semitism until something is done about
Christianity. It is as illogical for a follower of Jesus to persecute a Jew
as it is for him to commit any other sin of hate; the process by which he
rationalizes his anti-Semitism should be identical with the process by which
he rationalizes his other breaches of the code according to which his religion
orders him to live. The fact that the two processes are not identical is the
essence of the matter; the fact that a Christian is able to feel that anti-
Semitism is not a sin, and indeed may be a virtue, a participation in the
divine chastisement of a race of God-killers, is the evil which spreads and*

maintains and strengthens this Christian violation of the law of love. As long as so cool and Luciferian an assumption is resident in Christian thinking, the Jew is a marked man, with a yellow patch on the arm of his identity. . . .

Religious toleration in America is legal, but in practice it is a well-mannered fraud; bigotry and prejudice are in abeyance only, they are not diminished or dead; they can be stirred as easily as the waters of a pond.

Such is indeed the truth of anti-Semitism; all the rest is commentary, from the fifth-century Codex Theodisianus *where, according to both* Parkes *and* Hay, *the word "Jew" was "officially given for the first time the opprobrious significance it retained throughout Christendom for more than a thousand years" down to* Mein Kampf, *wherein Adolf Hitler insisted that he was but "fanning into a fighting frenzy the flames of anti-Jewish prejudice which the Church had kindled in the hearts of the European peasantry."*

Address at Convention of
National Community Relations
Advisory Council, Atlantic City, N. J., 1949

AFTERTHOUGHTS

Well, those thoughts were strongly brewed. To be sure, they had strong provocation—the very strongest conceivable. They derived from the inconceivable horrors of Nazidom which I then insisted—and insist still today—was the final fruitage of centuries of pent-up fury voiced and vented by the church against the so-called Jewish deicides.

In reviewing all this, I would still contend that the religious component—the immemorial teaching of Christianity that Jews are eternally damned for having allegedly murdered and rejected Jesus—is central to the consideration of anti-Semitism.

That religious teachings continue to play a most significant role in anti-Semitism was strikingly confirmed in a study by the Survey Research Center of the University of California. That report, based on questionnaire replies by members of Protestant denominations, found that 69 per cent of "church-oriented Christians" still believe that Jews are the group "most responsible" for the death of Jesus. Moreover, 81 per cent of the adult respondents believe that Pontius Pilate wished not to put Jesus to the cross. Some 48 per cent feel Pilate failed to save

Jesus because "a group of powerful Jews wanted Jesus dead." Of equal significance was the finding that 45 per cent assert that "Jews can never be forgiven for what they did to Jesus until they accept Him as the True Savior."

While I still insist upon this basic religious rudiment of anti-Semitism, I would not overlook the obvious fact that social, psychological, and economic factors do likewise enter into the tangled web of hatred of the Jew in our time.

It must be admitted that fundamental and formidable as is this religious factor, it cannot alone explain the feverish ups and downs of anti-Semitism. Nor can it, by itself, account for the obvious truth that anti-Semitism flourishes in times of emotional and economic crisis— depression, panic over Communist infiltration, and similar episodes wherein personalized bogeymen and simplified scapegoats are required.

Moreover, it is true that the major outbursts of anti-Semitism in our era, though stemming from the deep and remote recesses of religious hatreds, have frequently flourished in a decidedly anti-religious atmosphere. This was certainly true even of the Nazi nightmare which, in the end, consumed all religious groups in the flames of hatred. It is significant that today in the Soviet Union, that citadel of contempt for all religion, anti-Semitism continues to have a life and a dynamism of its own. Whereas the militant atheism sponsored by the Soviet Union despises all religious belief, the Soviet Union still manages to single Jews out for specialized harassment, discrimination, and stereotyping.

In America, happily, overt anti-Semitism has declined sharply since the 1930s. Today anti-Semitism has reached a low ebb as judged by the number and influence of its publications and organizations, the absence of any truly influential American leadership in its behalf, and the nervous zeal with which even the ultra-rightist organizations seek to dissociate themselves from this discredited position. Anti-Semitism has become disreputable in American life and its occasional outbursts in spewing speech or obscene scrawlings on synagogues is generally and vigorously repudiated and denounced by political, religious, and business leaders of all faiths who regard bigotry as un-American. Discrimination against Jews has been reduced, although still persisting especially in the upper reaches of big business (banking and insurance) and in posh social clubs and resorts.

Yet, despite these hopeful indices of progress, most Jews cannot help but feel that anti-Semitism is a monster which may be momentarily asleep, but has not yet been chloroformed to death. Let great tension fill the land and the ogre will rise and growl and stride abroad once more. Depression, war, political crisis—such traumas release the antagonism and fears which in normal times lie latent beneath the surface. If anti-Semitism is an irrationality, it should be no surprise that Jews sense its imminence through intuition—and perhaps insecurity—which owes at least as much to history as to reason. Thus, on November 22, 1963, American Jews were joined with their fellow Americans in shock and in grief at the assassination of President Kennedy. But I believe that for many Jews there was something else that non-Jews could not share: the visceral fear that when the ground collapses beneath our feet, the demon is likely to be aroused again.

The more liberal Christian churches have increasingly recognized their obligation to combat anti-Semitism. As already stated, many Protestant and Catholic scholars have labored diligently on the revision of Christian textbooks so as to eliminate the invidious and inciteful. The late Pope John XXIII took the initiative in deleting prayers offensive to Jews, going so far as to interrupt a service at St. Peter's when the prayer for the "perfidious Jews" was recited despite his ukase to delete this phrase. Institutes for Christian clergymen have been conducted in many synagogues, bringing together large numbers of Christian pastors to learn more about Judaism from leading scholars. The power of the mass media—television, magazines, books, radio, motion pictures, newspapers—has helped to convey a more accurate picture of Jews and Judaism to millions of non-Jews. And the National Conference of Christians and Jews, despite earlier preoccupation with superficial and sporadic sloganized brotherhood charades, is presently deepening its program to build some more solid bridges of dialogue, understanding and cooperation along interfaith lines.

Of course, the over-arching development is that which is occurring within the Roman Catholic Church. The labors of Cardinal Bea and his Commission, designed to extirpate from the Church the myth of Jewish deicide, have inspired a new spirit of Catholic-Jewish understanding. That the Church is marshalling the moral courage to cast off such historic malignancies is of towering significance. It is a break with the past which every Jew—and every other fair-minded person as well—must welcome. It is to be hoped that whatever declaration issues from the Ecumenical Council will be followed up in every land with an intensive reexamination of Catholic textbooks and literature so that the ancient stain may be obliterated once and for all. No one can expect the Gospels of the New Testament to be rewritten in accordance with this new rapprochement but there is now good reason to hope that the harsh edge of the Gospels will be softened by the warmth of understanding initiated by Pope John and which has been echoed by Pope Paul as well as by most of the Church fathers who assembled at the Vatican to renew and purify their Mother Church.

As a matter of fact, it may come as somewhat of a surprise to many of my fellow Jews, especially those who have suffered from anti-Semitic exclusion from medical schools, business opportunities, and housing that, in my opinion, anti-Semitism never struck as deep roots in American life as did anti-Catholicism. Jews have never tasted mass violence in America as did Roman Catholics in New York City, Boston, Philadelphia, and many other cities at the end of the nineteenth century when convents were burned, Roman Catholics were hunted down on the streets, and the militia had to be called out to protect life and property. Know-Nothingism, the American Protective Association, and the Ku Klux Klan were primarily directed at the so-called Papist, and this strain of anti-Catholicism left a strong mark on the American character.

My first serious encounter with such anti-Catholic bigotry was during the Smith-Hoover Presidential contest of 1928. New York Governor Al Smith was the Democratic nominee. I was then twenty-six years old, in my first pulpit in Charleston, West Virginia, having been ordained two years earlier at the Hebrew Union College in Cincinnati, Ohio. Fresh out of theological school—indeed, some of the members of my temple's Board of Trustees deemed me plenty "fresh"—I was still under the hypnotic spell of my professor of Bible, Dr. Moses Buttenweiser; I was also a bit more certain than I am now that every word uttered from my pulpit would bring God's Kingdom into being even in my own time.

Except for weekend student services that I had conducted in Owensboro, Kentucky, Charleston was my initial pulpit, and it exposed me for the first time to poverty in its bleakest and most baneful forms. Though reared in Chicago, whose West-Side slums and already overcrowded South-Side Negro ghettos had been quite literally at my doorstep, somehow my middle-class home had been insulated from these nauseating realities. My early concepts of injustice were derived from the stirring messages of Amos and Isaiah and not from the streets of my home town.

But in West Virginia I discovered poverty in all its naked proximity. I beheld those who "grind the faces of the poor," who "sell the needy for a pair of shoes" at outrageously exorbitant prices in the monopolistic mining-town company stores, and "those who add house to house and field to field until there is no room in the land"; those who add coal tipple to coal tipple until the land is expropriated and exploited, until once stately, tree-shadowed mountainsides are buried beneath filthy, sooty coal dust, and once crystal-clear streams are polluted with poisonous wastes. I saw men leave for their labors before dawn to crawl on all fours like animals into darkened caverns beneath the earth, risking their lives through inhumanly long hours and for a still more inhuman pittance of a wage, to return again in the dark of night with their little headlights illuminating the way to their huddled hutches, which few would be humorous enough to call houses, much less homes.

Such were the more realistic origins of my pulpit protest. And while there were murmurings and mumblings against my "socialistic" (read "Communistic," today) utterances, my liberal quotations of prophetic texts put to silence any incipient revolt against this so-called too radical young rabbi. I could invariably maintain that the issues were fundamentally moral and most assuredly had no bearing on partisan politics.

But the Al Smith matter was different. What text does one educe from Jewish law or lore to buttress the contention that a Catholic is entitled to become President of the United States? Wasn't one really exploiting the pulpit and opting for the Democratic candidate if one opposed the fanatical forces which were then mounting to defeat the "Happy Warrior," just because he was a Catholic?

I did not think so. I thought that, if ever America was to prove its sincerity that men "are endowed by their Creator with certain unalienable rights, that among these are life, liberty . . ."—yes, even the liberty to become President, regardless of religion or any other accident of birth—that time would be on Election Day, 1928.

Accordingly, I announced early in October that I would speak at a Friday evening Sabbath service in my synagogue on the subject, "Shall a Roman Catholic Become President of the United States?" That was one time during my ministry in that congregation when we had standing room only. The congregation, swollen by many interested or curious Christians, was bigger than that of the Day of Atonement.

The press was present likewise. A reporter asked me for my manuscript. Then—as now—I wrote out every word I spoke from the pulpit. The next morning my early Sabbath peace was broken by the constant jangle of the telephone. Under bold, black, banner headlines virtually my entire sermon was splashed across page one of the newspaper. There was general concern among many of my dearest friends —as well as considerable alarm on the part of my choicest adversaries.

A special board of trustees meeting was called for early in the following week. I had little anxiety for I knew that the sounder minds and saner spirits that guided the congregation would, like most of our congregational leadership, strongly uphold the "freedom of the pulpit" of which they had proudly boasted at my installation service just two years before.

Then came an unexpected, challenging, but most perplexing turn of events. That same Sabbath was broken once again in the afternoon by a telephone call from a person then unknown to me—the Chairman of the Speaker's Bureau for the West Virginia State Democratic Committee. He asked me if I would tour the state to speak on the subject of the right of a Catholic to occupy the White House as reported in the morning paper. I gulped and said I would think it over for a day or two.

Quite a dilemma! I knew that my temple board was scheduled to meet in a couple of days and I could delay any reply until then. I was certain that I could win majority support for the freedom of my pulpit. But to stump the state for the Democratic nominee, Al Smith—and that's the way it would seem to most—was courting disaster.

I felt confident that my own motivations were in no wise partisan. I realized that fear of the consequences could easily prompt me to take the line of least resistance, defer to my board, and allow them to prevent me from pursuing a course of action destined to educe much criticism. Yet I felt that it would be cowardly to take refuge in such a rationalization. I concluded that there was little, if any, moral distinction between preaching in a temple at which the general public is welcome, permitting one's pulpit utterance to be printed in the press, and actually saying these same things from the public platform. Thus, early in my career I learned that, while one must of course seek unofficial counsel from friends one trusts, there are, nevertheless, some issues of such magnitude that one must resolve them in the private sanctuary of one's own conscience.

Neither then nor since have I sought any special pulpit immunity. I have never essayed to allow the robe of some kind of esoteric priesthood to cloak the role of prophecy to which I believe the rabbi, however inadequate, is constrained to aspire. So, after confiding in my ever valorous-spirited wife—also wedded to me all of two years—and one or two trusted friends whose judgment I had learned to respect, I accepted the invitation into the political fray. My first experience at barnstorming began.

It started undramatically enough with a number of speeches in cities and towns where the halls were packed with predominantly Democratic regulars who, naturally, cheered my every point.

But then the Speaker's Bureau decided that I was expendable enough to risk sending into the rural areas—into those poverty-stricken, lean and hungry regions where the Ku Klux Klan flourished. Fiery crosses had burned on many of those West Virginia hills in years past and not a few citizens had been terrorized by white-hooded night riders. Now a Catholic running for the Presidency sent them into paroxysms of frenzied and lying propaganda. Many of those all too lamentably unschooled, illiterate countryfolk believed that a private line between the White House and Rome was already being installed (at least at the Vatican end) and that the election of Smith would ensconce the Pope at the right hand, if not of God, then at least of the President of the United States.

It was into this fanatical atmosphere that I was next sent. I was to speak in the public square in front of the courthouse—my first and never-to-be-forgotten speech in the open air. A large crowd had already gathered, some out of curiosity—for few, if any, had ever seen a rabbi before—but most came in undisguised hostility toward a Jew uphold-ing the right of a Catholic to be President of "Protestant America." Was not the KKK founded to save this "home of the brave" (brave, masqueraded Kluxers!) from just such a fate as this?

My wife was with me, as she was during most of my experiences, trying or triumphant. She was, despite her rare spiritual courage, ad-mittedly nervous. So was I. For the first and only time, she requested that I delete a passage from an address. She never again sought to sound such a word of caution, but instead always encouraged the honest expression of inner conviction.

But that day was different! Every face before us stared sullen, stolid, stony. Every lapel was adorned with a Hoover button. The very air was surcharged with tension. My wife leaned over and whispered the suggestion that I might omit my peroration wherein I stated that, "If I had to choose between being ruled by the Pope of Rome or the Grand Kleagle of the Ku Klux Klan . . ." (a fantastic choice, to be sure) ". . . I would choose the Pope of Rome." I made no commitment to her but promised I would let my decision rest upon my feel of the crowd when I reached that point.

I was grandiloquently introduced by some party hack. No applause. Only defiant silence. I tried out my most faithful, reliable sure-fire jokes (after all, wasn't I a veteran of two years on the Rotary cum Kiwanis cum Lions cum Optimists circuit?). Not a decibel of laughter, not even a scintilla of a smile.

So, I plunged into the speech itself. I detected tiny gleams of interest in a pair of eyes here and there. There was a scarcely discernible thaw. At least a few—well, one or two—seemed to be with me. That was all the encouragement I required. I ploughed on—Pope of Rome, Grand Kleagle, and all. A slight ripple of restrained applause ensued—and we were quickly hustled off to the next stop.

I had not elected Smith. Never will I forget that tear-filled night when, with a few fondly cherished friends, we huddled in front of the radio to try to catch from out of the thunderous crackle of static (from KDKA, Pittsburgh, our one-and-only reliable transmitter then) the election returns which revealed how well the KKK and the more "respectable" hate-mongers and poison-purveyors had done their job. But I had learned much. I had learned especially that no rabbi, priest, or minister should confine his messages to the protective asylum of the synagogue or church, but should rather let the word of justice well forth as water and the word of righteousness as a never-failing stream. No, my words did not elect Al Smith and the bigotry brewed in that bitter campaign was a long time in abating. In fact, it had to get a lot worse before it got better. We had to go through the throes of the Depression with the bitter truth of that maxim which is axiomatic to all minorities: "The last to be hired, the first to be fired." We had to witness the foulest fruitage of prejudice as a whole generation walked through the valley of almost universal death in Nazi concentration camps and crematoria.

But, at long last, right appears to be winning vindication: in the diminution of anti-Semitism, in the advance of Negro rights—however painfully, shamefully slow-paced—and in the election—thirty-two years after I faced that crowd in the courthouse square of a remote West Virginia hamlet—of the late John F. Kennedy as President of the United States.

But even that victory for interreligious understanding—more than three decades later—was a tight squeeze. Again, the forces of fanaticism tried to bar from the White House one who, though good enough, trustworthy enough, patriotic enough to have defended our country in its armed services, was deemed unworthy, because of his religious faith, to be considered for the Presidency of the U.S.

Sadly enough, it seems that for nations, as for little children, lessons must be repeated to be mastered. And so our more efficient press in

1960 poured forth their torrents of anti-Catholic vitriol—and some anti-Semitic and anti-Negro propaganda for good measure. For a time it looked as if the Klan was to demonstrate the traditional Jewish concept of the resurrection of the dead. This incipient revival of the most vicious bigotry was attended by not a few so-called respectable folk and forces. Thus, the widely serialized positive thinker, Norman Vincent Peale, seemingly gave his blessing to those who decreed that any male child born a Catholic was doomed to remain a second-class citizen, banned forever from the White House.

What I had done as a brash youth of twenty-six, I felt I could not eschew now in my safer haven of maturity. Again there were critics, of course. But now there were many more supporters. Together with my friend and spiritual brother, Bishop James Pike, I challenged the Reverend Peale publicly to debate this issue on TV. He beat a hasty retreat and recanted. And while the witches' brew of hate still boiled; while tons of vile and virulent propaganda flowed in torrential floods throughout the land, this time there were so many more decent-minded Americans determined that we had had enough of such disgusting fare. I used every opportunity available to me to condemn this kind of thinking and to plead for fairness in the campaign. I am proud that the Union of American Hebrew Congregations, as early as November of 1959, adopted a resolution at its Biennial Assembly in Miami Beach, Florida which declared:

. . . We express our dismay over statements made and positions taken by a few religious groups in outright opposition to the possible nomination for President or Vice-President of the United States of any person of the Roman Catholic faith. Without expressing any partisanship in favor of or against any candidate, we adopt the following principles which we deem essential to the preservation of a meaningful freedom of religion in the selection of persons for public office:

We oppose all religious tests for office, and deem the suggestion that the profession of any religious belief or disbelief should automatically disqualify a person from holding any office, to be fundamentally at variance with our democratic principle that religion lies within the realm of personal conscience. . . .

And while the election was won only by a hair, it was a day of victory for all Americans when a Catholic removed the "White Protestant Only" sign from the White House.

I believe John F. Kennedy, despite the tragic brevity of his administration, will live in history as a great President, and that his greatness will grow as the years give better perspective to his brilliant, inspired, inspiring and far too catastrophically foreshortened tenure. But one of his most important and lasting triumphs will be that he destroyed, once and for all, the "religious myth" in American politics. For here was a Catholic President who vigorously supported the letter and the spirit of the Constitution. He bravely defended the separation of church and state even in the face of hostile reactions within certain precincts of his own Church, as well as in some segments of Protestantism, to unpopular Supreme Court decisions. Not even the breath of favoritism for any religious group was ever attached to his ever fair and sensitive leadership. He was the President of all the people. The broken hearts and flowing tears of a united America at the moment of his tragic passing gave clear testimony that he had earned their full trust, confidence, and affection. And this, for our first Roman Catholic President, was no small contribution to justice and reason in American life.

While thus there has been undeniable progress in our interreligious relations, I confess I am still not entirely satisfied. There is much room for further improvement. True, we have grown as a nation beyond religious violence. We have attained a certain amount of civility in our relationships. The raw religious bigotry of the past has been much attenuated. We have become more sophisticated. But all this should not beguile us into thinking that the interreligious relations among Protestants, Catholics, and Jews are good enough. They are not, as the excellent book *A Tale of Ten Cities* demonstrates. The simple truth is that most of us are living in our separate ghettos. Though no grim walls of stone surround them as once incarcerated the Jews of the Middle Ages, they are socially and often economically sealed off nonetheless. While we may cooperate with persons of other faiths in our businesses or meet with them at Rotary luncheons or Community Chest dinners where fat contributions from all comers are avidly accepted, the five o'clock shadow falls over the land like three silken curtains, dividing Jews, Catholics, and Protestants into distinct communities—or into clearly demarcated ghettos still—even if no horrendous or concrete Berlin Wall fences some superciliously in and others disdainfully out.

Various studies confirm the growing tendency of each group almost exclusively to mingle socially with their own respective coreligionists. These studies reveal that Jews, for example, rarely dine in the home of Christians, that they prefer to live in neighborhoods with a strong percentage of Jews, that some at least are pressing for more Jewish parochial schools; that their doctors, insurance agents, and lawyers usually tend to be Jewish; that many of their rabbis today, lacking confidence in the staying power of their teaching, vigorously condemn mixed dating among the young. Catholics follow the same social pattern, but, in addition, the Church, as a matter of fundamental principle, has created a vast network of separate Catholic schools, universities, and institutions. While it cannot be denied, as these studies irrefutably attest, that much of this contemporary ghettoization is self-imposed, nevertheless, it would be a grave error to assume that all such isolation of one religious group from the other is a consequence of self-segregation. Such is the trap into which not a few—including some of my fellow Jews—are presently falling. The Jews "like it that way," say the complacent Christian commentators on the contemporary social scene, in somewhat the same tedious refrain as "the 'Niggers' were never happier or more content than in the segregated South." "We feel more at home among our own" echo the ape-like Jewish me-tooers who would create a lot of "little Israels," where alone—so they contend—the Jew can really be a Jew.

But it is not wholly so, and there is grave danger in such shallow analysis. There is danger that we will now all sit back content with this best of all possible worlds. But, let a single Jew try to break the invulnerably, vigilantly guarded portals of some exclusive "For Gentiles Only" neighborhood or country club, or start rising in some traditionally *Judenrein* vocation, and the hysterical reaction of fearful trembling will be tantamount to the panic which an invasion of Martians might induce.

To which the facile rationalizers will respond: "Who needs it?" Who needs the togetherness of golf braggarts and drinking bouts characteristic of too many of these select circles. Surely Jews and other excluded groups need not crave assimilation to some of the most obnoxious mores of America's jet set. But students of the socio-economic trends of our time who may be repulsed by the deteriorating values of these social citadels will confess that it is amid such surroundings—sordid though they sometimes are—that many of the decisions affecting political and financial affairs are determined. It is here that the firm's new vice-president is chosen. It is here that his wife is subjected to peering, microscopic evaluation. It is here that the huge new contract is awarded to this or the other bidder. It is here that the power structure of town and city, state and nation, is built—brick by brick; or rather, through careful screening, person by person.

So, while college quotas are diminishing, and "No Jews Need Apply" signs are disappearing in the lower echelons, this persistent social snobbery and exclusiveness will in time garner "For Gentiles Only" the topmost rounds of every ladder of success, as it has for a long time past succeeded in excluding Jews from the real financial strongholds of our land: the heavy industries, the big league of insurance, the foremost banking institutions, many of which are quite literally *Judenrein,* or at best, boast for sweet appearance's sake and by gentleman's agreement their single, solitary *"white* Jews." Though his concentration camps are gone, too much of Hitler's spirit is kept alive by such gentlemen's agreements maintained with far more genteel, but equally effective, techniques.

Granted, of course, that these goals of becoming president, or even vice-president, of giant steel, or aviation, or banking combines should not be the *summum bonum* of Jewish—nor of American—aspiration; nonethless, the opportunity should be available for all to compete. If "open skies" is our American policy overhead, let us opt for "open opportunities" underfoot for Christian and Jew, white and black, native and naturalized citizen.

While it is true that, even in the face of such an open society, individual Jews and Jews collectively may frequently prefer their own company, yet I maintain that any positive benefits of this admitted tendency toward voluntary self-segregation along religious lines are outweighed by the negative ones. To be sure, voluntary self-segregation may appear to help preserve the integrity of a group and to stem the tidal pressures toward assimilation. Such sentiment flows from a strong psychological need to be part of one's own group, in which one feels a greater measure of comfort. But, on the other hand, I believe that such rigid self-segregation along religious lines leads to the dull, flat, and fatuous uniformity which is already the bane of American life. If we live among people who look, act, and talk precisely the same as we do, frequent the same resorts, swarm the same spas, throng the same clubs, play gin or bridge with the same crowd, send our children to the same private schools—all of which are basically one-race, one-religion, one-class monochromes—it seems to me that we dilute into insipid, tasteless mush the rich variety of the democratic experience.

We ought not to be sheltered from differences, whether racial, religious, or social. I believe that living in homogeneous neighborhoods and isolating ourselves from other groups impairs our capacity for the growth of personality. And I believe, moreover, that such narrow and parochial patterns equip us very poorly for the world of dynamic diversity and color which we—and certainly our children—will inherit tomorrow. Many Jews—and no doubt this is true of other groups as well—avoid meaningful associations with non-Jews out of a fear of being hurt. But a certain amount of risk is inherent in life, not merely on the part of individuals but on the part of our religious movements as a whole. It is my contention—and conviction—that if the continued profession of our faith and the practice of its unique way of life are so fragile as to require the hothouse care of quarantine, if our survival depends solely on enforced or voluntary sequestration in a country of our own or in gilded ghettos in the pluralistic society of America, then the time-tested validity of our much vaunted "eternal values"—or even of our hallowed *mitzvot,* our practices, moral and ceremonial, of our unique way of life—must at long last be doubted.

It is better for Jews, while steadfastly and stubbornly insisting on the *right* of free entry everywhere and anywhere, nonetheless, to absorb occasional snubs and hurts and even exclusion from some of the supposedly rarefied planes in American life, rather than to buy insurance against anti-Semitism and intermarriage at the exorbitant price of rigid self-segregation.

The fact that our religious faiths are tending toward such respective self-imposed isolation does not mean, however, that there is an absence of tension and conflict among them. But, unlike the religious wars which revolved around matters of religious dogma, the interreligious conflicts of American life have to do, mostly, with social and civic issues. Conflicting interpretations of separation of church and state, birth control, censorship, divorce, gambling, child adoption, Sunday laws—these are the matters which stir fervent emotion and, frequently, religious tension in America. Such stresses and strains are inevitable in a religiously plural society and nothing worthwhile has ever been accomplished without tension, either by individuals or groups.

Pluralism means an acceptance, even a welcoming, of differences—real differences—and an understanding that competing notions among the faiths as to the "good society" will make for a certain amount of communal conflict. That is inevitable. But pluralism also means that such competition should be conducted within the bounds of fair play and mutual respect. It was natural that many Christians objected to the Supreme Court decisions on denominational or even nondenominational religious practices in the public schools, and now wish to see them overturned. But it was totally reprehensible that some distinguished Americans, in taking issue with the decisions, should have given vent to intemperate utterances which in effect impugned the religious sincerity of the Jewish community by identifying it with secularism and atheism, sometimes even suggesting that the opposition to prayer in the public schools stemmed from some brand of pro-Communism. Such talk makes pluralism and decent interreligious relations impossible. It is unworthy of the American tradition and of civilized discourse in a free land.

What *is* important is how these issues are confronted by the religious subcommunities. Are they candidly faced and frankly discussed? My impression is that frequently they are not. My impression is that Protestant, Catholic, and Jewish groups in most local communities are just beginning to establish such ongoing communication in earnest. Too often we still tend to see each other through periscopes, which are quickly raised or lowered as somebody rocks the boat and thus agitates the waters of our communal life. Even in controversial situations we are prone to address each other through press-release bombs lobbed into the newspapers from our respective battle stations. One who studied the matter said that in a recent bitter controversy over bus transportation in Connecticut, the religious leaders of the three faiths never bothered to get together on their own initiative to discuss personally the very religious issue which blackened the front pages of the newspapers and agitated the entire community.

Happily, at long last, we are witnessing the decrease of hypocritical cookie-pushing, back-slapping interfaith teas and sham interreligious dinners, replete with saccharine speeches that face no realities and build no substantial bridges. Happily, there is a growing thrust in the direction of candid and earnest interfaith "dialogue." But my experience is that these are still very limited in number, that they have not as yet burrowed beneath the layer of a few top clerics, and that it is still too early to assess whether these innovations represent merely—at best—a new vocabulary, a new semantics or—at worst—a last-straw *raison d'être* to save the interfaith movement in America from drowning in the sea of its erstwhile smugness and superficiality.

I have always felt—and still feel now—that talk is good but action is better. The only really effective interreligious communion and amity are to be found when Protestants, Catholics, and Jews labor together on concrete issues. United social action is the key to interfaith relations. It is deeply gratifying that churches and synagogues are finally—"late, late we come," as Dr. Eugene Carson Blake confessed at the March on Washington—joining hand in hand to work together for racial justice. The Negro revolution has produced, as a beneficent by-product, the beginning of an interreligious revolution. In dozens of communities and especially in our nation's capital, Christian clergymen and rabbis, together with their concerned laymen, have plunged into the thorny thicket of race relations. This may be the dawn of a new day of interfaith relations; it may also be the salvation of religion in America, rescued at a minute to midnight from the tolling of bankruptcy.

May God give us the strength to build on these relationships so that we can learn to work together—Protestant, Catholic, and Jew—to vindicate the ideals which underlie our separate faiths and our common heritage as Americans. What a blessing for America and the world if the leaders of Judaism and Christianity can find the courage and social imagination to break out of their organizational and institutional ruts, to see the moral crisis of an unredeemed world, and to join hand and heart in building God's kingdom here on earth. That is the real test of these times which try our souls and our faith.

The challenge is contained in a story—said to be true—which I heard when I was a rabbi in Toronto. It is said to have occurred in the prairies of the Canadian West where the fields grow high with the tall crop of waving, golden wheat. It relates how once a mother and a father and their little child set out from their native town to visit a neighboring village. In order to reach their destination, it was necessary for them to traverse one of the vast fields grown high with the fall crop of grain. To keep their child from straying off and becoming lost in this veritable forest of wheat, each parent took one of the child's hands as they wended their way together. After proceeding for some time in silence, the mother suddenly realized that the child was not with them. Evidently it had wandered away while they were walking along absentmindedly. In great consternation, the mother cried out, "Father, where is our child?"

The father looked down and he, too, noted for the first time that the child was gone. Hurriedly, they began to search this way and that—but to no avail. The child was nowhere to be seen. They returned quickly to their little village, called out all their neighbors and friends to join them in the search. All that day, all that night, all the following day and the following night they searched. But the child could not be found. On the morning of the third day, as they were standing about dejectedly, one man hit upon a brilliant idea. He said to his neighbors and friends, "Come, let us join hand to hand, forming a human comb— and we will stretch ourselves across the entire width of this field, and we shall tread across its full length and thus we shall cover every inch of ground. Surely, in this way we shall find the missing child." They hurriedly joined hand to hand, forming this human comb, and they began their silent, solemn and somber march down the field. Suddenly, someone stumbled over an inert object, lifted it, and placed it into the arms of the anxious mother. She gazed down into the pallid features of her own child's face and she beheld that it was dead. And all that grief-stricken mother could do was to cry out of the depth of her desolation and despair, "My God! Why did we not join hands sooner?"

"My God!" is my cry, is the cry of our whole anguished, agonizing generation. "My God!" is the cry of the bruised and battered and beaten multitudes of earth. "My God!" is the cry of the millions of maimed and mutilated, the downtrodden and oppressed, destined for destitution, destruction, and premature death. "Why do we not join hands—nation with nation, race with race, creed with creed, man with his brother man? Why do we not join hands before it is too late?"

12

RITES AND WRONGS OF RITUAL

FORETHOUGHT

There is a vast difference between treasuring those traditions which arise naturally out of the life and habit of a people, which are but the external expression of an inner and heartfelt need, and our latter-day tendency to shop around for some dramatic, or theatrical, or sentimental effects which are calculated to draw large numbers to the synagogue. Instead of treating worship as a living, growing organism, we ponder it as a bare façade to be dressed up with the addition of what we suppose to be more artistic words or enchanting rites than those at present available, with the result that what we achieve is not the burgeoning forth of some clear faith, but a vague kind of prettiness or sentimentality which frequently disguises, in the folds of traditionalism, the fact that we believe very little or do not know precisely what we believe.

An eminent historian of religion tells us that in every major religious movement three stages can be distinguished: first, a stage of moral enthusiasm, expressing itself in the purification of the personal life and in a holy zeal for the betterment of society; second, a stage characterized by the reflective formulation of those initial convictions and by precise theological definitions; and third, a period of waning moral energy directed toward the elaboration of ceremony and ritual.

"It is in this final stage," writes Dean Sperry, "that religion begins to be decadent." And with this conclusion the psychologists seem to concur. For they tell us that the aged suffer from a type of mind which they designate as "total recall," a state in which they seek to recapitulate every slightest detail of their past and to treasure every least significant relic of their earlier years.

And when Reform rabbis, once aflame with the passion of an Isaiah and a Jeremiah, now concern themselves with the world-tottering problem of how best to observe hamisha osor b'sh'vat *(the minor festival for tree planting) amid January's wintry gales, or how frequently to yield to our people's penchant for* yizkor *(memorial) services, forgetting that the original function of this ritual was to guard vigilantly the soul of the living, rather than to mumble superstitious incantations over the dead; when the essential is thus being lost amid the incidental, may it not be that our Reform Judaism too is becoming decadent and is being afflicted with a senile failure of nerve?*

"Retreat or Advance,"
Central Conference of American Rabbis,
Columbus, Ohio, 1937

AFTERTHOUGHTS

Let's be blunt about it. I no longer feel nearly so dogmatic about the role of ritual in Reform Judaism or in religion and life generally. I would take strong issue with the position I expressed in 1937. In fact, I think it's about time for a change of style in these essay-like presentations of thoughts and afterthoughts. A bit of forthright dialogue with myself might be a salutary and welcome change of pace. So let's imagine just such a face-to-face debate with my present thinking, known as Rabbi Now, leading off against my earlier thoughts, which we will identify as Rabbi Then (1937):

Rabbi Now: Look here, your thoughts of pre-World War II days were symptomatic of precisely what was wrong with Reform Judaism in its early days. You were so rationalistic, so universalistic that you reduced Judaism to a bloodless set of ethical principles. A *guf* without a *ruach*, a body without a soul, a brain without emotion. Isn't that why so many already within the ranks of Reform Jewry complained that Reform Judaism was "cold," and isn't that why so many outside— among the multitudes of unaffiliated—refused to join, protesting that your services reminded them of a Protestant church? Well, they were right—and you contributed to that situation of the "frozen people."

Rabbi Then: I'm not so sure. What is Reform Judaism anyway? In the first place, it is a bold proclamation that the *Halachah* (the whole of the law) is not literally and eternally binding upon us. It insists that Judaism must evolve and grow in accordance with modern knowledge and insights. It says that we must discard those ritual observances which are no longer meaningful in the life of the modern Jew, which have had the effect of obscuring the great ethical ideals stemming from the prophets and which had to be at the very heart of a vital, living Judaism.

Now: True enough, but didn't such thoughts lead to throwing out the baby with the bath? To cast off rituals and ceremonies which are no longer viable and which may even be offensive to our modern minds—such as a prayer for the restoration of animal sacrifices in the Temple at Jerusalem—is proper and understandable. But to declare war against all ceremonial as such is to squeeze all the color and emotion out of Judaism. It is to make Reform Judaism nothing more than a Jewish equivalent of Ethical Culture.

Then: Touché! And why do you think Ethical Culture developed in the first place? Why was it started by a former Reform rabbi? Precisely because of a despair that Judaism had ceased to be a religion of action, a way of life, a challenge to ethical living, a confrontation of society. Orthodox Judaism had been rendered immobile by encrustations of ritual observance which became ends in themselves. But Reform Judaism mounted a war of liberation against superstition and empty ceremonialism. It was, like most revolutions, slashingly destructive. It took literally the order of priority laid down by Jeremiah, to first "uproot and destroy"—to destroy all the vestigial remains of an outmoded past, to uproot outworn remnants of ancient and medieval superstitions that were suffocating the spirit and moral passion of Judaism and the Jew—before it could "plant and build" anew.

Now: Fear not. I have not forgotten my Jeremiah. But I maintain that Reform Judaism *has* planted and built. They are mistaken who dub our temples *goyische* churches. Our Union Prayer Book, created by the Central Conference of American Rabbis, is suffused with spiritual aspiration and moral challenge. We've planted and built the whole lovely ceremony of Confirmation and a host of other new ceremonial practices.

Then: But I condemned then—and I should think you would still join me in condemning—all those empty forms and hollow rituals which serve no spiritual or moral purpose.

Now: Aren't you being presumptuous? Aren't you assuming some kind of omniscience in cavalierly dismissing so many time-hallowed ceremonies as hollow and empty? Who is to be the final arbiter? Didn't some Jews—whole generations of them—choose death rather than relinquish some of these very *mitzvot* (commandments), including even

the dietary laws you disparage so frequently? Besides, aren't you talking as if ritual observances had no value in themselves? You must
realize . . .

Then: "Bring no more vain oblations! It is an offering of abomination
unto Me. New moons and convocations, I cannot endure iniquity along
with the solemn assembly. When ye make many prayers, I will not hear;
your hands are full of blood. Cease to do evil; learn to do well; seek
justice, relieve the oppressed, remove the shackles from the minds
and hearts of men." (Isaiah 1:13)

Now: I knew you would throw Isaiah at me. Classic Reformers have
always misinterpreted these prophets. Isaiah and Amos and Micah and
the others were not condemning *all* prayer, ritual, and observance. They
were condemning the *abuses* which were notorious in their time. They
were chastising their contemporaries for substituting means for ends,
for the hypocrisy of chanting hymns while doing evil. But you cannot
transmit the great moral imperatives of the prophets unless you touch
the emotions of man, quicken his spirit, and plumb the depths of the
human soul. Young man, you must feed the spirit as well as the mind.
This yearning of the spirit can be satisfied, ideally, by the significant
and deeply enriching observance of certain rituals which have meaning
for us in our time. Rituals properly viewed are intended to be reminders of the ethical demands the Lord requires of us.

Then: Reminders, did you say? Haven't you been observant enough
through all these afteryears to perceive how swiftly all such forms become ends in themselves? What sublime universal ideal is recalled by
the smashing of a glass at Orthodox Jewish weddings, for example?
What is the moral grandeur recalled by the slashing of a portion of
one's garment at traditional Jewish funerals, the putting on of the
yarmulke (headcovering) at prayer? Is it impossible truly to consecrate
a marital union, reverently to bury one's beloved dead, to worship
God without these outmoded external impediments? Yet some Jews
regard these as the very touchstones of faith.

Now: Yes, and some Reformers like yourself, in the first flush of
your revolutionary ardor, make just as great a fetish out of *not* doing
something as do the Orthodox in *doing* it. It's with some chagrin that
I recall what a fuss *you* made when you first went to Toronto about
taking off the *yarmulkes.* You were as rigid in your way as those you
are so swift to dub benighted for insisting upon putting them on.

Then: I disagree. There was a vast distinction between my attitude
then and that which characterizes the frozen rigidities of Orthodoxy.
I sought to impose *my* ways upon no one. The Orthodox insisted then,

as they invariably do, in our following *their* way regardless of our convictions, feelings, or background. That episode you have evoked to prove your point is, in my judgment, an affirmation of my own. It's quite illuminating. May I tell you about it?

Now: I shouldn't have brought up the subject. All right, but briefly, please! You have a tendency to be long-winded, you know.

Then: Well, that is one thing you and I have in common. Anyway, before my advent to Toronto, my impression of Reform Judaism was of a monolith, as inflexible and fixed forever as any Orthodoxy. The Reform congregations in which I had been reared and those that I had attended in Chicago and Cincinnati varied but little one from the other. They followed very much the same ritual, had similar mixed choirs (comprised mostly of non-Jewish choristers); the music by and large was a saccharine copy, if not a downright plagiarism, of the Christian composers of church liturgy. In the Midwest of my youth, it was utterly unheard of to have a cantor in a Reform synagogue. (For that matter, neither would a Reform congregation think of calling itself by so "Orthodox" a designation as "synagogue;" they were all called temples.) In that setting, to worship with head covered would have been most incongruous of all.

How unprepared I was for what was to confront me when I arrived in Toronto to become the rabbi of Holy Blossom Congregation! Even a preliminary week of orientation with my predecessor, Rabbi Ferdinand Isserman, did not prepare me adequately for what I encountered. At age twenty-seven, having been exposed exclusively to the classical pattern of Reform Judaism, restricted throughout those first three decades to association primarily with Reform Jews, I was suddenly plunged into a vibrant community of some forty thousand Jews of whom a bare couple of hundred families belonged to Holy Blossom Congregation, one of the three Reform congregations in the whole Dominion of Canada. Holy Blossom Congregation, founded in 1856, was older than the Hebrew Union College and the Union of American Hebrew Congregations, but it had been Reform only during the eight-year incumbency of my two predecessors. (Incidentally, and in response to the ubiquitous query that I have encountered everywhere, years of research on my part have failed to uncover the origin of the name "Holy Blossom." My best clue is that it is a free translation of *Pirche Kodesh,* a verse in Isaiah, which means "flowers of the Holy One.")

I recall how completely "shook up" I was when I first realized that there was a congregation in the ranks of Reform that still was so utterly "unreformed," so steeped in Orthodoxy, as not to remove its hats in prayer. And that congregation was mine!

Now: Served you right, you and your twenty-seven-year-old dogmatism.

Then: Well, I was definitely not going to be caught in the pulpit with my hat on. I should amend that to say caught in *my own* pulpit, for I had already officiated at "mixed" marriages (Reform with Orthodox) with my head dutifully covered if such were the wishes of the family. I would have felt like a hypocrite to pray and preach regularly, observing a practice which I had learned from my teacher, that master of Talmudic lore, Professor Lauterbach, was pure custom, or *minhag*, and in no wise *din* or prescribed law. If Orthodoxy criticized Reform for its *chukas hagoy* (following the "ways of the gentile") because it worshipped with head uncovered, I felt that it was really the Orthodox that were to be accused of this aping conduct. Surely, the prophets of Israel did not cover their heads when they proclaimed their truth to the populace; but Catholic Cardinals do. Who was imitating whom?

Now: Are you almost through?

Then: Not quite. I fumed and fretted. But I felt that I had not yet accumulated sufficient strength in the congregation to challenge this long-established practice, particularly since I was also engaged during those weeks in a heated controversy with the Zionist leaders of the community. Conscience dictated that I should resign. And yet, since it was the very eve of the Holy Days, conscience also demanded that I remain at least through those Days of Awe. But not with hat on!

I felt I had only one recourse. I went to the President of the congregation and laid all my cards on the table. To my great surprise—and relief—he was sympathetic to my plight. Although the eve of the New Year was near, and time short, he agreed to call a special meeting of the entire congregation. The official notice stated that the meeting was to consider a motion to the effect that henceforth "the covering of the head at worship would be optional." You see, my friend, how liberal I was. I asked only that those who desired to remove their hats be permitted to do so; those who felt otherwise, to wear them.

Now: Still seems like much ado over very little, but go on.

Then: The other officers were not nearly as indulgent as the President. The Vice-President, for example, told me quite candidly that he was categorically opposed to so sudden a change. But he said he would not vote against it; he would abstain. There were other discouraging comments from innumerable congregants during the brief interim prior to the meeting itself.

When the meeting convened, the notice of motion was read and seconded. The President, casting a calculating eye across the sparsely filled room to note the preponderance of "first families" (more hospitable to Reform, of course), was about to put the issue to a vote, when one of the more Orthodox members leaped to his feet and demanded the floor.

He had, undoubtedly, been sent as an advance agent by his faction to be their contemporary surrogate to "hold the fort" until the remainder of their contingent arrived. We had indeed slipped up on an indispensable preliminary bit of strategy. We had not demanded—as at that earlier juncture we might have—a time limitation on all speeches from the floor. So we were treated to a filibuster by this champion of the status quo. I was seated on the platform with the officers of the congregation, filled with trembling apprehension as, after about a half-hour of this flamboyant oratory, one after another of those known to favor the more Orthodox flavor of Holy Blossom drifted into the room. Hurriedly, I began to count noses. The vote was certain to be close. Noting the presence now of many of his cohorts, the speaker relinquished the floor and our side had its innings. I brought the debate to a close with as fervent a plea as I could make for an understanding on the part of all for the sensitivities and predilection of their fellow members—for each to follow his own conscience.

The vote was taken. As the "ayes" rose to their feet, it was obvious that it was going to be even closer than I had anticipated. And then one of the most touching things that has occurred during my rabbinic experience took place. My Vice-President, reared in strictest Orthodoxy, always hypersensitive to the opinion held of him by his Orthodox friends and boyhood associates (which accounted for his serving notice on me in advance that he could not vote in favor of such a radically Reform innovation), now surveyed the apparently insufficient number of "reformers" getting to their feet to vote affirmatively on the proposition before them. This sterling human being slowly rose to his feet and bravely stood up to be counted on the side of change. By the slimmest of margins, the congregation voted that in the future the wearing of hats would be optional.

Now: Thank goodness that's over. *Mazel Tov* (congratulations) on a puny victory!

Then: But it isn't over. The most unexpected chapter is still to come. The eve of the New Year was ushered in a few nights later. The congregation gathered, each member hesitating in the vestibule to wrestle with conscience or to argue with his parents or grandparents as to whether it was right to remove the hat within the house of worship. About 25 per cent of the congregation took the leap by so doing.

As they looked about the synagogue to take note of what their fellow congregants were doing, a few more, rather sheepishly, took off their head coverings. More than half did not. But up until then, most of the congregants had not yet seen their new spiritual leader (congregational meetings are as poorly attended in Canada as in the U. S.). The rabbi had not yet appeared. The first notes pealed out from the organ. The hubbub of conversation of many hundreds of worshippers was abruptly silenced. The rabbi entered the sanctuary—for the first time at any Holy Day service in the more than seventy years of Holy Blossom's history—with his head uncovered. A thousand gasps, gathering into bursts of whispers, spread through the congregation and exploded across the pews like a clap of long-delayed thunder. Just as I did not think to inquire in advance concerning the matter of "hats on or hats off," so not a single member of that congregation thought it necessary to write into that motion that such an option should not apply to the rabbi. As many among them were to tell me during that decade-and-a-half of richly fulfilling years that I spent among them, no one had the slightest premonition that a rabbi *"sans yarmulke"* would usher in the hallowed Jewish New Year.

The roar continued for some time after I had to plead again and again for silence and the reverential beginning of the service of worship. How many were able to pray that night without the nagging of turbulently disturbed emotions is anyone's guess. Few left the services promptly. The foyer long resounded with bitter arguments between advocates and adversaries.

But the next morning well over 50 per cent of the congregation emulated my example. By the Day of Atonement, less than a quarter of the congregation retained their hats. By Succoth (the Feast of Booths), that number was reduced to less than a tenth. During the course of the ensuing year, only one or two steadfastly kept their hats on their heads.

You see, *Now,* though this story has taken us on a long detour, it brings me directly back to our discussion and to my insistence that ceremonies and customs become ends in themselves and substitutes for the essential spiritual purposes and moral aspiration of our faith.

Now: Well, thank goodness you've finished. But, you know, I think it proves the very opposite of the point you are trying to make. I think it substantiates everything I've been trying to impress upon you. It proves that you did, as a matter of fact, make as much of a fetish out of taking off the hat as your Orthodox contingent made out of keeping it on, which was precisely my contention before you started on this filibuster. It also makes me wonder whether all that childish and fearful nonsense did not contribute much to the emergence of Conservative Judaism in this country. It was such spectacles which must have catapulted thousands of non-Orthodox Jews right into the Conservative synagogue.

Then: No. The controversy was important in demonstrating that covering of the head was not the *sine qua non* of worship. It emphasized how we tend to fasten upon some such externality and fix it forever in our minds—or rather in our emotions—as an indispensable requisite of our so-called religious expression. There are myriads of similar examples from every cult known to man: hastily scribbled notes which I saw so many Japanese in Tokyo hang on trees, confident that their petitions would be granted; the twirling of prayer wheels by the poverty-stricken peasants I watched in remote Nepal, who relied on these whirling discs to raise them out of their degradation rather than upon the scientific rotation of their crops which they stubbornly resisted as a foreign intrusion and a violation of their long-cherished faith; and the saffron-robed priests whom I heard and watched in a shrine in Rangoon as they struck their gongs and clapped their hands to dispel evil spirits. I would include even our own superstitious practice of reciting the *Kaddish* (Prayer for the Dead) for a precise, never varying, number of months no matter how slowly—or how swiftly—one's grief may be assuaged or how precious or despised the departed may have been, simply because Jewish legend decreed that the spirit of the dead hovered for that many months between Paradise and the Netherworld and could be dispatched to the abode of everlasting bliss only if those specific words were recited at the properly specified times.

Yet, these latter-day rituals of ours we regard as much more enlightened and less primitive than some of the practices I have just described.

Now: I don't think anyone would deny that there are some folks who substitute means for ends. But aren't you generalizing from the peccadillos of the few? And aren't you overlooking the fact that there are at least as many—undoubtedly multitudes more—who have been able to advance toward those ends you hold so dear, *by virtue* of some of these means that you so roundly condemned?

Then: The trouble with you is that you've quoted only part of that sermon of 1937 that I delivered to the Central Conference of American Rabbis—the part that so neatly suited your purpose. True, I denounced the trend then beginning in Reform to resurrect long-out-moded ceremonies. But I added in that same message: "This does not mean that I fail to appreciate the pedagogic and even the spiritual value of so many of the more beautiful ceremonies and symbols of religion in general and of Judaism in particular. I know that the psychologists warn us that abstract truth and ethical theories fail to satisfy the religious cravings of man—and of the child especially."

I went on to explain even more explicitly that, "man does not live by brain alone," but likewise, by everything that flows from the heart; he is lashed by an emotional hunger which lies too deep for words or theologies or creeds. I even quoted Plato who posited the need for Beauty as the first of his Universals, and to satisfy this yearning man has created ceremonies and symbols. You see, I was not nearly as iconoclastic as you suggest. I did not—as I confess some of our trail-blazing Reform revolutionaries tried to do—"throw out the baby with the bath," as you put it. But I think you will agree that, whereas in the first thrust of Reform the pendulum did swing too far in the indiscriminate casting aside of many beautiful and useful ceremonies and symbols, the pendulum may now be approaching dangerously close to the other extreme.

Now: But didn't you, yourself, contribute to this reverse action? Didn't your Union of American Hebrew Congregations encourage the revival of many once-discarded ceremonies and hasn't it had, together with the Central Conference of American Rabbis, a committee for the creation of new ceremonies?

Then: My Union of American Hebrew Congregations? Forgive me for again quoting from my address to the CCAR: "Religious ceremonies and symbols were never artificially concocted in committee rooms to serve as 'survival values' for a people that can apparently find no better *raison d'être* than to keep alive its folkways which in turn are kept alive in order to keep itself alive." That's what I said then and since you're trying so desperately to bring me up to date with yourself, I'd like to repeat that warning to you as well, lest your latter-day pleas for the recapture of some of the lovelier and more meaningful ceremonies of the past will once more lead our people astray and plunge us back into a veritable Orthodox attitude toward the accept-ance of such rites as ends in themselves.

Now: Do I gather from that remark that you share the apprehension expressed in so many Reform circles today that Reform is actually drifting back to Orthodoxy—a "viewing with alarm" which I don't for a single moment share?

Then: In the definitive words of one of my college professors I would reply "yes and no." No, I don't really think Reform is reverting to Orthodoxy as we understand that term today. To be sure, some of our extreme Reformists dub every departure from the norm, as they have known it, as such a capitulation to Orthodoxy. I recall a number of ludicrous examples—ludicrous were they not so tragically in error.

Let me recount just one from among many. This episode occurred some years later when I was asked to address a meeting at Temple Beth Ahavah in Richmond, Virginia. During the open forum that followed my formal presentation, that invariable question was hurled at me: "Isn't Reform reverting to Orthodox practices?" Again, my invariable countercharge: "Name one example." This time it was the argument that the establishment by the Reform movement of a School of Sacred Music for the training of cantors was proof positive of our abject surrender to Orthodoxy. "You had in this congregation," I replied, "a native son who left home and went to the big city of New York and made good. His name is Lewis Strauss, better known throughout America as Admiral Strauss. He happens to be President of Temple Emanu-El of the City of New York. Now so far as I know, Temple Emanu-El has never been without a cantor. And I doubt if Admiral Strauss would be particularly pleased—nor would his congregation—if that Temple were designated as Orthodox."

No, I don't think that the adoption or rejection of any particular rite or ceremony can be characterized as Reform or Orthodox. It's not what we do or don't do that makes us Orthodox or Reform. It's *why* we do it. It's the mood and motivation with which such a symbol is utilized or rejected. If we do it out of superstition and fear, or out of a misguided belief that every jot and tittle of the Torah was literally dictated by God on the crest of Sinai and that it is forever incumbent upon us to obey without deviation—that's Orthodoxy. But if, for example, we believe that the kindling of the Sabbath candles (which, by the way, no responsible leader of Reform ever mandated out of existence; its abandonment for a period came about solely by indifference and neglect) is a movingly beautiful and symbolic way in which to welcome the "Sabbath bride" and to distinguish that day of rest for the body and refreshment for the spirit from the rest of the week—then that's not Orthodoxy at all. Psychology discovered long before your afterthoughts came along that man's emotions, like an iceberg seven-eighths of which lies concealed beneath the sea, comprise the major part of his being. We cannot, therefore, ignore these submerged emotions in our religious appeal.

That's my negative reply to your query. No, to this extent I don't think we're swinging back to Orthodoxy.

The *"yes"* part of my answer rests on my growing apprehension that *some* of the practices being reintroduced into Reform ritual are once again becoming far from means to some noble ends, but are becoming ends in themselves and shamefully ignoble ones at that. The ceremony of *bar mitzvah* is a flagrant example. Even in my most iconoclastic days I was sympathetic to its reentry into the Reform temple or its perpetuation where it had never been relinquished. Thus I performed this ceremony without protest in my Holy Blossom pulpit, although I took every precaution to safeguard the Confirmation at the age of sixteen rather than thirteen. Nevertheless, I fear that this ancient rite is getting out of control and is becoming, through its extravagantly lavish receptions and wholesale gift-giving, the most striking example of supplanting good ends with vulgarized means and of squeezing all spiritual meaning out of a once lofty and appropriate ritual. Now you see why I was so apprehensive in 1937 and, despite my greater permissiveness through the intervening years, I'm somewhat apprehensive still.

Now: But since you obviously don't want to strip Reform of its more colorful and still-useful garments, how are you going to distinguish between the "still-meaningful," as you put it, and the outmoded? What criteria are you going to apply? Or are you content to let every rabbi, and every congregant as well, do precisely what he deems best?

Then: Most assuredly not. I have quoted a hundred times the fitting words on this subject spoken by Rabbi Isaac Mayer Wise, words uttered with a directness, even a vehemence, which few of our milder-mannered preachers would employ today: "Everyone does what is right in his own eyes. Some call this liberty—I call it license." I gave voice to this same sentiment in a message some years ago in Amsterdam before the biennial convention of the World Union for Progressive Judaism. "Hats on, hats off, rabbis robed, rabbis unrobed, one day Rosh Ha Shona and two days also; Ashkenazic pronunciation and Sephardic likewise—sometimes from the same pulpit; Kosher kitchens in so-called Reform social halls—all this and ham and bacon, too; *bar mitzvah* encouraged and *bar mitzvah* barred, confirmation at thirteen, fourteen, fifteen, and sixteen; Shavuos on the Sunday or Sabbath

before—and after; social action stressed and social action suppressed."
Yes, I too call this anarchy and that's the reason why I have so constantly urged the adoption of standards of practice—social, moral, as
well as ceremonial—to guide Reform Judaism.

Now: Come now! Aren't you being hopelessly inconsistent? Is not
the codification of any such practices the beginning of all Orthodoxy,
the very denial of the liberal spirit of Reform?

Then: That's what many of my rabbinic colleagues maintain. But
many of their congregants disagree, especially new members who flock
into our Reform temples looking for some guidelines to Reform
Jewish conduct in the home, in the synagogue—even in the market
place. They are hopelessly confused by the potpourri of practices
calling themselves Reform. A Reform Jewish guide to moral and ceremonial conduct that is not prescribed for all time, and is subject to
revision upon revision upon revision as has been the case with our
Reform Jewish Union Prayer Book, is not Orthodoxy. It does not
strike me in the least as being a betrayal of the spirit of Liberal or
Reform Judaism.

Now: Whether you recognize it or not, I think you're coming closer
to my own viewpoint which I tried to explain at the outset. I maintain, as you seem now to be doing, that Reform Judaism would have
died, and would have deserved to die, if it had sought to perpetuate
itself as merely a precious and pristine faith, deifying reason, reducing
Jewish experience to mere ethical preachment, and sundering the
bonds of flesh and bone which join every Jew to his fellows, living
and dead, and yet to be born, here and everywhere in the world. You,
too, have come a long way—fortunately—for if at least some of
your earlier views had prevailed, Reform would indeed have become a
new kind of Orthodoxy, fossilized and cold as a marble mausoleum.

Then: That's a very pretty sermon but what you're saying is really
quite cynical. It is that to succeed, Reform Judaism has to trim its
own principles by catering to the emotional and symbolic needs of the
masses. And I suppose that's why Reform has become so attractive to
so many former traditional Jews. Maybe some of the allegations concerning our contemporary "sell-out" are partially true. Maybe we *are*
tending to become mere imitators, compromisers, and nose counters—
all things to all men.

Now: A moment ago I thought we were quite close together but I
find that I must again disagree. The genius of Reform has been its
capacity to change, to create, to innovate. We weren't held captive
by a *Halachah* (The Law) which declared that all was handed down

for all time by God at Sinai. We have taken that genius and applied it—
not to imitating the Orthodox—but to the creation of new and vital
ceremonies and symbols which lend beauty and emotional power to
our services, our prayer, and our home observance. We have not
copied. We have pioneered in . . .

Then: But, don't you see . . .

Now: . . . creative services, in altogether new ceremonies. We
originated, as you said earlier and then so lightly dismissed, the Confirmation service which literally saved the holiday of Shavuos from
decay in America. We brought the music and the choir into the synagogue, enriching our worship with fresh dimensions of beauty and
drama, even though an incredible number of congregations split over
the question of whether an organ is proper in the synagogue. We introduced the candle-lighting and the *Kiddush* into the Friday evening
service in the synagogue and encouraged its resurrection in the home.
We gathered poets and writers and composers to create new prayers,
new songs, to give voice to man's yearning for God. You talk of imitating. Who has done the imitating? It is the traditionalists who have
emulated these practices. As they shed tears of wrath at the liberties
we have taken with the tradition, they have quietly introduced—I
almost said bootlegged—many of these same practices into their own
synagogues.

Then: Well, put it any way you want. What it adds up to is Reform
Judaism is getting more Orthodox all the time. There are some Reform
synagogues which actually have the men wearing hats. And the rabbis
more and more wear *tallesim*—I know you call them *atorahs,* but it's
the same thing. More and more Hebrew is introduced all the time. And
now it's becoming Sephardic yet! So what will remain of Reform?

Now: Don't be so fearful of the future. When you decry change, you
negate the basis of Reform. We refuse to call ourselves Reform*ed,* as
the Protestant Reformed Church terms itself, because we believe that
we are engaged in a continuous process of change and growth. It cannot be placed in glass at one particular moment in history, with the
declaration: this is it! No, we evolve; we grow; we mature; we enlarge
our vistas. We open ourselves to new and more profound spiritual experiences. We listen with eager ears to the seers of our own time.
We live. We are a living Judaism. Reform Judaism has been unafraid
of the future. New frontiers are to be explored with enthusiasm, not
approached with trembling. Who knows what we will be fifty years
hence, or a hundred years from now? Who knows what the world will
be? It is time we learned that we are more than intellect alone, more

than cool reason. Our spirit is compounded of tears, blood, grandeur of vision, and intoxication with God. Through prayer and meaningful ceremony and symbol we reach beyond ourselves. Through the outreach of our senses and our feelings, through the aspirations and meditations of our hearts as well as through the ratiocination of our minds, we give expression to our inmost dreams and our sublime yearnings for the living God.

Then: Now it's my turn to insist that we're really not as far apart as at times we have seemed and to echo your own sentiments to the effect that I've at last caught up with you. Maybe so—but I also think that you've retraced your steps somewhat in my direction. Perhaps it's time to invoke once again one of my—and I believe yours, too—favorite utterances: not "either-or" but "both-and." Not either all rationality or even all lofty moral principle as we must have both rites and rights, symbols and ceremonials wedded to spiritual aspiration and righteous conduct, the latter strengthened, sustained, and served by the former; the former guideposts, directional signals, instrumentalities for the attainment of the latter.

Now: Amen.

13

REFORM JUDAISM TODAY AND TOMORROW

FORETHOUGHT

Never did life permit our faith, even in its remotest origins, to remain static. It was the principle of continuous adaptation which changed the Judaism of Abraham into the Judaism of Moses; the Judaism of Moses into the religion of the prophets; the religion of the prophets into the religion of Ezra, and so on, through the many metamorphoses wrought by the Pharisees, the Talmudists, the Tosefists, the Exegetes, the Chasidim, the philosophers. Some of us are beginning to forget all these myriads of shifting forms and phases, as we are coming to regard all further progress and development as a sin; as, contrary to the counsel of Koheleth, *we do regard the former days as better than these.*

We likewise forget, or overlook, the fact that life, never so radically modified as within the past few centuries, had wrought vast transformations in Judaism and the Jew even before those pioneers of Reform, Jacobson or Geiger or Holdheim or Hirsch, came upon the scene. Thus Reform Judaism was not the cause, *but the effect of all these widespread transmutations; Reforms came "not to destroy, but to fulfill," to save Judaism for the Jew who was already adrift and well-nigh lost to the fold.*

Let some of our faint-hearted Reform rabbis, who would beat a retreat into those "former days" and who would lay at the door of Reform Judaism the responsibility for all the present drift and dereliction, read the myriad of remonstrances regarding the indifference and apathy of the multitudes even in the most rigidly Orthodox communities of yesterday or today; let them read their diatribes against their own flock's open violation of the laws of Kashrut. *Let them read the description of Orthodoxy's present plight as voiced by one of its own rabbis in a volume of sermons entitled* The Message of Israel: *"The dietary laws are almost universally discarded; the Sabbath has well-nigh disappeared; synagogue attendance is negligible; Christmas trees are becoming ever more popular and intermarriage shows no sign of abating." Let them appraise all such actual conditions and be realistic enough to confess with a leader of Conservative Judaism in America: 'We can no more be the Jews of "Hear, ye sons" than an aeroplane can be an oxcart. We may believe that type of living quaint and beautiful, but we cannot model our lives upon it. It is like a museum piece to be admired, but not emulated. In a nostalgic mood we may long for it, but when we are actually confronted with the choice, we will not choose it."*

Surely such words as these, coming from the strongholds of Orthodoxy and Conservatism, ought to give us pause, and persuade us to cease from our self-incrimination and from our presently most popular indictment of Reform as being responsible for having filched from Judaism all its erstwhile charm and loveliness. It is a romantic conceit, no less absurd than the mixed multitude of the desert, licking its chops and dreaming of that abundance of fish which supposedly they ate in Egypt, to imagine that Jewish life had reached the apogee of grace and beauty in the medieval period, the emancipation from which, so it appears today, was fate's "unkindest cut of all," as far as the Jew is concerned. . . .

And it is equally quixotic to presume that these shattered fragments are to be gathered together again; that the accelerated forces of life and change can be stayed, and that the myriads of young Jews and Jewesses who are seeking—and finding—salvation in national or racial movements can be won for a religious interpretation of Judaism merely by resolving that into the services of all Reform Jewish congregations be put "traditional symbols, ceremonies, and customs, such as the use of only Jewish music, the use of a cantor, the use of only Jewish singers," as if the surging songs, as if the musical genius of no other people could lift our Jewish souls "unto the hills whence cometh our help."

(From "Retreat or Advance"—1937)
Central Conference of American Rabbis,
Columbus, Ohio, 1937

AFTERTHOUGHTS

I believe now, as I did in 1937, that the capacity for change and growth has been the genius of Judaism and has saved it from decay. Reform Judaism has emerged as a response to the palpable need for change. It arose a century ago when Jewish life was centered in Europe. The French Revolution signaled the beginning of the end of the Jewish ghetto. Democratic revolutions, together with the emergence of a new industrial society fashioned by science and technology, destroyed the old life and released a new set of human problems and relationships. In the midst of this ferment, Jewish life had become uncharacteristically rigid. The *Shulchan Aruch* of Joseph Karo, (a detailed code of Jewish ritual practice), had become the "final" word on Jewish practice, thus stifling the historic process of adaptation which had kept Judaism alive through the ages. The *Shulchan Aruch,* first printed in 1567, could not cope with the revolutionary demands of a new era. At the very moment when Jews were being accepted for the first time in the countries of their sojourn, this code declared them to be in exile. When Jews were seeing new visions in science and democracy, it summoned them to await the miraculous arrival of a personal Messiah to redeem them. When Jews were beginning to relate in freedom to non-Jews, requirements of the *Shulchan Aruch* virtually necessitated the isolation of Jews from the non-Jewish world. Such an anachronistic, unworldly, and irrelevant Judaism could not have survived unless the juices of creativity were stirred within the crusted shell and liberated once again.

Reform Judaism arose as a flaming revolt by Jewish laymen in Germany against the intolerable rigidities of the Middle Ages. Rabbis recognized the need for change and joined with these laymen in the nineteenth century in freeing Judaism from the debilitating barnacles and dry rot of a fossilized orthodoxy. But it was on the free soil of America—and not Germany—where the seeds of rebirth took root and flowered into the swelling movement of Reform Judaism.

The changes wrought by the Reformers made Judaism relevant to the liberal and modern spirit of a pioneering America. It brought order and dignity to the religious service. It gave equality to women in the synagogue. It introduced the Friday evening service, the weekly sermon in the vernacular, and the beauty of organ and choral music. It rescued from virtual oblivion the holiday of Shavuos, marking the revelation at Sinai, by making it the significant occasion of Confirmation. It created a modern system of religious education for the young, with effective textbooks and other contemporary pedagogic techniques for attractive religious education. It established the first national federation of synagogues (the Union of American Hebrew Congregations) in 1873. It established the first seminary in America for the training of rabbis (the Hebrew Union College) in 1875. Its leaders were responsible for the formation of the interfaith movement, of the Hillel Foundation of B'nai B'rith, the Synagogue Council of America, the American Jewish Committee, the American Jewish Congress, the American Joint Distribution Committee, the United Israel Appeal, and a host of additional agencies for the service of *Klal Yisroel*—of the entire Jewish community.

It cast off outmoded prayers for a personal Messiah, prayers for the rebuilding of the ancient Temple in Jerusalem, entreaties for the restoration of animal sacrifice, antiquated caste rules regarding *Kohanim* (priests), the obligatory demands of the dietary laws, obsolete marriage and divorce practices, superstitious customs, and the unnecessary second days of festivals and holidays.

One of the myths about Reform Judaism—and a weapon used by its enemies—is that Reform was an aberrant faith, alien to the mainstream of Jewish tradition. Rabbi Jay Kaufman, able Vice-President of the Union of American Hebrew Congregations, has clearly demonstrated the inaccuracy of this charge:

A full and fascinating volume could be compiled of the critical and faith-saving reforms which were instituted in Judaism in an effort to adapt it to new circumstances. King Josiah "found" the Book of Deuteronomy in order to lessen the power of the priests and localize the excessive sacrifices. Synagogues were set up while the Temple yet stood, with the aim of establishing learning in place of sacrifices. To achieve this purpose the Torah was committed to a script legible to the non-priest and chapters and verses were added so the common man could read it. Simple prayer services were conducted in the synagogues at the very time the sacrifices were going on and the laymen were permitted to participate in them, not only the priests. . . . Hillel, living in a period of ascetic religious rigorism, reformed many impossible usages. . . . Jochanan ben Zakkai, in that era of great crisis, gave Jamnia new powers, and changed the treatment of converts and Gentiles. Rabbi Yehuda ha-Nassi abrogated the ban against writing down the Law and ignored the threat of a fearful punishment for so doing and also changed the laws concerning tithes and relations with Gentiles. Rabbi Yochanan gave voice to the theory so consistent in Judaism that rabbis have the right to abrogate, modify and institute, depending on the year, the place and the circumstance. The list is endless.

Only during the comparatively brief period when Jewry was completely ghettoized and cut off from free contact with the non-Jewish world did the process of internal change and external absorption cease. That stagnant era in Jewish history is not typical of Judaism. It is folly to accept that abnormal period as the norm for modern Judaism. It is well known that such stagnation breeds death. Only the constant interchange of thoughts and ideals with other societies, which kept Judaism virile and vigorous in the past, can create a viable Judaism for the present.

Reform Judaism had the daring to restore this pristine flexibility of our faith and thus to release the creative energies of growth and change that had been dammed up by ghetto incarceration and its inevitable severance of Jewish life from the living world outside its grim walls. Thanks to Reform Judaism, Conservative Judaism evolved as a middle-way between Orthodoxy and Reform. Its rationale was to counter the "extremism" of Reform. But, in actual practice, Conservative Judaism has quietly accepted many of the changes which the Reformers proudly—and rather truculently—proclaimed, including Friday evening services, a revised prayer book, Confirmation on Shavuos, use of the organ in the synagogue, Sunday schools, the weekly sermon, a Seminary, and parallel national institutions to advance Conservative Judaism. Conservative Judaism has flourished as has Reform. In my view, it has taken the easy road. It has made a virtue out of vagueness. It has carefully abstained from defining its own philosophy. It has been all things to all Jews. It has exalted compromise into a principle. It has introduced changes where absolutely necessary to placate its restless constituents (as in driving a car near to the synagogue on Sabbath). But it has made these changes quietly and almost diffidently in order not to arouse the wrath of the rabbis of the Jewish Theological Seminary who hold the Conservative movement in total intellectual and organizational subjugation.

A fascinating ambiguity of Conservative Judaism in America is that its Seminary leaders are heavily tradition-oriented and neo-Orthodox, but many of its rabbis and most of the laymen in its congregations are barely distinguishable from the congregants of Reform synagogues. Nevertheless, Conservative Judaism has played a positive and constructive role in American Jewish life. It has no doubt exerted significant influences on the dynamic evolution of Reform Judaism as both movements have also exerted a very real, if not quickly discernible, influence on modern Orthodox Judaism in America. But there would be no Conservative Judaism at all if the original Reformers had not broken open the locks which imprisoned Judaism in the musty caverns of the past.

As a matter of fact, I would not be at all surprised if a quarter of a century from now Reform and Conservative Judaism have merged into one powerful non-Orthodox movement. Increasingly, the philosophical differences are being narrowed. It is primarily the institutional factors compounded of avid competition for funds and followers which continue to divide us. Yet, as Jews move to the large metropolitan centers of America, changing their Jewish denominational labels with increasing ease, there will arise in the dwindling Jewish communities of small towns, especially in the Midwest and South, an irresistible tendency toward conserving resources and toward merging congregational forces. "Separate but equal" synagogue structures will yield to unified non-Orthodox institutions. This trend will ultimately make itself felt on the national level as well.

No doubt this prediction will bring cynical smiles to the faces of those who know the measure of existing institutional tensions between Conservative and Reform. But American Jewish life is dynamic, and startlingly new forms of organization are sure to emerge in a swiftly changing American milieu. I believe that the mainstreams of Reform and Conservative Judaism will ultimately flow together, despite the likely defection at that point of some "classical" Reformers on the one side and some neo-Orthodox Conservatives on the other, both die-hard groups regarding any such coalescence as anathema.

But the spirit of constant reformation, evolution, and change must survive and surmount any such coalition, for Reform Judaism has indeed been a revolutionary and constructive creative force in Jewish life. I believe that Reform Judaism has saved Judaism in America. Had it not been for Reform Judaism, American-born generations of Jews would, undoubtedly, have rejected the narrow, superstitious, and ritualistic Orthodoxy of their parents as they have done in so many other countries where, unfortunately, Reform did not arrive on the scene early enough to salvage those who, in revolt against and disgusted with an Orthodoxy that had become moribund both intellectually and spiritually, fled from our Jewish fold by the thousands. Though it is the favorite theme song of the foes of Reform that our presentment of Judaism is but a bridge to apostasy, a stepping-stone to Christianity, though our UAHC headquarters in New York City, which we call the "House of Living Judaism," is dubbed by our traducers as the "House of *Leaving* Judaism," the naked truth is that for the tens that have forsaken the Reform households and synagogues in which they have been reared in a rational appreciation of their faith, hundreds—even thousands—have abandoned the homes and houses of worship which have turned their faces like flint against the age in which we dwell.

In South America, for example, which I have recently visited, vast numbers of Jewish youth are forsaking both Judaism and Jewry as well. Their parents, though often likewise repelled by an outmoded Orthodoxy, remained staunchly, even zealously, loyal to the people of Israel through their labor and love for the Land of Israel. Today their children, bereft of the dreams of these *Hovevei Zion* (Lovers of Zion), are being lured from both folk and faith by the revolutionary passions of our time and of the lands in which they dwell. They are forsaking the synagogue in droves not because the advent of Reform has diluted their spiritual heritage, but because we have arrived too late to demonstrate that there is more revolutionary power in prophetic Judaism, in Moses and Isaiah, than in Marx and Khrushchev and Castro.

Whereas in virtually all other countries, including Israel, Reform Judaism is in revolution against the power of entrenched Orthodoxy, here in America the situation is altogether different. Here the revolution has been won. Reform Jewry needs no sanction from either government or any Orthodox authoritarians. Here, in church-state separation and religious freedom, Reform is at liberty to stretch to the limit of its own resources, free to build a new way, not merely for the synagogue but for society as well. Yet even in America Reform Judaism faces grave problems. And underlying all of them is the truth that, as with most revolutions, it is necessary to follow the revolutionary "tearing down" with the "building up" of a constitution, a system of order.

We have had our revolution. No longer do we pretend that we are in exile. Deep are our roots in our native soil of America. We are at home here as Jews are at home in England and in Israel. We await no Messiah. We are masters of our own Jewish destiny.

Now we must frame our constitution. We must fortify our cherished freedom with a measure of order. We must lift the standards of our synagogues and of individual Reform Jewish practice. The time has come—indeed, it is long overdue—to say finis to the situation in which religious indolence and apathy parade as Liberal Judaism; the time has come to mobilize our spirit and our faith so that we may fulfill in our time the ancient and ever-relevant mandate which God has thrust upon us.

But how build such a constitution? What are the goals to which Liberal Judaism must aspire if it is to win the future? What are the weaknesses to be overcome?

The first requirement is to recapture for the synagogue the passion which American Jews poured into the struggle for a Jewish homeland and into the struggle to save the displaced persons who survived Hitler. Only the Jewish religion can restore the spent zeal and the damped-down ardor of millions of Jews now without a cause or purpose.

As Martin Buber once warned: "Even if others can get along without God and His spirit, if the Jew should attempt such a course, he shall perish at his own hand. If the Jew stops believing in the might of the spirit and in himself as its artisan on earth, his existence will come to a speedy and inglorious end. He shall have no destiny or future." The late, great rabbi and Zionist leader Abba Hillel Silver rightfully pointed out (as early as 1929) upon the occasion of the twenty-fifth anniversary of the death of Herzl:

It is well that the political phase of Jewish Messianism is coming to a close in the upbuilding of the National Homeland. We shall not have to lay so much stress in the future on the importance of nationalism. We shall henceforth be confronted, not with its lack, but with its consequences. Hitherto wanting the full complement of the attributes of nationalism, we were constrained to over-emphasize its virtues. Many of the spokesmen of our cause were driven to extol nationalism per se which, after all, is a quite recent and, demonstrably, quite inadequate concept. It is not mankind's ultimate vision. Certainly it is not the substance of our own ancestral tradition, whose motif is not nationalism, but prophetism. Nationalism is not enough. It is a minimum requirement, not a maximum program. Nationalism will not suffice the eternally questing soul of our people. After its national life is secure, Israel must push on to the frontiers of the new world—the world of internationalism, of economic freedom, of brotherhood and of peace.

Where, then, is there an agency, a medium, an instrument, a vehicle for such a relevant and indispensible purpose better equipped by tradition, by practice, by experience, by the *gestalt* out of which it has arisen, than the synagogue? But it must be a synagogue radically different from the pale, anemic would-be replica of the synagogue of our fathers, reduced, as someone said of the church, in words equally applicable to too many contemporary synagogues, to "chicken broth for the ailing, a brief code for mating, and a few seemly words at the grave." Or as the always penetrating and provocative Mordecai Kaplan describes so much of the present-day synagogue as representing a place where the "high Holy Days have come to be observed by many of our people as a kind of *Yahrzeit* (Memorial) for the Judaism which died with their parents."

That kind of synagogue sufficiently buttressed to meet the crisis of our time must be a synagogue whose God is a living God—not a God who revealed Himself and His word once and for all time at Sinai and speaks no more. He must be a God whose revelation, not merely in the words of our ritual but in reality, comes continuously to us, whether out of distant times or out of the insights of the seers of our own day, no matter how much violence such insight might inflict upon some of our cherished but outmoded concepts. A God with whom Einstein and Freud and Dewey were not at war but rather in league as they brought us to a broader vision of His majesty rehearsed throughout the universe and a deeper insight into the struggles, the conflicts, the aspirations in the mind and soul of man. He must be a God not merely of the past, but of the present and the future, to whom we can pray in the idiom of our time, as Norman Corwin captured it in his "On a Note of Triumph":

Lord, God of test-tube and blue-print; Who jointed molecules of dust and shook them till their name was Adam,
Who taught worms and stars how they could live together,
Appear now among the parliaments of conquerors and give instruction to their schemes: Measure out new liberties so none shall suffer for his father's color or the credo of his choice:
Post proofs that brotherhood is not so wild a dream as those who profit by postponing it pretend: Sit at the Treaty Table and convoy the hopes of little peoples through expected straits,
And press into the final seal a sign that peace will come for longer than posterities can see ahead,
That man unto his fellow man shall be a friend forever.

Such a God, such a living, loving God must fill the synagogue with His *shechina,* with His ever-present being, and set the light of His countenance upon His God-intoxicated children.

Nothing static can survive in a dynamic universe. No synagogue can cope with crisis unless it admits the right, nay the duty, of each generation to reinterpret its faith and its religious forms in the light of its own time and thought. There are many among us today who have forgotten this essential element in Israel's persistence. It was Herbert Agar who, in his *A Time for Greatness,* said that democracy is not a station, but a road. So it is with Judaism—with Liberal Judaism especially. It is not a station already attained, a comfortable resting place where we can preen ourselves in the light of our past achievement. But it is a road; an endless, ofttimes arduous road along which we must constantly and persistently plod.

The faith and forms of the liberal synagogue must become again manifestations of a movement; not achieved or exhausted at one single historic moment, not forever frozen, but a process concerning which every decade will have something to add to or to subtract from that which has gone before. Reform was never intended to be a noun representing something already obtained—eternally fixed, coagulated, final—but an adjective describing a dynamic, progressive, ever-evolving, deepening, and developing faith. We dare not permit Reform to become itself an Orthodoxy admitting of no further change or variation within our fold, but we must make certain that we heed the spirit rather than worship the words of our dauntless Reform pioneers who solemnly warned us, in the language of Kaufmann Kohler, to ". . . guard against conferring upon the pioneers of Reform the claim of infallibility. We would sin against the spirit of progress, should we canonize their every word. Truth grows, and many a thing which seemed true fifty years ago, is no longer so today."

Here too, Dr. Julius Morgenstern, the President Emeritus of the Hebrew Union College, warned us that "whenever Reform Judaism over-emphasizes its own brief tradition and, with mistaken loyalty, endeavors to perpetuate its own past in this present age of swift and extreme change, it belies its own name . . . it ceases to be Reform and becomes Orthodoxy, of a peculiar type, it is true; but Orthodoxy nonetheless."

We want no such neo-Orthodoxy in Reform today. We crave a Liberal, Progressive Judaism resolutely declaring the right of our generation to change customs and rituals, to reclaim that which we may have cast aside, to restate doctrines in the light of the altered conditions of our day. All this we insist is not a reversion to Orthodoxy, but the only true and consistent Reform which today and always must refuse to worship at the shrine of so-called classical crystallization.

It must be a synagogue in which the prayers of our ritual also shall be matched with the intellectual and spiritual atmosphere of the world in which we find ourselves. Revision after revision of our prayer book has been made and yet, if we be scrupulously candid and not afraid to face the honest criticisms which occasionally our laity is not too timid to confess to its rabbis, we must admit that, in far too many instances, our people's hearts are not quickened nor their souls stirred by much of the verbiage of our liturgy. I do not know whether prayers can be written to touch the souls and move the hearts of a generation which, after all, is not living in an age of faith, but rather in one which still reflects the doubts and skepticism of the early Enlightenment. Yet, directors at youth camps who have experimented pragmatically with new forms of prayers, our chaplains in the armed forces who talked to men and women in their hours of greatest and gravest personal crisis, have indicated that there is some longing within the hearts even of our contemporaries which is not altogether satisfied with that which we have striven to give them. We have not yet approached this problem of prayer in our time with the tools and techniques of such scientific research as we utilize in all other areas. Widespread questionnaires, unlimited experimentation, the cooperation of the finest minds and spirits in the realm of poetry, drama, and art must be enlisted in our free uninhibited search for those forms and conditions, that quality and quantity of worship, which will win from our contemporaries some more satisfying response than is to be seen in our forsaken sanctuaries or even in those few exceptional synagogues which swarm with audiences of spellbound listeners to some especially gifted orators, but which, even in such instances, are devoid of devout worshippers.

I believe we must ascertain whether our present prayer book is the best possible vehicle for transmitting the reverence, beauty, and spiritual richness of our Jewish worship. Only Reform Judaism has had the daring to undertake such a search through scholarly revisions of many archaic and anthropomorphic passages. Orthodox Judaism, denying the right to tamper with that which it holds as revealed by God for all time to come, is imprisoned by its own dogma. Conservative Judaism, while claiming the right to revise the prayer book, has failed to recast even some of the most outmoded of prayers; even the anachronistic petition for restoration of animal sacrifice in the temple has only been amended so that the text refers to the fact that *in the past* such sacrifices were brought. The basic text of the Conservative prayer book remains unchanged. While the Reform prayer book much more adequately reflects the temper of the modern spirit, these revisions have consisted mostly of the deletion of some of the more blatantly objectionable and obsolete prayers. But in my view there are still a host of archaic expressions in the prayer book which must offend those who care about the meaning of the words they utter. Thus, we still proclaim that "God heals the sick," though millions of devout people are consumed by cancer. He "loosest the bonds," though the stench of Auschwitz still plagues our sleep. He still "givest them food in due season," though more than half the people of the world go to bed hungry every night. These passages can be looked upon merely as poetic license, but I see no reason why the prayer book should include any such impediments to the free and uninhibited expressions of the worshipful mood.

I agree with Rabbi Robert Kahn who called for a genuine reform of the Reform prayer book. Really to accomplish this, Rabbi Kahn wrote, would mean to "clear the ground and to start all over again with a master plan in which the salvaged riches of tradition would be cleansed, reshaped, planed, sanded, mitred and fitted into an organic whole, a structure of worship which would be less like a museum and more like a sanctuary. Its architects must be rabbis, its builders laymen, musicians, poets and playwrights." I have urged the Union of American Hebrew Congregations and the Central Conference of American Rabbis to reach out to those profound thinkers, creative spirits, sensitive poets, and gifted composers of our time so that we may be able to help the individual in the lonely secrecy of his heart, as well as the congregation in its exalted togetherness, to slake the thirst for the "fountain of living waters" which afflicts the whole of mankind.

Closely allied with the words of our mouths and the meditations of our hearts, there must be far more dramatic and thrilling pageantry in our synagogues if they are to win such adherents both in number and in fervor as may meet the crisis of our time. It is just here that we Reform Jews must confess that we have indeed sinned in our emasculation of too many of our traditionally rich and beautiful ceremonials. We did cast aside many precious gems together with some of their admittedly tarnished settings. Those symbols and forms which do still have significance today must be recaptured and refurbished; others must be created anew, not as a retreat to Orthodoxy as has been mistakenly alleged, not because dogmatically we believe they were all everlastingly ordained at Sinai, but because many of them have added dignity and beauty and have breathed loyalty and heightened morale into Jewish living. The findings of modern psychology, perhaps intuitively glimpsed centuries ago by our forebears, remind us that there must be feeling as well as thought, poetry as well as prose, for the wholesome life; and that we are frequently conditioned by that which appeals to our hearts even more than by that which persuades our minds. To be meaningful today, the synagogue must become an oasis of beauty and spirit amid the drab mechanics of life, just as the traditional house of prayer clothed the naked skeleton of doctrine and dogma with the warm and tingling flesh of pageantry and emotion.

This brings me to another and perhaps most controversial requirement for an effective Liberal Judaism of today and tomorrow. It is a recommendation with which, for many years, I was personally in strenuous disagreement. Whenever, at our conferences of rabbis or at the Union biennials, there has been urged upon us a consideration of some code of practice for Liberal Jews, my own spontaneous reaction, like that of many of my liberal colleagues, has been one of resistance to anything which might ever so slightly impede and inhibit the free spirit which is indeed the essence of our liberal faith. Wider experience, however, and a frank appraisal of the actual state of affairs within the hundreds of congregations which I have personally visited throughout this continent, have now convinced me that that which we have today in the synagogue, of the Reform Jewish movement particularly, is nothing which even remotely resembles true liberty but is rather unrestrained license which may soon cause our movement to degenerate into nothing short of self-destructive anarchy.

The end result of such *laissez faire,* which permits every rabbi and every layman to do that which is right in his own sight, was startlingly brought home to me not so very long ago when at a temple board meeting in one of the congregations I was asked in all seriousness whether Reform's capitulation and lamentable retreat to Orthodoxy were not manifested by the fact that their rabbi was urging upon them the introduction of a Sabbath morning service. That, of course, so I was told, would remove one of the principal criteria that marked that congregation as Reform.

Similar examples which tragically travesty the whole purpose and content of Reform Judaism might be easily multiplied. But this in itself is indicative of the irrefutable truth that no synagogue subject to the whim and caprice of this or that individual can do aught but make confusion worse confounded. Only that synagogue which hews to at least a minimum code of practice in Jewish knowledge, in ritual and ceremonial observance, and in moral conduct and social action will possess the authority and the effectiveness necessary to withstand the spiritual anarchy of our day. Liberty under some form of law can alone prevent freedom from degenerating into license. The comparative weakness of our contemporary synagogue must be frankly and courageously studied in the light of our stubborn insistence upon absolute congregational autonomy and self-interest. On the one hand, we have unified Jewish community councils in which almost every facet of Jewish life is bound together for the attainment of common objectives and, on the other hand, we have hosts of inviolately independent synagogues usually pitted against each other rather than working in cooperation with one another. Even within the relatively homogeneous ranks of our Reform movement, we have so worshipped this idol of autonomy as to be blind to the havoc which it is creating in many spheres of our religious life. Mammoth congregations with almost limitless resources and magnificent facilities flourish within a stone's throw of tiny, struggling congregations which languish for want of the most modest aid in manpower or means. Even more reprehensible and alarming is the fact that such flourishing synagogues frequently resist the establishment of sister congregations, be they ever so humble, anywhere near their own vigilantly guarded bailiwicks—no matter how many thousands of unsynagogued Jews may be within the shadow of their looming sanctuaries.

This is not merely the judgment of one who might be ungenerously accused of having a professional interest in the multiplication of congregations. After a painstaking and objective survey of conditions in one of our metropolitan centers, a committee, consisting primarily of disinterested laymen, indicated this sorry and abortive situation by stating:

. . . it is apparent that most congregations are more concerned with their own welfare, than they are with the growth and development of our movement . . . they positively object and actively resist the effort to organize new congregations unless they be as far away from their own location as possible, no matter how filled their own rosters may be, no matter how many thousands of unaffiliated Jews there are in their immediate vicinity, no matter how few prospects there might be in the remoter sections of the city to which they would restrict our missionary efforts.

Such a synagogue—or rather, such synagogues, because we cannot possibly use the generic term "synagogue" in the face of such unbridled chaos—cannot possibly meet the challenge of the future. As nations must surrender at least a portion of their anachronistic absolute sovereignty for the rearing of one world, so we must explore the possibility of creating a strongly unified American synagogue whereby the strong shall aid the weak and the rich serve the poor through the channel of community-wide and nation-wide coordination.

Does this mean that I am urging some rigid hierarchic system which has been so alien and repugnant to our liberal tradition? Most assuredly, I am not! The very contrary is in my mind and heart. I would insist that those standards of practice and conduct, those policies and programs pursued by the synagogue, must be democratically determined—and I do not mean merely "democracy from the top down." I mean democracy from the bottom up; democracy springing from the grass roots of our humblest members who would be drawn into the determination of the functioning of the modern synagogue. There is no greater mockery of the whole democratic process, in which both as Americans and as Jews we profess our belief, than that characteristic of most of our congregational procedure. Representation is given and policies are usually decided by that handful of individuals who frequently comprise many a self-perpetuating, and seemingly hardy perennial, Board of Trustees. Rarely are concrete and controversial issues placed squarely before our congregations as a whole, so that the will of the majority may be unequivocally expressed.

We, who realize that there may be tentative weaknesses and passing inefficiencies within democracy, are nonetheless sustained by an indomitable confidence in the ultimate wisdom of the people and must insist upon a religious structure that will be genuinely democratic, from its lowliest foundation in the humblest individual within the local congregation to the topmost levels of our national institutions. Basic policies, projects, and programs ought to be as democratically resolved within the synagogue as in the state. In this area, we do indeed take the name of democracy in vain when we are unprepared to yield to majority decisions and refuse to submit our fondly cherished nostrums and notions to the will of the people themselves.

It is with such a democratic practice alone that we can make our appeal to the swarming multitudes of unsynagogued Jews whom we have so woefully neglected and whose failure to affiliate has so palpably weakened the contemporary synagogue. No institution that caters to or draws from the upper middle classes only can hope to make an impact in the coming era. Only that synagogue, the heart of which will pulsate with the warm blood of the *masses* of our fellow Jews, can hope to meet the present crisis. Only those congregations that will throb with their enthusiasms, meet their needs, assuage their longings, and reflect their aspirations will prove adequate to cope with other ideologies and movements which do hold out some measure of hope and healing to the restive multitudes. Only a synagogue proclaiming and seeking to practice such a Judaism, adapted to the soil and soul of our time and clime, can win these masses and be strengthened by them. Only a synagogue fired with such missionary fervor to win the multitudes of Jews to our cause can face the future with confidence.

We must similarly face with utmost candor our failures in Jewish education. A recent study of Jewish education in America found that "Jewish education in the United States is like a river, a mile wide and an inch deep." Despite the pioneering role of Reform Judaism in modern Jewish education, we cannot wash our hands of our own grievous shortcomings. It is abundantly clear that the Sunday school system is not ample to transmit a heritage and to build Jewish motivation and commitment. Two and one-half hours a week are a pittance and a sham. Our children, by and large, do not take their religious schools seriously—and who can blame them? We do not have enough trained and inspired religious school teachers. And even the occasionally dedicated and creative teacher is frustrated by paltry hours, paltry salary, and by the debilitating indifference, if not downright resistance, of the parents. How can a parent transmit a heritage he does not possess himself? How much good can be derived from religious education of the young unless there is an equivalent program of adult education?

I believe we shall have to move in the direction of a two- or three-day-a-week religious school, intensified training programs for teachers, community-wide and professionally conducted academies of adult Jewish education, and a widely expanding network of Jewish religious camps (for young and old alike) where Judaism can be made relevant and exciting in a richly positive Jewish atmosphere. We are already making progress in some of these directions; for example, Reform Judaism already maintains seven such camps throughout the country where Jewish youth can see visions. But much more must be done. A bold and dramatic approach to Jewish education is an imperative for the future of Liberal Judaism in America.

As the synagogue must look inward, so must it proclaim its message and offer its ministration to the whole of our stricken world. The degrading depths to which the synagogue would be dragged by those who posit a false dichotomy between the secular and the sacred, the religious and the political, is shamefully driven home in a communication from a past president of one of our large congregations in the South, that I received in protest against what I thought was my innocuous commendation of racial integration. He wrote:

There are Americans of the Jewish faith who see danger in the concerted attempt of the Jew to pull the Negro's chestnuts out of the fire. The Jewish press has even depicted scenes of pluperfect democracy, in which Jewish children and Negro children might enjoy the common companionship which Rabbi Eisendrath so sadly misses in some parts of our country. But this gospel against the segregation of the races may some day bring action founded upon the proposition that "Jews are no better than niggers." If Jews follow this ideology, they are going to get just what they are looking for. But I ask, can we not find some message dedicated to a faith which this troubled world needs far more than an insistence which runs counter to the innate feelings of countless Americans? Why should Jewish leadership not attend to its own business?

Pertinent questions indeed—and impertinent as well! And to the urgent issue of race relations might well be added an almost endless list of similar problems: international peace, economic justice, adequate housing, minimum wage, religious freedom, and a myriad more about which the prophets of Israel gave us such sublime principles and which the rabbis incorporated into the most minute social and moral codes of individual and collective conduct. An ironic contrast to this effort to crib, cabin, and confine the synagogue to mere ecclesiasticism is to be found in the words of a communication which I received early in the war from one of the youngest and at that time most recently ordained rabbis. From a tiny atoll in the Pacific, he wrote:

There is in our synagogue too much thundering against evil more for the sake of the thunder than in any hope of affecting the evil. If modern religion is to attract the returning men and women, then in the spirit of the high ideals they proclaim, the various creeds must enter into the lists of modern social conflict, and decisively. They must take sides. The prophets of old spoke clearly and firmly upon specific problems which beset their generation. In their day it was the oppression of the widow and the orphan, the selling of the poor for a pair of shoes, the neglect of the manumission of slaves. In our day there may be a lack of prophets. There is no lack, however, of the problems they denounced. It is now time for our generation to take its stand and deliver its denunciation about our particular specifics.

Religious leaders must successfully move their congregations and the individual members who comprise them to abolish racial discrimination, or these leaders will have to admit that religion has lost its vigor and is destined to pass away. Pulpit and prayer book must declare that modern monopolies and cartels, by whatever name, must give way before the needs and rights of individuals, or else religion must give way. They must speak in definite terms, mention names, educe facts, and not be content with vaguely defined wrongs and glittering generalities. No sweetly worded brochures or pious resolutions will suffice. They must point the finger, they must name the name. The Bible is not to be merely fondled. We cannot be content to quote and requote its venerable parables and proverbs. When congregations read the proclamations of the truths of Scripture, but indulge in apathy, evil, and the wickedness of indifference, they are taking God's name in vain. If worshippers pray for justice and pick up their prejudices when they put down their prayer books, they are being traitors to centuries of their religious tradition. Religion which fails to effect the direction of human motives and actions for good in relation to the problems of human society is no religion and had better be cast into the discard. It becomes hokum and humbug and will be flung contemptuously aside by those who demand a brave new world for themselves and their children.

No synagogue, which fails to offer such a program of social and moral action, can be relevant to a changing world. But it must not devolve exclusively upon the rabbis. Laymen too must catch this prophetic vision and be inspired to consecrated action. The Commission on Social Action of Reform Judaism has stimulated more than 400 synagogues to develop such programs of social action and education. And our Religious Action Center in Washington, D.C., works with groups of all other faiths to bring the religious conscience to the nation's capital. But most of our people do not yet feel the connection between their religious faith and life itself.

Only a synagogue thus dedicated to the larger issues of mankind merits survival. The pallid shadow of the traditional synagogue offers little hope for redemption and neither does the Protestant-styled temple. We have too much of such "little Judaism," to quote a striking phrase from that rarest religious seer of contemporary Israel, the late Leo Baeck, who argued that we had contented ourselves with:

... a Judaism which exhausts itself in belonging to a congregation or perhaps to some association and which in such service deems to have fulfilled its share of Jewish duty. . . . If others find their fulfillment in such little Judaism, that is a deficiency in them; if we found our satisfaction therein, it would be a distortion of our nature, a denial of our supreme task.

The greater Judaism is our especial strength, our especial right. . . . Judaism must not stand aside, when the great problems of humanity which are reborn in every epoch struggle in the minds of men to gain expression, battle in the societies of mankind to find their way. We must not, as Jews, deny ourselves to the problems of our time, nor hide ourselves as Jews, in the face of them. We are Jews for the sake of humanity. We have our questions to raise and we have to give our answers. To rouse the conscience of humanity is our best title deed. We will have to speak often a No to much that happens on earth; to speak a No for the sake of our great Yes, of our great demand. We shall often have to accuse, for the sake of justice, of love, for the sake of the promise; to say No and accuse, because we are what we are and should be, the Lord's most loyal opposition on earth, the steadfast and the stubborn for God's sake.

The synagogue that would enable us to meet the crisis of our day, that will make for our Jewish survival in America and throughout the world, must indeed be stubborn and steadfast for God's sake; it must be saturated with that spirit which would consecrate our souls to God and our service to Israel and all our fellow men. When the tabernacle in the wilderness was dedicated, so our rabbis tell us, the evil spirits which had been harassing Israel were put to flight. Who knows but that through the synagogue reborn and revitalized, through the religious rebirth and reconsecration of our people Israel, the evil demons of our day—war and injustice and bigotry and homelessness and hatred—may likewise be put to flight. Through all the toilsome, turbulent centuries of our people, as the poet Bialik has told us:

> If you would know the spring whence strength of soul
> Was drawn in evil days, woeful as these
> By those who bravely walked to meet their death
> Bending their neck beneath the biting steel.
>
> If you would know the well where those who, crushed
> Between the straits of chaos and the grave,
> Drew comforts of the Lord, and mighty faith.
>
> If you would know the stronghold where your fathers
> Salvaged their soul's desire and held the Law
> Holy above all holies to be saved . . .
> Turn to the House of God.

14

WILL SUCCESS SPOIL THE SYNAGOGUE?

FORETHOUGHT

That there is a crisis to meet, not even the most casual observer of Jewish life can deny. But that the synagogue is capable of meeting such a deep and far-reaching crisis, even many of the most fervent proponents of the synagogue cannot but question.

This general derogation of the synagogue to a second-class role or, in some instances, to virtually no role at all in the contemporary American scene, was strikingly brought home to me by an experience not many weeks ago which, were it not so symptomatic, would not merit repetition.

This scene takes us to Atlantic City, New Jersey, where thousands of Jewish leaders from all over America are gathered to dedicate themselves to the admittedly holy task of succoring our brethren and of enabling the captive to return in joy unto Zion. Grandiloquent speeches are made! It is piously proclaimed that this is no mere matter of physical relief but a sacred crusade for the religious rehabilitation of our people as well. There are even cheers and deafening applause when Dr. Chaim Weizmann, in one of the most moving and prophetic utterances I have yet heard from any living statesman, solemnly warns that the only kind of state which Israel dares build in Eretz Yisroel must be one established by "a kingdom of priests and a holy people."

Yet, on the Sabbath eve, the synagogues situated within the very shadow of this vast assemblage were deserted. Hardly a single one of those who so fervidly called upon American Israel to join in this holy task of religious reconstruction and spiritual restoration elsewhere, whether in Europe or Zion, was present to prove the sincerity of his word by his deed. . . .

As a matter of fact, less is spent on both religion and philanthropy *in the United States than on alcohol and tobacco per person per year. The welfare of both man's body and soul rated about $1.50 out of every $100 spent by the average American.*

When it comes to the synagogue itself, even more humiliating are the paltry pennies that are flung to this diminutive poor relation of a David by that most formidable Goliath of our time, the Jewish federations and welfare funds which would so grudgingly mete out their mite to our Jewish religious institutions. While the fault may inhere somewhat in ourselves, for our weak and timid surrender to the monopolistic fund-raising machinery of our day, the startling fact remains that out of the tens of millions raised for overseas and local needs by our federations and welfare funds, the allocation to national Jewish religious institutions fell from the munificent fraction of .08 per cent in 1945 to .03 per cent in 1946, while the figure for 1947, when it is finally compiled, will in all likelihood approach the vanishing point.

"Millions for defense, but not one cent for 'tribute,' " as someone has facetiously, yet too truly, put it. Countless millions for relief and the fighting of anti-Semitism and hardly a penny for the true fortress of our faith and people: religion and the synagogue!

March, 1948

AFTERTHOUGHTS

Was it only sixteen years ago that I said those words? It is no longer the same world. As H-bombs, Khrushchev, Africa, jets, the cold war, astronauts, moon-shots, and Telstars have transformed and telescoped the whole universe as we knew it in 1948, so the Jewish world has also undergone radical alteration. Some of my worries of 1948 nag at me still. Others have been thrust aside by the race of events. Time no longer marches on; it swoops by on the wings of rockets, and the Jewish community I sometimes chastised—but only with the *"y'asurim she ahavah"* ("the wounds of love")—I still censure, but for different reasons.

American Jewry has not decayed. It has flourished. And the synagogue is no longer relegated to a second-class role. On the contrary, it has become the most important source of Jewish identification for American Jews. It has made a comeback of monumental magnitude.

More than 60 per cent of American Jewry is said to be affiliated with the synagogue—Reform, Conservative, or Orthodox. A report made at a recent meeting of the Conference of Jewish Federations and Welfare Funds revealed that, of all the Jewish children enrolled in Jewish educational institutions, as many as 90 per cent are in synagogue religious schools—in striking contrast to the far greater proportion previously attending non-synagogue schools. More and more of late we Jews are tending to regard ourselves as a religious community. Of course, we are more than merely a religious community. But it is as a religious group that our Christian neighbors see us—and it is also the way Jews increasingly conceive of themselves.

I still feel that the Jewish religious community does not get a fair share of Jewish funds, but my erstwhile tone of mixed anguish and indignation seems no longer warranted. Maybe it was not fully warranted even then. When I spoke in March, 1948, the entire Jewish community was understandably preoccupied with the gigantic task of binding up the wounds of hundreds of thousands of survivors of Nazi persecution. It was a moment replete with history; a few short weeks later, the rebirth of the Jewish State seized the imagination and commanded the spiritual and financial sacrifice of Jews throughout the world and, especially, of American Jewry. In that very year, United States Jewry poured out its support of the United Jewish Appeal to the extraordinary measure of $180 million—an impressive figure which continued, although in lesser amounts, through the earlier years of Israel's military and economic trials.

Looking back at my thoughts then, I am startled by what may have been some lack of historical perspective on my part. In those days I prayed—and hardly dared to believe that those prayers would be realized—that a shimmering dawn would break for the Jewish people after the bloodiest nightmare we had ever endured in our tortured history. Israel was that dawn and that miracle, and none should cavil at the sums required to help "pass that miracle." One can only regret that some of us hammered in vain at too many barriers, that we did not expend sufficient energies nor seek to raise even greater funds that the miracle might have been wrought sooner so that more of our brother Jews might have been rescued from Hitlerism and given a safe haven in Zion.

There are never enough funds—as I have articulated with all too puny results before fund-raising breakfasts, luncheons, dinners, teas, and cocktail parties from the Atlantic to the Pacific—but few Jews have given "until it hurts." Few have changed their standards of living, moved to more modest homes, relinquished their lavish winter holidays, or expensive world cruises, or pawned their Cadillacs and their minks in order to increase their contributions to Jewish causes. A survey conducted a few years ago revealed that, despite the desperation of our people's plight, despite all the high-pressure appeals, American Jewry had contributed less than 2 per cent (and American Jewry is in the vanguard of all other Jewries and of most non-Jewish philanthropic response) of its estimated gross income. A far cry indeed from the Biblical standard of tithing, still observed by the Mormons and certain other denominations!

Although the Jewish community can well afford to care adequately for all its needs, charitable, educational, and religious, the synagogue has not received its just proportion of Jewish resources available. Nevertheless, we must admit that our American synagogues have not been exactly starved. Glistening, modern, new sanctuaries have burgeoned in every community in the land (the well-known "edifice complex" in Jewish life). American Jewry has become comfortably middle class—undoubtedly the most affluent Jewish community in our history. It does give. What Jew can refuse the well-greased, efficient, and high-powered fund-raising apparatus of the Jewish community with its ubiquitous and obnoxious card-calling, the "big givers," and the "Men of the Year" affairs?

Fund-raising has become the special genius of American Jewish life, with God, as someone has put it, converted into a kind of "honorary chairman" of our vast philanthropic syndrome and Judaism transformed "from monotheism to money-theism." The "corruption of the best may well become the worst." With its not infrequent vulgarities, its exaltation of means as an end in itself, its tendency to inflate the man of wealth (however unexemplary) into a community leader, the dog-eat-dog competition for funds among Jewish groups—this idolatry of fund-raising may be corrupting Jewish life and the synagogue almost as much in the 1960s as the shortage of funds seemed to be starving American Judaism in the 1940s.

Our highly-developed fund-raising is, of course, an aspect of our new middle-class character. Jews have made a giant leap—in one generation—from the gruesome sweat shops and swarming tenements of the lower East Side to the plush suburbs of Westchester and Long Island, New York; Glencoe, Illinois; Shaker Heights, Ohio; and Beverly Hills, California; and to the new high-rise cooperatives of Miami, Florida, as well as to the lush penthouses of every major metropolis. Of course, not all Jews are rich—nor are even most of them

—as our traducers falsely claim; nor are our very wealthiest coreligionists in the same league with the American Bourbons who dominate the executive suites of our United States economy. But taken all in all, the financial status of the American Jew compares favorably with that of any other religious group (Episcopalians may rank a bit higher) in America. The once-thriving Jewish labor movement is disappearing, and the virtual slamming of the gate of immigration in 1924 has prevented replenishment from abroad. American Jewry has become middle class, native born, suburban, and highly Americanized.

We are paying a price—a heavy price—for our successful accommodation to American life, for our freedom and our prosperity. In large measure the criteria for success of the synagogue, too, are middle-class American values far removed from the traditional Jewish plumb line: "What doth the Lord require of thee?" What *is* required of the average member of our congregations today? Regular payment of dues is the first priority and it is a "must." Equally regular attendance at services of worship? Well, this is piously hoped and pleaded for by the rabbi, but rarely heeded and never *required* as a *sine qua non* of membership, even of *leadership* in that which is still called, anachronistically, the House of Worship. Is the pursuit of Jewish knowledge a qualification, if not for mere nominal membership, then at least for becoming a trustee, an officer, even a president of a congregation today? Hardly. Is a member obligated to a conscientious effort to translate the teachings of our Torah, of our moral law, into his personal life and the affairs of the society of which he is a part? Not really. Unhappily, here, too, the homogeneity of American and of Jewish life tends to dilute the spiritual and educational emphasis of the historic synagogue into another empty status symbol. Too much congregational achievement is measured today by numbers added to rosters rather than by souls brought nearer to God, rather than by spirits changed and charged and challenged to carry out His will; by sanctuaries remodeled or replaced, rather than by lives regenerated and a society redeemed.

The opulence of physical structure, the size and location of site, the character of the neighborhood, the charm of the rabbi—these are the measuring rods by which most Jews evaluate a synagogue. With some notable exceptions, the mantle of leadership in the synagogue is bestowed upon laymen of means. In all branches of Judaism, synagogue boards are—again with exceptions so sparse as to prove the rule—made up of prosperous businessmen who feel an obligation to help conduct the affairs of the synagogue in businesslike fashion.

Business being business, even in the synagogue, they tend to regard the rabbi as hired help employed to perform the religious duties of the institution, while they preside over its management and define its policies. Religious zeal, ethical sensitivity, and Jewish knowledge are, in the main, accidental and incidental desiderata. Leadership is not based on such criteria. One is reminded in striking contrast of the beautiful explanation, quoted by Rashi, to the verse 10:3 in the Scroll of Esther: "And Mordecai . . . was accepted by the *majority* of his brethren." Why only by them and not by *all* Jews? Because since the time he got involved in politics at the court of Ahasuerus and abandoned his study of the Torah, he was demoted from his righ rank in Jewish leadership. Thus, even a pious Jew like Mordecai was not exempted from living up to the virtues of true Jewish leadership which was unthinkable without knowledge and study of Torah!

It is no longer so. We live in a climate in which many temple board members rarely attend religious services, would not be found dead at an adult education course, never read a Jewish book, and whose economic affluence, in some instances at least, may stem from what may be generally accepted but are nevertheless highly questionable ethical practices. Do such board members really exist? In embarrassing numbers—and if this catalogue of failures is insufficiently damning, I should add that there are among the trustees of our Jewish religious institutions more than a few estimable gentlemen who have no more belief in God than they have in flying saucers.

In many congregations, I have found a wide and disturbing gap between the thinking of the board and the thinking of the congregants at large. In many instances the board tends to regard itself as a Hamiltonian buffer against the passions and the desires of the people. Is the board of trustees of the American synagogue really representative of its membership? Sometimes yes, more often no. It seems to me that most boards of trustees arrogate to themselves altogether too much authority. Perhaps all congregations should emulate the practice which a handful of congregations have introduced—frequent congregational "town meetings" for the debate and resolution of major issues.

Why should a "small group of willful men," to quote Woodrow Wilson, decide, for hundreds of members, such significant issues as the kind and amount of instruction to be taught in the religious school and what stands to take, if any, on social problems in the community, or what is more frequently the case, to decide arbitrarily to take no stand at all—to sit it out in silence though other religious institutions raise their voices loud and clear, and though a large majority of their skillfully suppressed members may yearn that their synagogue speak with prophetic passion and act with courageous collective resolution? Why should such an oligarchy, often Jewishly illiterate, fix standards for confirmation and *bar mitzvah,* and similar matters? Although elected (usually perfunctorily) by the membership, the board of trustees can nonetheless become autocratic. If so they cut themselves off from the thinking of the congregation at large. An infusion of democracy into the synagogue is indispensable. Democracy is a process of controversy and accommodation and there is no better way to inspire and challenge the congregants at large than to involve them in the experience of shaping policies on basic questions. There are risks always in the democratic process and the procedure can be cumbersome. But we are all acutely aware of the greater abuses of any system in which a small group exercises an iron rule over matters which vitally affect policy, and congregational society is no exception.

The grievous failings of American culture—the worship of money, power, status, success—have inevitably permeated the spirit of the synagogue in America. We have only to be honest with ourselves and examine ourselves with unclouded eye. Our synagogues have become middle-class institutions. In order to maintain a large plant and a growing staff, dues must necessarily be set so high that Jews of lesser means are unable to belong. To be sure, most congregations loudly boast that "no Jew is turned away" from their doors (unless he doesn't have a ticket on the Holy Days), that there is plenty of room for the poorest of the poor at every Sabbath service (*especially* Sabbath mornings when attendance is sluggish), and that no child will be refused admission to the religious school regardless of his parents' financial condition in life.

But exalted as all such talk and policy admittedly are, candor compels the confession that there is a golden curtain drawn between the financially disadvantaged and the synagogue unless they are willing to subject themselves to some—however subtle and gentle—demeaning "means test," unless they are prepared to face the indignity of pleading poverty. Some congregations—though not enough of them yet—have moved in the direction of a flexible dues system in which each family pays in proportion to its ability to pay. This I regard as a healthy trend, worthy of greater emulation.

Notwithstanding this general "bowing the head and bending the knee" before the altar of mammon, rabbis are generally accorded a free pulpit. But the leaders of not a few temples have a low tolerance for political and economic dissent. In many congregations, particularly in the South, certain topics are definitely taboo, like *trefe* (non-kosher) food in a strictly Orthodox home.

Social action is repugnant to many trustees who cannot see what race relations and civil liberties have to do with religion and who, in any event, regard controversy as the ultimate heresy in the synagogue. Thus, even when a social action committee is finally and after prodigious effort authorized by the Board, it is more than likely that any strong proposal for public action on a controversial issue will be laundered and bleached into vapidity before it emerges from the wringer of the board of trustees. It is no wonder that there is a rapid turnover of social action chairmen in most synagogues. Characteristically, the idealistic and socially sensitive social action chairmen and the members of the board of trustees function on two different conceptual planes. Social action is, by its nature, an uphill struggle in the contemporary American synagogue. A popular social action committee is probably doing nothing important.

In the face of such general apathy, and even of active opposition, I am especially proud of the role of resolute leadership played by the Union of American Hebrew Congregations. From its very founding, it sought to relate religion to life and to apply Judaism's prophetic teaching to the social, political, economic, national, and international problems of the day.

The social action program of Reform Judaism has made good and rather impressive progress. Our national Commission on Social Action has become the social conscience of the Reform movement, and most Reform synagogues now have social action or community affairs committees. But this progress has been made despite considerable apathy and even resistance which mounts formidably whenever decisive forward steps are contemplated.

A striking illustration of this was the mammoth controversy which erupted in Reform Judaism when Mr. Kivie Kaplan, a distinguished member of the national Commission on Social Action, made a generous contribution to make it possible for the Commission to establish a center in Washington, D.C. Mr. Kaplan was responding to a need I had frequently expressed, that the voice of Reform Judaism should be heard in the nation's capital where the crucial decisions of our time are shaped. A powerful opposition mobilized to reverse the decision of the Union of American Hebrew Congregations to accept the gift and establish the center. Led by a few large and powerful congregations in the North, the opposition won support from some Southerners rankling over our position on integration, as well as from some sullen bastions of classical Reform. So fierce became the opposition that the entire Reform movement was convulsed for two years, during which the battle lines were drawn and the propaganda war mounted. In a highly charged and dramatic confrontation at the Biennial Assembly of 1961, the moment of truth arrived. An enthusiastic message of support from then Secretary of Labor Arthur Goldberg gave encouragement to the social action forces, but it did not lessen the furious attacks upon the idea of a social action center in Washington. Finally the debate ended. The vote was overwhelming—approximately 1200 to 100 in favor of the center. Today, the Religious Action Center in Washington works side by side with many Protestant and Catholic social action agencies functioning in the nation's capital to elevate the moral standards of American political life.

In the effort to apply Judaism to life, the rabbis, on the whole, have played vital roles. As a matter of fact, there was a time when the rabbis enjoyed a virtual monopoly in this realm, when almost every rabbi was himself a veritable social action committee. And while most rabbis have long lamented the absence of laymen in this genuinely Jewish enterprise, there are others who would like matters to remain that way everlastingly, and who appear to resent the "intrusion" of the laymen into their once sacrosanct precincts. But this is to perpetuate a newly risen evil in Jewish life: the altogether un-Jewish distinction between laymen and rabbi.

It was not so throughout most of our Jewish past. Traditionally, the rabbi was only a more highly educated layman—better versed in the Torah and in the teachings of Judaism. That "only," of course, marks an important distinction; yet it did not create the hiatus which is presently developing and which is another manifestation of Jewish acculturation, of our accommodation to the mores of our environment. Thus aping our Christian culture, too many rabbis passively accept or actively pursue the role of pastor or priest, a category unto themselves.

As a consequence, what is happening to the American rabbi? He is allowing himself to be shaped in accordance with the laymen's conception of what a rabbi should be—preacher, counsellor, ambassador to the Christians, community relations expert, public speaker, temple bulletin editor, administrator, and fund-raiser. The rabbi is becoming all things to all men. His salary, in many instances, is commensurately high; his effectiveness is, too frequently, low. His public status is relatively high; his level of scholarship is lower than it should be—and than it used to be. The rabbi is a busy, frustrated, harassed public figure who has almost ceased to be the teacher of Torah. Rare is the rabbi who has the time to achieve scholarship. He has become too easily assimilated to the anti-intellectual atmosphere of our day, to the climate in which irrationalism has been enthroned and the egghead has become the butt of every snide and sniveling sneer.

Again, with some inspiring and notable exceptions, too many rabbis have capitulated to the clamor of the crowd and have ceased to be "the eternal student," as demonstrated by Elijah Gaon who, from his tiny "house of study," and without radio and television to aid him, exerted more influence over an entire generation of Jews and of the generations to follow than all the public relations rabbis of our day.

The peculiar merit of the rabbis of the past was their resolute resistance to the bread and circuses, the gladiatorial spectaculars, and the popular pastimes which were part and parcel of the culture of those centuries (there was card playing in their day, too—read the denunciations of this long-favorite pastime among Jews by the rabbis of the Middle Ages). While the masses of Jews invariably, then as now, followed the multitude and slavishly adopted the ways of the gentile, Jewish leadership consistently repudiated such imitation which deprived the rabbi of his birthright of scholarship.

It is unhappily not generally so today. Too frequently the hankering after a superficial, first-name popularity—on the golf course, at the bridge table, or the cocktail party—is filching from the contemporary religious leader the time that he might otherwise spend in the learning which, certainly in Judaism, is the title deed to his lofty designation as rabbi (teacher). The criteria of pulpit committees—rotund voice, graceful gestures, affable manner, pleasant countenance, safe on politics, soft on social action, and not too exacting of his flock—give a clue to what too many laymen seek in their so-called spiritual leaders and to which I fear some of our rabbis too cravenly capitulate.

Especially revealing of this distressing portrait was the report of the Executive Vice-President of the Central Conference of American Rabbis, Rabbi Sidney Regner, growing out of his years of experience in pulpit placement. He tartly observed that,

... the image of the rabbi today, in the eyes of some people, has something of the Madison Avenue tint and the Organization Man touch. Rabbis, full of vim, vigor and vitality who, in popular parlance, will "sell" themselves and their personalities, neither too meek nor too aggressive, who by all means should not be too far out of step—those are the desiderata most frequently stressed. . . . I have *never yet* had a congregation tell me that they wanted a *scholarly rabbi*. [author's italics]

Surely the committed rabbi must rouse himself to rebel against such an incongruous denouement to so noble a calling. We cannot permit this stultification of the descendants of Hillel and Akiba, of Jochanon Ben Zaccai and that long line of teachers whose title the rabbi proudly bears.

As the desire and demand for learning are thus being diluted, so is the voice of social action being muffled. By every canon of our Jewish tradition the rabbi is called upon not only "to learn and to teach," but perhaps even more persistently "to observe and to do." Familiar to even the most superficial student of Judaism is the stubborn insistence that "Not study is the chief ingredient, but action." And did not Rabbi Eliezer in Pirke Aboth warn that "he whose wisdom exceeds his works, to what is he likened? To a tree whose branches are many but whose roots are few and the wind comes and plucks it up and overturns it on its face." Still further did one of our sages go when he dared to assert that "he who occupies himself with study alone is as if he had denied God Himself."

There are too many of us who thus deny God today, who are victims of this creeping, even leaping, indifferentism of our time. The same infection is seizing our theological students as well. William Whyte bemoaned the fact that American college students, in striking contrast to the radical revolt of youth characteristic of the thirties, in contrast also to the still flaming youth in Africa, in Asia, in South America, and in Israel, find their outlets too frequently in panty pilfering, in destructive games and riots, crowding into telephone booths, and bed-pushing antics.

No cause seizes them. They seem fed up with all this political jazz . . . this applies to theological students as well. Without exceptions, those heads of seminaries I have interviewed find the present generation less inquiring of mind, more ready to accept authority, and indeed most anxious to have it laid on the line.

Here, too, Jewish life absorbs the worst in its surroundings, rather than the best. As with American youth in general, so is it with Jewish youth, according to an intensive survey conducted a few years back by one of our leaders of the Reform Jewish youth movement, Rabbi Jerome Davidson:

No rebellion or discontinuity takes hold of them. No cry for ideals in any way foreign to typical American middle-class rouses them. The majority interviewed are not really bothered by the problems of poverty or segregation. "The people wouldn't live in slums if they didn't want to," they superficially assert as they smugly conclude that the prophets would indeed approve the conditions of twentieth century America.

And as it thus seems to be with the average run of American Jewish youth, so too does it appear to be tragically true in our seminaries. It was not so in the now long, long ago when I sat in the classroom. Not only were we constantly inspired and challenged by the vivid presentation and contemporary application of the prophets, but the then-popular social gospel of Christendom also wielded its potent influence upon us. Today the pages of Rauschenbusch and John Haynes Holmes are unread and unheeded, while the habit of accommodation to things as they are has become contagious. Pastoral counseling rather than prophetic preaching is *de rigueur* now. I am not against pastoral counseling. But I am opposed to the altogether un-Jewish, distinctively Christian overemphasis on the salvation of the individual—which in our time often salves the conscience through the confession of one's sins on one's knees, or the outflow of free associations on the couch—rather than the galvanizing of the individual's resources for the redemption of society.

I do not claim to have definitive knowledge of all our theological students. But I do know that whenever I have had open-end discussions with them and have encouraged the utmost frankness and complete freedom to make me a target for searching and even embarrassing questions, rarely do the interrogations deviate from those minutiae having to do with the mundane problems of individual security.

It was not so when the founders of our theological schools brought them into being. Isaac Mayer Wise constantly urged his "boys," as he affectionately called them, to "break asunder wherever we can the chains of the bondsman, the fetters of the slave, the iron rod of despotism, the oppressive yoke of tyranny. Let us banish strife, discord, hatred, injustice, oppression from the domain of man," was his rallying cry. And Stephen S. Wise, the founder of the Jewish Institute for Religion in New York City, pleaded with his students to help transform our synagogues into "forces of righteousness rather than farces of respectability in the community."

No peace-of-mind palliatives did these founders of our theological schools prescribe for those upon whom they placed their hands in prayerful ordination. They craved no automated, mass-produced, ecclesiastical mechanics, taught and trained for push-button synagogues and schools, institutional promoters, organizational men in robes, dilettante psychoanalysts, pulpit puppets oozing sweetness and light. Modern Maccabees, "Hammerers of God," they sought, summoned to smash the world's evil on the anvil of justice, kindlers of divine discontent with things as they are, bearers of light to a morally baffled and spiritually bewildered generation. Not purveyors of unctuous pastor oil, but descendants of God's angry men, not hesitating to go into the counting house, the factory, or the governmental office to exclaim, with the prophet Nathan, "Thou art the man!"

It was said of Tolstoy that he "stabbed men awake." There are times—and surely this is just such a time—when we require nothing quite so much as those who will thus stab men into wakefulness, who will "light a spirit bomb," who will "jolt our apathetic generation out from under the husks of old dead meanings," who will dynamite us into knowing where we are and whither we must go. Of whom can we expect such an ennobling, sometimes lacerating, mission, if not of our spiritual leaders? In a world of shame, the *eved adonoy,* the servant, the "porter of God," as the Hebrew poet phrased it, dare not slink supinely and silently to the sidelines. "Jerusalem was destroyed," say our sages, "because men no longer rebuked one another." So will our world be destroyed if it hears, especially from its rabbis, its ministers, its priests, its divinely ordained and consecrated "men of God," only the soothing syllables of those who pant after and pander to popularity rather than apply the scorpion sting of moral rebuke and challenge.

To be sure, the picture is not altogether black. Although I still insist the situation is indubitably foreboding, there are, of course, nevertheless, many elements of promise in the contemporary synagogue. In the first place, a majority of American Jews now identify themselves with the sanctuary. Regardless of the diverse motivations which bring them to the temple, the fact that they belong presents an unparalleled opportunity to strengthen their Jewish commitments and to deepen their knowledge. Moreover, the frank dissatisfaction which rabbis and sensitive lay leaders feel in the quality of the contemporary American synagogue, touching off a wave of self-searching which sometimes amounts to self-flagellation, is itself a healthy augury. This restlessness is resulting in new emphasis on adult education, rising standards for religious school instruction, creative ventures in a religious camp experience for adults as well as youth, an awakening interest in social action, a fresh approach to the teaching of Hebrew, a budding taste for the utilization of the arts and the best of Jewish and world literature within the synagogue. In addition, the status of the synagogue, despite all its shortcomings, has risen sharply in the Jewish consciousness.

A generation ago, the American Jewish community consisted of the Zionist groups, the lodges, the philanthropic and welfare funds, the civil defense bodies, the Yiddish cultural agencies, plus the synagogue.

Today the American Jewish community consists of the synagogue, plus the others. Debates as to whether or not the synagogue should receive primacy or centrality in the American Jewish community still break out from time to time, but such debates deal with sterile abstractions. The reality is that the synagogue *is* becoming central and will be even more so in the future as Christians identify Jews—and as Jews identify themselves—as, primarily, a *religious* community. Beyond any other Jewish institution, the synagogue is the embodiment of the total Jewish way of life. And this great promise makes it all the more incumbent upon us to examine ourselves with the utmost frankness.

We have got to cease our preoccupation with numbers. Our current predilection toward the counting of noses is no more healthy than the tendency of a past generation to change their noses, to "cut their noses to spite their race," as the great rabbi of Temple Sinai, Chicago, the late Emil G. Hirsch, once phrased it. It is not important that we have 1,000 or 500 or 200 families in our respective synagogues, or that we have one million or two million persons in our Reform movement as a whole. What *is* important is what the synagogue does for them and to them, how it affects the quality of their lives and their dynamic urge to transform the lives of others, the very life—or death—of mankind. We need to rise above the lowest common denominator—a standard so low it is almost invisible—to aim at standards of excellence. To be a lay leader of a synagogue, one should be required to undertake a regimen of Jewish learning, to live an ethical Jewish life in business and community alike, and to participate in the religious as well as the fiscal tasks of the congregation. It seems to me we do not expect enough from our people; we do not demand enough or challenge enough. We settle too easily. We aim too low. We are too afraid to fail. Such timidity, such short-selling of synagogue membership and especially of its leadership is, according to a well-known Midrash, a gross transgression. "Just as it is forbidden to utter the name of God in vain, so should you not assume a public office if you are not worthy of it."

At the same time, the potential of what we could achieve is almost limitless. We are free in America to fashion whatever Jewish life we will. The financial resources are here. So are the human resources— a Jewish community of five million persons, almost all of them eager to identify themselves as Jews, many of them hungry for moral and spiritual guidance of a meaningful kind. Our three-faith culture has invested the synagogue with an unparalleled prestige. The existence of the State of Israel can be a fructifying force for American Jewry. Our camps and youth programs offer hope for a new and committed generation.

But this much I think remains crystal clear: the future of American Jewish life depends on what the synagogue becomes. If the synagogue can shape itself into an effective vehicle to carry the timeless values of Judaism, Jewish life in the year 2000 will be vigorous and distinctive in America, and Judaism will be a faith by which men live. But if—as present trends portend—the American synagogue becomes a blend of Jewish country club and Protestant church, if we continue to reward leadership on the basis of un-Jewish criteria, if we confuse busyness in the synagogue with the true business of Judaism, if we allow the synagogue to become a comfort station in a world of challenge and change, then the synagogue may nevertheless survive, but only as a forsaken shrine of a forgotten past. And the fires of faith which warmed a hundred generations of the covenant people will become ashes cold and dead on the free soil of America.

We must be vigilant to make certain that the American synagogue does not meet the fate portended in an ancient rabbinic story. We are told that in the old Temple at Jerusalem there was a flute fashioned out of reeds, an old flute dating back to the time of Moses. Its sound was sonorous and sweet, exalting the hearts of all worshippers who heard it. One day the priests of the Temple decided to decorate the flute—after what was, no doubt, a high-pressure, card-calling, fund-raising campaign among the status-seeking populace. The appeal was evidently successful for the flute was overlaid with heavy and costly gold. Its appearance was superb. But its once mellow resonance was now metallic and jarring. Gold had debased its former ravishing tone.

God grant that this will not be the destiny of the American synagogue. Let us pray and work that its long-hallowed courts will not be spoiled by success.

15

CAN JEWS UNITE?

FORETHOUGHT

*Our quest for unity must not be limited to our own admittedly re-
stricted Reform fold. The founder of our Reform Jewish movement
in America, Isaac Mayer Wise, really sought a much larger unity. It
is interesting to point out that Wise's first call for union was not addressed exclusively to his sister congregations of the Reform wing of
Jewry; nor even to congregations only, but rather "to the ministers and
all other Israelites" of America.*

*I do not believe that in so crucial an hour as this, Wise would
have relegated to any other person or body the special privilege of
summoning "all the ministers and other Israelites" of our day to organize themselves into some manner of congress, assembly, conference,
or whatever one might wish to call it. "What's in a name?" Wise would
have affirmed, so long as Jews confer with one another on problems
of mutual concern. A conclave of Jews by any other name would have
seemed just as sweet to him whose one consuming passion was to see
all his fellow Jews united as the brethren they boast of being. He
would have taken the initiative now as in the year 1848. Wise did not
possess all the advantages which it is the proud privilege of our Union
to command, with names upon its roster that include those of utmost
influence on the American Jewish scene. He did not have a following
of some several hundreds of thousands of adherents. "I am a stranger
among you, unknown and unimportant," he stated. But that did not
deter him from insisting that "as God is a unity, so has He charged
Israel to unite all mankind. But before Israel can proceed with its sacred
mission," he logically argued, "it behooves us to be united as one man."*

If our Union of congregations would be true, not to this incident

270

or that in the life of its founder, but to the spirit that he sought to breathe into it, we must not grudgingly or apathetically or falteringly follow, but eagerly and constructively take the lead in molding an American Jewish unity. And if I see at all the etzbah Elohim *("the finger of God") in the selection of my humble self for a high and honored post in this great Union then it is in this perhaps more than in aught else besides: it was my lot to be instrumental in forging in the Dominion of Canada just such a united Jewry. As variegated as the hues of the rainbow are the multifaceted aspects of Canadian Jewish life. Yet, we learned the lesson of unity amid diversity, of speaking with a single voice, of acting in harmony toward a common end. If I can be of some little service in bringing to the American scene the fruitage of my decade and a half of labor in this direction across the border, then will the Union's choice of leader, for just such a challenging time as this, not have been altogether in vain. In the words of Wise once more: "In God's name, let us unite and do our work."*

Founder's Day Address,
Cincinnati, Ohio,
Hebrew Union College, 1943

AFTERTHOUGHTS

If anything, I feel even more strongly on this subject now than I did in 1943. The American Jewish community is flourishing and, I believe, highly creative. It is freer, more comfortable, enjoying the most hospitable climate, suffering less hostility and discrimination than any other Jewish community in the history of the Diaspora. It has achieved much and promises more. But, in its inability to achieve cooperation and unity, the American Jewish community betrays a scandalous immaturity and a shameful failure of nerve.

Why should not the largest Jewish community in the world be able to transcend—not obliterate, but transcend—its legitimate differences? How can we hope to meet the challenges of leading the Jewish world if we continue to be divided against ourselves and to make a principle out of anarchy? It is notable that other Jewish communities throughout the free world have achieved a higher measure of unity than we have. The British Jewish community has its democratically constituted Jewish Board of Deputies. France has its Conseil Representatif des Juifs de France. Argentina is served by its Delegacion de Asociaciones Israelitas

Argentinas. And, the example I know best, Canada, maintains an effective Canadian Jewish Congress which has the support of the B'nai B'rith, the American Jewish Congress, the synagogue bodies, and the entire organized Jewish community.

As the rabbi of Holy Blossom Congregation in Toronto, Canada, I had participated in initiating the Canadian Jewish Congress, an agency which brought together all facets of Canadian Jewry. It had been a difficult, fascinating, and immensely instructive experience— one which, as I indicated in my forethought, anticipated some of the very issues which I was to face years later in the leadership of the Union of American Hebrew Congregations. Reform Judaism in Canada was, at the inception of the Canadian Jewish Congress, a minuscule movement, consisting of three congregations. Reform Jewish leadership was largely non-Zionist. In view of the passionate Zionist sentiments of the overwhelming majority of Canadian Jewry, there was real concern among the Reform Jewish delegates at the founding conference that we would be "majorized"—that is, that our conscientious dissent on the Zionist (or any other) issue would be brushed aside by the zeal of the majority. Although I could not deny the reality of this danger, I felt the pressing need for Jewish unity in those tragic days outweighed the risks.

The opening session of the Congress seemed to confirm the fears of my laymen. A resolution was presented, putting the Canadian Jewish Congress on record in favor of the "establishment of the Jewish commonwealth in Palestine." This resolution was obviously an implementation of the classic Zionist theory that Jews throughout the world live in *galut* (exile) and that only the reestablishment of a Jewish nation in Palestine would normalize Jewish life and eliminate the constant danger of anti-Semitism, that *only* in Zion could all Jews find and found their "homeland." My delegates and I rejected the implication that we were thus in exile or that there could be no future for Jews unless and until such an all-inclusive single homeland would be restored in Palestine.

I proposed a simple-sounding amendment: substitution of "a" for "the homeland." Pandemonium broke loose. I was booed and hissed as if I had revealed myself as a traitor to Israel. My amendment was scornfully brushed aside. Sadly, our delegation left the hall in protest against what we regarded as an abuse of minority rights. The unpleasant incident, which threatened momentarily to disrupt the Congress, proved a blessing in disguise. The Congress leaders, realizing that a Canadian Jewish Congress without even a small minority could not presume to speak for a united Jewish community, called upon us to work out a procedure which would respect any dissenting view without at the same time stifling the will of the majority. Thus, it was agreed that any policy statement in the name of the Canadian Jewish Congress had to have the assent of all the constituent groups that comprised the Congress; should one agency dissent, its dissent had to be noted in any statement by the Congress. From that day to this, the Canadian Jewish Congress has legitimately represented every element of the Canadian Jewish community. Its accomplishments for Canadian Jewry, and for Canada itself, have been substantial.

To those who argue that such unity is not applicable to the United States because of the comparative numerical insignificance of Canadian Jewry (which even today numbers only 254,000), let me state that such matters are never really determined on a quantitative basis. Tiny Jerusalem was destroyed because of the acrimony between the factions of its population which, in the main, shared the same ancestry and historic background. There can be discord among a handful and unity among a multitude. Are there truly differences as deep-rooted or as valid among the admittedly diverse segments of American Jewry as prevailed among the inhabitants of the thirteen original colonies of the United States? And yet, they did form the Union. And who among the leaders of these sacrosanct American Jewish organizations, who argue that their autonomy and integrity are so hallowed and inviolate that they cannot be subordinated to some form of unified deliberation, decision, and dedication to the common good of American and world Jewry, would dare compare our differences with those of the more than one hundred sovereign powers that constitute the United Nations?

The corollary is likewise true: if we Jews, a mere fraction of a fraction of humankind, cannot find a formula where we can act in concert for our respective and common good, then how can we continue with any sincerity to pray in our synagogues that our supplication will be fulfilled: "Oh, may all, created in Thine image, recognize that they are brethren so that one in spirit and one in fellowship, they may be forever united before Thee."

Neither the Canadian Jewish Congress, the Board of Deputies of British Jews, nor the many other viable bodies of united Jewries infringe upon the *voluntary* character of Jewish life, its democratic temper, or the rights of individual conscience. Rather, each demonstrates that there is a Jewish community bound together by common needs and goals, capable of speaking with one voice when necessary, rising above the clamorous plethora of individual lodges, chapters, and committees. Jewish dignity and purpose cannot survive the jungle of organizational competition for credit and publicity, the irresponsible jockeying for power, the Babel of voices drowning each other out, and the unconscionable squandering of limited and exigent resources in arrant duplication of purposes and programs. Yet that is roughly the situation of American Jewry in 1964.

Examples of Jewish organizational chaos can be multiplied. When Chairman Khrushchev came to the U.S., a number of Jewish organizations went into feverish competition with each other to arrange a conference with the Soviet Chairman on the plight of Russian Jewry. The effect of all the unilateral overtures was predictable. None saw Khrushchev. Likewise, when George Lincoln Rockwell, the penny-ante American photostat of Hitler, sought a permit to speak at Union Square, New York, Mayor Wagner was treated to a barrage of conflicting demands on the part of many Jewish organizations, most of whom had never consulted with each other before admonishing the Mayor as to what the Jewish community wished. Similarly, I believe that former President Truman's well-known disillusionment with American Zionists stems from the host of conflicting pressures applied by Jewish organizations seeking to assist Israel.

Yet a great deal more progress has been made in *local* Jewish communities in the U.S. than on the *national* scene. Virtually every Jewish community of any significant size maintains a united Jewish Welfare Fund. In fact, this drive for local solidarity has marked one of the major Jewish contributions to America as a whole. These efforts and successes in Jewish unity which forged the all-inclusive and community-wide Jewish Welfare Funds became the model for the United Community Chest of the general community. In addition, local Jewish communities maintain Jewish Community Councils or Jewish Community Relations Councils through which all local Jewish groups cooperate in setting joint policies and discussing common problems—cooperation virtually taboo in the national arena. In most of our large cities, Jews recognize that there is something more than an American Jewish Congress or Committee chapter, or a B'nai B'rith Lodge or a Council of Jewish Women chapter, or a Zionist party or a specific synagogue, with which they may be associated. There is an organized Jewish *community,* with responsible procedures, which is capable of considered and combined action.

From the first moment I was called to the leadership of the Union of American Hebrew Congregations, I determined to do all in my power to overcome any unnatural isolationism which had developed in American Reform Judaism—despite its founder's admonitions to the contrary—and which was divorcing us from the mainstream of American Jewish life. There was nothing, however, in the principles or history of Reform Judaism to justify this tragic separatism. Certainly there was naught in the thinking or activity of Isaac Mayer Wise to justify setting Reform Jews apart from their brethren. Just two years after his arrival in America in 1846, as an unknown immigrant speaking little English, he had the moral valor to issue his summons for a synod, not merely of his Reform coreligionists, but of "all Israelites in America."

Though this first venture ended in failure, Wise was neither disheartened nor detoured from this dominant desire. He never did succeed in his ambition, despite his willingness to compromise with the Orthodox Jews on the authority of the Talmud. After twenty-five years of ceaseless, ofttimes heartbreaking, effort, he had to content himself with the establishment of the Union of American Hebrew Congregations as the central body for *Reform* synagogues. It was not, therefore, this towering giant of early Reform in America who was the isolationist, but the leaders, especially those of a then totally anarchic Orthodoxy, as well as certain disdainful Reform "patricians," rabbinic and lay, who refused to join forces with the upstart from Bohemia. Nor did Wise ever intend the Union to be some sort of sect sequestered from its fellow Americans.

A bare five years after its inception in 1873, under Wise's guidance—and goading—the Union undertook to sponsor the Board of Delegates of American Israelites which represented the total Jewish community of that time in the protection of Jewish rights. And at the 1905 Biennial Council of the UAHC, the first call for an American Jewish Congress was issued. Through the years, again and again, the UAHC, often with the Central Conference of American Rabbis, bent its energies to the creation of such national instrumentalities as the American Jewish Committee, the American Jewish Congress, the Hillel Foundation, the Synagogue Council of America, and a host of other institutions designed to effectuate greater unity throughout the whole of American Jewish life. Thus did the Reform movement seek to remain true to the behest of its founder. In 1880, Reform Judaism was undoubtedly the dominant force in American Jewish life.

But as the tides of Jewish immigration to the United States at the turn of the century began to inundate American synagogues, Reform Jewish leadership seemingly became alarmed and sought to insulate itself from what some regarded as the "hordes" from Eastern Europe. In panic, some of the Reform Jewish leaders drew in the hem of their garments from any chance contact with that "mixed multitude." As a consequence of their failure to embrace the vital East European masses, the synagogues abdicated many of their traditional functions. A network of new secular agencies sprang up to meet the needs of the immigrants. Regrettably, in those years the preponderantly Reform synagogue seemed incapable of responding to dynamic change. By 1930, representing perhaps less than one-tenth of American Jewry, Reform Judaism had slipped to the periphery of American Jewish life— weak, sterile, uncertain of itself and its future, and dangerously cut off from the main current of Jewish energy and idealism.

This was the bleak prospect confronting me when I was requested to leave my pulpit in Toronto on a temporary basis, to become the "Interim Director of the UAHC." At that time a great new call to American Jewish unity had just been sounded. But this time it came neither from the UAHC nor from the synagogue in general. A forceful Jewish leader named Henry Monsky, then President of the B'nai B'rith, called upon American Jewry to turn its back on "business as usual" and come together to face the unparalleled threat of Nazi Germany.

In December, 1942, Monsky had called the heads of all major Jewish organizations to join with him in a single delegation to wait on President Roosevelt at the White House. The delegates appealed to the President to issue a stern warning to the Nazi leaders that "they will be held to strict accountability for their crimes." In addition, they requested that an American commission be appointed at once to receive and examine all evidence of Nazi barbarities against civilian populations and to submit that evidence to the bar of public opinion and to the conscience of the world. These actions led, ultimately, to the inquiry into German war crimes, climaxed by the Nuremberg war trials.

But that single ad hoc act was not enough to satisfy Monsky. He issued another call to the leaders of all Jewish organizations to meet with him in Pittsburgh on January 23, 1943, to make plans for unified Jewish action after Hitlerism was destroyed. Thirty-two organizations attended. Two—the American Jewish Committee and the Jewish Labor Committee—refused to participate. Patiently, Monsky negotiated with the American Jewish Committee and finally persuaded it to join on the understanding that the over-all body would be called the American Jewish "Conference" instead of "Assembly." Assembly implied a separate political enclave, the American Jewish Committee stated. They were also apprehensive that the right of an individual organization to dissent would not be fully recognized or honored. But Monsky's negotiating skill triumphed and not only the AJC but thereafter the Jewish Labor Committee joined also. For the first time, the entire spectrum of Jewish life—Reform, Conservative, Orthodox, Zionist, non-Zionist, labor, and business—had been gathered under one umbrella.

The Union of American Hebrew Congregations was present at that planning session and concurred in the call for a general plenary gathering representing all these organizations as well as communities at large. That decision, however, was taken by the Executive Board of the UAHC only and not by its General Assembly. When the Anglo-Jewish press carried the official call for the Conference in August, a fury of controversy erupted within the Reform movement. I was immediately faced with the question of whether to speak or not to speak on the issue. I was not given much time to debate this matter with myself as almost immediately upon my arrival in Cincinnati to assume the directorship of the UAHC, Dr. Julian Morgenstern, then President of the Hebrew Union College, graciously invited me to give the address on Founder's Day, which occurs each year at the end of March. I accepted.

The temptation was strong to eschew all things controversial, to make a pleasant beginning by rubbing no one's fur the wrong way. I had such a convenient alibi with which to evade the entire issue: I was only an *interim* Director, anticipating my return to Holy Blossom Congregation in time for the Holy Days in the fall. Who expected any major pronouncements from one assigned so tentative a task?

And yet the predicament of the Union, torn by indecision, cried out for some decisive word and the compulsion to speak became "like a burning fire within my bosom," which, strive though I did, I was unable to resist.

I addressed myself to the controversy welling up in the ranks of Reform and throughout the whole of American Jewry over the forthcoming American Jewish Conference. I sought to bring to bear the experience I had gained in the founding of the Canadian Jewish Congress. I strongly urged the Union not to reject that most promising step toward American Jewish unity.

My address was promptly printed—with a most generous foreword by Dr. Morgenstern who strongly endorsed its sentiments—and was widely distributed among the approximately 300 congregations that comprised the Union at that time. As was to be expected, it met with a mixed response. There were those, among some of the Reform rabbinate especially, who coveted a more than 100 per cent Jewish nationalism. One colleague condemned my comments as "vague, nebulous, watery." They were so vague, nebulous, and watery that, as I subsequently wrote in an article printed in the *Hebrew Union College Monthly* of June, 1944, they resulted in a number of resignations from the Union Board and a more severe financial loss than any other Jewish organization had suffered from a similar controversy.

On the other side were ranged the die-hard and uncompromising anti-Zionist, anti-*K'lal Yisroelites,* anti-collectivists who fiercely attacked my proposed deviation from the Pittsburgh Platform's anti-Zionism and my plea for an all-inclusive deliberative body. They feared, as had my Canadian Reform Jewish leaders a decade earlier, that such a body would "majorize" our Reform minority.

I called a high-level conference of the rabbinic leaders of both sides. Several of the leading Zionist rabbis in our Reform ranks refused to sit down at the same table with members of the American Council for Judaism (whose leaders regretfully had abounded in the leadership of the Reform movement until that time). But a number of outstanding leaders of American Zionism, such as Rabbi James Heller and the late Rabbi Barnett R. Brickner, did attend, notwithstanding the presence across the table of such American Council spokesmen as Rabbi Morris Lazaron, the late Rabbi Louis Wolsey, and others.

One would have thought that we had a group of mutually hostile Arabs and Jews around the table. It was imperative at the outset to carry on conversations with each side separately. But, gradually, the icy atmosphere thawed and some frank talk and back talk—and maybe a bit of double talk—ensued. We were finally able to hammer out an agreement to be submitted to the General Assembly scheduled for July. It was based upon the unanimous conviction that the Union should be saved from the schism which immediately threatened; that the anti-Zionists should retreat from their insistence that the Union wash its hands completely of the so-called Zionist "taint" of the American Jewish Conference; and that the more fanatical Zionists should cease trying to dragoon the Union into the Zionist camp. What evolved was a position of "neutrality" in the face of the cold war then raging which threatened momentarily to erupt into a feverishly hot one.

This position of neutrality was severely condemned by some of my more avid Zionist colleagues. I pointed out that the then Chairman of the Zionist Emergency Council himself, the late Rabbi Abba Hillel Silver, strongly agreed with the position at which that conference arrived (though he had not been present at its deliberations), that it was "more essential to preserve Reform harmony than to commit an organization with as mixed a constituency as we possess to a patricular platform upon which there was developing even then in Zionist circles much mixed feeling." It was Dr. Silver who asserted publicly on more than one occasion that, dedicated Zionist though he was, insistent as he was upon the passage of the Commonwealth resolution by the American Jewish Conference-to-be, he would never ask his congregation to go on record one way or another on the controversial political issue of Zionism. And what he would not ask of his congregation, he would not ask of the Union.

On August 29, 1943, at the Waldorf-Astoria in New York, the American Jewish Conference was convened. It was the most representative, the most inclusive gathering ever held in American Jewish history. It consisted of some 500 delegates representing 64 national organizations and 375 Jewish communities.

The controversy opened to the identical refrain that had accompanied the Canadian drama, the never failing chant of "Behold, how good and pleasant it is for brethren to dwell together in unity." It was with these all too-familiar words that Henry Monsky called its sessions to order. In his kneynote speech Henry Monsky said:

One of the essential virtues of this gathering is that it comprises leadership democratically chosen from the ranks of the whole of American Israel. It is the antithesis of the prevalent practice of representation by *shtadlanim* [self-appointed leaders]. The spirit of democracy and the development and appreciation of democratic processes have changed the whole concept of Jewish leadership. Leaders must be responsible to the yearnings, the aspirations, and the hopes of those for whom they presume to speak.

But Jewish unity again proved to be a fragile shoot. It was shattered by contention as to whether the Conference should recommend the reconstitution of Palestine as a Jewish national homeland. The overwhelming majority of the delegates voted for this so-called "Jewish Commonwealth" resolution. The definite article, "the," however, had this time been wisely abandoned in the hope of procuring unanimous agreement.

And there was still another lesson imparted by the experience of the young Canadian Jewish community to the then almost 300-year-old American Jewry. Knowing in advance the position of the Union of American Hebrew Congregations, Henry Monsky, Stephen Wise, and other Zionist leaders at the Conference sat down with the numerically negligible minority which our Union delegation comprised to work out a formula by which all future statements, deputations, and resolutions would respect the dissent of the UAHC. This agreement was not always honored throughout the existence of the American Jewish Conference, but the few mistakes were corrected and honesty of purpose prevailed throughout. It was hoped that this pattern of frankly acknowledged diversity would vouchsafe the continued adherence of all the organizations there represented. But it was not to be. The American Jewish Committee, under the leadership of Judge Joseph Proskauer, quit the Conference, charging that it endangered their organizational autonomy.

Again, tremendous pressures mounted to have my own organization join in this walk-out. It must be noted that many of our leaders were also prominent members of the American Jewish Committee. Fierce lobbying raged in the rooms and corridors of the Waldorf. I had learned the power of a determined minority. I believed that the Union, by honestly registering its dissent from the majority decision, could provide a new pattern for American Jewish unity, could demonstrate the centuries-old Jewish insistence that democracy stands only so long as such minority status is recognized, so long as the recognized minority does not peevishly and petulantly refuse to accept the majority decision.

The first session of the American Jewish Conference was over, but my own difficulties in relation to this issue continued. The conflict continued to agitate the Union family. There were additional resignations from our Board of Trustees, including a distinguished Eastern jurist, an influential newspaper tycoon, and two prominent Baltimore businessmen. Congregations, too, threatened to withdraw from Union membership and schism within Reform Jewry once more loomed as a dire possibility. Much of my writing, speaking, and travel during that period was necessarily devoted to this subject. Upon all I urged the acceptance, both as Jews and Americans, of the democratic process and promised another full-dress debate on this matter at the next General Assembly, delayed again, because of the exigencies of the war and its unsettled aftermath, until 1946.

That momentous gathering was held in Cincinnati, birthplace of American Reform and citadel then of much of the anti-American Jewish Conference sentiment. I made my first definitive statement as President of the Union. My remarks in that "State of Our Union" message which were pertinent to the problem of American Jewish unity sought to trace the true, and not the more recently contrived, purposes of the very founding of the Union itself and its deep historic—and moral—commitment to Jewish unity.

My position was supported by some illustrious leaders of American and Reform Jewry and bitterly opposed by others. But the decision of the delegates was overwhelmingly in favor of our continued adherence to the American Jewish Conference.

In 1947 the Conference faced mounting pressures from within. Some of its constituent organizations were determined to broaden the scope of the Conference and make it a permanent body. Others felt that the Conference should not go beyond the particular areas in which it was authorized by its charter and that it should not become a permanent organization.

I remember this bitter period with poignancy because it was my fate to be Chairman of the Committee on Future Organization. The report, which became known as the "Eisendrath Report," embroiled the Conference in the conflict which spelled its death. For a while, however, we had reason to be sanguine. Hours of patient, painstaking give and take had finally resulted in a call for reconstituting the American Jewish Conference without in any way infringing upon the autonomy of any member organization.

The day of decision had arrived when I was to present my report.

The date was May 15, 1948. The scene was the Chicago Opera House, which was filled to the rafters long before the meeting was due to begin—an occurrence of punctuality virtually unprecedented in Jewish history. The audience had gathered to listen to the eloquent words of that unmatched tribune of the Jewish people, Stephen S. Wise.

For that very morning the State of Israel had been proclaimed. Who, then, was in a mood to listen to any mere report—even one that held promise of forging an American Jewish unity—when the vision of Zion restored had been miraculously fulfilled in our own time? Under the circumstances, I suggested that my report be deferred to the following morning and that the evening program be confined to a *single* speech by the one who, above all, had dreamed this dream and labored so assiduously for its fruition. I willingly bowed out and looked forward to hearing the words of Wise alone that night.

But I couldn't be that fortunate. The immutable ways of *The New York Times* had not been taken into account. Just before I proceeded to the platform, the ubiquitous Irving Spiegel, gifted veteran of that newspaper, rushed up to me wildly waving a copy of a release of my remarks. He was almost hysterical in his protest. "You can't do this to the *Times*," he shouted at me. "The presses are rolling. *You* have to speak tonight. I'll be fired if tomorrow's paper carries an account of something that never happened." I compromised by reading the tiny paragraph the majestic *Times* was at that moment printing, plus one sentence expressing the hope that on the morrow American Jewry would prove worthy, through its unity, of what had just occurred in Israel. It was the shortest speech of my career—and the most popular.

My report the next day was overwhelmingly and enthusiastically approved. But Monsky's death a few months earlier had foreshadowed the collapse of the AJC. Although as President of B'nai B'rith he had supported me throughout the difficult deliberations, the next session of B'nai B'rith voted to withdraw from the Conference and it became an item of history.

Monsky had died at one of the sessions considering the future of the Conference. His passing and that of the Conference are not unrelated because it is my conviction that, had it not been for his untimely death, the Conference might have persisted, notwithstanding the admitted fact that it was established on an ad hoc basis and could be perpetuated only by unanimous consent. With Monsky's death, however, and his vision and passion for a united Jewish community, national Jewish organizations reverted to their habitual narrow and petty bickering and the pursuit of their vested interests.

Although it suffered and collapsed from internal bleeding, the American Jewish Conference rendered a distinctive service to Jewish life. Representing the Conference, a number of us served as official consultants to the United Nations, and helped persuade the UN to incorporate human-rights pledges into the Charter. The Conference worked closely with the victorious Allied nations to relieve the suffering of the survivors of Nazi persecution. It brought to the conscience of the world the necessity of a haven for the Jewish homeless. It brought a modicum of unity to Jewish life in a critical and desperate time.

There was another by-product of this which affected me personally. Those stormy meetings, reflecting the grave crises in Jewish life, convinced the Union leadership that so significant a body could not be directed in absentia. The actual director, for whom I was acting as surrogate, was fulfilling an assignment in Israel. He was asked to choose between that assignment and the Union. He chose the former and I was asked to become the directing leader on a permanent basis.

The next test for American Jewish unity revolved around the National Community Relations Advisory Council, (NCRAC) which was established in 1944. Here, too, the crisis of Hitlerism was the real sponsor—the NCRAC was fashioned in order to realize coordination among the civic defense agencies. Its original member agencies were the American Jewish Committee, the Anti-Defamation League of B'nai B'rith, the American Jewish Congress, the Jewish Labor Committee, the Union of American Hebrew Congregations, and the Jewish War Veterans. The NCRAC was conceived as a "fish-bowl" instrumentality for the development of common policies, joint planning, and the elimination of duplication. NCRAC was a frank compromise between those who wanted to merge all the civic defense agencies into one "unitary" agency and those who cherished the status quo (which has been defined as "the mess we are in").

Although the NCRAC made some progress, it was obvious over the years that duplication of work and funds, competition for credit, and occasional unilateralism among the large agencies had not been eliminated. Some said these defects were inherent, the price of democracy. Others—and especially those whose job it was to raise the communal funds which provided the sinews for the civic defense agencies—insisted that the NCRAC must be given enlarged powers so that coordination and cooperation could be strengthened further.

As a result of these pressures, it was agreed by all to call in a disinterested social scientist to make an objective study of the entire field of Jewish community relations. Dr. Robert MacIver, distinguished social scientist of Columbia University, was the unanimous choice. After months of intensive study, MacIver presented his report which recommended thoroughgoing changes in the field of Jewish community relations to provide for joint program planning, reassessment of common goals, and the allocation of various functions among the organizations. Thus, work with veterans groups would be allocated to the Jewish War Veterans, work with other faiths to the Union of American Hebrew Congregations and other Jewish religious bodies if they were working in this field, legal work to the American Jewish Congress, etc.

The MacIver report was adopted, overwhelmingly, at a tense and harrowing convention of the NCRAC in Atlantic City in 1952. After hours of debate and desperate efforts to avoid a break, the climax was reached in the early hours of the morning. Irving Kane, then Chairman of the NCRAC, presided. Kane is undoubtedly one of the most eloquent and devoted Jewish lay leaders I have ever met. He was the personification of graciousness and courage as he presided at that unforgettable occasion. But when the decisive vote was announced, it did not resolve the issue.

Frank Goldman, President of B'nai B'rith, approached the microphone. He was followed by Jacob Blaustein, President of the American Jewish Committee. Again the litany of "voluntarism," the new Holy of Holies of Jewish life, was chanted. In a hall electric with a sense of tragedy, each leader announced that, by virtue of the vote just taken, his agency now felt compelled to withdraw from the NCRAC.

Irving Kane made a deeply moving, last-minute appeal to the dissident presidents to reconsider. His dramatic words filled the auditorium and brought a catch to the throats of the delegates:

If you should withdraw, I only urge you to consider what it is you are escaping from and where it is you are escaping to. You are escaping from the only instrument that the American Jewish community has ever forged which has some possibility for bringing about some degree of common sense, the only instrument we have which provides for some degree of fellowship in this field of work and which preserves, and yes, protects, your autonomy. You would be escaping to highlands of loneliness and isolationism from the American Jewish community. I cannot quite remember when I have been sadder than I am at this moment. For those who tried and failed, my continued regard and affection, and the prayer on my lips that we will meet again some day, somehow, somewhere, to work together in a common cause.

To no avail. The bridge collapsed. I found Kane an hour or so later, alone and weeping. Inwardly, I wept with him for I, too, had once again fought as vigorously as I could for a continuation of this united front. Again, the Union was pressed to follow the AJC, now buttressed by the Anti-Defamation League, out of the NCRAC. But again the Union, despite its many leaders prominently identified with both, remained firm. In the months that followed, I criss-crossed the country urging communities to persist in their efforts to reconstruct this broken unity.

The NCRAC survived the breach. It has now grown to include, among its national agencies, the United Synagogue of America (congregational body of the Conservative movement) and the Union of Orthodox Jewish Congregations (Orthodox), and some sixty local Jewish Community Councils from all parts of the United States. It has provided increasing service to the Jewish community in policy guidance, joint planning, and in the reassessment of the assumptions upon which the field rests. But the absence of the two largest Jewish civic defense agencies leaves a serious void. At this writing, there are hopeful signs that the Anti-Defamation League may yet rejoin the NCRAC. Despite the importuning and the periodic appeals of the Council of Jewish Federations and Welfare Funds and other concerned bodies and individuals, the American Jewish Committee continues its recalcitrance. It still insists that it is contrary to democratic principles to establish a "central voice," to submit to "majorizing," and it insists that "voluntarism" in Jewish life requires that each agency be completely free to follow its own distinctive philosophy,

I believe, in all deference, that these are rationalizations and shibboleths. The hard truth is that some Jewish leaders believe they can sustain their membership and raise their funds more easily if their own image is not blurred through cooperative enterprises. They believe that wisdom begins—and undoubtedly ends as well—with them. They have contempt for the processes of communal decision by majority vote. The fear of being "majorized" is an arrogant slogan which conceals an unwillingness to subject one's judgment to the free interplay of debate and decision. If not by majority decision, how then shall the Jewish community reach responsible decisions? By fiat? By the *fait accompli* of the self-appointed spokesmen? By the "take-it-or-leave-it" effrontery of the influence peddlers?

What kind of a so-called Jewish community do we have when some of our largest agencies (who derive their funds from the total Jewish community) make a fetish of interfaith relationships, going to all lengths to confer jointly with all manner of Protestant and Catholic agencies, while staunchly rejecting all proposals that they extend at least the same effort to exchange views with their sister agencies in the Jewish community? Our tasks are too vast—and our opportunities for service too great—to permit this squandering of communal funds, this vitiation of the strength which comes from united action. The American Jewish community deserves better of its agencies than a continuation of organizational chauvinism and institutional narcissism.

Since every Jewish organization is autonomous, each has a right, if it chooses, to reject cooperation with other Jewish groups in the pursuit of common causes. The American Jewish Committee cannot be compelled to rejoin the NCRAC, for example. But neither does the American Jewish community have an obligation to subsidize and reward intransigence. If the American Jewish Committee derived its funds from its own members, it could thumb its nose at the larger Jewish community. But that is not the case. It receives the bulk of its funds from community-wide Jewish welfare efforts, from Jews of all segments of Jewish life. The tragedy is not merely that one or another Jewish body refuses every request for cooperation. It is that the entire Jewish community has not yet had the courage to say: you choose to go it alone? Then, you will go it alone financially as well! Until such courageous discipline is exercised, the total Jewish community is, in effect, rewarding isolationism and penalizing those who cherish cooperation and community.

I believe a new day will yet dawn for the entire Jewish community —a day in which the loyalty of each Jew will not be consumed by his particular organizational segment but will reach out with pride to an overarching expression of Jewish interests, ideals, and values. Intra-Jewish relations will one day command the same enthusiasm within the Jewish community which is today reserved for interfaith relations.

To be sure, it is my hope that such unity may be subsumed under the aegis of our Jewish faith. By this I do not mean exclusively under rabbinic authority which some mistakenly believe is intended by the term "religious leadership." That is a Catholic pattern of organization where the priest is everywhere regnant. In Judaism, by contrast, both laity (Jewishly literate) and rabbinate labor together in our religious enterprises.

Our religious commitment must be embodied and expressed in a deepened, enriched, and expanded synagogue and reach outward toward the achievement of American Jewish unity. Only thus will we rise above the exclusively adventitious approach to Jewish life, eschew the altogether pragmatic criterion of "good will at any price," and seek instead to fulfill the prophetic mandate of God's will at any cost.

Until that day comes, we must strive tirelessly to improve communication and frank dialogue among all segments of American Jewry. We need not envy its hierarchical and authoritarian structure to recognize the creativity and spiritual fellowship with which the Roman Catholic Church has animated the Vatican Ecumenical Council. If a new structure of American Jewish unity seems too quixotic to contemplate, let us at least see to it that we do not continue the sin of refusing to sit down with our fellow Jews. I propose that the presidents of major Jewish organizations come together to plan a special conference to which will be invited representatives of every national Jewish organization, religious and civic, as well as representatives from every local Jewish community council in the land. This conference will be informational only, enabling Jewish representatives to exchange views and program plans on the overriding problems confronting American Jewish life. It will set up no permanent organization or structure, with the exception of a chairman and committee to plan the ensuing conference. Such a conference, to be held annually or biennially, could deal with such varied topics as civil rights, Israel, world peace, Jewish education, American immigration policy, Jewish fund-raising. In addition to plenary sessions, special workshops could address themselves in more detail to particular fields of Jewish interest. Since this would not be a formal structure, involving a new organization, no resolutions would be adopted, or actions taken, in the name of the conference but only in the name of those participating organizations which would desire to join in a particular statement or action in their own names. This would not meet the crying need for genuine Jewish unity. But it would, I believe, be a first, tentative step away from the chaos of Jewish separatism. It would build mutual confidence and would create a forum, where none now exists, for every segment of American Jewry to sit down at one table to examine and discuss the vexing problems which confront us all.

That the leaders of major Jewish organizations can thus come together, at least under the pressure of crisis, was vividly demonstrated by the extraordinary Jewish unity which marked the Conference on Soviet Jewry in April, 1964, in Washington, D. C. There, 500 delegates, representing all major Jewish groups, spoke out with one voice against the persecution of three million of their brethren in the Soviet Union.

Once more, in the words of Wise: "In God's name, let us unite and do our work." Not merely in the name of sweet—or bitter—expediency, not only when the enemy threatens our brethren or ourselves with extinction. But because "before we can hope to unite mankind, it behooves us to be united as one man." If I may be permitted the poetic license to paraphrase the prophet Amos: Thus saith the Lord, I hate, I loathe your proclamation of my unity, your affirmation of: "Hear, O Israel, the Lord is One" when you yourselves are riven with rancor and steeped in strife. Take away from me the cacophony of your conflicting and competing hymns, the strident noise of your *Sh'mas* as long as they arise from the lips of those divided into discordant camps, who refuse to become one even as you proclaim Me one. May we instead bend every effort of mind and will and heart to stand all of us this day—and all days—before the Lord as the united hosts of Israel.

May we remember the prophetic promise that those hosts, if steadfastly united, would become "like the sand upon the shore of the sea." What manner of reward was that? asked our rabbis. Are not such grains of sand the most fragile of God's handiwork which even the slightest breeze can blow away? Indeed, so they are, another sage replied. When they are separated one from the other they are powerless to resist the gentlest wind. But let them cling unto each other, one grain unto another grain, and they form the strongest strand against which the most powerful gusts beat in vain.

16

CAN FAITH SURVIVE?

FORETHOUGHT

It is sheer persiflage and pious pretension to maintain that there is no conflict between this new universe and the "old-time religion" of our fathers which still frantically maintains that God has created this far-flung universe for man's special delectation and delight; that this old earth as we know it is the chosen planet of the Divine, and its inhabitants the peculiar possession, the pampered pets of Providence; a religion which blandly and blindly asserts that not a sparrow drops to the ground, nor a single hair doth fall, but what it is God's concern. We, sophisticated generation that we are, accept nonetheless credulously a God who is a sort of universal messenger boy, a cosmic valet, a mighty medicine man, who prescribes for his petted children's every ache and pain and who, despite all man's mischievous pursuits, despite all evil, all poverty, human wretchedness, and inhuman battle, will see to it that all shall be well in the end. Such a faith science has demolished.

What then is man? Man is dust, but glorious and magic dust which has swept through unnumbered eons of time; slowly, painfully, tortuously passing through myriads of changing forms, at first chaotic and unconscious as to whence it came or whither it was going, but emerging at last into consciousness, into personality, into spirit, into God. What is man? Lowly dust become divine! In his heart reside deep-rooted principles of right, passionate yearnings for love, fervent longings for brotherhood and peace, mighty hungering and thirsting after the good, the beautiful, and the true—all that we have ever meant, or should have meant, by God.

God lives, and so does religion, so long as there whispers that "still small voice" within, which no mortal tyrant or fiendish ruler can ever really stifle, that unquenchable, irresistible, undying voice of true re-

ligion which so softly, and yet so sternly, enjoins: "Let justice flow forth as water and righteousness as a never-failing stream . . ."

Toronto, 1930

AFTERTHOUGHTS

I recall how surprised I was by the reaction—or rather by the lack of reaction to those words after I had spoken them from the pulpit of Holy Blossom Temple during the Holy Days of 1930. In voicing my conviction that a Reform or Liberal Judaism, that any faith, in fact, can survive the corrosive acids of our day only if it refuses to remain coagulated by ancient and outmoded theological concepts which had not been re-examined in the light of modern knowledge, in expressing my amazement at the ironic self-contradiction of congregants who found little difficulty in casting off outworn ceremonies but who clung to equally antiquated beliefs, I expected to be subjected to the argument that one should let sleeping dogs lie and not disturb slumbering concepts of God, no matter how much out of harmony they might be with the scientific findings of our time. I was prepared to counter that, aside from the intellectual dishonesty and spiritual hypocrisy involved, Reform Judaism, Judaism, religion itself could not survive nor be accepted by an increasingly sophisticated generation, unless it were firmly established upon the rock of truth. I felt that another flash fire of antagonism might burst around this treatise; but the sermon fell like a dud. There was neither commendation or condemnation. Just a blank, cold, neutral indifference. Yet, beyond a momentary sense of relief, I felt a troubled disappointment. Why?

I expected my fellow Jews to be as excited about a discussion concerning God as they had been over my political and economic points of view. I assumed they would manifest at least as much interest in the challenging of pet and pat theories about the Divine as they had in my questioning the status quo of the social order. This was one of my first lessons, confirmed a hundred times since, that a rabbi can take all manner of liberties with notions about God, but he had better be mindful of the contemporary mandate: touch not our sacred gospels regarding the supposedly sacrosanct economic arrangements of our society, our patterns of race relations, and the problems of international affairs.

Or maybe Jews generally, whether they are aware of it or not, have absorbed from their instruction in Yeshiva, in Talmud Torah, in religious school—however superficial that training may have been—something of the historic emphasis of Judaism on *mitzvot,* on the commandments of God and man's duties toward His creatures, rather than upon the effort to fathom His nature.

Levi Ben Gerson (known as Gersonides) was one of the foremost Biblical authorities of the fourteenth century and, at the same time, a brilliant scientist. "The Torah," he said, "is not a code that compels us to believe in falsehood." In contrast to Christianity, Judaism had little difficulty in accepting the new truths and challenges of science. Although Baruch Spinoza was accused of heresy by the Jewish leaders of Holland in the seventeenth century, this was a rare and extraordinary event which cut against the grain of normative Judaism. Moreover, the motivation for the trial was social and political rather than theological. Because Judaism is a non-dogmatic religion, stressing study and deeds rather than creeds and articles of faith, Judaism was not threatened by the truths uncovered by science. Anti-intellectualism has been repugnant to Judaism, making for a compatibility between the Jewish religion and science.

How different from the confrontation between Christianity and science which reached its dramatic and despotic climax in 1633 when a shaken Galileo stood before the Inquisitional tribunal in Rome and was constrained to recant his insistence that the earth was, like all other planets, an orb that revolved about the sun.

"I, Galileo, being in my seventieth year, being a prisoner and on my knees, and before your Eminences, having before my eyes the Holy Gospel, which I touch with my hands, abjure, curse and detest the error and the heresy of the movement of the earth."

According to legend, the apparently humbled and repentant Galileo was, in reality, still the scientist seeking only the truth and, as he rose to his feet, he still defiantly whispered: *"Eppur si muove!"*—"and yet, it does move!"

Although the bitter conflict between truth-seekers and close-minded "defenders of the faith," reflected in that sorry spectacle, has waned in our time, it must be admitted it has not been wholly resolved. The eternal wrangle is partly the consequence of the misunderstanding of the true nature and respective functions of religion and science.

In that message of 1930, I sought to bring to bear upon the knowledge of our Jewish faith some of the new wisdom and insights which the stupendous discoveries of our age had brought to light. Much of that wisdom and many of those insights had, in my college days, all but shattered my own earlier beliefs, but by the lights of these very revelations of modern science I had subsequently found my way to a deeper and more abiding faith.

What about today? One might expect that ideas and concepts fashioned in the struggle between age-old religious teaching and modern scientific advance would survive at least the thirty years that have intervened. Yet nothing in our swift-changing contemporary intellectual climate can be so easily taken for granted. Little can long be regarded as so inviolately axiomatic. It has been correctly stated that during the past three tumultous decades there have been more earth-shattering discoveries than in all preceding ages of man. If Galileo upset the seemingly eternal teachings of his day, and if Darwin toppled prized and precious beliefs that had been vigilantly guarded for more centuries still, then our contemporary Einsteins, Freuds, Plancks, Shapleys, and Oppenheimers have exploded still more supposedly irrefutable concepts not only of science but of religion and theology.

Yet, I find little in that discourse on "The Never Failing Stream" that does not stand the test of at least this tiny slice of time. The very title, selected from the prophet Amos, conforms to all that science presently reveals. In Amos' striking simile, that righteousness shall flow forth as a never failing stream, there is a divinely intuitive grasp of what Matthew Arnold later defined as that "Power not ourselves which makes for righteousness" or, what Rabbi Roland Gittelsohn in his *Man's Best Hope* perceptively refers to as "that Power *within* ourselves—and within the universe—that makes for righteousness."

At the time I first delivered this address, it was in conflict with the orthodoxies of both religion and science. It challenged both the religious concept of God as a Person apart from His universe and His ultimate creation, of Man, as well as of the then generally accepted scientific thesis that the universe and all that is within it, including man, are the product of sheer blind chance or of inevitable, irrevocable, unqualified laws of cause and effect. Chairman Khrushchev's language may have been contemporary when he stated that his cosmonauts had explored endless space in their speeding satellites and yet had found no trace of God. But he was far from being alone or even original in our day's expression of atheism. For the time of my youth and early manhood was replete with the same frequently iterated taunt phrased in one way or another: We have examined with our microscopes every organ, every cell of man's body and we have not come across his so-called soul. We have explored with our mightiest telescopes the farthermost reaches of the skies and have discovered heretofore unknown stars and planets whose rays are but reaching us today though they may have been burned to cinder eons ago, yet we have found nowhere through these boundless reaches any trace of God or of his ministering angels.

Mechanism and materialism were triumphant. Man not only descended from the ape—which many of us were ready to believe—but he in no wise differed from him in kind even though in degree he may have been endowed with a larger brain and hence a greater capacity to learn and to be taught. There was nothing other than matter and force either in man or in the universe: no heart, no spirit, certainly no God; no goal, no purpose, no plan. Given sufficient time and experiments the scientific laboratories might yet succeed, by the sheer concatenation of enough turns of the wheel of chance, in inducing a group of monkeys to compose a Brahms concerto, to create a Shakespeare's *Hamlet,* to write a Twenty-third Psalm. There was nothing unique in man to account for these purely accidental achievements.

I took issue with that earthrooted theory of science as I did with the heaven-concentrated theology depicting God mounted on His throne, a statistical clerk, a supreme Univac recording life and death, sickness and health—as our liturgy for the most sacred and most deeply spiritual of all our solemn Holy Days still portrays Him. Now science has wrought more havoc with many of the scientific notions of yesterday than it has with what I then outlined as my concept of that "divinity which shapes our ends"; of that power, force, spirit which is not apart *from* but a part *of* both the universe and oneself, as well as of everything that lives and breathes and whose being derives from the primal and pulsating energy suffusing the whole of life, which some of us still call God.

In this connection, I shall never forget how disillusioned I became with one of my youthful idols whom I had once regarded as the epitome of liberality of thought, freedom of spirit, capaciousness of heart, and wisdom of mind: the renowned lawyer and champion of virtually every worthy cause during the early years of this century, Clarence Darrow. When barely in my teens and impressionable enough to be influenced in ordinary circumstances by the consensus about me, I nevertheless remained totally unimpressed by the rabid newspaper headlines yapping for his scalp because of his defense of Leopold and Loeb. In retrospect, I think it was Darrow's daring defiance of that bloodthirsty mob, his masterful summations and truly religious pleas for understanding that first awakened my aversion to capital punishment, my first convictions about the hidden motivations of crime, and the power not alone of the human body but of the human spirit. His boundless compassion and humanity when I heard him speak so movingly concerning the plight of the American Negro likewise impressed me deeply.

But it was during my avid following of the Scopes "monkey trial" in 1925 that Darrow emerged in my mind as a staunch intellectual liberal and a foe of all bigotry. He was defending the mind of man against those who, in our century, like the self-appointed guardians of God's truth in the time of Galileo, were striving to put it into a strait-jacket and to incarcerate it within the prison of their restricting creeds. But my illusions concerning Darrow were promptly though regretfully dispelled when I myself tangled with him in a symposium in Toronto on the subject "Agnostic, Christian, and Jew."

The massive reaches of Massey Hall were thronged to the rafters with Christians, Jews, and agnostics—the vast majority of whom un-doubtedly came to hear the ever-controversial and widely known Dar-row. He was to speak first; my friend Reverend G. Stanley Russel next, and I last. As Darrow lifted his hulking frame from his seat and advanced to the rostrum in his proverbial unpressed clothes and baggy trousers, a hush that was almost reverential came over that over-crowded hall.

Darrow began by identifying religion, all religion, with the literal infusion of that initial anesthetic administered by God to Adam. He took refuge in the stale and long-outworn jibe, asking the males in the audience to feel their bodies in order to try to locate the exact spot from which the rib was stolen. More in earnest than in jest, he inquired of the ladies how they liked being the consequence of this first act of grand larceny. He asked what clothes we might be wearing when we will be ushered through "those pearly gates." I realized with a jolt that this man whom I had so esteemed did not have the foggiest idea of what constituted much of contemporary philosophy and religion. He didn't begin to realize that there were at least some forces in religion that had kept pace with the progress of scientific advance. Of course, William Jennings Bryan, against whom Darrow had so brilliantly contended in his defense of the teacher Scopes, had hosts of funda-mentalist followers; there were still religious leaders and myriads of their parishioners who opposed those who would not accept literally every word of Scripture. Nevertheless, it shocked me that so sophisti-cated a spirit as Darrow could identify religion exclusively with these benighted notions of an outmoded religious teaching. I was amazed that he should so unfairly have set up this antiquated concept as a straw man for his shafts of blazing, burning satire in which he sought mercilessly to obliterate not merely outgrown notions *about* God, but God himself. Not even a passing bow of recognition did he offer to the prophets of Israel or to the compassionate teacher of Nazareth, from whom, whether he would confess it or not, so much of his own passion for righteousness must have derived.

The Protestant minister, with more years and maturity than I, then presented a dispassionate apologia for the liberal Christianity which his own United Church of Canada represented (a church, by the way, which had achieved its remarkable liberal position largely out of the broadening experience resulting from the merger of three formerly distinct denominations: Methodist, Presbyterian, and Congregational). I was less indulgent than my ministerial colleague. I had been disillusioned by Darrow's unjust caricature of religion in general and of Christianity in particular. But I had been far more disillusioned in the man himself who, if he did not know better, should have; and if he did know better, was guilty of a deliberate hoax. Emboldened by anger, I threw away the manuscript I had carefully prepared and attempted to pick up the pieces of the battered body and heart of religion which Darrow had strewn about the hall. I subjected his own impish heresies to the same satire as he had so successfully exploited.

I traced the evolution of religion from the primitive brutalities of "eye for an eye and a tooth for a tooth"—which Darrow had also singled out for his target of attack—to the all-enduring mercies of Hosea and the all-pardoning compassion of Jesus' "Forgive them, Father, for they know not what they do." I sketched the development of Judaism from a narrow henotheism of tribal national gods in battle with one another to the Father of all mankind. I traced the delusion that His hunger could be sated and His thirst slaked by the slaughter of myriads of animals and the offering of their flesh and blood on His bespattered altars, to the Divine mandate "The Holy One is sanctified by justice." I revealed how little Darrow actually knew about religion and that, far from religion standing still, as he had sought to demonstrate, it was *he* who had not moved in the quarter of a century of an otherwise scintillating career. A low angry growl of his displeasure became audible to me as I spoke.

At the evening's close he stalked angrily from the auditorium without observing even the convention of a handclasp and huffily declined to attend a reception to which we had all been invited.

I have not rehearsed this tale to denigrate one to whom I still owe a large intellectual and spiritual debt. I have done so to show that too much of the historic hostility between religion and science is based upon such outlandishly false impressions of the nature of true religion and an equally fallacious notion of the limits and purpose of science.

Contemporary scientists have become more humble than some of their arrogant predecessors. Many realize today that they do not know all the answers and that "the leap of faith," as the basis of religion is frequently described, is not only well warranted but is as exigent for science as it is for religion. Many have come to recognize that science has its own questions as to the "what" and the "how" of terrestrial and cosmic phenomena, and even of human behavior. But they are now more willing to confess that the "why" and the "for what purpose" and the "to what end" lie primarily in the domain of religion. Nor need there be a cold war between these two sets of queries. Today's scientists understand that the two must meet, with far greater mutual sympathy and appreciation of each other's methods, goals, and objectives than has heretofore been the case.

As science probes the frontiers of outer space, the paramount purpose of religion should be to sanctify inner space. Where science aspires to send missiles to the moon, religion must recharge and challenge men anew to its mission to mankind, its mission of peace and brotherhood on this earth—this earth which God called good, but which men threaten to make vile, to make extinct. Where science seeks the rocket's red glare, the imperative task of religion is to bring a different kind of "light unto the nations"—a light of compassion, of justice, of creativity, of the liberated power of the individual human spirit.

Religion and science should be partners in building a better life. Science is method; religion is a guide to life. Science tells us what is; religion tells us what *should* be. Science has to do with knowledge; religion has to do with values. Religion without knowledge is fanaticism. Science without religion is dangerous. It is the proliferation of our scientific tools, without an equivalent growth in moral direction, which has thrown mankind into the crisis of our age. Unless religion can impart values and purposes to channel our scientific knowledge, we will face increasing social deterioration and dehumanization.

It is primarily religion which sustains the vision of human brotherhood which is indispensable to human survival. Rabbi Robert Gordis has described religion as "the improved hypothesis, the personal reaction, the faith beyond the evidence." But religion is also the goad to conscience and the champion of human dignity. It reminds us that life is purposeful and not accidental and that man's intelligence can create a better, more peaceful world. It gives dimension to human life. It is what made a scientist say: "I never expect to understand most of the things I value most highly—the thrill of a sunset, a symphony, the love that I have for certain persons."

For powerful as science is, it will never by itself answer the ultimate questions which have always plagued man: Who am I? Where am I going? What do I want? What is the purpose of my life? Nor will science ever determine any of the crucial questions of a person's life—it will never provide the computers to select a marital partner, it will never furnish think machines to supplant a parent's guidance to and love for his children, it will never grind out of a Univac an ethical code nor offer a synthetic substitute for friendship and life-long loyalties and love. These will be determined by one's value stance—what is most important to each individual. And values are derived, first and foremost, from religion.

Albert Einstein, perhaps the greatest scientist of our time, wrote these words:

The most beautiful emotion we can experience is the mystical. . . . He to whom this emotion is a stranger, who can no longer wonder and stand rapt in awe, is as good as dead. To know that which is impenetrable to us really exists, manifesting itself as the highest wisdom and the most radiant beauty, which our dull faculties can comprehend only in their most primitive forms . . . this knowledge, this feeling is at the center of true religiousness.

John L. Fischer of Tulane University writes:

If religion means an active faith in the future of mankind, reverence for those saints of the past who have devoted their lives to the pursuit of right-eousness, truth, meaning, if it means an organized dedication of men to the idea of universal brotherhood—then, surely, such a humanistic religion is not to be ruled out. . . .
Such a religion would have the advantage of being totally free from the defensive attitude toward science characteristic of most churches today. Its adherents would not fear any kind of knowledge. Its churches would not be a refuge for those who hide their heads in the sand and refuse to face the difficult and complex facts of the world today.

As the scientists of our time have thus grown more humble and confess that the more they come to know the more they know they don't know, as they admit that every mystery unveiled reveals even greater mysteries beyond, so the religionists of our generation must forego their erstwhile dogmatism. Religion doesn't know all the facts of life either; far from it. While churches and priests—and synagogues and rabbis, too, though less frequently—have often arrogated to themselves the possession of the exclusive truth, even the most superficial survey of the history of religion presents not a single ray of evidence to substantiate so preposterous a conceit.

Did the father of the patriarch Abraham possess the truth of which he undoubtedly dogmatically prated, or did his son, who so savagely slashed his idols to splinters? Did those who posited a God exclusively the possession of the hosts of Israel, who fought "the battles of the Lord" in His name, and who were unable to worship Him on any soil other than Zion have the truth—or did the Psalmist who chanted: "Whither shall I go from Thy spirit?" Did those who drove Spinoza from the synagogue, because he found the Divine permeating the whole of creation, harbor the truth, or did their excommunicated victim who was but echoing the deeper meaning of the prophet's affirmation "Holy, Holy, holy is the Lord of hosts, *the whole earth is full of His glory*"?

As religionists, we have made too many mistakes in our purblind and intolerant presumptions and prejudices. We have spilled too much blood in tyrannical and totalitarian defense of warped and biased orthodoxies. And while Judaism has not been as riven as other religions with such sectarian squabbles and theological wars, nevertheless we have had our occasional Spinoza and our Acosta. Maimonides, it is true, set forth the essence of a more tolerant Judaism when he refused to dogmatize about God and permitted himself only to describe Him in His negative attributes. He also evinced an extraordinary liberalism for his day when he bade his brother Jews to recognize the truths inherent in the teachings both of Jesus and of Mohammed. And though the books of Maimonides were burned and his teachings were proscribed as heretical, he is enshrined in Jewish history, partly because of his humility before the great unanswered dilemmas of life, before that which the more modest scientists of today admit may well be the great *Unknowable*.

Teachers of religion must strive more intelligently to know what science is all about. Too many religionists set up straw men, which they proceed zestfully to destroy. Listen to the voices of so-called religion which in most sections of our country monopolize the air waves. You will be appalled by what passes for religion and an alleged knowledge of the world in which we dwell. Hear those sanctimonious sermons flaying the dead horses of a vanished past! No serious man of science in our time any longer talks about not finding God in his microscope. Yet this is the kind of nostrum which these flamboyant preachers set up as the target of their snarling attacks. For if religion has not stood still, then how much the more is this true of science. If religion has taken a step or two forward, science has taken giant strides in its mammoth seven-league boots, leaving too many spokesmen of religion so hopelessly behind that they have given up the attempt to keep pace and take refuge instead in anti-intellectual surrender of the mind.

Not so the scientist who not only experiments and explores matter but thinks and feels as well in the context of our time. Thus, Professor Theodosius Dobzhansky of Columbia University, commenting on the uniqueness of man, has written:

An egg cell, from which every man and woman has developed, weighs approximately one twenty-millionth of an ounce. An adult is roughly fifty billion times heavier. This fifty-billion-fold increase in weight has resulted from the consumption and assimilation of food. It is quite literally true that a man is a conglomeration of transformed groceries. . . . *But he is most surely not only that.* [author's italics] This pile of groceries perceives, thinks, feels joy and suffering, and accordingly deserves the following description given to it by the author of one of the Dead Sea Scrolls: "So walk I on uplands unbounded, and know that there is hope for that which Thou didst mold out of dust to have consort with things eternal."

When it comes to man the complexity is overpowering. Can a complexity so great, and yet so orderly arise by a mere arrangement of atoms in the materials which are kept on the shelves of grocery stores?

And his answer? Both yes and no. Nothing from the outside has supernaturally, artificially entered into man. But today's scientists do find evidence throughout the long chain of evolution that things altogether unprecedented and unanticipated occur and that man has developed a nature, a spiritual nature if you please—an expression not opposed by many of the scientists of our time; the spirit of man who "stands with one foot in his biological past and with the other in his divine future."

"The spirit of man is the light of the Lord," chanted the Biblical poet centuries upon centuries ago. How satisfying that the scientists of today affirm the same truth: that this spirit which has evolved from stars and suns and seas and primordial ooze, from bird and beast and flower and fruit, must be the fruition of a similar though greater and inexhaustible spirit within the universe itself.

George Russel Harrison, Dean of the School of Science at the Massachusetts Institute of Technology, writes:

It is not difficult for a scientist to see *The Hand of God* [author's italics] in the patterns which the protons, neutrons, and electrons take in forming atoms, and those which the atoms take to form the molecules, molecules to form cells, cells to form tissues, organs, and bodies, and bodies to form social aggregates. The basic tenets of all great religions, the distilled spiritual wisdom of humanity, coincides closely with what science reveals in nature. The universe is based on order, not on chaos and chance.

Science, which once was viewed at being engaged in a total war against religion, now corroborates most of the deeply held convictions of liberal religion and of Reform Judaism in particular. Of course, there is only an impregnable refutation of the literal interpretation of God's walking in a garden and with His very hands forming the first man out of the dust of the earth; of his performing a skillful surgical operation upon that lone inhabitant, removing and fashioning out of his rib the first female, and the entire creation of the world being completed in six days of twenty-four hours each. All these latter-day attempts to square Scripture in a literal way with the finding of modern scientific research, anthropology and archeology, sociology and psychology, are acrobatics of the imagination.

For the Bible is not really a textbook of modern science, unquestionably as history, and not even altogether valid as biography. But its spiritual insights, its discoveries of the moral equations, inexorable as those which operate in the realm of physics and mathematics and astronomy —these are indeed undergirded by the explorations of our day. The poet who wrote that "it is not good for man to dwell alone" had an intuitive psychological wisdom. The spiritual emphasis of Judaism upon corporate responsibility rather than upon individual salvation is amazingly prescient of what only now the mind of man is beginning to comprehend. Only starry-eyed and deluded idealists dared to share Judaism's belief in the indispensability of cooperation and in "separating not thyself from the community." Today, science, on the track at last of the nature of cancer's ravaging scourge, has learned that its cause is to be found somewhere in the as yet unfathomed phenomenon which constrains certain cells to behave in an altogether individualistic, anarchistic, rampaging manner, refusing to behave in harmony with their disciplined fellow cells. Cancer, it is presently believed, is the consequence of just such cellular chaos.

And, as the cells are to the body, so is the individual to society. Hence, Ralph W. Burhoe, of the American Academy of Arts and Sciences, tells us:

The scientific picture says that I am in reality nothing apart from the cosmos and my fellow human beings. My own true being lies inextricably bound to the whole. To serve my fellow beings and to serve the programs of evolving life is to serve my deepest and most significant self. This is my "true," my "spiritual" being, or my "soul."

So, too, with the Jewish concept of the oneness of body and spirit, of the impossibility of declaring the former vile and the latter alone worthy and godlike. "This is not to say," continues scientist Burhoe, "that the body is evil or illusory. On the contrary, it is an essential part of the system which is I and is equally as divine and sacred as anything."

And does not the Hebrew affirmation of the Oneness of all creation, as adumbrated in the unceasing declaration of the *Sh'ma,* capture the endless panoply and pageantry of creation? This, too, is sensed in scientist Burhoe's warm and truly religious peroration:

This core or soul of my being, the sciences reveal, is older than the hills, a growth of hundreds of millions of years, still conceived as living value in my genotype—[It takes] me back thousands of years—links me to the evolution of all life on earth, past and future. To serve this deeper self is not to discount the body—for all this part of my being. All life is sacred, as Schweitzer says.

What a pity our own rabbinic teachings are not better known. It is this interpretation of the scientifically revealed world as sacred, including our own nature, which we need to recognize if we are ever to get away from our idiotic schizophrenia that spirit and values lie in one world and matter and knowledge reside separately and independently in another. That is the great lie, the grave error of our times. Our Jewish heritage, too, in contrast to so much in Christianity and other faiths, long since declared this a grave error, a lie, a libel on our Creator.

And what about our Jewish concept of man as coworker with God? This also, in the earlier mechanistic era, seemed a presumption and in the contemporary theological retreat into orthodox obscurantism is still held to be an act of flagrant human arrogance and pretense, as wrong as those early Church Fathers who insisted that man is too vile, too tainted with original sin ever to hope to better his lot unless the grace of God magically and mysteriously descended upon him. Their contemporary echoes—the present-day existentialists—wander hopelessly about in this alleged *Emek Habakha,* this "vale of despair," weighted down with apocalyptic foreboding, awaiting the crack of doom which no effort of man but only the compassion of God can possibly avert.

The existentialists dwell upon the absurdity and tragedy of the human situation. Will Herberg has even gone so far as to import into Judaism the totally alien Christian notion of "original sin." Implicit in the saturnine ruminations of the existentialists is the worthlessness of man, his gross absurdity, and his impotence to know and do right without supernatural intervention. To me, the resurgence of orthodox theologies does not manifest a growing maturity of religious thought but rather a traumatic and wounded response of withdrawal from the painful realities of a haunted world. The new theologies tend to shrink man to a melange of ambiguities, perversities, and immobilizing contradictions. While pursuing the nature of God they impugn the nature of man. And by embarking on voyages into the mysterious and the inscrutable, they turn their backs upon the urgent challenges of the here and now. What has been hailed by many as religious depth strikes me as a sinking into obscurantism and a perilous failure of nerve. What is required of religious leadership is more than theological speculation; what is required is also social creativity and a bold confrontation of all the evil forces which now conspire to dehumanize men. Science, which might once have supported such a denigration of man, no longer has any sympathy whatsoever with this dirge-like refrain that "man is but a race of worms" incapable of lifting himself by his bootstraps from his low estate.

Today's leading scientists take strenuous issue, as does our Jewish teaching, with this frantic flight from reality and responsibility onto the intellectual and spiritual opium pads of self-imposed narcosis. Neither contemporary science nor historic Judaism have anything in common with these peddlers of the dope of futility—the divinely fated doom with no escape for man caught by the carapace of his innate and inescapable mortality, groveling helplessly and hopelessly in his darkened cave unable to climb up and out unless God's ladder of supernatural salvation is lowered down to him.

The kinship of spirit which has arisen between recent scientific assumptions and ancient Jewish faith is astounding. They now join in an harmonious duet of affirmation that we ourselves are the builders of that ladder, "fashioning its rungs out of wood discovered by the searching parties of the mind in the forests of reality."

In accord with the age-old teaching of Judaism, that man is the *shutafo shel ha-kodosh* (the coworker with God) in the continuing task of creation, is the comment of C. Judson Herrick, of the University of Chicago, who writes: "We already know enough about our natural cosmos to be humbled by the stupendous magnitude and splendor of it." And this scientist's concept of "to be humbled" does not mean to be reduced to a groveling spawn of evil; it means to be awed but not overawed, for he adds: ". . . and to be inspired by the fact that *the human population plays a part in the cosmic evolution that is by no means insignificant.*" [author's italics]

I acknowledge that, like the early Reformers, I was too sanguine and too unqualified in my own initial and adolescent optimism about man. Our generation has witnessed the slimy depths of bestiality to which some men can sink, and our simplistic confidence in the inexorability of human progress has been cruelly shattered. In portraying man as the crowning achievement of Creation, as copartner with God, as being fashioned only "a little lower than the angels," I undoubtedly under-emphasized the frailty and the cruelty which equally constitute the nature of man. No doubt we failed, in our messianic zeal, to balance such roseate texts as "And God made man in His own image" with the many countervailing Biblical reminders that "the inclination of man's heart is evil from his very youth." In our insistence on man's limitless potential for good, we did not emphasize enough that man possesses a *yetzer ho ra* (an evil spirit) as well as a *yetzer ha tov* (a good spirit). We neglected the teachings of our tradition that as God needs our help so do we require His. By our well-warranted revolt against salvation by faith alone we went to the other extreme in seeking redemption by works only. Though it is true as I have stated in the Introduction that "in Judaism we do not begin with belief," we tended unintentionally to diminish the role of any such faith and too many among us have abandoned it altogether. Preoccupied, as admittedly we are bidden to be, with religion's concern for man's relations with man, we tended, mistakenly, to move God off center stage, to reduce Him to an abstraction in much the same way that the *Christian Century* magazine lamented that "God, says the unwritten glossary of American politics, is a word in the last paragraph of every political speech."

This caveat notwithstanding, science does attest to the truths of Judaism, in contrast especially to its daughter faiths. Was Paradise the portion of Adam and Eve alone and is man doomed forever to be punished by everlasting exile from establishing God's kingdom on earth? Were the Jews blind, deluded, stubborn, stiffnecked because they denied that the messiah had come and insisted instead that the messianic era lay in the future? Professor Alfred E. Emerson, also of the University of Chicago, seems to concur with our Jewish vision of the days ahead when he asserts categorically: "We have to accept a change toward a better existence rather than a deterioration from a golden age or from a perfect life in the Garden of Eden." No, neither man's task nor God's was completed in the past so that they might rest content with their achievement.

Paul E. Sabine of Palo Alto, California, ingeniously suggests "a simple change in tense in the Biblical account of cosmic and human origins." All that is necessary, according to Sabine, is to translate that majestic first line of Genesis to read: " 'From the beginning God *is* creating the heaven and the earth,' and thus get a stereoscopic view of the scientific and scriptural accounts of the process of creation. In like fashion we can read, 'God *is* creating man in His own image' and arrive at a satisfying synthesis of the two supreme mysteries of existence, God and the human soul."

I have quoted these several scientists not because I believe that religious faith can be *proved* in the test tube or the laboratory, or with the telescope or microscope, or by the soaring of satellites through space. These men of knowledge and those astounding extensions of their eyes, ears, hands, and minds can no more establish the existence of God, of the soul, of the ultimate purpose of life than can the fundamentalist preacher demonstrate the validity of these beliefs by the profuse quotation of so-called proof texts from the Bible. For faith in these finalities cannot be proved by either of these procedures. Faith must be found in the inner recesses of one's own heart and spirit. Faith, as Ian G. Barbour of Carleton College defines it, is "man's ultimate trust, his most basic commitments, what he bets his life on, the final basis by which he justifies his other values. The religious question is precisely about the object of a person's devotion; it asks to what or to whom a person gives his ultimate allegiance."

And if I seem to be at war with orthodoxy, I am. I am embattled, however, as one who might oppose the mistaken ideas and action of a brother or as one convinced that his own father or mother has been in error. I would stand against them as Abraham did when he smashed the idols of Terah—not in anger but in the belief that only by such honest removal of the rotting husks of illusion can the kernel of truth be revealed.

It is this faith that great and growing numbers of the foremost thinkers of our time are confirming. It is such a faith alone that can and will survive even the critical barrages of our day. It is the same faith which is affirmed by Rabbi Roland Gittelsohn, one of the all too few of my rabbinical colleagues who has dared to place every facet of our faith in the perspective of the present. Rabbi Gittelsohn concludes his aforementioned *Man's Best Hope* with these stirring words:

There is nothing cold or abstract about glimpsing my role in the great cosmic adventure of life. I feel the deepest, warmest kind of stirring within me when I listen to the Shostakovich Fifth and reflect that this ineffable beauty is what man—product of protozoan though he be—is now capable of creating and appreciating. My heart beats faster with excitement when I stand on a New England knoll in October, breathing the glorious color of leaves and somehow sensing that they and I alike are manifestations of a universal life-force which unites us. I can tremble with excitement at the dawn in my mind of a new truth, knowing that it makes me a partner to every searcher for truth from the beginning of time and relates me intimately to the ultimate source of Truth. I have been moved almost to tears by the realization that a turbulent struggle within me, followed by the choice of an ethically good act instead of an evil alternative, was my way of saying *yes* to God, of becoming truly His creative partner on earth.

Strangely, despite all that has happened to the world since I preached that sermon in 1930 as a young neophyte in the rabbinate, I believe that my basic views of God and man have not significantly changed. Does this mean that I have closed my mind, that I have failed to grow intellectually and spiritually, that rigidities of mind and prejudice have sealed off my faith from reality? Some readers will undoubtedly think so. I do not.

Many of my rabbinic colleagues, impatient with such concepts, are summoning us to recover our faith in a personal God, and they warn us direly that our people are losing (if they have not already lost) that profound sense of religious commitment which gives purpose and order to one's life. They are right in their warning. Jews, especially, maintain an almost complete indifference to theology. Jews are returning to the synagogues in impressive numbers, but every rabbi knows that it is not an uncompromising God-orientation which is bringing them back. Prayer has become a lost art for millions of Jews. Every survey indicates that American Jews are at the bottom of the totem pole, well below their Protestant and Catholic neighbors, in "church" attendance and in the regimen of personal prayer and worship. Jews may be God's chosen people, but the blunt reality is that most contemporary Jews (in Israel as well as here) have chosen to be spectators not worshippers, that they lack a deep commitment to a God to whom they feel personally accountable. Jews live their lives—and I am afraid most synagogues do, too—by secular values rather than by that stern guide of Jewish history: "What does the Lord require of me?"

But, I believe, this religious emptiness which vulgarizes and impoverishes Jewish life cannot be cured by a campaign to persuade our constituents to recover the God of their fathers. In the first place, such a campaign will not succeed; it is tantamount to bailing out the ocean with a sieve. Whether we like it or not, we must be honest enough to recognize that neither exhortation nor persuasion will win American Jews back to the consciousness of the Jewish Covenant with God. Most Jews in America could not even define that Covenant. Education could bring knowledge. I doubt that it would bring commitment to a personal God of Israel who knows and cares about the fate of the individual.

No, I think a great part of our difficulty is precisely that most Jews believe that the choice is between accepting a personal God or nothing. And, in such a choice, to affirm such a God is to raise a plethora of unanswered questions, such as: Why did God permit the slaughter of the 6 million? Why do the innocent suffer and the evil so often prosper? Does God hear my prayers?

Belief in a personal God is, to most Jews, unacceptable, and the rather easy rabbinic aphorisms about the inscrutability of God's will do not satisfy. But rejection of God—atheism—is no solution either. Such negativism is not compatible with the genuine, though inchoate, yearning of American Jews for positive spiritual values which can give meaning and purpose to their lives. Our generation needs God but it must be a concept of God attuned to the best of our scientific knowledge, as well as to the sharp demands of our reason and conscience.

Is this so heretical? To many no doubt it is. But let's face it. Man's ability to comprehend the ultimate has constantly evolved and expanded. Men once found gods in the rocks and the trees and in the sun. Later generations worshipped idols as gods, and Abraham, smashing his father's idols, must have appeared a fire-eating heretic to his contemporaries. Until men understood the rotation of the seasons, they naturally ascribed this miracle to God. Ideas of God have changed constantly in Judaism as well. Various notions held about the Divine were regarded as unworthy of Him by later generations. When Moses Maimonides, the eminent Jewish thinker of the twelfth century, described God as pure spirit, indefinable and ineffable, his books were publicly burned by his shocked fellows. In our own generation, Mordecai Kaplan's iconoclasm has earned him similar honors. God must be reinterpreted in every age. Even our earliest sages, commenting on the familiar Hebrew phrase "God of Abraham, Isaac, and Jacob," insisted that this often iterated expression connotes the fact that, though God is Himself ever the same, the conception of Him differed in the respective generations of Jacob, Isaac, and Abraham. Most assuredly this must be true of our own age, which dares not cling superstitiously to outmoded descriptions of the Divine. Any religion which isolates itself from the swiftly changing drama of human experience dooms itself to irrelevance and decay.

Our generation is rejecting, not God really, but an immature and childish concept of Him. It is well-portrayed in the story told by Rabbi Jacob Shankman, President of the World Union for Progressive Judaism.

Once in a park I saw a little child running away from its mother. The mother called the child back, but the youngster ran on. Then the child fell and scraped her knee and began to cry. And the mother shrieked, "See, God punished you because you did not answer me." I do not believe in that mother's kind of God. My God does not go around in parks shoving little children who don't answer their mothers. That child fell because she lost her balance—it is as simple as that, and no theology is involved.

I believe now—as I did thirty years ago—that God is that spark in man, that spark which suffuses the whole of His creation—which makes for cosmos rather than chaos, for cooperation rather than for competition, for righteousness rather than iniquity and inequity. I believe that God is that Supreme Force in a world which is distinguished by law and order, purpose and plan. I believe that the human personality is a spiritual as well as a physical entity, derived from dust but destined for divinity. I believe that the deepest, the greatest, and the grandest aspirations of the human spirit are compatible with, and supported by, a moral force in the universe itself. I share the view of the ancient rabbi who said: "All that the Holy One, blessed be He, created in the world He created in man."

And I believe that our generation would respond to a religious faith which, while never offending reason, affords each human being the opportunity to fulfill the potential of his own personality by searching constantly for the ultimate context in which he, as a child of God, belongs, and which takes God as goad to the good and ethical life. "Seek Me and live!" For such a faith rests on that searching foresight, that revelation—divine revelation, if you will—of the Psalmist who proclaimed that which we are just beginning to comprehend in all its magic, its mystery, its magnificence, through the God-given discoveries of the mind of Man. Only such a faith can and will survive. Fortified by such a faith we may still affirm with the Psalmist:

When I behold Thy heavens . . . the moon and the stars which Thou hast established (and today we must add the satellites and the satellites of satellites and the depths of the seas and the unseen atoms and electrons); What is man, that Thou art mindful of him? . . . Yet Thou has made him but little lower than the angels, and hast crowned him with glory and honor. Thou hast made him to have dominion over the works of Thy hands; Thou hast put all things under his feet: sheep and oxen, all of them, Yea, and the beasts of the field . . .

Thou hast endowed him with the potential of knowing Thee, the source of his life, of my life, of all life, and Thou hast made him Thy partner in the never-ending work of creation.

INDEX

Aaron, 110
Abbott, Lyman, 196
Abernathy, Ralph, 144
Abraham, 18, 99, 117, 236, 297, 303, 305
Abyssinia, 77
Acosta, Uriel d', 297
Agar, Herbert, 244
Agrippa, 81
Akiba, Rabbi, 63, 144, 173, 200
Albee, Edward, 36
Ambrose of Milan, 182
America, 95, 101-103
American Academy of Arts and Sciences, 299
American Civil Liberties Union, 27
American Council for Judaism, 51-52
American Jewish Committee, 135, 239, 274-277, 280, 283-285
American Jewish Conference, 60, 276-277, 279-284
    Committee on Future Organization, 281
    "Eisendrath Report," 281
American Jewish Congress, 135, 140, 239, 272, 274-275
American Joint Distribution Committee, 239
American Nazi Party, 119
American Protective Association, 208
American Way of Death, The (Mitford), 32
Amos, 6, 75, 188, 195, 198, 208, 224, 291
Another Country (Baldwin), 128
Anti-Defamation League, 135, 284
Antiochus, 73
Anti-Semitism, 29, 65, 81, 128, 136-137, 204-207, 212-213, 272
Anti-Zionism, 49-51, 53, 60, 278
Arabs, 51-53, 55-57, 64
Arendt, Hanna, 79-80
Argentina, 120, 271
Aristotle, 111

Arnold, Matthew, 36, 291
Atlantic Monthly, 26
Azaryah, Rabbi Eliezer ben, 173

Baeck, Leo, 39, 65, 79-80, 189, 253
Baldwin, James, 126, 128, 133
Barabbas, 183-184
Barbour, Ian G., 303
Bar Kochba, 76
Bea, Augustine, Cardinal, 207
Beer Tuvia, 56-57
Ben-Gurion, David, 11, 56, 64, 66-67
Berger, Rabbi Elmer, 55
Berlin, 78, 80
    wall, 82
    West, 81
Bettelheim, Bruno, 79
Bible, 36, 95-96, 106, 117, 172-173, 299
    Douay, 99, 104
    King James version, 99, 104
Bible and Universal Peace, The (Gilbert), 74
Black, Eugene, 157
Black Muslims, 146
Blake, Rev. Eugene Carson, 134, 218
Blaustein, Jacob, 284
B'nai B'rith, 274, 276, 282, 284
    Anti-Defamation League, 283
    Hillel Foundation of, 239, 275
Board of Delegates of American Israelites, 275
Board of Deputies of British Jews, 273
Bombay, University of, 84
Brav, Rabbi Stanley, 154
Brazil, 120
Brickner, Rabbi Barnett R., 278
British Royal Commission, 174
Bryan, William Jennings, 293
Buber, Martin, 171, 243
Buddhism, 21, 75
Bunche, Ralph, 145
Burhoe, Ralph W., 299-300

ABOUT THE AUTHOR

Maurice N. Eisendrath, rabbinical President-for-life of the Union of American Hebrew Congregations, the congregational body of 662 Reform Jewish synagogues in the Western hemisphere, was ordained in 1926 from the Hebrew Union College–Jewish Institute of Religion, which awarded him an honorary D.D. in 1945. He was graduated from the University of Cincinnati in 1925. He was elected to Phi Beta Kappa in his senior year and honored by his alma mater in 1957 with an honorary LL.D. In September, 1964, he was awarded an honorary LL.D. from Brown University. He is noted as one of the foremost proponents of interfaith understanding in the United States and in Canada where he served as rabbi in the pulpit of Holy Blossom Temple, Toronto, from 1929-1943. He is the recipient of the first Four Freedoms Award, the Gandhi Peace Award, and the Clergyman of the Year Award as a "fearless defender of justice . . ." He has been called "a Jewish Thomas Paine" for his vigorous and unequivocal championship of civil rights.